CRITICAL ISSUES IN EDUCATION

A READER

FIRST EDITION

EDITED BY **Kisha R. Cunningham, PhD**
Savannah State University

cognella®
academic publishing

Bassim Hamadeh, CEO and Publisher
Michael Simpson, Vice President of Acquisitions
Jamie Giganti, Senior Managing Editor
Miguel Macias, Graphic Designer
Zina Craft, Senior Field Acquisitions Editor
Gem Rabanera, Project Editor
Elizabeth Rowe, Licensing Coordinator
Allie Kiekhofer, Interior Designer

First published in the United States of America in 2016 by Cognella, Inc.

Trademark Notice: Product or corporate names may be trademarks or registered trademarks, and are used only for identification and explanation without intent to infringe.

Cover image copyright © Depositphotos/Wavebreakmedia.

Printed in the United States of America

ISBN: 978-1-63487-290-4 (pbk) / 978-1-63487-291-1 (br)

www.cognella.com   800-200-3908

Contents

PART FOUR
Curriculum and Instructional Foundations of Education   183

DEDICATIONS

To my parents, Willie and Marilyn Cunningham, my grandmother, Rena Paisley, and Dr. Elazer J. Barnette for their love and encouragement. Thank you for providing me with the richness and meaning of life and teaching me to make a difference.

FOREWORD

BY MARSHALITA SIMS PETERSON, PHD

This book is the culmination of years of research, teaching, and administrative activities, as well as trial and error linking educational theory to practice. This gathering of educators converged on a single mission—to address the critical issues impacting education today. As such, this text provides a framework for examination and analysis of issues involving educational systems and stakeholders. For some, the topics in this text are an introduction (first exposure) to education issues; for others, this text is a refresher and a reminder that challenges in education continue to plague our communities, our schools, and our nation. As captured in the various presentations by the chapter authors, this text brings to the forefront complex issues in education, drawing attention to the need for purposeful discussion.

I frame this textbook as a call for *conversation* involving critical issues in education. This text lends itself to a knowledge base regarding these issues and key topics that serve as a springboard for *conversation*—critical issues for critical *conversation* in education.

One of the most daunting issues in the 21st century involves education and the challenges impacting children and schools on a daily basis. This text speaks to these topics, leading to probing questions and inquiry involving learning communities, successful pedagogy, and transformational experiences for students. As a pragmatist and optimist, I assert that there are essential questions with innovative solutions to the problems in education. It is significant to recognize that these issues are not necessarily new, but represent the increased need for student engagement through dialogue and educational research. Thus, this text serves as the foundation for *conversation* and identifying potential solutions.

The motivation for this text is also associated with navigational tools for professional development and extended research in addressing the challenges experienced at the community and national levels. Analysis, research, and reflection can prompt innovation in education and serve as a driving factor for those who are passionate as well as committed to successful learning communities and quality educational experiences for all students.

I frame these remarks with focus on associative factors impacting exceptional educational experiences inclusive of curriculum programming, poverty, achievement gaps, graduation rates, student retention, state/federal agencies, teacher education preparation programs, parents, and communities. I think of Dr. Vanessa Siddle Walker, a distinguished historian and scholar of education (and former colleague), whose work generates a framework around parents and community in education, equity in schools, and historical examination of "schooling" in the context of educational dilemmas today. The relationship between school and community and the intersection of responsive pedagogy, nurturing learning environments, educational leadership, performance standards, and communal engagement brings us to examine the dynamics and challenges of education. As Dr. Cunningham suggests, current challenges and opportunities reflect the past. In agreement, I expound to suggest that similar issues, concerted efforts, and *real conversation* provide for purposeful experiences of student success in our educational systems today.

In closing, the importance of creating space for critical conversation cannot be overstated as the dynamics, subtleties, and underlying forces of education have positioned us in either a state of urgency or a home of complacency. It is through exposure and the unraveling of issues that space for conversation has the propensity for deliberate and systematic processes in effectively addressing indicators of student success. It is therefore essential that readers of this text position themselves to analyze, advocate, and give voice to their thoughts regarding critical issues in education. If thought-provoking *conversation* ensues, then this text has served its purpose.

Marshalita Sims Peterson, PhD
Interim Dean, School of Teacher Education
Savannah State University
Savannah, Georgia

Preface

"It must be remembered that the purpose of education is not to fill the minds of students with facts ... it is to teach them to think."

—Robert M. Hutchins

There are critical issues facing teachers, school administrators, and parents. This book explores and analyzes some of the major issues in education and how educational trends are shaping our future. This text is designed to examine historical and philosophical conceptions of education, theories of learning, issues of diversity, and social justice through critical lenses. Students will also explore the roles schools play in American society and the aims of education. It is organized around the conceptual framework of educational reform. By examining the teaching profession from multiple vantage points—both within and outside the school—students will be able to reflect on and interpret the meaning of education.

The first section of the book examines the "known" and helps readers classify and interrogate a range of suppositions that undergird education. Who are our students? How do historical contexts affect their learning experiences, both in and out of the classroom? What are the purposes of education? "Study the past if you would define the future." This phrase from Confucius asserts the importance of knowing ourselves and our history in the context of developing aptitudes for reading and responding to education critically today and in the future.

The second section of the book examines social context issues and how they affect the learning experience both in and out of the classroom. Issues relating to school choice, the academic achievement gap, students and their families, and schooling in a diverse culture are examined, and the moral and ethical responsibilities of teaching in a democracy are discussed.

The third part examines issues and perspectives emerging from reform initiatives, educational equity, school finance, federal and state policy, and legal aspects of education. The general hierarchy of influence of political sources (local, state, and federal) relevant to American education is discussed, and a general description of the relationships of these bodies regarding influence on education in America is presented.

Part IV examines issues in curriculum and instruction. This section focuses on the challenges of knowing our students. It also examines the relationship between the individual needs of students and deepening our understanding of pedagogy. Issues relating to standards, classroom management, and motivation are also presented.

The final section examines the ins and outs of the teaching profession. The struggles and strategies of the profession are provided. Readers are reminded of the call and need for educators and the importance of those in the profession to engage in continuous discussion of these important topics, to strive for excellence in our teaching fields, and to make a difference in the lives of students.

This book will be beneficial for students who are considering teaching at the elementary, middle, or senior high school level. It will also be valuable for all preservice teacher candidates and those returning to school for a postbaccalaureate program in education.

PART ONE

Historical and Philosophical Foundations of Education

CHAPTER 1

A Brief History of Education in the United States

BY KISHA R. CUNNINGHAM, PHD
SAVANNAH STATE UNIVERSITY

> "... the true business of the schoolroom connects itself, and becomes identical, with the great interests of society. The former is the infant, immature state of those interests; the latter, their developed, adult state. As "the child is father to the man," so may the training of the schoolroom expand into the institutions and fortunes of the state."
>
> —Horace Mann

It is difficult to understand teaching today without becoming familiar with America's educational past. Knowledge of our educational history is important for two reasons. First, such knowledge can be used to evaluate current issues facing the profession today. Second, an awareness of how America's educational system has developed is an important part of teacher preparation. American education can be divided into seven periods, each one with predominant educational concerns and the contributions made by its most influential educators.

The Colonial Era (1620–1750)

Education in colonial America has its roots in English culture. Early colonial elementary curriculum stressed religious objectives. The primary objective of elementary schooling during the colonial era was to learn to read so that one might read the Bible and religious catechisms and thereby receive salvation. Those who taught could do so with minimal qualifications and for little to no pay. Schoolmasters were typically men, who usually taught students who were boys. The most common types of schools were dame schools, reading and writing schools, and the Latin grammar schools. Dame schools were usually held in the homes of widows or housewives for teaching children basic reading, writing, and mathematical skills. The first Latin grammar school (Boston Latin School) was established in 1635. Harvard College, the first higher education institution in the United States, was established in Newtowne, Massachusetts, in 1636. Latin grammar schools were established to provide male students a precollege education that is comparable to today's high school. In reading and writing schools, boys were offered a religiously oriented curriculum education that went beyond what they learned at home or in dame school. These schools were supported by public funds and fees paid by parents. In 1690, the first New England primer was printed in Boston. Primers, with very explicit religious and moral messages about the proper conduct of life, were used by colonial children to learn to read.

In the United States today, compulsory education laws require that parents, or those who have custody of children between certain ages, send their children to school. Two political forces led to mandated public education in America: the Massachusetts Act of 1642 and the Massachusetts Act of 1647. The Massachusetts Act of 1642 required each town to determine whether its young people could read and write. The 1647 act mandated the establishment and support of schools. This act was often referred to as the Old Deluder Satan Act because education was seen as the best protection against the wiles of the devil.

The Revolutionary Period (1750–1820)

Education in America during the revolutionary period was characterized by a general waning of European influence on schools. Benjamin Franklin founded the Philadelphia Academy in 1751, which was aligned with "Proposals Relating to the Education of Youth in Pennsylvania," a pamphlet written by Franklin in 1749. This school had a curriculum that was both classical and modern, including courses in history, geography, navigation, surveying, and classical languages. The academy ultimately became the University of Pennsylvania. On July 4, 1776, the Declaration of Independence was adopted by the Continental Congress. To preserve these hard-won freedoms, a system of education became essential. In 1779, Thomas Jefferson proposed a two-track educational system. The plan called for state-controlled elementary schools that would teach—at no cost to parents—three years of reading, writing, and arithmetic to all white children. Although Jefferson's proposal was unsuccessful, it was understood that through education, citizens would learn how to become intelligent, participating members in the new democracy.

The Struggle for State-Supported Schools (1820–1865)

The first state-supported high school in the United States was established in 1821. While the Boston English Classical School marked the beginning of the struggle for state-supported common schools (free state-supported schools that provided education to all students), it also marked an awakening among those in the profession to provide an education system that touched on the needs of students. Those in favor of free common schools tended to be city residents and non-taxpayers, democratic leaders, philanthropists, and working persons. Those opposed were rural residents and taxpayers, members of the old aristocratic and conservative groups. Notable events in the history of education during this era include:

- In 1827, the state of Massachusetts passes a law requiring towns of more than 500 families to have a public high school open to all students.
- The New England Asylum for the Blind opens in Massachusetts in 1829, becoming the first school in the United States for children with visual disabilities.
- The first of William Holmes McGuffey's readers is published in 1836. Their secular tone sets them apart from the Puritan texts of the day. The McGuffey readers were an immensely popular series of reading books for students in grades one through six.
- A visionary educator and proponent of public (or "free") schools, Horace Mann (1796–1859) works tirelessly for increased funding of public schools and better training for teachers.

- Mount Holyoke Female Seminary, the first college for women in the United States, opens in 1837.
- The oldest institution of higher learning for African Americans, the African Institute (later called the Institute for Colored Youth), is established in Cheyney, Pennsylvania, in 1837.
- In 1839, the first state-funded school specifically for teacher education (then known as normal schools) opens in Lexington, Massachusetts.
- Massachusetts enacts the first mandatory attendance law in 1852.
- The first kindergarten in the United States is started in Watertown, Wisconsin, in 1856.
- The National Teachers Association is founded by 43 educators in Philadelphia in 1857.
- The first Morrill Act, also known as the Land-Grant Act, becomes law in 1862. It provides federal land that states could sell or rent to raise funds to establish colleges of agriculture and mechanical arts.

The Expansion of Common Schools (1865–1920)

From the end of the Civil War to the end of World War I, publicly supported common schools steadily spread westward and southward from New England to New York. In 1867, the Department of Education was created in order to help states establish effective school systems. After hearing of the desperate situation facing schools in the South, George Peabody funded the two-million-dollar Peabody Education Fund to aid public education in southern states. Notable contributions to the field of education during this era include:

- Boston creates the first public day school for the deaf in 1869.
- The Panic of 1873 causes bank foreclosures, business failures, and job loss. The economic depression that follows results in reduced revenues for education. Southern schools are hit particularly hard, making a bad situation even worse.
- In 1874, the Michigan State Supreme Court rules that Kalamazoo may levy taxes to support a public high school.
- The first Indian boarding school opens in Carlisle, Pennsylvania, in 1879.

- The second Morrill Act is enacted in 1890. It provides for the "more complete endowment and support of the colleges" through the sale of public lands. It leads to the creation of 16 historically black land-grant colleges.
- In 1892, the Committee of Ten (formed by the National Education Association to establish a standard secondary school curriculum), recommends a college-oriented high school curriculum.
- The Carnegie Foundation for the Advancement of Teaching is founded in 1905.
- In 1909, educational reformer Ella Flagg Young becomes superintendent of the Chicago Public Schools.
- The Smith-Lever Act establishes a system of cooperative extension services connected to land-grant universities and provides federal funds for extension activities in 1914.
- The American Federation of Teachers (AFT) and the American Educational Research Association (AERA) are founded in 1916.
- The Smith-Hughes Act passes in 1917, providing federal funding for agricultural and vocational education. It is repealed in 1997.
- In 1919, all states have laws providing funds for transporting children to school.

As common schools spread, school systems began to take on organizational features associated with today's schools: centralized control; increasing authority for state, county, and city superintendents; and a division of labor among teachers and administrators at the individual school site (Button and Provenzo Jr., 1989).

The Progressive Era (1920–1945)

From the end of World War I to the end of World War II, American education was influenced by the progressive movement. John Dewey's *Democracy and Education: An Introduction to the Philosophy of Education* was published in 1916. Dewey's views helped advance the ideas of the progressive education movement. In 1919, the Progressive Education Association is founded, with the goal of reforming American education. It went on to devote the next two decades to implementing progressive theories in the classroom. Notable events in the field of education during this time include:

- In 1922, Abigail Adams Eliot, with help from Mrs. Henry Greenleaf Pearson, establishes the Ruggles Street Nursery School in Roxbury, Massachusetts, one of the first educational nursery schools in the United States.
- In 1925, *State of Tennessee v. John Scopes* (commonly called the Scopes Monkey Trial) captures national attention as John Scopes, a high school biology teacher, is charged with the heinous crime of teaching evolution. The trial ends in Scopes's conviction. The evolution-versus-creationism controversy persists to this day.
- The Scholastic Aptitude Test (SAT) is first administered in 1926.
- The Great Depression begins with the stock market crash in October 1929. Public education funding suffers greatly, resulting in school closings, teacher layoffs, and lower salaries.
- *Alvarez v. the Board of Trustees of the Lemon Grove (California) School District* (1931) becomes the first successful school desegregation court case in the United States, as the local court forbade the school district from placing Mexican American children in a separate "Americanization" school.
- In 1939, Frank W. Cyr, a professor at Columbia University's Teachers College, organizes a national conference on student transportation. It results in the adoption of standards for the nation's school buses, including the particular shade of yellow.
- The United States enters World War II after the Japanese attack Pearl Harbor on December 7, 1941. Education is put on the back burner as many young men quit school to enlist; schools are faced with personnel problems as teachers and other employees enlist, are drafted, or leave to work in defense plants; and school construction is put on hold.
- The GI Bill of Rights, officially known as the Servicemen's Readjustment Act of 1944, is signed by President Franklin D. Roosevelt on June 22. Roughly 7.8 million World War II veterans take advantage of the GI Bill during the seven years benefits are offered. More than two million attend colleges or universities, nearly doubling the college population. About 238,000 become teachers.

In spite of its short life, the progressive education movement had an unmistakable impact on American education (Cremin, 1961). Many practices today have their origins in the experimentation of the progressive era: inquiry or discovery learning; self-paced instructional approaches;

field trips; flexible scheduling; open-concept classrooms; nongraded schools; small activities; and school-based counseling programs—all contributed to the changing expectations of schools.

The Modern Postwar Era (1945–1990)

The decade after World War II saw a series of profound changes in American education. The computer age began in 1946: the Electronic Numerical Integrator and Computer (ENIAC), the first vacuum-tube computer, was built for the US military by J. Presper Eckert and John Mauchly. With thousands of veterans returning to college, the President's Commission on Higher Education was given the task of reexamining the role of colleges and universities in postwar America. The first volume of its report, often referred to as the Truman Commission Report, was issued in 1947 and recommended sweeping changes in higher education, including doubling college enrollments by 1960 and extending free public education through the establishment of a network of community colleges. This latter recommendation came to fruition in the 1960s, during which community college enrollment more than tripled. Teachers and educators were put in the spotlight in 1957 when the Soviet Union launched the first satellite, *Sputnik*, into space. Occurring in the midst of the Cold War, it represented both a potential threat to American national security, as well as a blow to national pride. At least partly because of *Sputnik*, science and science education became important concerns in the United States, resulting in the passage of the National Defense Education Act (NDEA), which authorized increased funding for scientific research, as well as science, mathematics, and foreign language education.

A number of important court cases contributed to the changes and forced answers to several questions:

1. How could equal opportunity be extended to all groups?
2. What knowledge and skills should be taught in schools?
3. How should knowledge be taught?

The federal government and the courts played a great role in promoting equal educational opportunities for all groups after World War II. Some of the rulings from 1945–1969 include:

- In the landmark court case *Mendez v. Westminster and the California Board of Education* (1946), the US District Court in Los Angeles rules that educating children of Mexican descent in separate facilities is unconstitutional, thus prohibiting segregation in California schools.
- Recognizing "the need for a permanent legislative basis for a school lunch program," the 79th Congress approves the National School Lunch Act in 1946.
- In the case of *Everson v. Board of Education* (1947), the US Supreme Court rules by a 5–4 vote that a New Jersey law allowing reimbursements of transportation costs to parents of children who ride public transportation to school—even if their children attended Catholic schools—does NOT violate the Establishment Clause of the First Amendment.
- In the case of *McCollum v. Board of Education* (1948), the Supreme Court rules that schools cannot allow "released time" during the school day, which allows students to participate in religious education in their public school classrooms.
- Public Law 81-740 (1950) grants a federal charter to the Future Farmers of America (FFA) and recognizes it as an integral part of the program of vocational agriculture. The law is revised in 1998 and becomes Public Law 105-225.
- Public Law 550 (1952), the Veterans' Readjustment Assistance Act of 1952, modifies the GI Bill for veterans of the Korean War.
- On May 17, the US Supreme Court announces its decision in the case of *Brown v. Board of Education of Topeka* in 1954.
- Federal troops enforce integration in Little Rock, Arkansas, as the Little Rock Nine enroll at Central High School in 1957.
- In the case of *Engel v. Vitale* (1962), the US Supreme Court rules that the state of New York's Board of Regents' prayer violates the First Amendment. The ruling specifies that "state officials may not compose an official state prayer and require that it be recited in the public schools of the State at the beginning of each school day …"
- In the cases of *Abington Township School District v. Schempp and Murray v. Curlett* (1963), the US Supreme Court reaffirms *Engel v. Vitale* by ruling that "no state law or school board may require that passages from the Bible be read or that the Lord's Prayer be recited in the public schools … even if individual students may be excused from attending or participating …"

- The Elementary and Secondary Education Act (ESEA) is passed on April 9, 1965. Part of President Lyndon Johnson's War on Poverty, it provides federal funds to help low-income students, resulting in the initiation of educational programs such as Title I and bilingual education.
- The Higher Education Act is signed at Southwest Texas State College on November 8, 1965. It increases federal aid to higher education and provides for scholarships, student loans, and establishes a National Teacher Corps.
- Project Head Start, a preschool education program for children from low-income families, begins as an eight-week summer program in 1965.
- In 1966, the Equality of Educational Opportunity Study, often called the Coleman Report because of its primary author, James S. Coleman, is conducted in response to provisions of the Civil Rights Act of 1964. Its conclusion that African American children benefit from attending integrated schools sets the stage for school busing to achieve desegregation.
- The Bilingual Education Act, also known as Title VII, becomes law in 1968. After many years of controversy, the law is repealed in 2002 and replaced by the No Child Left Behind Act.
- The Scopes Monkey Trial is revisited in 1968. In the case of *Epperson et al. v. Arkansas*, the US Supreme Court finds the state of Arkansas' law prohibiting the teaching of evolution in a public school or university unconstitutional.

During the 1960s and 1970s, issues that grew out of the civil rights movement and affected education include busing, affirmative action, and reverse discrimination. In response to the large number of Cuban immigrant children arriving in Miami after the Cuban revolution, Coral Way Elementary School started the first bilingual and bicultural public school in the United States in 1963. Also in that year, Samuel A. Kirk used the term "learning disability" at a Chicago conference on children with perceptual disorders. The term sticks, and in 1964, the Association for Children with Learning Disabilities, now the Learning Disabilities Association of America, was formed. Today, nearly one-half of all students in the United States who receive special education have been identified as having learning disabilities.

The 1970s was a decade mixed with conflict and struggle for American education (Ravitch, 1983). The decade was marked by drops in enrollment, test scores, and public confidence, as well as progressive policy changes that promoted a more equal education for all Americans. Schools found themselves in financial trouble, and the ability to meet the needs of students was further reduced. SAT scores were experiencing a downward trend, and there was a call for "back to basics" and accountability. This period also led to many parents responding to the crisis by establishing alternative schools or joining the home school movement.

The first half of the 1980s saw an escalation of the criticisms of the 1970s. In 1983, "A Nation at Risk" was released, a report that cites the high rate of illiteracy among 17-year-olds and minority youth, a drop in SAT scores, and a need for colleges and businesses to offer remedial reading, writing, and computation classes. This report and others that swept the nation during the 1980s made a lasting imprint on education in the United States. Though it was a daunting period of frustration for educators, teachers recognized that they could rally in support of education and the profession for those still interested in becoming teachers.

The push for reform continued into the 1990s and into the new century. New steps have been taken to empower teachers and to restructure schools. Teachers have contributed to the discussion on reform. Their decisions have led to many changes in curriculum, textbooks, standards for students, behavior, evaluations, budgets, and staff development (Parkay and Stanford, 1992). While it is too early to evaluate this empowerment push for teachers or the restructuring of schools and the system as a whole, it appears that the trend of reform will continue.

Each period illustrates how current problems and opportunities reflect the past. When we look to the future and contemplate ways to make our educational system even better, we must acknowledge the debt we owe to those who have shaped the history of American education up to the present. We must be willing to be students of our past if we are to improve education in the future. The United States has set for itself an educational mission of truly ambitious proportions. We realize fully this mission will be difficult, but an examination of our history shows it is not impossible. In little more than 370 years, our educational system has grown from one that offered only minimal education to an advantaged minority, to one that now provides maximal educational opportunities to the majority.

References

Button, H. Warren, and Eugene F. Provenzo Jr. (1989). *History of Education and Culture in America*, 2nd ed. Englewood Cliffs, NJ: Prentice-Hall.

Cremin, Lawrence A. (1961). *The Transformation of the School: Progressivism in American Education, 1876–1957*. New York: Knopf.

Parkay, Forest, and Beverly H. Stanford (1992). *Becoming a Teacher*. Massachusetts: Allyn & Bacon.

Ravitch, Diane (1983). *The Troubled Crusade: American Education, 1945–1980*. New York: Basic Books.

DISCUSSION QUESTIONS

1. How does teaching today differ from teaching in colonial America?

2. What are the major social forces that have shaped American education?

3. What are the major political forces that have shaped American education?

CHAPTER 2

New and Old Myths in Education

INTRODUCTION
BY KISHA R. CUNNINGHAM, PHD

"School days, school days; dear old golden rule days. Readin' and 'ritin' and 'rithmetic; taught to the tune of a hick'ry stick."

—from "School Days," Will D. Cobb, composer

In education, there are many new and old myths that have developed throughout the history of education. It has been said that the education system today lacks depth and doesn't explore different world views. The term "technolizing learning" is used today to describe how the classroom and teaching profession have changed because of technological devices. Teaching today has acquired a reputation of being like fast food, with knowledge given out quickly through programs like Google, Twitter, and Bing. In addition to technolized learning, issues of equal opportunity, cultural deprivation, and the learning curve continue to be prevalent in education reform conversations today. This chapter examines both new and old myths in education and false ideologies often directed at those issues.

New and Old Myths in Education

BY PETER McLAREN

LIFE IN SCHOOLS: AN INTRODUCTION TO CRITICAL PEDAGOGY IN THE FOUNDATIONS OF EDUCATION

Technologizing Learning

Many mainstream approaches to curriculum development and implementation offered to classroom teachers are politically laundered and culturally sterile programs of learning in which students are taught to think in fragments isolated from the flow of everyday experience.[1] Students develop a mechanistic cognitive style within classrooms that appears at times to conform to Henry Ford's rust-proofed assembly lines. The file keepers, accountability- mongers, and "knowledge specialists" at both state and local levels have instructed teachers to segment behavior, measure fluid social activity in terms of "inputs" and "outputs," and reduce human beings to computer printouts. They inscribe the terrain of our crisis- ridden classrooms with the logic of domination through an insistence that teachers take the experiences, values, and cultural capital of working-class and minority students *less seriously than they do those of the dominant culture.* This situation often unknowingly helps perpetuate the reproduction of social and cultural inequality. As teachers, we are encouraged to be good "systems people," to create synthetic environments for our students. We dish out knowledge like fast food; burger specials arrive limp and overcooked from the Insight Kitchens of Google, Twitter, and Apple.

Today, technocratic consciousness is looked on as the new educational mechanism for generating classroom health. Teachers often give technocratic theories the benefit of the doubt and exhibit at times an incredulous penchant for following instructions and deferring to the "experts." Some of the new curriculum technologies have even been "teacher-proofed," which only contributes further to the devaluing and deskilling of teachers by removing them from the decision-making process. As teachers, we need collectively to demythologize the infallibility of educational programmers and so-called experts, who often do nothing more than zealously impose their epistemological assumptions on unassuming teachers under the guise of efficiency and procedural smoothness. What we are left with is an emphasis on *practical* and *technical* forms of knowledge as opposed to *productive* or *transfor-mative* knowledge. We are left without the chance to explore other epistemologies, other worldviews from indigenous histories and cultures. This is largely due to the epistemicide of Western imperialists with white settler mentalities who to this day demonize, hellify, and destroy the languages and ways of knowing of indigenous peoples, a practice that began with the genocide of indigenous peoples of Las Americas by the Spanish and continued into North America with the European genocide of First Nations peoples and Native Americans.

A particularly serious problem with the technocratic mentality is its appearance of objectivity and value-neutrality. What its adherents don't tell you is that a hidden political agenda oftentimes informs new policy and program directives.

Our classrooms need theory, but not the life-obstructing theories that are embedded in a technocratic worldview linked to the com-modification of human labor under capitalism. We need theories that provoke teachers to question the value assumptions that underlie their technocratic cultural terrain and throw open to scrutiny the classroom practices and social relations linked to the capitalist law of value that future teachers are forced to acquire during their teacher education.

Neoconservatism and the Myth of Democratic Schooling

Rarely discussed—or even considered—in proposed solutions to the plight of students in our nation's schools are the many invidious myths that underlie current approaches to urban education. By myths, I refer to the resurgent "truths" of conservative educational thinking that were temporarily buried in the sixties but began stirring their bones again in the educational compost during the seventies and continue to be embraced even today.[2] One of the most dangerous of these is the myth of *equal opportunity*, which maintains that the educational system is the glorious equalizer of our free society. Success can be achieved by intelligence, hard work, and creativity. Like many myths, this one forms part of our everyday perception, even though it has been proved untrue again and again.

Believers in this myth suggest that inequality results from our established form of "meritocracy," which provides students who are more capable—who try harder and have more innate intelligence—with their rightful rewards and excludes those who are less able. Some neoconservatives even claim that biology is at the root of class division, and that minority and working- class students are at the greatest disadvantage because of their unfortunately deficient gene pool. In other words, culturally and economically disadvantaged students have *inherited* a lower intellectual aptitude. It is only natural and desirable, then, that our society rewards the brightest and most able students differentially. This "intellectual impediments model" stresses that different racial and class groups are endowed with different intellectual capacities, which regrettably inhibit the success in school of minority and economically disadvantaged students.

Neoconservatives choose to ignore or misinterpret recent research that indicates that one of the greatest determinants of academic success is parental income. Referring to this cruel reality as the "Frankenstein and Einstein" syndrome, Paul Olson (1986, p. 78), a critical educational theorist, points out that parental background makes a greater difference to school achievement than measured IQ. The myth of equal opportunity therefore masks an ugly truth: The educational system is really a loaded social lottery, in which each student gets as many chances as his or her parents have dollars.

Neoconservatives argue that the desire for parity is in reality a "cult of envy." They equate the liberal vision of equality for all with their racist perception of Chinese society: zombielike, conformist, and emotionally malleable. What a dull world equality would bring. But no one argues that individual differences don't exist. The real issue is that *the education system gives those who begin with certain advantages* (the right economic status and thus the right values, the right speech patterns, the right mannerisms, the right behavior) *a better chance to retain those advantages all through school, and ensures that minority and economically disadvantaged students will remain at the bottom rung of the meritocratic ladder.*

Neoconservatives will tell you that not everybody can be president of General Motors or a CEO for Microsoft. What you can read between the lines translates somewhat differently: Why waste good taxpayers' money on the lesser breeds? They're hardly going to lead this country, except maybe at the head of the welfare rolls. This view completely ignores Noam Chomsky's argument that "success is also correlated with traits much less sanguine than intelligence: manipulativeness, greed, dishonesty, a disregard for others, and so on" (cited in Olson, 1986, p. 78).

Neoconservatives predict a resurgence of the individual. Horatio Alger, we are told, will be resurrected from the cultural woodwork where he has lurked for decades. In this atmosphere, the perennial failure of the ghetto student can often be blamed on a lack of motivation and will to succeed. Though most mainstream educational pundits fortunately don't ascribe to the myth of genetic inferiority or lack of natural ability, they do continue to rationalize the failure of lower-class, minority, and immigrant students by blaming their home environments.

This is the myth of *cultural deprivation*, which interprets social and educational problems in terms of student failure to "fit" into the social milieu. As a result, economically disadvantaged and minority students are labeled "deviant," "pathological," or "impulse- ridden" when they don't behave in the ways expected by middle- class teachers. Of course, this theory cannot account for why "deficiencies" are consistently grouped along class lines. Schools foster programs to correct these problems, to build up the skills and attitudes of ghetto children, to make up for their so-called cultural deficits and motivate their lazy, apathetic souls—rather than consider structural changes in the wider society, changes in school policy, negative teacher feeling, or curriculum implementation that might be exacerbating the problems in the first place. This again amounts to blaming students for their own miseducation.

Please don't let me be misunderstood: A student's self-image and a teacher's attitude in school do play important roles, but they are not as likely to alter the ghetto student's class position as they are to affect where he or she resides within a particular class grouping. Those within the critical tradition know that the majority of parents among the working poor do hold reasonably high expectations for their children. Nevertheless, these parents have a *realistic expectation* of how schools work for their own children, as distinct from how they work for more privileged children.

As Feinberg and Soltis (1985, pp. 34–35) point out, some advocates of the "cultural impediments model" claim that since achievement is largely the function of class culture, and since it is believed that little can be done to alter behav-ior that is rooted in class culture, compensatory school programs will have a negligible effect on school achievement. These same advocates claim that schools may even make matters appreciably worse in trying to change the social standing of the working poor, since by catering to the poor, educators water down the entire curriculum and relax academic standards for everyone. These theorists argue that inequality is the natural outgrowth of urban development, an attitude that effectively undercuts the imperatives for equality of opportunity and equality of outcome.

Once educational programs have been shrouded in these myths, they need not be abandoned when they fail. Failed programs can be—and are—used by the dominant culture as evidence to support the myth-based definitions of academic failure: that failure lies in the genes, character traits, or home lives of the students themselves. Even good programs can fail because the clientele is unreachable, hence unteachable. Failure, therefore, simply proves the assumptions on which the policy was based.

Life chances are *socially conditioned* by capitalist social relations of production, exchange, and circulation to a greater extent than they are determined by individual effort. Yet we live in a culture that stresses the merits of possessive individualism, the autonomous ego, and individual entrepreneurship. In this prevailing view, social conflicts are reduced to individual, subjective concerns rather than problems having to do with social and material inequality, the structure of capitalist society, and collective greed and privilege.

Disabilities and Discrepancies: The False Ideology of the Normal Curve

The education system has not been kind to special education students and students with disabilities. These students have suffered the most at the hands of the educational establishment that has been traditionally wedded to the notion that there is something scientifically valid about a "normal" developmental curve that ranks human beings according to hierarchically based quartile ranges. One would perhaps expect the notion of a "normal" developmental curve to be met with the liveliest incredulity, depreciation, and denunciation by teachers and educational administrators, but astonishingly this has not been the case. However, scholars in critical pedagogy and critical disability studies have risen to the occasion and are challenging the use of the normal curve as a representation of variation of human behavior within the general population and its use in labeling and characterizing specific groups of individuals. Of course, the idea of a normal curve reeks of a stance of moral superiority, with the idea of the "abnormal" (or being on the less desirous side of the curve) often considered synonymous with the excrementitious subject—the perverse, the unnatural, the diseased.

Critical educators do not believe that learning outcomes are normally distributed simply because so-called scientifically "objective" measures produce normal distributions. What is being measured, however, does not necessarily distribute normally among the human population. According to Curt Dudley-Marling and Alex Gurn (2010), the normal curve—which can be traced to the applications by Carl Gauss and Pierre-Simon Laplace of Abraham de Moivre's mathematical theory of probability and the efforts of the astronomer Adolphe Quetelet to apply the "normal curve of error" to the social realm of human beings—is a product of random measurement errors. Human behavior, however, is never completely random and is always influenced by social factors. The "mean," therefore, is not necessarily a meaningful representation of groups and individual group measures, and deviations of the mean do not signify human imperfections. For instance, the tails of the bell-shaped normal distribution do not represent "brilliance" at one end or "feeble-mindedness" at the other (Dudley-Marling and Gurn, 2010). The concept of normality, in which diverse human traits are characterized by a bell-shaped curve and the idea of a statistical norm, is, according to Dudley-Marling and Gurn, an ideological construct that "has been used to justify persistent social, economic, vocational, and academic inequalities that plague contemporary American society" (p. 19).

If, for instance, we believe Richard Herrnstein and Charles Murray's (1994) pernicious notion that extremes of income distribution and competence are viewed as natural manifestations of the normal curve, then why bother to pursue public policies aimed at eliminating poverty (Dudley-Marling and Gurn, 2010, p. 19)? (We don't need to rehearse here the storied career of Charles Murray, who participated in a Pentagon counterinsurgency operation applying counterinsurgency strategies tested in rural Thailand to US urban centers, his promotion of greater incarceration rates in the 1970s, his eugenicist work on behalf of the white elite, his attack on social welfare programs, and his argument that America's elite are genetically endowed with greater intelligence and need to pass on their value systems to the nonelite underlings to preserve the moral fabric of the country.) Studies of mean differences have been used to distinguish students with learning disabilities from students who are not learning disabled based on categories of exceptionality. Such studies have caused students from nondominant cultures to be disproportionately represented in special education classes; have supported the use of a discrepancy model and its normative assumptions for assessment and placement practices that associate a student's measured academic performance to his or her global ability measured by IQ tests that have been shown to be biased in terms of race and class; have identified best practices for students in special education classes; have justified a one-size-fits-all curriculum under the assumption that the academic performance of similarly aged students tends to cluster about the mean; and have led to the assumption that a fraction of students will necessarily fall at the lower end of the normal distribution (Dudley- Marling and Gurn, 2010; see also Valle and Gabel, 2010). Yet psychological phenomena are not inherently distributed normally, and there are plenty of behaviors that do not follow a Gaussian or normal curve. The normal curve applies only to truly random events, and in the social worlds of which we humans inhabit, most phenomena are not the result of random events and do not distribute normally. In fact, in the world of human affairs, you are likely to see nonnormal distribution in the form of right-or positive- skew distributions (Dudley-Marling and Gurn, 2010). Hence we see too little descriptive and adaptive approaches to classroom pedagogy and an overwhelming preponderance of peda-gogies related to effectiveness and prediction in terms of normative distribution. While the passing and reauthorization of the Individuals with Disabilities Education Act recommends that states adopt response to intervention (RTI) models and abandon discrepancy models, Valle and Gabel (2010) warn that the RTI models should not be used to identify children with disabilities, since such approaches can amplify an adherence to the discourse of normativity (Gurn, 2010).

Endnotes

1. For a fuller discussion of this point, see McLaren (1982).
2. See McLaren (1981).

References

Dudley-Marling, Curt, and Gurn, Alex. (2010). "Troubling the Foundations of Special Education: Examining the Myth of the Normal Curve." In Curt Dudley-Marling and Alex Gurn (Eds.), *The Myth of the Normal Curve* (pp. 9–23). New York: Peter Lang.

Feinberg, W., and Soltis, J. F. (1985). *School and Society*. New York: Teachers College Press.

Gurn, Alex. (2010). "Conclusion: Re/visioning the Ideological Imagination in (Special) Education." In Curt Dudley-Marling and Alex Gurn (Eds.), *The Myth of the Normal Curve* (pp. 241–256). New York: Peter Lang.

Herrnstein, Richard J., and Murray, Charles. (1994). *The Bell Curve: Intelligence and Class Structure in American Life*. New York: Free Press.

McLaren, P. (1981, October 15). "Education as Myth." *Ontario Public School Teachers' Federation News*, p. 17.

McLaren, P. (1982, April 1). "The Technocratic Classroom." *Ontario Public School Teachers' Federation News*, p. 11.

Olson, P. (1986). "Methods, Interpretations, and Different Views of Aspirations." *Interchange*, Vol. 17, No. 1, pp. 76–81.

Valle, Jan, and Gabel, Susan. (2010). "The Sirens of Normative Mythology: Mother Narratives of Engagement and Resistance." In Curt Dudley-Marling and Alex Gurn (Eds.), *The Myth of the Normal Curve* (pp. 187–204). New York: Peter Lang.

DISCUSSION QUESTIONS

1. What does the term "system people" mean? What effect does it have on education?
2. How is equal opportunity viewed in education today?
3. Why is the normal learning curve considered false?

Social Context in Education

CHAPTER 3

School Choice

INTRODUCTION
BY KISHA R. CUNNINGHAM, PHD

"Alice came to a fork in the road. 'Which road do I take?' she asked.
'Where do you want to go?' responded the Cheshire Cat.
'I don't know,' Alice answered. '
Then,' said the Cat, 'it doesn't matter.'"

—Lewis Carroll, *Alice in Wonderland*

Prior to the legislature of Section 105 of the School Aid Act, students could enroll in other districts by enrolling as tuition students. The No Child Left Behind Act provides new education options for families and allows students to leave their current district of residence to enroll in a school within the same district if their child attends a school that needs improvement or the school their child attends is unsafe. This federal law also allows parents to take advantage of free tutoring. The law requires that states and local school districts provide information to help parents make informed decisions regarding their child's education. This chapter focuses on schools of choice in the United States, particularly open enrollment, and discusses their advantages and disadvantages.

Schools of Choice

MICHAEL F. ADDONIZIO AND C. PHILIP KEARNEY
EDUCATION REFORM AND THE LIMITS OF POLICY: LESSON FROM MICHIGAN

Following passage of Public Act 362 of 1993 and subsequent legislation that created Michigan's charter school program, the Michigan legislature expanded the state's educational choice initiatives by creating a schools of choice program in 1997.[1] This legislation, Section 105 of the School Aid Act, required all local school boards to decide whether or not they would accept nonresident students in their schools. Those districts opting into the program were required to publish the schools, grades, and programs open to nonresidents and then accept applications. If the number of applicants exceeded available slots, enrollees would be selected by random lottery.[2]

Prior to this legislation, students could enroll in other districts as nonresidents in one of two ways. First, they could enroll as tuition students, with tuition calculated according to a (nearly incomprehensible) section of the School Aid Act.[3] Alternatively, the student's district of residence could release the revenue associated with the student to the enrolling district, enabling the student to receive free tuition. As one would expect, such permission was rarely granted. The new "schools of choice" law allowed students to leave any district of residence to enter a choice school within the same intermediate school district (ISD), and the associated revenue (i.e., foundation allowance) followed automatically. Specifically, the enrolling district receives the lesser of the foundation allowance of the resident district and the enrolling district. Further, the enrolling district is prohibited from charging tuition in any form to make up any revenue differences.

Michigan's schools of choice program was expanded in 2000 to include contiguous districts outside the ISD and to include districts in any contiguous ISD the following year.[4] As with the 1997 legislation, local school boards electing to enroll nonresidents were required to select such students by lottery if their district was oversubscribed and, again, the enrolling district receives the lower of its own and the resident district's per pupil foundation allowance. Districts electing to enroll nonresidents are not required to provide transportation to choice schools, although anecdotal evidence reveals that some districts do send school buses into neighboring districts for this purpose.

While adopting both charter schools and schools of choice, Michi-gan legislators and voters defeated two efforts to institute school voucher programs in the state. In 1999, Senate Bill 31 was introduced to give vouchers to students in cities with a population exceeding 750,000. The proposal, of course, would have impacted only the Detroit school district. Students from families earning less than 150 percent of the federal poverty level would have been eligible for the vouchers. The bill, however, died in committee.

Following the demise of Senate Bill 31, business executive and former Michigan Board of Education member Richard DeVos led a coalition of education, civic, and business leaders in forming Kids First! Yes! which sought to amend the Michigan Constitution to give parents whose children attend school in districts that failed to graduate two-thirds of their students a publicly funded voucher worth one-half of the district's per pupil expenditure to attend a school of their choosing. As a sweetener, Proposal 1 would have guaranteed that public school spending would never fall below the current level and would have required teacher testing in academic subjects.[5] Opponents of the proposal organized under the name All Kids First! On November 7, 2000, Michigan voters defeated Proposal 1 by a margin of more than 2 to 1.

Among the various forms of K–12 school choice, voucher programs, which encompass private as well as public schools, are easily the most controversial. This controversy stems primarily from the use of public revenue to fund religious school education, a practice prohibited by most state constitutions, including Michigan's.[6] In addition to constitutional issues regarding the separa-tion of church and state, critics cite the potential of vouchers to increase social stratification along racial, ethnic, academic, and socioeconomic lines (Goldhaber and Eide 2002). Concern over such stratification has also been raised in connection with charter schools and interdistrict choice, but the objections have been less strident, probably because these reforms involve only public schools, which are tuition-free and, with rare exception, equally accessible to all appli-cants.[7] Consequently, these public choice initiatives have enjoyed much more public support in Michigan and across the states.

Rationale for Schools of Choice

This form of educational choice, often referred to as open enrollment, appears on the surface to be a more modest policy reform than charter schools.[8] These programs do not alter school gover-nance, as do charter schools, and may not hold the same potential for curricular and instructional innovation as the more autonomous charter schools. Rather, open enrollment programs enlarge geographic school attendance boundaries, so students are not limited to their neighborhood schools. The first state open enrollment law was adopted by Minnesota in 1987. Since then, the number of states with open enrollment programs has grown to 42. Of these, 19 states have mandatory laws and 23 have voluntary programs. Mandatory laws require local school boards to promulgate open enrollment policies, while voluntary laws allow such local district policies (Witte, Carlson, and Lavery 2008).

In essence, open enrollment breaks the link between household and school location. In so doing, these programs could reduce the socioeconomic and racial stratification of students, allowing students to cross boundaries of local districts that segregate families along these lines. On the other hand, interdistrict choice could exacerbate such segregation as families further sort themselves without having to change their place of residence.

Advocates of these and other market-based education reforms, including charter schools, vouchers, and tuition tax credits, generally assert that the resulting competitive pressures exerted on schools will improve the productivity of the educational system as a whole (see, e.g., Friedman 1955; Chubb and Moe 1990; Hoxby 2000, 2002). That is, competition among schools will benefit not only those students who actively choose to participate in these programs, but also those who remain in their traditional, neighborhood schools. This argument, which often emphasizes the private rather than public (or civic) benefits of education, rests on the notion that traditional public schools essentially enjoy a monopoly over students living in their attendance areas, and that monopolies, protected as they are from competition, do not use resources efficiently. Choice advocates further assert that if the money follows the student, a market-based choice program will cause good schools to prosper and grow, while bad schools will either improve or disappear (Hoxby 2000).

By this line of reasoning, school choice advocates see the potential for particularly substantial educational gains for minority and low-income children who traditionally attend low-performing schools. Indeed, studies show that support for school choice, whether open enrollment, charter schools, or vouchers, varies by racial/ethnic group and with the quality of available public schools. For example, a 1993 survey of Michigan residents revealed greater support for a proposed public school choice plan among Detroit residents, particularly lower-income minority residents and those less supportive of their neighbor-hood schools (Lee, Croninger, and Smith 1994).

At the same time, however, these market-based reforms have been criticized on the grounds that they may compromise the public purposes of schools, particularly those regarding civic participation and social cohesion. That is, the idea that schools should contribute to equality of social, economic, and political opportunities for people of different racial and socioeconomic backgrounds suggests that all students be exposed to a common educational experience that ought not be left to the vagaries of individual or family preferences (Levin 1991, 2000; Fiske and Ladd 2000; Gill et al. 2001). For example, school competition could exacerbate the stratification of students across schools by race, class, and ability or deemphasize preparation for citizenship. Such an instance of market failure could arise if schools and parents are interested not only in school quality, but also in the characteristics of the student body. Specifically, if parents select schools at least partly on the basis of the socioeconomic profile of the student body and schools have some ability to influence their applicant pool (e.g., by selective advertising or social networking), then competition could increase stratification (Epple and Romano 2000; Ladd 2002).

Critics say that the school choice initiatives can impair the effi-ciency of schools that lose students to their competitors. First, more motivated students and parents may be more likely to actively choose their schools, leaving their less motivated counterparts concentrated in the less attractive schools (Levin 1998; Witte 2000). These schools would then become increasingly less capable of competing in the educational marketplace as their positive peer influences leave. Second, as revenues decline in tandem with enrollments but operating costs do not, these schools are forced to cut programs and services, triggering further losses (Fiske and Ladd 2000).

Impacts of Open Enrollment Programs

Although open enrollment is arguably the least innovative of the school choice initiatives, more closely resembling the traditional system of local public schools than either charter school or voucher programs, as a form of school choice, open enrollment can be expected to exert several important effects on students and communities, and these effects may be interrelated. In addition to the straightforward fiscal effects of school choice, other important but less obvious effects are those on school performance and student sorting. In examining these effects, we must consider why families value school choice. To the extent that parents choose schools on the basis of their educational quality, one could expect that school choice would improve school efficiency. That is, schools can be expected to strive for improvements in teaching and learning to attract new students and the resources that accompany them. Conversely, to the extent parents choose

31

schools on the basis of the socioeconomic profile of the student body, choice could compromise school efficiency as school incentives are directed away from academic performance and toward selective advertising and recruitment activities (Ladd 2002; Rothstein 2006).

Despite the widespread adoption of open enrollment programs across the states, researchers have focused primarily on the effects of the alternative school choice mechanisms of vouchers and charter schools. Moreover, although we now have a fairly substantial body of research on the effects of school competition on educational outcomes, much of this work examines the effects of competition from nearby private schools or neighboring public school districts. Reviewing more than 40 studies in the United States, Belfield and Levin (2002) find that competition has modest positive effects on student achievement. The research literature on the effects of open enrollment programs, in contrast, is relatively scant. A study of well-established open enrollment programs in Minnesota and Colorado finds that students tended to leave districts with higher proportions of low-income and low-achieving students and enroll in districts with greater concentrations of middle-class and higher-achieving students (Witte, Carlson, and Lavery 2008). Such effects are not unexpected, but the full array of short-and longer-term impacts of open enrollment programs continue to unfold.

FISCAL EFFECTS

The most immediate effect of children moving from one district to another is the accompanying transfer of revenue and creation of financial winners and losers. The common practice across the states of paying for schooling by the student ignores a number of important realities about the costs of operating schools. First, almost all instruction takes place in classroom groups, so the actual personnel costs of adding a single student to a classroom are essentially zero. And this is certainly so if the open enrollment program is limited to filling empty classroom seats, as is generally true in Michigan. Similarly, overhead costs for such things as buildings, administration, and even transportation are not increased by the addition of even a substantial number of students if seats are available for them. Conversely, the district of residence sees no reduction in operating costs as it loses students to neighboring districts.[9]

As a result, an open enrollment program such as Michigan's, in which a full per pupil foundation allowance follows the child, provides a windfall for the enrolling district and a corresponding loss for the sending district. Further, to the extent students seek transfer to schools in more afflu-ent or more academically successful districts, such a program will likely exacerbate the quality differences between districts and encourage further transfers. At the same time, however, the absence of such financial rewards and penalties would give public school districts little incentive to improve their programs and respond to parents' educational demands.[10]

EDUCATIONAL EFFECTS

Empirical evidence on the academic effects of school choice is mixed. Those studies that do find positive effects also tend to find that minority students living in urban areas benefit the most from school choice (e.g., Goldhaber and Eide 2002). On the other hand, choice reforms could adversely impact such students as enrollments and resources shift from one set of schools to another in these communities (Addonizio 1994). The distinction, of course, depends on who elects to change schools and who does not.

Some evidence of the educational effects of competition among public schools is taken from large-scale intradistrict choice programs in New York City and Chicago. Community District 4 on the upper east side of New York City has been widely acclaimed as an example of a high poverty district serving predominantly minority students that has seen dramatic improvements in student achievement following the introduction of school choice. Starting in 1973, the district formed more than 20 alternative schools from which parents could choose. In creating these alternative schools or programs, District 4 leaders severed the traditional correspondence between buildings and schools. Several programs, usually employing different educational approaches and serving different age groups, were housed in the same building (Elmore 1990).

Most research on District 4 points to the dramatic improvements in student achievement, but researchers disagree as to how much of the gains are attributable to choice and competition. Other possible contributing factors cited by researchers include higher achieving students attracted to the district by the innovations, increased resource levels, and school downsizing (Teske et al. 1999). One could argue, however, that these additional factors are themselves desirable attributes of any well-conceived school choice program that provide educators the resources and latitude to offer new educational alternatives.

One study of Chicago's high school open enrollment program that used distance from a student's home to school of attendance to identify active choosers reveals little impact on academic outcomes district-wide, but it does find a small positive impact on graduation rates for some students attending career academies, a type of vocational school (Cullen, Jacob, and Levitt 2000). A second study comparing academic outcomes between lottery winners and losers in

Chicago's high school choice program finds little evidence that attending sought-after programs improves students' academic outcomes, whether standardized test scores, attendance rates, or credits earned.[11] Further, while the study finds some evidence that lottery winners attending sought-after schools were less likely to report that they were disciplined at school or arrested, they were not more likely to expect to graduate college, enjoy school, have positive interactions with peers or teachers, or feel safe at school (Cullen, Jacob, and Levitt 2003).

PEER EFFECTS

In addition to the impact of school choice on student achievement, a second question dominating the school choice debate is whether choice results in greater student sorting or stratification. That is, given a choice of school or district, will families sort themselves by race, socioeconomic class, or some other characteristic in a way that would weaken community bonds and social cohesion? And one could easily imagine such sorting also impairing the educational achievement of particular student groups.

Prior to about 1990, school choice for families in the United States consisted almost exclusively of choosing the school district in which to live or sending children to private school. Accordingly, much of the research on school choice focused on this type of "Tiebout choice," or "voting with one's feet."[12] Clotfelter (1999) finds evidence of student sorting across districts, but Hoxby (2000) and Alesina, Baqir, and Hoxby (2000) conclude that more student sorting occurs within districts across schools. Urquiola (2005), examining the effects of school district concentration and competition in U.S. metropolitan areas, finds that competition among school districts does contribute to student stratification, but adds that this observed sorting may also reflect residential segregation patterns possibly unrelated to schooling and school district boundaries.

The introduction of open enrollment and charter school programs in the 1990s created new avenues for student sorting, as families were no longer restricted by school district boundaries when choosing their public schools. This new sorting could occur in two general ways. First, as noted earlier, households may differ in their interest and ability to exercise this newfound choice. More specifically, choosing households may be of higher socioeconomic status than nonchoosing households, raising the possibility that white students, more academically able students, and students from families with more educational resources will leave their traditional public schools for schools of choice. This hypothesis is supported by a substantial body of research (e.g., Lee, Croninger, and Smith 1996; Armor and Peiser 1998; Witte 2000). Second, active choosers may sort themselves as well, possibly along racial or class lines. Less research is available on this question, but a rigorous study by Weiher and Tedin (2002) of school choice in Texas finds that race is a good predictor of the school choices made by choosing households. Analyzing the choices of 1,006 charter school households, the authors find that whites, African Americans, and Latinos transfer into charter schools where their groups comprise between 11 and 14 percentage points more of the student body than the traditional public schools they are leaving. Further, the vast majority of choosing households transfer their children into charter schools with *lower* performance on the state achievement test than the traditional schools they left. Interestingly, this observed behavior largely contradicted preferences expressed by these households on surveys designed to elicit their criteria for choosing a school.

Impacts in Michigan

Following passage of the schools of choice legislation, many Michigan school districts saw an opportunity to increase their operating revenue. By the program's second year, 45 percent of districts were accepting nonresidents and by the fifth year, fully 80 percent of Michigan's districts had signed on. Statewide pupil counts, however, were quite modest in the program's early years, with schools of choice enrollments rising from 7,836 in 1997 to 33,506 in 2001, about 2 percent of Michigan's K–12 enrollment (Cullen and Loeb 2003). Examining the first two years of the program, Arsen, Plank, and Sykes (2000) find participation highest in rural and central-city school districts.[13] It was much lower in suburban districts and lowest of all in high-income districts and districts with growing resident enrollments. This finding is not surprising. While the fiscal effects are unambiguously positive for a district enrolling nonresident students to fill otherwise empty desks, some districts may decline to participate in the program because of concerns over peer effects, real or perceived. Put simply, local boards of education may fear that without the authority to screen applicants, the district runs some risk of enrolling undesirable students, including low achievers, those with behavioral problems, or racial minorities.[14]

Arsen, Plank, and Sykes (2000) also find that transferring students were moving to districts with higher family incomes, higher MEAP scores, and lower concentrations of minority students than their home districts. For rural districts as a group, student outflows were roughly offset by inflows, while central cities sustained an average 0.7 percent enrollment loss. For some urban districts, however, the net loss of students and revenue was much larger.[15]

RECENT TRENDS

Michigan's schools of choice program has grown in recent years. We obtained data from the MDE on Sec. 105 and Sec. 105C enrollments (full-time equivalent student counts [FTEs]) from the program's inception in 1996–97 through 2008–09.

With the exception of 2001–02, statewide participation in Michi-gan's schools of choice pro-gram has risen each year since its inception. This steady growth in schools of choice enrollments, moreover, has occurred during periods of both growth and decline in Michigan's total public school enrollments. These data are presented in Table 6.1.

As the data show, the rate of participation in Michigan's schools of choice program has grown steadily since its inception and is now approaching 5 percent of Michigan's K–12 enroll-ment.[16] This growth is undoubtedly fueled by the growing financial pressure on local school districts, a topic discussed in Chapter 3. Because local districts can control the scope of their participation in the program, designating the schools, grades, and number of slots available to nonresidents, they can essentially seek to fill empty desks, thereby gaining revenue while controlling operating costs.

COUNTY AND LOCAL IMPACTS

These totals, while showing steady annual growth statewide, conceal the very uneven impact of schools of choice across localities. The majority of local districts in Michigan are largely unaf-fected by the program, neither losing nor gaining enrollments to any substantial degree. But many districts in major metropolitan areas are significantly impacted, with some districts enroll-ing substantial numbers and proportions of nonresident students. Much of this interdistrict student movement has occurred in the tri-county region of southeastern Michigan, consisting of Wayne, Oakland, and Macomb counties. Table 6.2 lists the 28 local districts whose schools of choice enrollments numbered at least 500 and accounted for at least 15 percent of total district enrollment in 2008–09.

Table 3.1. Statewide Participation in Schools of Choice, 1996–97 through 2008–09

Year	Nonresident enrollment	Total enrollment	Nonresident as % total enrollment
1996–97	7,386	1,680,693	0.44
1997–98	10,576	1,694,320	0.62
1998–99	14,413	1,709,892	0.84
1999–00	19,045	1,714,815	1.11
2000–01	33,506	1,720,335	1.95
2001–02	33,248	1,731,092	1.92
2002–03	39,800	1,750,631	2.27
2003–04	50,247	1,734,019	2.90
2004–05	57,671	1,708,585	3.38
2005–06	63,279	1,697,900	3.73
2006–07	66,673	1,678,480	3.97
2007–08	74,091	1,648,540	4.49
2008–09	76,650	1,615,371	4.75

Source: MDE.

While Michigan's total schools of choice enrollment accounted for less than 5 percent of the state's total K–12 enrollment in 2008–09, this 13-year-old state program is the source of a substantial share of student enrollments and operating revenue for some local districts. As noted earlier, participation in the choice program is a local decision, and success in attracting nonresident students depends on local marketing efforts as well as reputation. As a result, local impacts vary, even for neighboring districts. Indeed, competition for students is often most intense among neighboring communities, fostering local rivalries and resentments not seen in the charter school movement. An example of diverse impacts on neighboring districts is provided by Highland Park, which enrolls fully 57 percent of its students from outside the district (with the vast majority of these choice students living in the Detroit Public School District), and

Table 3.2. Districts with High Schools of Choice Enrollments, 2008–09

District	Sec. 105 enrollment	Total enrollment	Percent Sec. 105 enrollment
Highland Park	1,563	2,747	56.9
Inkster	1,526	3,005	50.8
Clintondale	1,758	3,647	48.2
Vandercook	540	1,302	41.5
Carrollton	703	1,792	39.3
Oak Park	1,467	3,771	38.9
Westwood	685	1,923	35.6
Dearborn Heights	1,013	2,847	35.6
Madison (Oakland)	523	1,520	34.4
Riverview	838	2,641	31.7
Corunna	764	2,438	31.4
Lakeview	875	3,132	28.0
Essexville-Hampton	537	1,923	27.9
Pennfield	535	2,029	26.4
Melvindale-N. Allen	654	2,800	23.4
Ypsilanti	898	3,877	23.2
Western	659	2,865	23.0
West Bloomfield	1,567	6,845	22.9
Bangor	553	2,540	21.8
Ferndale	758	4,033	18.8
Southgate	988	5,467	18.1
Lakeview (Calhoun)	685	3,790	18.1
East Lansing	604	3,417	17.7
Berkley	776	4,407	17.6
Allen Park	639	3,730	17.1
Fraser	772	4,802	16.1
Warren Woods	517	3,391	15.3
Saginaw Twp.	805	5,334	15.1

Source: MDE.

neighboring Hamtramck, which enrolls a mere 8 percent from outside the district. A local school board's decision about enrolling nonresidents is multifaceted, involving educational, financial, and political considerations. Moreover, for those local districts choosing to participate, success in enrolling nonresidents depends on the aggressiveness of the district's marketing efforts and the district's image, socioeconomic characteristics, and academic reputation. And, of course, districts must be concerned with loss of resident enrollment whether they pursue nonresident students or not.

Some insight into the dynamics of Michigan's schools of choice program can be gained by examining participation at the county level. Fully 17 of the 28 local districts listed in Table 6.2 are located in the three counties of Michigan's southeastern region, with Wayne, Oak-land, and Macomb counties claiming 8, 5, and 4 of these 28 high choice enrollment districts, respectively. At the same time, however, while nonresident enrollments are quite high in these 17 local districts, participation rates are considerably higher in several other counties and zero or near zero in others. Nonresident enrollment rates for selected counties for the past five years are presented in Table 3.3.

The counties (each an ISD) are ordered by their 2008–09 schools of choice enrollment rates, from high to low. The three most active counties in 2008–09, Jackson, Berrien, and Saginaw, were also the most active in each of the last five years, in terms of participation rates. Moreover, nonresident enrollment rates have increased in each of the past four years in each of these counties. Indeed, the numbers and proportions of nonresident enrollments have increased steadily across most of these counties, reflecting the state's steady growth in open enrollment activity. Notable exceptions, however, include Kent and Genesee ISDs, which have eschewed the state's choice program in favor of their own cooperative student transfer programs.

At the same time, nonresident enrollment rates vary considerably across local districts within each county, again reflecting the localized nature of school choice in Michigan. These local district rates are presented for Jackson County in Table 3.4.

As a percentage of total public school enrollment, the level of open enrollment activity in Jackson County has been the highest in the state for each of the past five years. Local districts enrolling the highest proportions of nonresidents have been Vandercook Lake, Western, East Jackson, Hanover-Horton, and Michigan Center. It is no coincidence that each of these districts has recorded high school graduation rates among the highest in the county and well in excess of Jackson Public School District.[17] Jackson City Schools has been the big loser in the county's schools of choice program. The district's enrollment gains and losses in schools of choice are

Table 3.3. Nonresident Enrollments Selected Counties 2004–05 through 2008–09

County	2004–05		2005–06		2006–07		2007–08		2008–09	
	FTE	%	FTE	%	FTE	%	FTE	%	FTE	%
Jackson	2,918	10.95	2,997	11.26	3,226	12.19	3,379	13.11	3,516	13.94
Berrien	2,429	8.77	2,631	9.69	2,879	10.73	3,009	11.38	3,130	12.01
Saginaw	3,457	9.78	3,526	10.18	3,627	10.75	3,816	11.55	3,855	11.91
Ingham	3,196	6.59	3,364	7.05	3,563	7.56	3,719	8.01	3,847	8.48
Midland	799	5.49	834	5.83	393	2.79	961	6.88	1,011	7.39
Macomb	4,782	3.48	5,703	4.10	6,545	4.69	7,822	5.64	9,244	6.68
Oakland	7,490	3.68	8,056	3.95	8,679	4.24	9,175	4.54	9,452	4.71
Washtenaw	1,229	2.58	1,508	3.15	1,585	3.31	1,695	3.60	1,971	4.19
Wayne	9,307	2.60	9,721	2.76	9,914	2.90	11,893	3.59	11,791	3.70
Kalamazoo	138	0.40	152	0.45	222	0.65	219	0.65	252	0.75
Muskegon	161	0.58	566	1.74	669	2.09	1,100	3.49	165	0.53
Genesee	56	0.07	70	0.08	79	0.10	109	0.14	119	0.15
Kent	0	0	0	0	0	0	0	0	0	0
Group	35,962	3.13	39,128	3.41	41,381	3.65	46,897	4.21	48,353	4.43
State	57,671	3.38	63,279	3.73	66,673	3.97	74,091	4.49	76,650	4.75

Source: MDE.

Table 3.4. Local Districts in Jackson County nonresident Enrollments 2004–05 through 2008–09

Local district	2004–05		2005–06		2006–07		2007–08		2008–09	
	FTE	%	FTE	%	FTE	%	FTE	%	FTE	%
Western	551	19.5	554	19.2	619	21.0	644	22.2	659	23.0
Vandercook Lake	473	35.5	471	35.0	498	36.8	506	38.3	540	41.5
Columbia	154	8.6	140	7.8	168	9.4	171	9.8	203	12.0
Grass Lake	91	7.8	98	8.3	115	9.5	155	12.5	181	14.2
Concord	118	11.8	110	11.1	136	14.1	150	15.5	160	17.4
East Jackson	315	19.6	312	20.1	310	20.8	329	22.7	297	22.3
Hanover-Horton	218	15.5	247	18.0	255	18.7	275	20.4	306	22.7
Michigan Center	324	22.0	316	21.4	291	20.1	284	20.3	311	22.1
Napoleon	129	7.9	148	8.9	166	10.1	216	13.3	220	13.8
Northwest	143	4.0	143	4.1	158	4.7	183	5.7	174	5.7
Springport	107	10.1	129	12.1	128	12.2	128	12.4	147	14.2
Jackson	296	4.4	329	4.9	381	5.7	338	5.2	318	5.0

Source: MDE.

Table 3.5. Jackson Public Schools Enrollment Losses Due to Schools of Choice, 2000–10, Fall Pupil Counts (FTE)

Year	Enrollment gain	Enrollment loss	Net loss
2000	102.30	831.01	728.71
2001	92.00	888.67	796.67
2002	162.80	1,052.39	889.59
2003	186.34	1,186.75	1,000.41
2004	251.95	1,345.32	1,093.37
2005	295.52	1,500.68	1,205.16
2006	329.30	1,486.50	1,157.20
2007	381.03	1,527.45	1,146.42
2008	338.00	1,587.00	1,249.00
2009	318.25	1,646.40	1,328.15
2010	284.06	1,756.83	1,472.77

Source: MDE.

given in Table 3.5. Jackson City was losing enrollment prior to the inception of schools of choice, but the choice program has managed to accelerate this trend in recent years, starting in 2004–05.

BERRIEN COUNTY—A TALE OF THREE DISTRICTS

Two of the three local districts in Berrien County where nonresidents exceed 200 FTEs and 20 percent of enrollment are Coloma and Eau Claire. (The third is Bridgman.) And the district with the smallest nonresident enrollment is Benton Harbor, with a mere 12 nonresidents, or 0.3 percent of enrollment. A five-year history of nonresident enrollments for local districts in Berrien County is presented in Table 6.6. Benton Harbor schools are open to nonresidents but few families in neighboring communities have shown interest in enrolling. Clearly, the movement of choice students has been away from Benton Harbor and toward Coloma and Eau Claire, among other districts. We can track this migration of students from Benton Harbor with administrative data compiled by the MDE for their state aid payment system. Table 6.7 provides

Table 3.6. Local Districts in berrien County nonresident Enrollments 2004–05 through 2008–09

District	2004–05		2005–06		2006–07		2007–08		2008–09	
	FTE	%	FTE	%	FTE	%	FTE	%	FTE	%
Benton Harbor	4	<0.1	3	<0.1	4	0.1	17	0.4	12	0.3
St. Joseph	5	0.2	75	2.7	140	5.0	215	7.6	234	8.2
Lakeshore	15	0.5	57	2.0	102	3.5	145	4.9	161	5.5
River Valley	96	9.6	91	9.8	91	10.5	87	10.7	81	10.6
Galien Twp.	33	18.9	58	32.6	67	38.3	58	31.0	61	37.0
New Buffalo	182	26.5	192	29.6	195	29.3	185	28.1	164	24.9
Brandywine	194	13.1	202	14.0	228	15.5	212	14.5	235	16.5
Berrien Springs	235	14.5	283	16.6	363	20.5	389	22.2	457	24.3
Eau Claire	205	24.0	221	26.0	248	30.0	252	31.1	207	28.1
Niles	198	4.9	195	4.8	208	5.2	204	5.2	247	6.3
Buchanan	199	11.3	190	11.1	189	11.0	205	12.0	201	12.0
Watervliet	231	16.8	234	17.5	230	17.3	255	19.2	244	19.1
Coloma	512	23.2	510	24.0	482	23.4	425	22.2	424	22.9
Bridgman	233	22.7	231	22.2	238	23.8	267	26.7	292	29.6
Hagar Twp.#6	49	71.0	37	52.2	40	58.0	31	54.4	45	73.8
Sodus Twp.#5	38	61.3	52	80.0	54	84.4	64	85.3	65	91.5

Source: MDE.

a historical profile of the district's student exodus from 2000 to 2010 under the state's schools of choice program.

Such movement of students across public schools in and around Benton Harbor has been of enormous social, political, and legal consequence for decades. The Benton Harbor, Coloma, and Eau Claire districts were principals in a 35-year federal desegregation case that spanned the period of 1967–2002. The case originated with a lawsuit filed against the Benton Harbor School District by the parent of a student and the NAACP, claiming the district was discriminating against and segregating black students. Specifically, plaintiffs alleged that black teachers were

Table 3.7. The Exodus of benton Harbor Residents under Schools of Choice, by Enrolling District, 2000–01 through 2010–11

Year	Coloma	Eau Claire	Berrien	Watervliet	Bridgman	St. Joseph	Other	Total
2000	78	70	14	10	5	0	14	191
2001	138	76	10	27	10	0	28	289
2002	167	102	48	41	17	0	54	428
2003	191	102	68	44	35	1	80	521
2004	280	153	100	42	36	0	63	674
2005	378	121	105	53	40	3	86	786
2006	363	166	138	54	29	45	124	919
2007	365	192	207	43	22	100	146	1075
2008	299	194	218	56	28	161	172	1127
2009	270	164	274	63	23	173	175	1142
2010	289	230	315	86	13	177	263	1373

Source: MDE.

assigned to black schools and white teachers to white schools, and that in the junior high and high schools, which were more integrated than the elementary schools, students were tracked, with most black students placed in the slower sections (Kotlowitz 1998).

The litigation dragged on for 15 years before the plaintiffs eventually prevailed. In 1981, Judge Douglas Hillman of the Western District Court of Michigan found that officials of the predominantly white Coloma and Eau Claire school districts promoted "white flight" from the largely black Benton Harbor School District by taking transfer students, mostly white, from the district on a tuition basis and ordered the desegregation of Benton Harbor, Eau Claire, and Coloma schools. The court order called for voluntary busing between Benton Harbor and the two heavily white neighboring districts "whenever such transfer would result in decreasing segregation in each school system" (*Berry v. School District of City of Benton Harbor* 1981).[18] The court also ordered extraordinary state payments to Benton Harbor for magnet educational programs.

The desegregation order remained in force until April 4, 2002, when Judge Hillman granted the state of Michigan's motion for "unitary status," a declaration that all remaining effects of past segregation in Benton Harbor had been eliminated.[19] The ruling phased out the program of court-ordered state payments, which had totaled more than $116 million, to the district and effectively ended the 35-year-old case.[20]

Since Judge Hillman's decision terminating the federal desegregation efforts in Benton Harbor, the racial composition of the district has changed little, with the proportion of children who are African American remaining about 94 percent. These students, however, have become even more poor, with the proportion who are economically disadvantaged (i.e., eligible for free or reduced price lunch under the national school lunch act) rising from 79.6 percent in 2002–03 to an astronomical 98 percent in 2008–09. Over this same period, the proportion of African American students has fallen in both Coloma and Eau Claire, and the proportion of economically disadvantaged students has fallen dramatically in Eau Claire. These data on the racial and socioeconomic composition of the students in these districts, along with neighboring Bridgman Public Schools and the public school academies of Berrien County, are presented in Tables 6.3A and 3.8B.

Although these descriptive data do not establish a causal relationship between the advent of schools of choice and the growing socioeconomic stratification across the local districts involved in the court order, the correlation between Michigan's schools of choice program and the increasing socioeconomic isolation of the children in Benton Harbor Public Schools is unmistakable. This phenomenon is depicted in Figure 1.

Table 3.8A. Percent African American Students Selected Districts in berrien County

District	2000–01	2001–02	2002–03	2003–04	2004–05	2005–06	2006–07	2007–08
Benton Harbor	92.7	93.9	93.6	94.0	94.8	94.4	94.0	94.3
Coloma	18.9	16.8	14.2	14.6	15.4	14.3	15.0	12.7
Eau Claire	17.4	15.8	14.4	14.2	13.2	15.0	15.8	14.0
Bridgman	0.7	0.7	0.4	0.6	0.7	1.2	0.8	1.4
PSAs					67.1	71.3	72.8	73.4

Source: MDE. PSA figures are enrollment weighted averages.

Table 3.8b. Percent of Economically Disadvantaged Selected Districts in berrien County

District	2000–01	2001–02	2002–03	2003–04	2004–05	2005–06	2006–07	2007–08
Benton Harbor	84.5	80.5	79.6	86.8	89.0	74.3	87.5	92.2
Coloma	40.4	40.7	42.0	50.2	51.0	44.9	52.3	41.6
Eau Claire	51.8	54.4	56.2	58.7	67.0	51.8	27.9	27.0
Bridgman	12.9	11.9	15.2	19.2	19.0	23.6	27.0	23.8
PSAs					76.1	85.5	67.8	59.5

Source: MDE PSA figures are enrollment-weighted averages

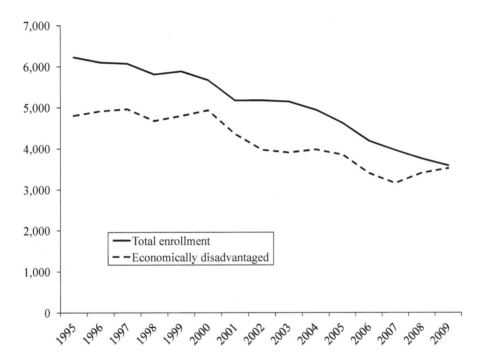

Figure 1. Benton Harbor Area Schools Enrollment History
Source: MDE.

The data draw a stark picture of a school district beset by steadily declining enrollment and rising poverty. Over this period, Benton Harbor Area Schools has lost nearly half its enrollment, while the percentage of its students who are economically disadvantaged has risen to an astonishing 98 percent by 2009, as noted above. Certainly this outcome is not entirely attributable to the state's open enrollment program. Outmigration, charter schools, and generally declining economic activity have all played a role. Nevertheless, it is equally clear that open enrollment activity has contributed substantially to the school district's plight of racial segregation and poverty. A history of the exodus of Benton Harbor residents to neighboring school districts is depicted in Figure 2, with the most popular destinations individually identified.

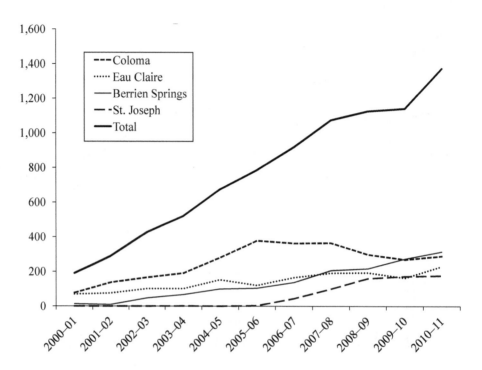

Figure 2. Benton Harbor Area Schools Enrollment History
Source: MDE.

SAGINAW COUNTY

Saginaw County public school districts are the third most active county group in terms of participation rate in the state's open enrollment program. This is so despite the nonparticipation of two of the county's 13 local districts. One of the nonparticipants, Frankenmuth, is by far the wealthiest district in the county as measured by residential property wealth per pupil, while the other nonparticipant, Freeland, ranks fourth.[21] A history of open enrollment in the county is presented in Table 3.9.

Systematic effects of the county's relatively high rate of participation are not readily apparent from these data. For example, Carrollton, with the greatest proportion of nonresident students, ranks last among the county's local districts in residential property wealth, just ahead of Saginaw City. Further, while Saginaw City School District has steadily lost enrollment since 1991–92 (except for a slight increase in 2002–03), these losses do not appear to have been exacerbated by the state's open enrollment program. Saginaw Public Schools' open enrollment history is presented in Table 6.10 and the district's total enrollment history is depicted in Figure 3.

DETROIT PUBLIC SCHOOLS

In absolute numbers, no Michigan school district has lost more students through schools of choice than Detroit Public Schools (DPS). Moreover, this enrollment loss has been just a part of an unprecedented student exodus also fueled by Michigan's charter school program and general demographic trends. These broader trends and their attendant fiscal and political difficulties are discussed at some length in Chapter 7. Here we will focus exclusively on the DPS experience with the state's open enrollment program. A history of DPS enrollment gains and losses stemming from schools of choice is presented in Table 3.11.

The data reveal that DPS is far from a desired educational destination for families in neighboring school districts. The schools of choice traffic has been almost entirely outbound. Where are the students going? Again, state administrative data reveal the enrolling districts for these residents of DPS. A 10-year history of the DPS schools of choice exodus is presented in Table 3.12, with the more popular destinations identified.

While the district's total number of outbound students has grown more or less steadily since the fall of 2000, the distinction of most preferred destination has cycled across several neighboring districts. Throughout most of this 11-year period, Highland Park Public Schools has been the preferred destination, with enrollments from Detroit peaking in 2008 at nearly 2,200 and more than doubling Highland Park's enrollment that year. Highland Park's Detroit enrollments plummeted in 2010, however, as educational and financial issues mounted in the district. By that time, Oak Park and Inkster had become the destinations of choice for Detroit residents, while the traffic to Westwood Public Schools reached a new high.

Table 3.9. Local Districts in Saginaw County, 2004–05 Through 2008–09, Nonresident Enrollments

District	2004–05		2005–06		2006–07		2007–08		2008–09	
	FTE	%	FTE	%	FTE	%	FTE	%	FTE	%
Saginaw City	1,007	8.7	1,006	9.2	989	10.0	1,042	10.9	1,096	11.9
Carrollton	486	29.3	512	31.7	581	33.5	646	37.2	703	39.3
Saginaw Twp.	709	13.7	780	15.1	831	15.7	863	16.0	805	15.1
Buena Vista	245	19.5	196	17.6	202	18.6	142	14.6	173	18.3
Chesaning	107	5.3	76	3.9	73	3.9	91	4.9	89	4.9
Birch Run	62	3.3	66	3.5	119	6.3	143	7.7	157	8.5
Bridgeport-Spaulding	334	15.5	323	15.1	256	12.6	185	10.1	124	7.3
Frankenmuth	0	–	0	–	0	–	0	–	0	–
Freeland	0	–	0	–	0	–	0	–	0	–
Hemlock	90	6.1	106	7.1	103	7.1	128	8.9	115	8.4
Merrill	53	6.2	47	5.7	59	7.1	74	8.8	83	10.5
Charles	67	5.6	68	5.7	74	6.2	81	7.0	72	6.4
St. Swan Valley	298	17.1	346	19.4	341	19.3	423	23.3	438	24.5

Source: MDE.

Table 3.10. Enrollment Losses for Saginaw Public Schools Due to Schools of Choice, 2000–10, Fall Pupil Counts (FTE)

Year	Enrollment loss	Enrollment gain	Net loss
2000	987.13	353.68	633.45
2001	1,004.55	450.16	554.39
2002	1,194.67	653.34	541.33
2003	1,274.31	713.78	560.53
2004	1,459.07	890.16	568.91
2005	1,605.17	1,006.82	598.35
2006	1,694.71	1,005.84	688.87
2007	1,741.05	988.74	752.31
2008	1,778.28	1,041.72	736.56
2009	1,760.66	1,096.38	664.28
2010	1,825.32	1,059.37	765.95

Source: MDE.

Table 3.11. Enrollment Losses for Detroit Public Schools Due to Schools of Choice, 2000–10, Fall Pupil Counts (FTE)

Year	Enrollment loss	Enrollment gain	Net loss
2000	1,466.33	0	1,466.33
2001	3,081.86	0	3,081.86
2002	3,871.04	0	3,871.04
2003	4,005.27	0	4,005.27
2004	6,009.79	210.83	5,798.96
2005	6,587.53	363.56	6,223.97
2006	7,258.60	0	7,258.60
2007	7,605.72	0	7,605.72
2008	9,061.82	6.00	9,055.82
2009	8,606.78	11.00	8,595.78
2010	8,458.46	27.50	8,430.96

Source: MDE.

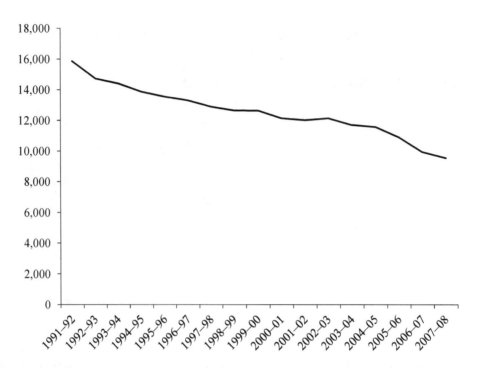

Figure 3. Benton Harbor Area Schools Enrollment History
Source: MDE.

These year-to-year fluctuations in cross-district student movements may be explained by a host of factors, including the adoption of an attractive new program in a district (e.g., full-day kindergarten), enhanced pupil transportation service, favorable press coverage, or more aggressive marketing. District leadership may also choose to suspend or discontinue their open enrollment programs, maintaining their continuing nonresident enrollments but accepting no new enrollees. And while it is unlikely that these annual fluctuations in nonresident enrollment levels are reflective of real changes in the academic quality of the schools involved, a steady outflow of students and revenue from a school or district is likely to damage the reputation of those institutions, spurring more departures of students and resources and eventually inflicting real damage on the academic programs. Undoubtedly, this has been the case in DPS.

Table 3.12. Districts Enrolling DPS Residents, 2000–10, Fall Pupil Counts (FTE)

Year	Ferndale	Oak Park	Dearborn Hts. #7	Highland Park	Redford Union	Westwood	Inkster	Other
2000	2.00	145.00	209.60	965.84	0	0	7.00	136.89
2001	306.11	344.00	225.60	1,327.06	0	15.00	146.00	718.09
2002	328.63	468.66	243.00	1,503.62	225.83	17.00	84.50	999.80
2003	354.50	612.66	483.00	606.32	270.07	44.00	40.50	1,594.22
2004	577.01	720.97	532.00	1,364.78	502.48	222.00	49.00	2,041.55
2005	747.50	670.33	492.50	1,513.38	642.34	278.00	50.00	2,193.48
2006	983.58	593.67	488.83	1,468.13	622.11	341.00	245.00	2,516.28
2007	444.77	1,418.82	467.14	1,551.56	527.00	385.15	120.90	2,691.28
2008	310.00	1,628.40	473.50	2,162.70	410.66	406.00	685.00	2,985.56
2009	330.29	1,285.28	447.50	1,504.03	296.50	337.50	1,122.70	3,282.98
2010	360.00	1,012.49	420.50	791.32	218.50	631.00	1,270.90	3,753.75

Source: MDE.

Schools of Choice: Added Value or Zero-Sum Game?

Michigan's schools of choice program is best viewed as part of a broader state movement toward choice and entrepreneurship in K–12 education, one strand in a multifaceted strategy to create incentives to improve public schools. And although it receives less attention than the state's expansive charter school program, Michigan's open enrollment program has had a substantial impact on school enrollments and funding levels in metropolitan areas across the state, including those in Berrien, Jackson, Saginaw, Oakland, Macomb, and Wayne counties.

As a school improvement strategy, however, open enrollment suffers from several shortcomings. First, unlike the charter school program, the open enrollment initiative lacks any supply-side strategy to encourage new school creation. Rather, schools of choice is a zero-sum game in which the gains of the winners in the quest for enrollments and revenue are offset by the losses of the other competitors. Indeed, for those local communities on the losing side in the hunt for student bounties, more than money may be lost. As families remove their children from schools in the communities in which they live, the bonds between school and community are weakened. In particular, this schism jeopardizes public support for local schools, including support for district millage requests for capital projects. Further, such student movement threatens to polarize communities and further segment students by race and socioeconomic status. Evidence of such strains has surfaced in communities in Berrien, Oakland, and Wayne counties, among others.

Finally, the educational effects of Michigan's open enrollment program are not easily discernable and certainly elude the level of public scrutiny given to the performance of charter schools. That is, student achievement data are routinely reported at the school and district level, thereby facilitating the evaluation of charter schools but obscuring the impact of open enrollment on student achievement. As a result, the future of Michigan's schools of choice program will likely depend less on evidence of educational outcomes than on ideology and political preferences. At this time, the long-term effects and policy implications of open enrollment are somewhat ambiguous. The program may result in the further segregation of students by socioeconomic characteristics and academic achievement in metropolitan areas. On the other hand, the program may continue to provide some families with an opportunity to enroll their children in a more desirable school system without the need of relocating their residence. This potential benefit may suffice, at least in the near term, to maintain current levels of political support for the program.

Endnotes

1. Public Act 300 of 1997.

2. Exceptions were made for siblings of children already enrolled in the district. Also, a district could refuse to enroll an applicant who has been suspended within the preceding two years or who has ever been expelled.

3. Sec. 380.1401 of the School Aid Act states: "Tuition for grades K to 6 shall not exceed 25 percent more than the operation cost per capita for the number of pupils in membership in grades K to 12. Tuition for grades 7 to 12 shall not exceed 12–1/2 percent more than 115 percent of the operation cost per capita for the number of pupils in membership in grades K to 12 .... The per capita cost used shall not include moneys expended for school sites, school building construction, equipment, payment of bonds, or other purposes not properly included in operation costs as determined by the state board."

4. Public Act 297 of 2000.

5. At the time this proposal was being debated, data on high school graduation rates in Michigan were notoriously unreliable, and the list of districts falling below the two-thirds standard was the subject of much dispute.

6. On July 27, 2002, in a 5 to 4 ruling, the U.S. Supreme Court upheld the constitutionality of a voucher program established by the state of Ohio for families residing in the Cleveland City School District. Many families used the vouchers to send their children to Catholic schools. The court ruled that the Cleveland voucher program did not violate the First Amendment's separation of church and state because the state was not providing the funds directly to the church-run schools. Rather, the state gave the funds to the parents who then paid them to the sectarian schools (*Zelman v. Simmons-Harris* 2002). Although *Zelman* would appear to pave the way for voucher programs that allow parents to choose church-run schools, such programs are prohibited by many state constitutions. Michigan's constitutional prohibition is particularly stringent.

7. Indeed, another reason for the unpopularity of vouchers in the United States is that many proposals have called for relatively small voucher amounts, falling far short of tuition at most good private schools. As such, these plans have been often viewed by the public as more of a "giveaway" to affluent families with children already enrolled in these schools than an opportunity for the less well-heeled to enroll their children. Programs targeted to low-income households, on the other hand, have enjoyed some measure of support in a few states. State-funded voucher programs currently operate in Maine, Ohio, Vermont, Utah, and Wisconsin, along with a federally funded program in the District of Columbia.

8. The term *open enrollment* has been used to refer to *intradistrict* public school choice programs, a form of choice that predates the *interdistrict* choice created by Michigan's schools of choice program. Here we will use open enrollment to describe the more recent and more expansive interdistrict programs as well as notable intradistrict programs such as those in New York City and Chicago.

9. In microeconomic terms, the marginal cost of educating an additional student is near zero and, conversely, the marginal cost reduction of losing a student is likewise near zero.

10. Intradistrict choice, of course, would generally not create such a powerful economic incentive, since districts can shift funds from school to school or change school attendance boundaries to compensate for enrollment shifts across schools.

11. Because lottery winners are selected at random, winners and losers have the same set of background characteristics on average. Therefore, any observed differences in academic outcomes between lottery winners and losers can be attributed to winning the lottery and not to other influences, either observed or unobserved.

12. Economist Charles Tiebout, in a seminal 1956 article, "A Pure Theory of Local Expenditures," described a mechanism by which individuals choose their community of residence according to that community's combination of local taxes and services. If there are many localities, each with a unique tax/service package, individuals will be able to select their most preferred package in the same manner that they buy goods and services in a private market. This analogy with private markets suggested by Tiebout implies that resources may be allocated efficiently in the public sector as well as in the private sector, a proposition that had been previously dismissed by most economists.

13. In this context, "participation" refers to students attending public schools in districts other than their district of residence. In this way, a student may participate in schools of choice even if his district of residence does not.

14. A 2006 study published by the Harvard Civil Rights Project identified Michigan as one of four states with the highest levels of black segregation in its public schools (Orfield and Lee 2006). This state of affairs is not lost on the residents in many urban areas. As one African American student in author Addonizio's economics of education class at Wayne State University observed, a district may resist the financial incentive for enrolling nonresidents in order to "keep Snoop in the hood."

15. These districts experiencing relatively heavy enrollment losses included Saginaw, Jackson, Pontiac, Niles, Adrian, Inkster, Ecorse, and Hillsdale. Michigan's three largest urban districts, Detroit, Grand Rapids, and Flint, experienced net enrollment losses of less than 1 percent (Arsen, Plank, and Sykes 2000).

16. Section 105/105C is a state program. Alternatively, local districts within the same ISD may develop their own interdistrict plans that operate independently of the state's schools of choice program. While these cooperative programs allow some student movement across local district boundaries, they generally restrict such movement, resulting in fewer interdistrict transfers as compared with the more competitive state program. Notable examples of these more cooperative choice programs are found in the Kent and Genesee ISDs (Arsen, Plank, and Sykes 2000). Indeed, Kent County public schools report zero participation in the state program (see Table 3.3).

17. The five-year, 2008 graduation rates for these districts, as reported by the Michi-gan Center for Educational Performance and Information, were Vandercook Lake, 89.0; East Jackson, 86.8; Hanover-Horton, 94.4; Michigan Center, 87.0; and Jack-son City, 63.8. Western, with a graduation rate of 72.5 percent in 2008, is somewhat anomalous among this group.

18. In 2007, however, the U.S. Supreme Court ruled that school assignment systems cannot be based on race alone (*Parents Involved in Community Schools Inc. v. Seattle School District* 2007).

19. This ruling was reflective of a general reluctance of the federal courts in the last several decades to insert themselves into the governance of public schools, now viewed as the province of state and local governments. In 1991, the U.S. Supreme Court began to authorize school districts to return to segregated neighborhood schools (*Board of Education of Oklahoma v. Dowell* 1991). The court issued two subsequent rulings that further relaxed desegregation standards. In *Freeman v. Pitts* (1992), the court allowed school districts to terminate desegregation plans even though the schools had not yet become integrated. In *Missouri v. Jenkins* (1995), the court emphasized local control over desegregation as the primary goal of school governance.

20. In his 50-page decision, Judge Hillman wrote, "I accept [the State's evidence] that after adjusting for [socio-economic] factors and first grade test scores, no statistically significant gap exists between the performance of white and minority students in the Benton Harbor schools. In other words, no 'achievement gap' exists ... that is attributable to the race of the students ..." *Berry v. School District of the City of Benton Harbor* (2002).

21. In 2007–08, residential (i.e., homestead) state equalized value per pupil in Fran-kenmuth was $243,311, far exceeding the corresponding value of $167,152 for Hemlock, the county's second-wealthiest district.

DISCUSSION QUESTIONS

1. Why is open enrollment considered the least innovative of school choice initiatives?
2. What were some of the educational effects of school choice?
3. What is the greatest effect of children moving from one district to another?

CHAPTER 4

Academic Achievement Gap

INTRODUCTION
BY KISHA R. CUNNINGHAM, PHD

"The tragedy of education is played in two scenes—incompetent pupils facing competent teachers and incompetent teachers facing competent pupils."

—Martin H. Fischer

Commonly identified as a strategy for promoting deep learning and understanding, active learning instructional strategies include a wide range of activities that share the commonality of student engagement. Implementation of those strategies is sometimes impeded by student and faculty preferences for stimulus-response learning. Implementation of strategies also requires a greater amount of time to address course materials. This chapter examines the academic achievement gap, active learning, and strategies for promoting deeper learning.

Enhancing Academic Achievement by Identifying and Minimizing the Impediments to Active Learning

BY ROBERT A. PETERS
WESTERN MICHIGAN UNIVERSITY

Introduction

The education and teaching literatures have extensively discussed active learning strategies and the benefits of implementing them, but have accorded minimal attention to the barriers to implementation. More specifically, active learning strategies such as application, discussion, group work, journaling, service learning, simulations, and students responding to questions or posing questions arising from the readings (Dietz-Uhler & Lanter, 2009; Hattery, 2003, Novak, 2002; Pollack & Motoike, 2006; Sands & Shelton, 2010; Schaefer & Zygmont, 2003) are credited with producing greater rates of deep learning and understanding than passive learning (Candela, Dailey, & Benzel-Lindley 2006; Novak, 2002). However, maximizing the rates of deep learning and understanding is dependent on counteracting student and faculty preferences for the polar opposite of active learning which is passive or stimulus-response learning. In the absence of overcoming these preferences, the inclusion of active learning strategies in MPA courses entails placing a thin veneer of active learning over the foundation of passive or stimulus-response learning. Under these conditions, faculty continue to minimize course preparation time while students are able to perpetuate the learned behaviors of limiting their responses to the procedures, knowledge, and skills addressed by the course while ignoring elements from other courses, knowledge, and skills that may be more appropriate or generate a deeper understanding of the topic. Due to operating within these parameters, the linkages developed between material discussed in the course and the students' preexisting knowledge structure are artificially limited along with the probability of recalling and utilizing the information at a later date. Nor is it possible to identify the components of the students' responses that are conditioned reactions to the stimuli generated by the assessment mechanism or indicators of deep learning and understanding

(Billing, 2007; Connor-Greene, 2000; Doyle, 1988; Hay, 20007; Hay & Kinchin, 2008; Lithner, 2008; Taylor & White 2006; Watters & Watters, 2007).

There also are few instances in which the literature has examined the curricular implications of implementation even though it is a significant issue in the introduction of active learning strategies. The central challenge in executing active learning strategies is that they consume more time than stimulus-response/passive learning. Unless there is sufficient slack in the curriculum, the integration of active learning strategies into the MPA curriculum therefore necessitates a reduction in the volume of knowledge and skills addressed by the curriculum or an increase in the number of required credit hours.

Given the role of stimulus-response learning in inhibiting the realization of active learning's benefits, the next section provides a brief synopsis of stimulus-response learning and a description of the student and faculty preferences for this approach to education. The section also delineates some of the strategies for counteracting the preferences and thereby maximizing the extent to which active learning strategies foster deep learning and understanding. Due to active learning strategies requiring a greater amount of time to address topics, the subsequent section addresses strategies for prioritizing curriculum components, reducing the breadth of coverage, and integrating the remaining course materials. The final section summarizes the findings and examines the implications for MPA programs.

Identifying and Counteracting Barriers to Active Learning

As implied by the nomenclature, stimulus-response learning entails students generating the appropriate responses to instructor-furnished stimuli. The process begins with lectures and the accompanying PowerPoint presentations that define the portions of assigned readings the instructor deems to be important and reinforces the definitions, methods, and interpretations conveyed by the assigned readings. Additional reinforcement is provided by problem sets, quizzes, objectives, and questions raised by the faculty member and the readings. By the time students sit for their exams, they have been conditioned to base their responses on the materials addressed by lectures and subsequent exercises, to disregard insights and relevant information gleaned from other courses and personal experience, to apply the same strategies for answering questions that were used for the problem sets and similar exercises, and to provide responses that replicate the ones generated by each of the previous steps. Due to students being conditioned to respond to key words and cues embedded in each step of the learning process, those who review the answers to exam questions cannot determine the extent to which the responses are unconscious reactions to stimuli or indicative of learning and understanding (Billing, 2007; Connor-Greene, 2000; Doyle, 1988; Lithner, 2008; Ogilvie, 2009; Taylor & White 2006; Watters & Watters, 2007).

BENEFITS OF STIMULUS-RESPONSE LEARNING ACCRUING TO STUDENTS

Even though stimulus-response learning is not a vehicle for promoting deep learning and understanding or traits such as creativity and critical thinking, the benefits of stimulus-response learning produce a preference for the approach and a barrier to fully achieving the promise of active learning. One of the primary benefits accruing to students is the faculty assuming responsibility for the learning process and thereby enabling students to be passive recipients of the knowledge and skills their instructors pour into their heads (Albers, 2009). The perspective is reflected in the students' contention that the instructor did not explain the material in ways students could understand and course evaluation questions asking whether difficult material was explained to the students' satisfaction. In both instances, the absence of statements regarding the students' efforts to read and understand the material suggests insufficient comprehension and understanding is primarily the faculty's fault; they should have been a better teacher. Learning therefore is implicitly defined as a function of the instructor's abilities rather than a responsibility shared by both teacher and students.

The perception of faculty and student responsibilities is also reflected in the assumption that the instructor will tell students what they need to know (Brost & Bradley, 2006; Clump & Doll, 2007; Lord, 2008; Marchant, 2002). Under these conditions, students can choose to (1) forego, with impunity, reading the assigned materials, (2) read, but not invest sufficient time and energy in comprehending the materials, or (3) read and comprehend the materials. The frequency of students choosing the first option is suggested by the prevalence of aliteracy, i.e., the ability to read but the decision not to do so. Burchfield and Sappington (2000) concluded that a majority of undergraduates and approximately one-third of graduate students do not read the assigned materials. The preference for not reading or investing minimal effort in comprehension (Sappington, Kinsey & Munsayac, 2002) is also suggested by student responses to the author's open- end course evaluation questions. When asked to define the advantages and disadvantages of submitting concept maps before each set of assigned materials is discussed in class, approximately one-quarter of the students in a section of public budgeting and finance indicated the assignment forces them define the major concepts discussed in the readings and to map the relationships among the concepts. The use of the word "forced" suggests developing a deeper understanding of the material prior to class sessions was not a customary activity.

A second "benefit" accruing to students is minimizing the volume of material they are expected to study, know, and apply (Boesen, Lithner & Palm, 2010; Brost & Bradley, 2006, Clump & Doll, 2007; Ogilvie, 2009). Since the lecture and PowerPoint slides define components of the readings the instructor thinks are important (Adams, 2006), the students can, with minimal risk, focus on these elements and ignore the remainder of the readings. The power of the unwritten agreement is evidenced by a student's response to one of the author's open-end course evaluation questions. At the conclusion of the semester in which the author experimented with basing the course grade entirely on class participation, the student indicated he preferred the traditional exam format for determining course grades because he perfected the skill of predicting the material that would appear on tests and therefore earned good grades on each exam (Peters, 2008).

Although the perspective surfaced on only one course evaluation, the literature suggests the sentiment is shared by a number of students. Many successful students (those who earn A's and B's) learn the rules of stimulus- response learning early in their academic careers. Due to the impact of GPA's on the tracking of primary and secondary school students and their role in higher education admissions decisions, the rules of stimulus-response learning become deeply ingrained and, due their contribution to the students' success, develop devotees to stimulus-response learning (Albanese, 2000; Albers, 2009; Ogilvie, 2009; Raidal and Volet, 2009). The sentiment can be summarized in the adage "dance with the one who brung you."

The ingrained preference for instructors differentiating between important and unimportant material (Adams, 2006; Clump & Doll, 2007; Lord, 2008) is also evident in student responses to an open-end question concerning the advantages and disadvantages of PowerPoint presentations. Less than one-third of the students in each of four sections of the author's courses indicated they did not review the PowerPoint presentations the author posted online prior to each class session. Of the remaining students, several in each section stated the PowerPoint presentations defined the information the author thought was important. A few also indicated the presentations provided a framework for organizing their thoughts about the material and assisted in developing their concept maps. Although the author would like to believe that graduate students are more self-directed than instructor-dependent, the evidence suggests the distribution of PowerPoint slides prior to class sessions reinforces many of the students' preference for stimulus-response learning.

Stimulus-response learning is also suggested by student comments regarding exams and classes. Although the statement "it's not fair to include material on the exam that was not discussed in class" is more pervasive among undergraduate than graduate students, it nevertheless is symptomatic of the presumption that the instructor and PowerPoint presentations will provide signals defining material that is important or unimportant (Adams, 2006; Lord, 2008). A student also observed that one of the MPA courses required a considerable amount of reading, but the challenge of preparing for exams was significantly reduced by the fact that there was only one correct answer; the one discussed in class. The student therefore was able to focus on class discussions rather than develop a deep understanding of the material addressed by the readings.

A common theme of each of the preceding benefits is efficiency. The definition of topics that are important and unimportant enables students (1) to forego reading the assigned materials or to read, but not invest sufficient time to comprehend the materials and (2) minimize study time by focusing on topics the instructor defined as important and ignoring or briefly examining the remaining information. Additional efficiencies can be achieved whenever an instructor signals there is only one correct answer. Students can focus on replicating information discussed in class and thereby minimize the amount of time and energy invested in thought and analysis. However, each of the efficiencies is achieved at the expense of achieving deep learning and understanding.

STRATEGIES FOR COUNTERACTING THE BENEFITS ACCRUING TO STUDENTS

Efficiencies and "benefits" resulting from the students' dependence on instructors can be undermined by the introduction of active learning mechanisms at each phase of the learning process. Prior to discussing the assigned materials in class, the incentive to read the materials can be enhanced by the use of quizzes (Gier & Kreiner, 2009; Narloch, Garbin & Tumage, 2006), concept maps, and issue papers. Since faculty determine the content of quizzes and students define the composition of concept maps and issue papers, the latter two options shift the greatest responsibility for learning from faculty to students. In the case of concept maps, students are responsible for selecting the concepts discussed in the readings, diagramming the relationships among them, and defining the links between each pair of concepts (Hay, 2007; Hay, Kinchin & Lygo-Baker, 2008). Although several respondents to the author's open-end course evaluation questions contended concept maps can be completed without understanding the materials, the outcome is not feasible for issue papers. In this instance, students use concepts they have selected from the readings to analyze situations they have encountered at work or read in the media. Due to these attributes, pre-discussion quizzes, concept maps, and issue papers provide incentives for students to assume greater responsibility for reading and interpreting the assigned materials and thereby promote active learning by reducing the rewards of stimulus- response / passive learning.

When the assigned materials are discussed in class, the preceding incentives can be enhanced by minimalist PowerPoint presentations. Several critiques of PowerPoint suggest detailed slides focus discussions on the bullet points and unconsciously absolve students of the responsibility for developing additional items or perspectives (Adams, 2006; Gabriel, 2008; Klemm, 2007). To combat this tendency, and inject greater flexibility into class discussions, the author has gradually reduced the amount of information on the slides. On occasion, the author has developed six slides for a three-hour class and most of the slides contained only one sentence or phrase.

The breadth of class discussion can also be expanded by the instructor refraining from adding items that were in the readings but were not raised by the students. By following this strategy, responsibility for defining items is gradually shifted from the instructor to the students.

The benefits of parsimonious PowerPoint slides and participation by the instructor were measured during a semester in which a Smart board was in the author's classroom. Each time a student participated in the discussion, their contribution was summarized in a phrase that was written and stored on Smart Board. A subsequent review of the material revealed that five to ten percent of the items were not addressed by any of the readings but were the product of personal experiences at the students' place of employment and, less frequently, the material covered in other classes.

BENEFITS OF STIMULUS-RESPONSE LEARNING ACCRUING TO FACULTY

Stimulus-response learning is also a function of benefits accruing to faculty. Whenever instructors assume the role of conveyers of knowledge along with the responsibility for the learning of students, they can recycle information with minimal revisions. Consequently, the first time a course is taught, a significant investment of time is required to develop the reading list, PowerPoint slides, and notes for each class session. With the exception of periodically updating the reading list and the related revision of the PowerPoint slides and notes, stimulus-response learning enables instructors to invest minimal time in course preparation by the third or fourth iteration of the course.

A faculty member's research time also can be protected by foregoing implementation of the previously discussed incentives for students to assume a more active role in their education. Although quizzes, interactive sessions, concept mapping and issue papers provide incentives for students to read and analyze the materials (Benedict & Anderton, 2004; Choudhury, Gouldsborough & Gabriel, 2010; Padilla-Walker, 2006), e-leaning cannot be utilized to grade the latter two options and therefore require a weekly commitment of faculty time to review, grade, and provide feedback to students.

Similarly, developing detailed PowerPoint slides serves to minimize preparation time. By providing a script for each class session (Gabriel, 2008; Klemm, 2007), the prompts and transitions among topics enable instructors to minimize the amount of time dedicated to reviewing the materials and preparing for each class session. Detailed slides also constrain the range of discussions and therefore provide fewer opportunities for tangents (Adams, 2006; Gabriel, 2008; Klemm, 2007). For example, when one of the author's class sessions focused on state constitutional provisions affecting budgeting and financial management, the use broad headings provided sufficient flexibility for students to raise questions such as the use of eminent domain for economic development and the term of office for county drain commissioners.

However, the opportunity to examine a broader range of topics is not appreciated by a subset of students. Each semester, student responses to the author's open-ended course evaluation questions reveal a preference for focusing exclusively on the information addressed by the readings. Any discussion or question outside of this parameter is defined as an unnecessary tangent. Several students also perceive the flexibility to introduce personal work experiences as a chance for others to enhance their class participation grades by "showing off" their expertise instead of viewing the flexibility as an opportunity to relate theory to practice. The comments demonstrate the deeply ingrained preference of some students to limit the discussion to the "important" information. These feelings also surface on course evaluations as negative comments concerning the instructor's classroom management capabilities.

Whenever the learning strategies encourage greater participation and flexibility, the instructor is at greater risk of not knowing the answer to some of the students' queries. There have been a few instances each semester when the questions have been beyond the author's scope of knowledge (e.g., the term of office for county drain commissioners) and therefore required additional time for researching the questions. However, it is important to note that these instances do not appear to have appreciably affected the course evaluation ratings of the author's subject knowledge.

The evidence therefore indicates that detailed slides reinforce stimulus-response learning, they enable instructors to minimize preparation time, to stay on message, to avoid charges of "going off on tangents," and to virtually eliminate the necessity of addressing questions that are beyond the instructor's scope of knowledge.

The incentives to accentuate the role of stimulus- response learning are magnified by the reward structure of many colleges and universities (Brainard, 2007; Hannan, English & Silver, 1999). The primacy of research and publication in tenure and promotion decisions and a reliance on course evaluations to measure teaching effectiveness are factors that push teachers toward instructional strategies that reinforce stimulus-response learning and thereby reduce the benefits of active learning.

Given the current emphasis on assessment and accountability, an unintended effect of these initiatives is an additional incentive for engaging in stimulus-response/passive learning. The probability that a high proportion of students will demonstrate mastery of the material is maximized when (1) the lectures or classroom activities narrow the amount of material students must study, (2) problem sets or case studies reinforce the materials addressed by lectures or classroom activities (Benedict & Anderton, 2004; Boesen, Lithner & Palm, 2010; Choudhury, Gouldsborough & Gabriel, 2010, Padilla-Walker, 2006), and (3) the assessment mechanism incorporates key words and cues communicated in the first two steps (Boesen, Lithner & Palm, 2010).

The impact of the process is supported by student responses to two semesters of mid-term and final exams. Each of the exams included questions that evaluated the students' ability to replicate information addressed in the readings and class sessions, use knowledge gleaned from the course to analyze a "real world" event or organization, and address a question devoid of keywords or cues from the course. As expected, the percentage of students demonstrating mastery of the material is greatest for the first category of questions and least for the third type of questions. In fact, responses to the third type of question often raised questions as to whether most of the students attended any of the class sessions.

An example of each category of questions is as follows.

Replication: List and briefly describe the criteria for evaluating revenue sources.
Application: One of the tax proposals being floated by the governor and legislators is to impose a sales tax on services, eliminate the Michigan Business Tax (MBT) surcharge, and reduce the MBT tax rate. Identify the criteria for evaluating

revenue sources that would be used to support and oppose the tax proposal and the rationale for using each criterion.

Absence of key words and cues: One of the tax proposals being floated by the governor and legislators is to impose a sales tax on services, eliminate the Michigan Business Tax (MBT) surcharge, and reduce the MBT tax rate. Since you have been given the task of selling the plan to the public, describe the strategy you would use to secure public support for the proposal.

The first iteration of the question embodies each of the benefits of stimulus-response learning. The question uses the same terms as those included in class discussions and PowerPoint slides. Students therefore were alerted to the fact that there was a high probability the topic would appear on the exam and they therefore should be prepared to respond to the cues, i.e., terms used in class and on the slides. Due to the reliance on the stimulus (keywords) to elicit the desired response, most of the students demonstrated mastery of this subset of material.

The second version requires students to search state government websites for a description of the Michigan Business Tax, recall the information sought in the preceding version of the question, and determine which criteria would be used to support and oppose the tax proposal. Since the author did not use this or other tax proposals to demonstrate the use of the criteria in tax policy debates, stimulus-response learning could be utilized for the recall portion but not the application portion of the question. If, on the other hand, one or more tax proposals would have been used in class to demonstrate the role of the criteria in selling or opposing the initiatives, then the application portion of the question would have mimicked the problem set component of stimulus-response learning. Under these conditions, it would not be possible to determine the extent to which the students' responses to the application portion of the question were the product of replicating the examples discussed in class or a deep understanding of the material.

The third iteration eliminates the problem of disentangling the extent to which the responses are a replication of class work or an indication of deep understanding and a propensity to apply the material in a work or volunteer setting. Due to the generic nature of the question, it is devoid of the keywords and cues that serve as stimuli for eliciting the desired responses. The responses therefore measure the students' understanding of the material (Boesen, Lithner & Palm, 2010), the extent to which it has been linked to their preexisting knowledge structure (Hay, 2007; Hay & Kinchin, 2008), and the propensity to creatively apply the course materials (Boesen, Lithner & Palm, 2010) to settings outside of class.

In this respect, the results were quite humbling. On each of two occasions when the author included the third iteration of the question on exams, most of the students did not use materials from the readings or class sessions to address the questions. They relied on prior experiences, preferences, or similar bases for their answers. Their answers therefore were more reminiscent of responses provided by individuals who never attended class than those who completed a portion of the course. These outcomes do not bode well for the transference of information from the classroom to the place of employment and public service.

Curricular Implications of Active Learning Strategies

The instructors' selection of teaching strategies not only affects the extent to which deep learning and understanding occurs but also impacts the amount of time that is required to cover the material. Since the goal of graduate public administration programs is to enhance the higher level skills of Bloom's taxonomy, i.e., application, synthesis, and evaluation (Anderson & Krathwohl, 2001), effectiveness in this instance is measured by the proportion of students demonstrating mastery of the second and third types of questions discussed in the previous section. Even though lectures convey a greater amount of information within a given timeframe than is the case for active learning strategies, efficiency is achieved at the expense of the proportion of students who demonstrate mastery of questions involving application and the absence of cues and keywords. Active learning, on the other hand, requires a greater amount of time to cover similar volumes of information but also produces a greater proportion of students demonstrating mastery of higher level skills (Albanese, 2000; Dailey, Candela, & Benzel-Lindley, 2008; Schaefer & Zygmont, 2003; Watters & Watters, 2007).

Given the tradeoff between efficiency and effectiveness, implementation of active learning strategies requires a greater amount of time for conveying knowledge and building skills. As is the case for other professional programs such as construction (Bemold, 2005) and nursing (Dailey, Candela & Benzel-Lendley, 2008), the information explosion and replacing lectures with active learning approaches necessitate the process of decluttering the curriculum, i.e., prioritizing public administration skills and knowledge and jettisoning those components for which there is insufficient time to address.

An example of the prioritization and culling process is provided by the University of Baltimore's MPA program. The program's faculty responded to the state government's emphasis on outcomes measurement by defining essential knowledge and skills and aggregating the items into categories and courses. Due to the external pressures generated by state government policy, the tendency of faculty to protect their turf and areas of specialization was minimized throughout the curriculum revision process (Durant, 1997). The tendency to protect one's courses and areas of specialization can also be minimized by the active participation of alumni, practitioners, and employers in the curriculum revision process or emphasizing the data generated by surveys, focus groups, and advisory committees (Peters, 2009).

The author's evolving efforts to de-clutter his courses and the feedback generated by a Teaching Public Administration Conference paper session suggest the next step in the process involves the categorization of knowledge and skills by their half-lives. Since knowledge and skills with short half-lives are rapidly evolving, addressing the current literature and practices are not sufficient. A variant of the information literacy approach (Frand, Borah & Lippincott, 2007; Jacobs, Rosenfeld & Haber, 2003) suggests the course materials should identify sources of information that will enable the students to continually update and expand their knowledge and skills. The author's initial efforts involved listing sources such as professional organizations on the syllabus and, during one of the class sessions, providing an opportunity for students to examine and categorize the materials available on the organizations' websites. With the exception of the observation "I did not know I could find this information on the National Governors Association web page", anecdotal evidence suggests students were fulfilling the letter but not the purpose of the exercise. They were, in other words, complying with the requirement to categorize the information (e.g., legislative alerts, educational materials, certification, and training) but did not appreciate the role the sources of information could play in their professional lives or the pursuit of life-long learning.

In response to this assessment, the effort to cultivate an appreciation for the information's long-term value incorporates three initiatives. The first is to replace and supplement some of the assigned journal and textbook readings with materials generated by organizations listed on the syllabus. For example, materials on the Government Accounting Standards Board (GASB) website are viable substitutes for journal articles discussing recent changes in financial reporting standards, and the best practices section of the Government Finance Officers Association webpage provides valuable supplements to textbook materials. A second, and related, initiative is to increase the share of take-home exam questions for which students consult the web pages of professional and governmental organizations. Last semester, student responses to a government budgeting final exam question were based, in part, on information gleaned from the web pages of the Michigan House and Senate Fiscal Agencies and the Michigan Department of Budget. A previous health care policy question was based on health care reform legislation summaries posted on congressional websites and the web pages of advocacy groups such as The Henry J. Kaiser Family Foundation. The goal of integrating information from professional and governmental websites can also be expanded to include questions for class discussions. In this instance, the frequency of students accessing websites can be maximized by distributing the questions at least one class session before discussing them in class, scheduling class sessions in a computer lab, or establishing groups so that each group has access to a laptop.

The final initiative is to require students to collect a portion of their oral presentation and research paper materials from foundation, government, and professional organization websites. Since there is a rapid expansion and evolution of information and skills in public administration subfields such as health and transportation, students also are encouraged to access web pages of the organizations associated with their subfields. Even though the requirement is intended to increase the students' appreciation for the range of information provided by the sites, there is a surprising reticence to use the sources. Future syllabi therefore will include a requirement that more than a specified portion of the references must include the web pages of foundations, governments, and/or professional organizations.

As is suggested by the topics listed in Table 1, there often are overlaps between knowledge with short and long half-lives. Even though several budget formats have been used during the past fifty years and performance budgeting has been evolving for more than two decades, the political and economic variables affecting budget formats and the variables underlying an organization's reticence to implement budget initiatives have not significantly changed during the same time periods. In similar fashion, the Government Accounting Standards Board, over the past several decades, has generated several significant changes in accounting standards, but the blurring of distinctions between government and private sector financial reports has unfolded for more than two decades. Similarly, even though the sources and strategies for securing additional revenue have changed, the underlying message of the taxpayer revolt of the 1970s and 1980s has not changed: people are liberal when they can afford to be.

Since these examples, and many others, confirm the adage the more things change, the more they stay the same, a discussion of knowledge with short half-lives, such as the items listed in Table 1, should be interwoven with the related knowledge with long half-lives. By placing short half-life knowledge within a broader context of knowledge with a long half-life, a deeper understanding of the current context and the capacity to understand the ongoing evolution is enhanced.

Table 4.1. Examples of Knowledge and Skills with Short and Long Half-Lives

	Knowledge	**Skills**
Short	Budget formats	Generate expenditure requests
	Statutes, regulations, court decisions, and accounting rules	Develop financial policies
	Politics of revenue requests	Devise financing strategies
Long	Politics of budget formats	Identify expenditure data sources
	Legal and accounting trends	Conduct legal research
	Politics of revenue requests	Interpret political environment

The topics listed in Table 1 exhibit a similar intersection between skills with short and long half-lives. The sources of information that are the basis of expenditure requests have been stable over time but the formats for conveying the requests to the budget bureau/department and the legislative body have changed over time. In similar fashion, an analysis of the political environment is essential for developing a strategy for securing additional revenue even though the options for generating funds, especially in the case of capital projects, is continually evolving.

The table is also constructed to convey the linkages among knowledge and skills with short and long half-lives. The first item in each cell relates to the generation of expenditure requests, the second addresses the development of financial policies, and the third focuses on the revenue portion of the budget.

Summary and Implications

Although the literature recognizes the effectiveness of active learning in promoting deep learning and understanding, maximizing the benefits of these teaching strategies is impeded by the ingrained allegiance to stimulus-response/passive learning on the part of both students and faculty. The basis for this allegiance can be summarized in one word: efficiency. The greater the reliance on stimulus-response learning, the less time students need to devote to reading and studying and the less time faculty need to allocate to course preparation, grading assignments, and providing feedback to students. Since the academic success of many students and faculty can be attributed, in part, to learning and playing by the rules of stimulus-response learning, the preference for stimulus-response learning is reinforced by many students' predilection to minimize their responsibility for learning and the faculty's propensity to implement pedagogical techniques that were used by their instructors. Due to these factors, there are disproportionately few rewards for implementing active learning strategies that are not constrained by the parameters of stimulus-response learning, i.e., limiting the permissible range of solutions to those emanating from the assigned readings, lectures, and class discussions, utilizing case studies that reinforce the concepts addressed by the readings, setting parameters/instructions that limit the discussion and potential breadth of questions, and establishing grading criteria that do not encourage the synthesis of information from a variety of courses. The probability of implementing active learning strategies within the constraints imposed by stimulus-response learning is also augmented by university reward structures that encourage faculty to minimize the time demands of teaching so that research and publication can be maximized.

Given the preferences for stimulus-response learning and the resulting constraints on active learning, the limitations can be reduced and the benefits of active learning can be enhanced by two measures: consensus among the faculty and buy in by college and university administrators. Whenever faculty members identify the constraints imposed by stimulus-response learning and agree on strategies for overcoming the restraints when implementing active learning strategies, students experience greater consistency in instructional techniques and expectations. Since active learning requires a greater amount of faculty time for course preparation, and the time demands are augmented by the implementation of strategies that minimize the constraints imposed by stimulus-response learning, the shift toward the purer form of active learning is also dependent on tenure and promotion policies that reflect the added time commitment for instruction. One option is for a greater number of colleges and universities to adopt a two-track tenure and promotion system in which there is a track for teaching and one for research. The distinction would provide an incentive for those in the teaching track to invest a greater amount of time in course preparation and providing feedback to students. However, the extent to which the establishment of a teaching track contributes to the adoption of stimulus-response counter-measures is dependent on the criteria for measuring teaching effectiveness and the composition of assessment mechanisms.

The probability of adopting stimulus-response countermeasures will also be encouraged by the market. The capability of organizations to adapt to a rapidly changing environment is dependent on employing MPA program graduates who have developed critical thinking skills, creativity, the related capacity to "think outside of the box," and information literacy. Given the fact that active learning, not stimulus-response learning, develops these traits, the capacity of MPA programs to produce the skills demanded by the market is dependent on building on the work of ASP A (Henry et al., 2009; Raffel, 2009) and NASPAA (NASPAA Standards 2010) and minimizing the constraints stimulus-response learning imposes on the implementation of active learning strategies. MPA programs that do not unilaterally pursue these goals are in danger of replicating the current situation for MBA programs. Due to the increasing gap between the knowledge and skills needed by the market and those developed by MBA programs, the leading MBA programs are currently in the process of reducing this gap by dramatically revising their program orientations (Case Studies, 2010; Gosling & Mintzberg, 2006; Jackson, 2009).

When active learning and the stimulus-response countermeasures play an increasing role in MPA programs, there is an accompanying need to de-clutter the curriculum. Given the impact of turf, areas of specialization, and reluctance to retool on the curriculum revision processes, the probability of downsizing the curriculum is enhanced by the presence of external pressures or the commitment of MPA chairs/directors to give preference to the inputs of students, alumni, and employers collected through surveys, focus groups, and advisory councils.

Due to the increasing rate of change in knowledge and skills, the adaptability of MPA graduates can also be enhanced by examining the half-life of the knowledge and skills and utilizing this information to develop course content. The author has utilized a derivation of the information literature to develop the course content for knowledge and skills with relatively short half-lives. Instead of emphasizing information literacy's traditional components of identifying the requisites types and sources of information and assessing the information's validity (Frand, Borah & Lippincott, 2007; Jacobs, Rosenfeld &

Haber, 2003), the author has integrated into the course materials information that is gleaned from a variety of professional organizations. The approach is intended to familiarize students with sources of information that can be used throughout their careers to update and expand their knowledge and skills. Since the course also includes knowledge and skills with greater half-lives, the foundation is established for students to place the short-term knowledge and skills within the context of the longer term evolution of the profession.

Active learning facilitates deep learning and understanding and thereby enhances the probability that the course material will be recalled and used at a later date. However, achieving these outcomes is influenced by the extent to which the benefits of stimulus-response learning are neutralized, the curriculum is de-cluttered, students are guided to sources for updating their knowledge and skills, and an appreciation for the evolving knowledge and skills is generated by the interweaving of components with short and long half-lives.

References

Adams, C. (2006). PowerPoint, habits of mind, and classroom culture. Journal of Curriculum Studies, 38(4), 389–411.

Albanese, M. (2000). Problem-based learning: Why curricula are likely to show little effect on knowledge and clinical skills. Medical Education, 34(9), 729–738.

Albers, C. (2009). Teaching: From disappointment to ecstasy. Teaching Sociology, 37(3), 269–282 Anderson, L. W. & Krathwohl, D. R. (2001). A Taxonomy for Learning, Teaching, and Assessing: A Revision of Bloom's Taxonomy of Educational Objectives. New York: Longman

Benedict, J. O. & Anderton, J. B. (2004). Applying the just- in-time teaching approach to teaching statistics. Teaching of Psychology, 31(3), 197–201.

Billing, D. (2007). Teaching for transfer of core/key skills in higher education: Cognitive skills. The International Journal of Higher Education and Educational Planning, 53(4), 483–516.

Bemold, L. E. (2005). Paradigm shift in construction education is vital for the future of our profession. Journal of Construction Engineering and Management, 313(5), 533–539.

Boesen, J., Lithner, J. & Palm, T. (2010). The relation between types of assessment tasks and the mathematical reasoning students use. Educational Studies of Mathematics, 75(1), 89–105.

Brainard, J. (2007). The tough road to better science teaching. The Chronicle of Higher Education, 53(48), A16

Brost, B. D. & Bradley, K. A. (2006). Student compliance with assigned reading: A case study. Journal of Scholarship of Teaching and Learning, 6(2), 101–111.

Burchfield, C. M. & Sappington, J. (2000). Compliance with required reading assignments. Teaching of Psychology, 27(1), 58–60.

Candela, L., Dailey, K., & Benzel-Lindley, J. (2006). A case for learning-centered curricula. Journal of Nursing Education, 45(2), 59–66.

Case studies: Like the companies their professors study, the world's business schools are have to adapt to a more difficult market. (2010, May 5). The Economist, 396(8681).

Choudhury, B., Gouldsborough, I. & Gabriel, S. (2010). Use of interactive sessions and e-learning in teaching anatomy to first-year optometry students. Anatomical Sciences Education, 3(1), 39–45.

Clump, M. A. & Doll, J. (2007). Do the low levels of reading course material continue? An examination in a forensic psychology graduate program. Journal of Instructional Psychology, 34(4), 242–246).

Connor-Greene, P. A. (2000). Assessing and promoting student learning: Blurring the line between teaching and testing. Teaching of Psychology, 27(2), 84–88.

Dailey, K., Candela, L. & Benzel-Lindley, J. (2008). Learning to let go: The challenge of de-crowding the curriculum. Nurse Education Today, 28(1), 62–69.

Dietz-Uhler, B. & Lanter, J. R. (2009). Using the four- questions technique to enhance learning. Teaching of Psychology, 36(1), 38–41.

Doyle, W. (1988). Work in mathematics classes: The context of students' thinking during instruction. Educational Psychologist, 23(2), 167–180.

Durant, R. F. (1997) Seizing the moment: Outcomes assessment curriculum reform, and MPA education. International Journal of Public Administration, 20(2), 397–429.

Frand, J. L., Borah, E. G. & Lippincott, A. (2007). InfoIQ: Targeting information and technology lifelong needs. Public Services Quarterly, 3(3–4), 95–113.

Gabriel, Y. (2008). Against the tyranny of PowerPoint: Technology-in-use and technology abuse. Organization Studies, 29(2), 255–276.

Gier, V. S. & Kreiner, D. S. (2009). Incorporating active learning with PowerPoint-based lectures using content-based questions. Teaching of Psychology, 36(2), 134–139.

Gosling, J. & Mintzberg, H. (2006). Management education as if both matter. Management Learning, 37(4), 419– 428.

Hannan, A., English, S. & Silver, H. (1999). Why innovate? Some preliminary findings from a research project on 'innovations in teaching and learning in higher education'. Studies in Higher Education, 24(3), 279–289.

Hattery, A. J. (2003). Sleeping in the box, thinking outside the box: Student reflections on innovative pedagogical tools for teaching about and promoting a greater understanding of social class inequality among undergraduates. Teaching Sociology, 31(4), 412–427.

Hay, D. B. (2007). Using concept mapping to measure deep, surface and non-learning outcomes. Studies in Higher Education, 32(1), 39–57.

Hay, D. & Kinchin, I. (2008). Using concept mapping to measure learning quality. Education and Training, 50(2), 167–182.

Hay, D., Kinchin, I. & Lygo-Baker, S. (2008). Making learning visible: The role of concept mapping in higher education. Studies in Higher Education, 33(3), 295–311.

Henry, N., Goodsell, C. T., Lynn, Jr., L. E., Strivers, C. & Wamsley, G. L. (2009). Understanding excellence in public administration: The Report of the Task Force on Educating for Excellence in the Master of Public Administration Degree of the American Society for Public Administration. Journal of Public Affairs Education, 15(2), 117–133.

Jackson, D. (2009). Undergraduate management education: Its place, purpose and efforts to bridge the skills gap. Journal of Management and Organization, 15(2), 206– 223.

Jacobs, S. K., Rosenfeld, P. & Haber, J. (2003). Information literacy as the foundation for evidence- based practice in graduate nursing education: A curriculum-integrated approach. Journal of Professional Nursing, 19(5), 320–328.

Klemm, W. R. (2007). Computer slide shows: A trap for bad teaching. College Teaching, 55(3), 121–124.

Lithner, J. (2008). A research framework for creative and imitative reasoning. Educational Studies in Mathematics, 67(3), 255–276.

Lord, T. (2008). Dam it, professor. Just tell us what we need to know to pass your course. Journal of College Science Teaching, 37(3), 71–73.

Marchant, G. T. (2002). Student reading of assigned articles: Will this be on the test? Teaching of Psychology, 29(1), 49–51.

Narloch, R., Garbin, C. P. & Tumage, K. D. (2006). Benefits of prelecture quizzes. Teaching of Psychology, 33(2), 109–112.

Novak, J. D. (2002). Meaningful learning: The essential factor for conceptual change in limited or inappropriate propositional hierarchies leading to empowerment of learners. Science Education, 86(4), 548–571.

Ogilvie, C. A. (2009). Changes in students' problemsolving strategies in a course that includes context- rich, multifaceted problems. Physical Review Special Topics - Physics Education Research, 5(2), Article 020102.

Padilla-Walker, L. M. (2006) The impact of daily extra credit quizzes on exam performance. Teaching of Psychology, 33(4), 236–239.

Peters, R. A. (2008). Facilitating interaction to promote learning. The International Journal of Learning, 15(7), 159–166.

Peters, R. A. (2009). Using focus groups and stakeholder surveys to revise the MPA curriculum. Journal of Public Affairs Education, 15(1), 1–16.

Pollack, S. & Motoike, P. (2006). Civic engagement through service learning at CSU Monterey Bay: Education multicultural community builders. Metropolitan Universities, 17(1), 36–50.

Raffel, J. A. (2009). Looking forward: A response to the ASPA task force report on educating for excellence in the MPA. Journal of Public Affairs Education, 15(2), 135–144.

Raidal, S. L. & Volet, S. E. (2009). Preclinical students' predisposition towards social forms of instruction and self-directed learning: A challenge for the development of autonomous and collaborative learners. Higher Education, 57(5), 577–596.

Sands, E. C. & Shelton, A. (2010). Learning by doing: A simulation for teaching how congress works. PS: Political Science and Politics, 43(1), 133–138.

Sappington, J., Kinsey, K. & Munsayac, K. (2002). Two studies of reading compliance among college students. Teaching of Psychology, 29(4), 272–274.

Schaefer, K. M., & Zygmont, D. (2003). Analyzing the teaching style of nursing faculty: Does it promote a student-centered or teacher-centered learning environment? Nursing Education Perspectives, 24(5), 238–245.

Taylor, C. & White S. (2006). Knowledge and reasoning in social work: Educating humane judgement. British Journal of Social Work, 36(6), 937–954.

Watters, D. J. & Watters, J. J. (2007). Approaches to learning by students in the biological sciences: Implications for teaching. International Journal of Science Education, 29(1), 19–43.

CHAPTER 5

Students and Their Families

INTRODUCTION
BY KISHA R. CUNNINGHAM, PHD

"The most influential of all educational factors is the conversation in a child's home."

—William Temple

Capturing What Matters Most: Engaging Students and Their Families in Educational Planning

BY DEBORAH ESPINER AND DIANE GUILD

TEACHING EXCEPTIONAL CHILDREN

Many authors in the self-determination literature emphasize that students must be given every opportunity to be part of the decision making that impacts their lives. Students with high support needs are often not afforded this opportunity. The 3EPlan, a student-centered educational planning strategy, promotes culturally appropriate engagement and inclusion of all participants. The three Es of the process relate to the fundamental elements of student-centered planning: *engage, envisage,* and *enact.* Students and their support team work together to develop a vision for the student's future learning and identify supports that provide the student and the team the courage to enact the plan. Using this approach enables students to identify and express personal dreams and be actively involved in developing goals that reflect their choices.

The 3EPlan combines the Circle of Courage philosophy (Brendtro, Brokenleg, & Van Bockem, 2002; see box, "What Is the Circle of Courage?") with the technique of graphic facilitation (Sibbet, 1977; see box, "What Is Graphic Facilitation?"). The Circle of Courage philosophy (Brendtro et al., 2002) identifies four elements necessary for positive development: belonging, mastery, independence, and generosity. Graphic facilitation is an effective way of gathering information and guiding discussion through combining words and simple graphics, developing a visual language that is easily understood and remembered (Horn, 1998). Figure 1 describes the three essential Es of the planning process: engage, envisage, and enact. The practical skills of facilitation and graphic recording underpin each of these stages.

Introducing Three Students

We facilitated the 3EPlan process with three students. Pere, Malia, and Dana were attending a school in New Zealand that supports students between the ages of 5 and 21 who have a very high level of special needs. New Zealand adopts a noncategorical approach to disability, defining disability in relation to student need. A student with very high needs may require significant curriculum adaptations and support from specialist staff, additional teaching time, and instructional aide support. These needs are likely to remain high or very high throughout their schooling and may be in the areas of learning, vision, hearing, mobility, or language use and social communication (New Zealand Ministry of Education, 2012).

PERE

Pere was a 12-year-old Samoan boy. He lived at home with his parents, five siblings, and his paternal grandmother. Pere attended one of the school's satellite classes at a general education intermediate (Grades 7 and 8) school. Pere's mother, teacher, teacher aide, and speech language therapist also participated in his planning meeting.

MALIA

What Is the Circle of Courage?

The Circle of Courage (Brendtro et al., 2002) is a model of positive youth development based on Native American educational and child-rearing philosophies. It integrates indigenous wisdom with current research on resilience, brain science, and strength-based strategies. The value base is universal across diverse cultures and groups. The Circle is based on a medicine wheel and comprises four quadrants—the universal human needs of belonging, mastery, independence, and generosity. All parts of the Circle must be in balance if the child is to live in harmony. The Circle of Courage approach creates respectful connections among both adults and peers fostering climates for positive youth development.

Malia was 10 years old and lived with her mother and father. She was in one of the classes for students with very high needs at the specialized school. Because the family had recently moved to New Zealand from Samoa, there was no family support and they had not yet established community networks. Malia's mother and teacher participated in her planning meeting.

DANA

Dana was 18 years old and during the school week lived with three other students from the school in a house coordinated by a disability support service; she returned home most weekends.

What is Graphic Facilitation?

Effective student-centered planning processes are unique and creative, and are designed around an individual student (Amando & McBride, 2001; Dick & Purvis, 2005; Kincaid & Fox, 2002). Student-centered approaches often incorporate the technique of graphic facilitation (Sibbet, 1977). Graphic facilitation involves capturing ideas at the time they are discussed in a graphic and colorful way. The graphics used must be meaningful and understood by all participants.

The graphic facilitator records ideas on a large chart in full view of everyone participating. The chart provides a canvas on which the conversation is captured and developed and provides a vehicle for thinking together, and capturing and linking multiple perspectives. This can provide better results than using a traditional written format (Kim & Mauborgne, 2002) and acknowledges and accommodates different learning and processing styles (Gardner, 1985). Grove and McIntosh (2002) emphasized the importance of making information accessible by providing formats that reflect individual learning and communication styles. The use of graphics, photographs, and symbols understood by the student, promotes a sense of ownership and control, generating and motivating self-direction.

She attended the specialized school in a class that provides a transition program for students in their last 3 years of schooling. Dana's caregiver from the support service and her mother participated in the meeting, along with her teacher.

Dana's experience was selected as a case study as it clearly demonstrates the approach and the process. While Dana is a unique young woman, she shared many of the attributes of other young people at the school and has significant behaviors that people who interact with her find challenging.

Engage
DANA'S PREPARATION MEETING

Dana and her teacher met before the planning meeting to review Dana's progress and prepare for the meeting. They discussed the purpose of and procedure for the 3EPlan meeting; the four elements of the Circle of Courage; and Dana's strengths, dreams, needs, and possible goals. In addition, Dana nominated whom she would like to have join them for her planning meeting:

her mother, her residential caregiver, and the transition coordinator.

ENGAGE

Preparation with student

Discuss
- Strengths and interests
- Dreams
- *Ideas for getting there*
- The meeting process
- Who to invite

Consider
- Date, time, refreshments
- Room (accessibility, comfort, privacy, suitability)
- Invitations
- Facilitators
- Transport

Before participants arrive
- Ensure room is welcoming
- Set out refreshments
- Prepare paper and pens
- Obtain photograph of student
- Prepare and hang template

The planning meeting
- Welcome and introductions
- Culture of being together
- Purpose of and procedure of meeting

ENVISAGE

The planning meeting

Facilitate each element
- Belonging
  - Dreams
  - Now
  - Goal/s
- Mastery
  - Dreams
  - Now
  - Goal/s
- Independence
  - Dreams
  - Now
  - Goal/s
- Generosity
  - Dreams
  - *Now*
  - Goal/s
- Feed back the story at the end of each element

ENACT

The planning meeting

Feed back the chart retelling the complete story

Photograph the
- Chart/plan
- Student in front of the chart
- Student and participants in front of the chart

Present chart/plan to student

Close the planning process

Convert the plan to a program*

Implement the program*

Review and evaluate the program*

(*not part of this article)

Student-centered facilitation style

Recording through graphic facilitation

Figure 1. The 3EPlaning Process

83

The Planning Room

The room where Dana's meeting was to be held was selected for its accessibility, privacy, and suitability. An individualized chart (Figure 2) listing the four elements of the Circle of Courage (i.e., belonging, mastery, independence, generosity) hung on the wall; Dana's name and photograph on the chart would provide the focus for the meeting. Comfortable chairs of the same height in a semicircle enabled participants to see one another and to view the evolving chart.

Facilitating the Planning Meeting

After we explained the purpose of the 3EPlan meeting, we discussed possible timeframes and the participants decided to plan for 1 year. The team discussed the philosophy of the Circle of Courage. Dana was familiar with the Circle of Courage, as she had studied it in class. We listed the names of those participating on the side of the chart; Dana chose a color (red) to represent the graphic of herself, and selected colors to represent her family and friends (purple and green). Dana's caregiver thought the graphic representation was helpful because Dana "could see herself in red and knew that the points were about her."

Envisage

The Circle of Courage elements of Dana's chart (i.e., belonging, mastery, independence, generosity) provided a structure for the meeting's discussions. Dana and her team first examined *belonging* and what connections and relationships Dana wanted to maintain and develop over the next year, creating a vision for this element. We used graphics to record the Dream in an outer corner of the chart. The team then discussed what "belongings" (relationships and connections) Dana currently experienced (Now), and depicted these in the inner circle of the Belonging segment. Ideas for supporting Dana to progress from the "Now" to the "Dream" for Belonging would form the goals for the coming year and were recorded in the middle section of the circle. For example, one of Dana's "dreams" was to develop friendships. She suggested that one way of achieving this was to "belong" to a course of study, and identified a certificate course for students with special needs offered at the school she attended. So, one way for Dana to progress from

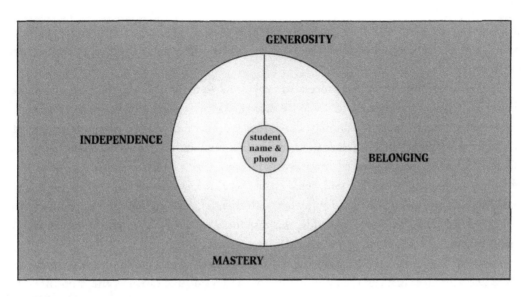

Figure 2. The Planning Meeting Chart

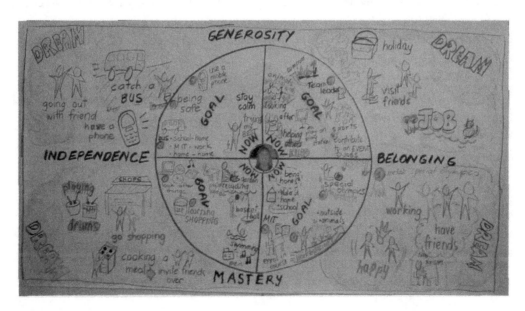

Figure 3. Dana's Completed Chart

the "Now" to the "Dream" of belonging (i.e., a short-term goal) would be for her to research the course, with the support of her transition coordinator, with a view toward applying for admission to the course.

The team followed the same process to explore all four elements of the planning chart. Figure 3 is Dana's completed chart; Table 1 illustrates a script typical of that when developing a Goal from a Dream. Once the planning of each element (quadrant of the Circle) was completed, the chart was fed back in a different progression: first retelling the "Now," then describing the "Goals" and how they progressed toward the "Dream." One of Dana's short-term goals was obtaining a cell phone, which she said would enable her to achieve several of her goals safely (e.g., shopping independently, visiting or going out with friends). Although her mother and teacher were skeptical about her ability to handle this responsibility, for Dana it later became a highly motivating factor in her working towards achieving several goals.

As with all student-centered planning, the 3EPlan meeting is focused on the student. We asked Dana for ideas first and then gave her mother and residential caregiver the opportunity to add their ideas before opening the discussion to the whole group. Although in her daily life Dana was usually very vocal, at the beginning of the meeting she was a little reticent. This was the first individualized education program (IEP) meeting in which she had participated. However, her teacher supported her by referring her to the preparation notes the two of them had made prior to the planning session. Dana soon relaxed, volunteered ideas, and appeared to enjoy the process. Dana's mother commented that

> The whole process was good for [Dana], to have her input and the things she wanted to do and the future for her ... . For me personally it was hearing [Dana's] dreams for herself. I know she is loud and boisterous but when it comes to serious talking about herself she is usually very drawn—doesn't say much—but for me to see the input she put into it was stunning.

Dana's teacher noted that this type of planning process also can be revelatory; "Her love of animals—I didn't know about that; it was new to me." Figure 4 provides possible questions and prompts to help encourage and aid discussion.

Table 5.1. Planning One of Dana's Goals for Independence

Developing the Dream →	Capturing the "Now" →	Planning the Goal (s)
Q: What do Dana and her family want to happen for her, in the near future?	**Q:** What skills, experience, and knowledge does Dana have now that can be built upon, to work towards the Dream?	**Q:** What does Dana and her team need to work on, to help her reach her Dream?
A: Dana wants to be able to take a bus into town to meet up with her friends.	**A:** Dana is currently trying her best to stay calm in situations she finds difficult or uncertain. This is an important skill to build upon when taking the bus; she'll need to be patient while waiting and adjust to changes in traffic and timing.	**A:** To help her ultimately be able to take the bus downtown, Dana and her support team first needed to achieve her riding the bus between home and school, between her parents' home and her weekday residential living location, and between work and her weekly class.

Enact

Towards the end of the process, when all four elements had been planned, we summarized the entire chart, narrating the plan as a story about what Dana would be focusing on over the next year. Emphasizing the interrelationship of the elements and the plan as an entity helped to create a highly motivating picture of Dana's following year. In closing, participants commented on how they felt about the meeting, which gave Dana and her support team the opportunity to share delights and concerns and to clarify or follow up queries.

We summarized each element as it was completed, presenting it as a progression: first retelling the "Now," then describing the "Goals" and how they progressed toward the "Dream."

At the end of the meeting, Dana took possession of the completed chart. (All participants later received a photo of the plan and Dana also had a laminated hard copy for her desk at school.) Immediately receiving a copy of the plan promotes enacting and related action. Dana posted her plan on the classroom wall the afternoon of the planning meeting, and related the "story" of her meeting and the goals to her classmates. After school, she took the plan home and asked the caregiver to mount it on the wall of the dining room; this in itself was an accomplishment. Her caregiver noted that "in the home [Dana] destroys things and that is an ongoing problem .... Normally things would get ripped off the wall and shredded, ... but with the plan she hasn't."

The Role of Facilitation

Ideally this process involves two facilitators: a *process facilitator* who develops a relationship with the participants, drawing out ideas, issues, and What would you like to be able to do by yourself? themes; and a *graphic facilitator* who records the ideas expressed in the form of graphics, symbols, and words. To increase student participation and involvement it is important to use a process with which the student can engage and follow (Konrad, 2008; Mason, McGahee-Kovac, & Johnson 2004). The commitment of facilitators is a powerful influence on the likelihood of students receiving a plan, having choices respected, and increasing involvement in community activities (Robertson et al., 2007). The facilitator must be committed to a student-centered philosophy, be an aware and conscious listener, and be able to communicate clearly (O'Brien & O'Brien, 1998; Sanderson, 2000). An understanding of group dynamics and using cooperative and collective decision-making strategies (Hunter, 2007) is essential. The facilitator needs to be able to guide the group towards a common understanding while encouraging the student and other participants to share information, learn from one another, remain focused, solve problems, make decisions, and plan work. Table 2 provides a list of strategies for implementing a student-centered planning meeting that incorporates graphic facilitation; Table 3 outlines the overall process.

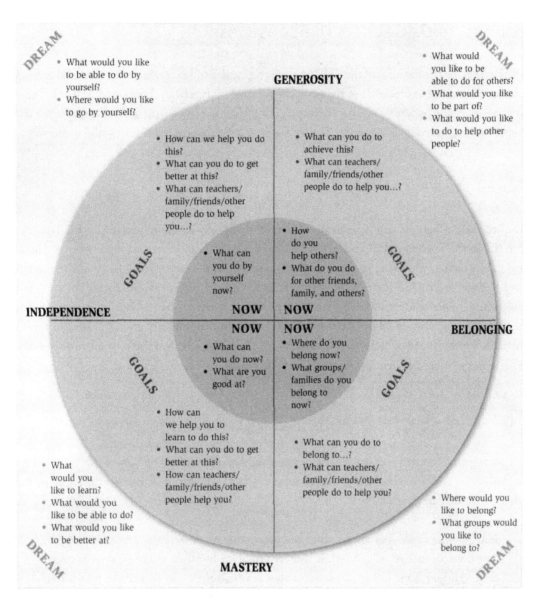

- What would you like to be able to do by yourself?
- Where would you like to go by yourself?

GENEROSITY

- What would you like to be able to do for others?
- What would you like to be part of?
- What would you like to do to help other people?

- How can we help you do this?
- What can you do to get better at this?
- What can teachers/family/friends/other people do to help you...?

- What can you do to achieve this?
- What can teachers/family/friends/other people do to help you...?

GOALS

GOALS

- What can you do by yourself now?

- How do you help others?
- What do you do for other friends, family, and others?

INDEPENDENCE

NOW NOW

NOW NOW

BELONGING

- What can you do now?
- What are you good at?

- Where do you belong now?
- What groups/families do you belong to now?

GOALS

GOALS

- How can we help you to learn to do this?
- What can you do to get better at this?
- How can teachers/family/friends/other people help you?

- What can you do to belong to...?
- What can teachers/family/friends/other people do to help you?

- What would you like to learn?
- What would you like to be able to do?
- What would you like to be better at?

- Where would you like to belong?
- What groups would you like to belong to?

MASTERY

Figure 4. Circle of Courage Questions, Prompts, and Thought Starters

Parents' and Teachers' Perspectives

To ascertain the effectiveness of the 3EPlan strategy, an independent evaluator interviewed parents and teachers at the end of each of the planning meetings (i.e., Dana's, Pere's, and Malia's). These interviews revealed seven main aspects: the process, the use of visuals, engagement, focusing on the whole student, individuals' expertise, developing positive and optimistic futures, and ownership.

About the Process

The process was "comfortable" (physically and emotionally), encouraging, and respectful. Teachers also found the process to be "student-and parent-friendly," with increased input from students and parents when compared to previous planning processes. Teachers also felt that the process gave them a better understanding of what was happening in the home and during the student's leisure time. One teacher remarked on how affirming it was to be involved in a process that fostered reciprocity of learning between school, home, and community contexts. Another commented: "For me it gave a better picture of what was happening. It was the way it was done—the visuals, the writing, the structure—it was very informal."

About the Use of Visuals

All participants commented that the use of visuals and graphic recording was an effective method of facilitating and recording the plan and supported the student in being more engaged in the process. Dana's caregiver said that

> Having someone doing the graphics and presenting made it a lot more interesting ... . The drawing fascinated [Dana]. It is more visual for her than talking ...; it was colorful and bright. One of her comments about it which made me realize she was taking an awful lot of notice was: "I wish I could draw like that." "How do you draw drums like that?" she would say. She just loved it ... . You have to have the visuals for her.
> (Caregiver)

Table 5.2. Practical Strategies for Teachers

Facilitation	Keep the focus on the student.
	Adopt a student-centered philosophy.
	Understand student-centered planning processes and match the correct process to the student.
	Use language that is understood by all participants.
	Be open and supportive; ask open-ended questions and seek clarification.
	Foster a welcoming environment that supports creativity of thought.
	Encourage engagement through group process.
	Plan for action and encourage that participants leave with a support role.
	Work with the group and the recorder.
Recording through graphic	Be prepared, have a selection of colored pens and good-quaiity paper available. Select a recent and appropriate photograph of the student for the chart.
	Be creative, know the student, think about content that might arise during the planning and practice on a small graphic for these ideas.
	Use culturally relevant imagery to foster connection with, and participation in, the process. The personalized design of each chart will reinforce ownership of the plan for the student and participants.
	Use a color coding for key participants, chosen by the student, which both empowers the student and helps him or her interpret the plan.
	Listen for the key messages and record the main points.
	Remember to summarize each element when it has been completed, checking for accuracy and asking if there are any more ideas to add.

Another participant felt that the visuals

> worked very well ... . [It's] the way to go. When I go to her home it is there and I can look at it and see where she is up to ... if it is just typed on paper it is just not the same.

About Engagement

One of the main advantages of this process was increased engagement for the student and other participants. The 3EPlan process provides multiple opportunities for students to express and discuss their ideas. Seeing the ideas recorded in a (visual) way that they can follow reminds the students of their role as the central participant.

About Focusing on the Whole Student

Participants felt that discussing the elements of belonging, mastery, independence, and generosity covered all aspects of students' well-being. This type of planning encompassed a wider discussion than previous IEP meetings. The discussion "brought out the needs and the areas for development from the perspective of home, school, and community" and enabled the exploration of options and associated fears and possible risks. Dana's caregiver remarked:

> This plan looked at everything—Dana's whole well-being—whereas an IEP didn't always have that and you relied more on the teacher and the teacher saying where [Dana] was at. [This process! involved the home where she is currently living; having that input—just everyone's input. I came away talking about it because it did look at the whole person.
>
> (Caregiver)

About Individuals' Expertise

Parents and caregivers commented that the process placed greater value on their own roles than other IEP meetings they had experienced. Whereas previous planning processes had focused more on school experiences and teacher expertise, this process uncovered and deepened the understanding and appreciation of the student. Participants commented that they had been able to listen to dreams, needs, and interests that previously had not been considered. One teacher noted that it "gave staff a lot of ideas on so many different things that we hadn't thought of or sat down and spoken about." Dana's mother echoed this idea of the meeting process revealing more about the student; "What I found interesting was [discovering] the things that Dana is doing at school and just how much she is [capable of] doing."

About Developing Positive and Optimistic Futures

Participants considered the 3EPlan affirming because it looked past the current and immediate situation and painted a picture of an encouraging future. Parents, caregivers, and teachers found this to be a valid and optimistic feature of the process:

> It looked at the future—not just where [the student] is at for the rest of the year, but the future. (Caregiver)

> Often you just look at the next year. I think [the process] looks more at the big picture and possibilities .... It is a valuable ongoing reference document and a checkpoint. (Teacher)

Participants felt that the process enabled them to see a pathway from the present to achievement of the students' dreams. The process is structured so that ideas from the 3EPlan meeting, incorporated into IEP transition programming as specific, measurable goals, help students realize this future. One teacher noted that the structure enabled participants to "see what were the essential or important goals and what [student] can do, and what we need to do to help."

Table 5.3. Checklist for Graphics Facilitation of Individualized Education Program/ Transition Planning Meetings

Task	Who will do this?	By when?	Date completed
PREPARATION: BEFORE THE MEETING			
Identify possible dates for meeting(s)			
Identify potential participants (discuss with student and parents)			
Include student in reviewing current program and establishing current levels			
Gather information: Provide opportunity for anyone who works with the student to contribute information, especially if unable to participate in the meeting			
Meet with the student: design and organize the event			
Identify meeting location (consider familiarity, accessibility, facilities)			
Develop agenda; roles and materials/resources, refreshments			
Schedule meeting for a time that is (most) suitable for parents/caregivers			
Invite participants			
Make sure everyone has relevant information			
Check transportation needs and put support in place if necessary			
Send out/phone reminders			
Set up the room (hang chart; seat participants in semicircle facing the chart)			
Make sure everyone is at the same height and included in the semicircle			
PLANNING: AT THE MEETING			
Welcome, introductions, ground rules, timeframes			
Establish a common understanding; outline purpose of 3E planning			
Create and maintain a safe planning environment and explain who will be doing what			

Keep the focus on the student			
Encourage involvement and acknowledge input			
Pace the meeting; allow time to process (pauses)			
Keep on track			
Create breaks as needed			
Be open and communicate effectively with everyone			
Facilitate and feedback each element: Belonging, Mastery, Independence, Generosity			
Where to now? (Review first steps and plan follow-up meeting)			
Celebrate the plan—congratulate participants			
Schedule next meeting			
Bring meeting to positive conclusion (e.g., a wish for the student, photo of group in front of graphic)			
Present the plan to the student			
Seek feedback: How was that for you?			
PROGRAMMING: AFTER THE MEETING			
Send photo of completed plan to all participants			
Work with relevant people (e.g., student, parents, specialists/therapists) to develop the IEP			
Make relevant adaptations as needed			
Develop precision teaching and monitoring checklists			
Develop resources			
Organize support			
Allocate responsibilities and timeframes			
Create and maintain motivation and energy			
Implement the program			
Monitor the program and data gathering			
Review student's progress regularly and make necessary changes			
Review and evaluate student progress and the program with all participants			
Evaluate and prepare for next planning session			

About Ownership

Participants commented that the process gave the students a sense of ownership of their plan. The students were given possession of the plan itself, so they could share and talk about it with other students, family members, and others who supported them. The students in this study took their plans home to hang on a wall. Having a personal copy of their plans made it more real and tangible. Dana's mother noted that "When Dana first did this she was so proud of it. Everyday we got up and it was on the wall of the dining area and Dana was always talking about it."

Final Thoughts

Participation in planning meetings by the students involved in this project had previously been limited. The 3EPlan ensured a high level of engagement because the planning was facilitated through the students and included input from parents, caregivers, and school staff.

The 3EPlan lays the groundwork for IEP development, and provides an important and meaningful platform for programming. The plan must be kept at the forefront to ensure that it continues to provide the impetus for the education and support the student receives, while remaining sufficiently flexible should circumstances and needs change.

Although the time required to facilitate the 3EPlan process (about $1^{1}/_{2}$ hours) was longer than in previous years (using other approaches), the meeting was scheduled to suit participants' time preferences. Parents and caregivers expressed overwhelming appreciation for the

Whereas previous planning processes had focused more on school experiences and teacher expertise, this process uncovered and deepened the understanding and appreciation of the student.

time taken as this enabled increased participation by students and parents and a more meaningful dialogue. A high level of engagement and participation from the student, and a greater reflection of the student voice, results in programming and an IEP that is more relevant to the student.

Students with high and very high needs are often not consulted or asked what is important to them or how they would like to spend their day. Dana's caregiver commented, "from what Dana said afterwards she liked talking about her dreams—and having everyone there talking about her dreams." Dana's mother noted that the next step was to "Make the dreams come real." Her final comment provided a succinct summary of the 3EPlan: "It captured what matters most."

References

Amando, A. N., & McBride, M. (2001). *Increasing person-centered thinking: Improving the quality of person-centered planning: A manual for person-centered planning facilitators.* Minneapolis, MN: University of Minnesota, Institute on Community Integration.

Brendtro, L., Brokenleg, M., & Van Bockem, S. (2002). *Reclaiming youth at risk: Our hope for the future.* Bloomington, IN: Solution Tree.

Dick, D., & Purvis, K. (2005). Total communication, person-centred planning and person-centered services. In P. Cambridge & S. Carnaby (Eds.), *Person-centred planning and cane management with people with learning disabilities* (pp. 100–117). London, England: Jessica Kingsley.

Gardner, H. (1985). *Frames of mind: Theory of multiple intelligences.* New York, NY: Basic Books.

Grove, N., & McIntosh, B. (2002). *Communication for person centred planning.* London, England: King's College.

Horn, R. E. (1998). *Visual language: Global communication for the 21st century.* Bainbridge Island, WA: MacroVU Press.

Hunter, D. (2007). *The art of facilitation.* Auckland, New Zealand: Random House.

Kim, W. C., & Mauborgne, R. (2002). Charting your company's future. *Harvard Business Review,* 80(6), pp. 77–83.

Kincaid, D., & Fox, L. (2002). Person-centered planning and behavior support. In S. Holburn & P. M. Vietze (Eds.), *Person-centered planning: Research, practice and future directions* (pp. 29–49). Baltimore, MD: Brookes.

Konrad, M. (2008). 20 ways to involve students in the IEP process. *Intervention in School and Clinic, 43*, 236–239. http://dx.doi.org/10.1177/1053451208314910

Mason, C., McGahee-Kovac, M., & Johnson, J. (2004). How to help students lead their IEP Meeting. *TEACHING Exceptional Children, 36*(3), 18–24.

New Zealand Ministry of Education. (2012). *Support for students with the very highest needs*. Retrieved from http://www.minedu.govt.nz/NZEducation/Education Policies/SpecialEducation/AQuickGuideToExtraSupport/LearningDifficulties/SupportForStudentsWithHighestNeeds.aspx

O'Brien, J., & O'Brien, C. (1998). Learning to listen. In J. O'Brien & C. O'Brien (Eds.), *A little book about person-centered planning* (pp. 15–18). Toronto, Canada: Inclusion Press.

Robertson, J., Emerson, E., Hatton, C., Elliott, J., McIntosh, B., Swift, P., … Joyce, T. (2007). Person-centered planning: Factors associated with successful outcomes for people with intellectual disability. *Journal of Intellectual Disability Research, 51*, 232–243.

Sanderson, H. (2000, November). *Person-centred planning: Key features and approaches*. Retrieved from http://www.familiesleadingplanning.co.uk/Documents/PCP%20Key%20Features%20and%20Styles.pdf

Sibbet, D. (1977). *7 see what you mean!" A guide to group graphics*. San Francisco, CA: Grove Consultants.

Deborah Espiner, *Principal Lecturer. School of Counseling, Human Services & Social Work, University of Auckland, New Zealand. Diane Guild, *Assistant Principal, Mt. Richmond Special School, Otahuhu, Auckland, New Zealand.*

Address correspondence concerning this article to Deborah Espiner (e-mail d. espiner @auckland. ac.nz).

The authors would like to thank the group of students and their support teams who participated in this research project. Without their energy, ideas, cooperation and critique this article would not have been possible. Thanks are extended to Dr. Bruce Kent for facilitating the interviews and coding and analyzing the interview data.

PART THREE

Governance, Support and Legal Foundations of Education

School Reform

INTRODUCTION
BY KISHA R. CUNNINGHAM, PHD

"School reform is not enough. The notion of schooling itself must be challenged."

—John Taylor Gatto

As educators, we often support school reform, yet struggle with authenticity and advocacy. It is hard to detach authenticity and advocacy. Chapter 6 follows a Harlem teacher during the late 1970s. She explains how complicated it was to implement certain things to low-income students and how she saw herself in many of these children. While many teachers understand how to relate to their students despite race, class, or gender, authentic relationship building is hard to achieve due to inauthentic societies and institutions.

School Reform, Authenticity, and Advocacy

BY GARY L. ANDERSON
ADVOCACY LEADERSHIP

As a young, idealistic teacher in Harlem in the late 1970s, like many urban teachers I struggled with how to integrate my political commitments to poor and working class students with my teaching. Having myself grown up working class and having struggled academically in school, I saw myself in many of my students. The alternative school I taught in was located in the old Hotel Theresa in New York City, a high rise building in central Harlem that at one time was an elegant hotel where jazz greats like Duke Ellington and political figures like Fidel Castro stayed. In those days it housed mostly city offices and our community-based school called College Adapter Program (CAP). It was a "second chance" school for youth who had dropped out of their high schools but showed promise. Our job was to get them ready for nearby City College, which at the time had open admissions and free tuition.

In those years as a teacher in Harlem, I struggled with the age-old problem of rigor and relevance. I knew I needed to teach students the skills to succeed in college. At the same time, I wanted them to have a relevant and empowering education. In the five years I taught there, I learned that students can be taught rigorous skills using an empowering curriculum, and Harlem was alive with relevant history. I remember teaching *The Autobiography of Malcolm X* in a classroom that was rumored to have once been Malcolm's office.

I hadn't chosen to teach in Harlem. Newly arrived in New York City, I didn't even know I was in Harlem until someone told me during my interview. I wondered how my mainly African-American and Puerto Rican students would view me. I was young, White, and from the Midwest, with only two years of teaching experience. I had read about the need to put on a tough front for so-called "innercity" kids. I was never good at posturing and was far from "hip," so I decided to just be myself, hoping that being authentic would set a tone in which my students could be authentic with me. I used a lot of humor, poking fun at myself and joking about my lack of urban sophistication. As one of the few White teachers in this alternative school, I think I was a bit of a curiosity.

These were not only kids of color; they were uptown kids who felt out of place downtown (where they seldom ventured). In the Manhattan of the 1970s, the designations "uptown" and "downtown" had class and race implications. As I laced my teaching with stories of my own struggles in school and with a sense of not measuring up, my students, especially the male students' tough fronts (necessary body armor for urban survival) melted away. As they saw my vulnerabilities, they also began showing me theirs. They laughed at my stories about growing up in Iowa, and their own stories flowed into the journals they kept for class. In many ways, I was their conduit to the mysterious White world they had little contact with, other than through the media. It was during those years in the old Hotel Theresa that I fell in love with my students and with teaching.

During those years, I learned how to teach a rigorous and empowering curriculum in spite of standardized tests. I taught English and knew that their success in college would depend on their ability to write competent papers. But since most of my students also had to pass the GED exam, a standardized test of high school academic skills, I learned how to help them demystify the exam and taught them the skills they would need to pass it. I told them not to confuse test prep with education, and we bonded around our plot to outwit the test. Together we were "getting over" on the system. Though at the tender age of 25, I was, in many ways, naïve and paternalistic, I saw myself as their advocate in a world in which few were looking out for their welfare. But, at a broader level, I had only a partial understanding of the vast economic and political changes that were occurring around us during the 1970s and 1980s, changes we would later refer to with terms like the *new economy*, *new capitalism*, and *neoliberalism*.

As a political activist and veteran of Students for a Democratic Society (SDS) and the anti-Vietnam war movement, I knew that the country was moving to the political right. New York City went bankrupt during this time, and while the financiers were bailed out, the city took a huge hit (Harvey, 2005). Nationally resources were being reallocated away from Great Society programs. This tendency culminated in Reagan's massive tax cuts for corporations and individuals as part of a "revolution" that resulted in the most massive reallocation of wealth upward, the country had seen since the 1920s. The top tax rate for individuals was reduced from 78 to 28% and tax adjustments on depreciations on investments for corporations allowed many corporations to pay no taxes at all. Just as African Americans were finally beginning to enjoy the benefits of the welfare state, including programs like CAP, it was coming under attack.

During the years I was teaching, I also worked some evenings with an organization led by Michael Harrington, author of *The Other America*, a book that helped inspire John Kennedy's war on poverty in the early 60s and later Lyndon Johnson's Great Society programs. In the 1970s his Democratic Socialist Organizing Committee (DSOC), which was also led by Cornel West and Gloria Steinem, worked within the Democratic Party to bring about prolabor policies. But I was never able to understand the connections between my work with DSOC and my work with my students in Harlem. I saw them as two separate worlds. By day, I tried to provide my students with the skills and cultural capital they would need to have any chance of success in an unequal system; by night, I worked to try to stop the unraveling of social gains achieved by decades of social activism, an unraveling that would leave an even more unequal society. Little did I know then how unequal we would become as a nation.

Around 1980, the funders of CAP mandated a shift from college preparation to vocational training and our funding was severely cut. Th e CAP acronym stayed the same, but instead of College Adapter Program, we became Career Advancement Program. Instead of teaching English classes to prepare students for college, I began teaching business English. We prepared keypunch operators just as the job was becoming obsolete. At CAP we had worked hard to "pump up" students psychically for a future that included a college education. Now, that excitement was gone. I left CAP to direct a program in the South Bronx, but the America that I had grown up in was changing in ways few of us grasped at the time.

Authenticity and Advocacy are Inseparable

I had struggled in those years with the twin themes of *authenticity* and *advocacy* that are central to this book—themes that seem lacking in our current discourse on teaching, leading, and reforming schools. I learned that authentic teaching wasn't essentially about cognition, learning theory, and teaching methods, though good teachers know these things. It was essentially about relationality and connecting in authentic ways with students. It was both the cognitive and noncognitive dimensions of teaching that were essential. Good teachers figure out how to relate to kids in authentic ways—despite differences of class, race, or gender, and without giving up their authority as teachers.

But I also sensed that building authentic relationships with students was not enough. Authentic teaching could not make up for inauthentic institutions or an inauthentic society in which discourses of equity contradicted vast and growing inequities. To paraphrase Paulo Freire (1970), being authentic with students means helping them to read the word *and* the world. To be authentic with low-income students, teachers needed to help them develop curiosity about the world, including why some struggle while others enjoy obscene privilege. As Freire has argued, this cannot be a pedagogy of answers. Such a pedagogy is indoctrination, no matter what side of the political spectrum it is taught from.

Beware of the leader who has lots of answers and few questions. Many administrators are taught to problem *solve*, not problem *pose*. There are entire courses in educational administration programs in universities on "decision making," which is largely an exercise in solving problems. But seldom are the skills of problem posing taught. And yet we know that how a problem is framed or understood will determine the way we go about resolving it. And even when problem posing is taught, problems are seldom understood in a social or historical context.

The moral of these stories is that it is hard to separate authenticity and advocacy. Authenticity at the interpersonal level is exceedingly difficult unless we create authentic institutions and an authentic society in which the values of equity and democracy can be practiced. Building relationships in schools, whether with students or teachers, becomes more difficult as reforms demand more scripted classrooms and more stressful workplaces.

Zero tolerance policies are a good example of divorcing authenticity from advocacy. We think we can solve problems by "getting tough" instead of doing the hard work of using teachable moments with children and youth. Increasingly in schools, incidents that in the past would have been handled with a meeting of principals, parents, teachers, and the students involved, are too often handled by the juvenile justice system. Once the police are on the scene—and their presence is ubiquitous in urban schools—the principal's authority is usurped. Not only do students miss out on the opportunity to be taught moral and ethical lessons by caring adults, they are getting criminal records at earlier ages, entering what is now being called the pipeline to prison. These youth are also disproportionately poor and of color.

I myself have struggled and continue to struggle with how to link authenticity and advocacy. My own teaching and leadership in Harlem was aimed at helping individual students become upwardly mobile, and our program was successful in sending many struggling students to college. Yet political forces occurring at another level were chipping away at the collective gains of 40 years of social struggle, and our program became a victim of those very forces.

Today as we struggle to get more students to graduate from high school, public funding for higher education is decreasing, leaving fewer affordable seats for low-income students. The average public subsidy for higher education has plummeted from over 30% to an average of 12%. State subsidies have dropped so low that what we used to call state-funded universities are now referred to as state-assisted, and in cases like Virginia, where state subsidies represent a mere 7% of budgets, some are referring to them as "state-located" universities.

While I tried to teach an empowering curriculum in Harlem, exposing students to writers of the Harlem Renaissance and the history of the civil rights movement, I'm not sure how well I got across the notion of becoming empowered democratic citizens in the political context in which my students were living. Juggling teaching, leadership, and advocacy is an ongoing puzzle to solve, and is best done collectively with other professionals struggling with the same issues.

We didn't have participatory action research or learning communities in those days, and many of these teacher and principal support groups today are more about feeding the system than challenging it. But the potential is there. Once leaders decide to take seriously the challenge of being an authentic advocate for low-income children of color, they will need the support of other colleagues to work through the complex dilemmas such advocacy will unearth.

Authenticity, Advocacy, and School Reform

In Harlem, my teaching experience ultimately morphed into administration as I became a bilingual coordinator, a program director in the Bronx, and ultimately took a principalship elsewhere. As an administrator, as in the classroom, I found I was sometimes able to create authentic spaces with teachers and students and advocate for the things I cared about. I learned to recognize when a window of opportunity opened up in the bureaucracy, and I could slip through some policy or practice that supported the kids with the least power. Later, I went on to do a doctorate, and in my early years working as a professor in the ivory tower, I oft en missed the adrenaline rush of being in a school with all of the sense of busy accomplishment one felt at the end of the day. Sometimes I had secret fantasies of returning to work in schools. As a professor I have spent a lot of time with aspiring and practicing principals, enviously listening in my classes to their stories about their teaching and leadership dilemmas, interviewing them for research projects, or visiting them as they interned in schools.

About seven or eight years ago though, when I was teaching at a university in Los Angeles, I began to notice a shift in the dilemmas I was hearing from my students. Both teachers (who were aspiring principals) and practicing administrators were beginning to frame their dilemmas differently. Whereas before they were confident that they could transform their schools along a vision that they believed in strongly, now they seemed discouraged and less hopeful—even cynical. Th is was particularly true of those teachers and administrators who saw themselves as advocates for those in the system who were most marginalized. Despite the rhetoric of decentralization and school autonomy, teachers reported that new reforms were forcing them to eliminate those activities they and their students most enjoyed and around which they were able to bond. I found my own fantasies of returning to work in schools dissipate. It didn't look like fun anymore, and the few authentic spaces in schools where one could create a true learning community seemed to be drying up. These teachers and principals, mostly in low-income schools in the Los Angeles Unified School district, were struggling with mandated reforms that involved scripted curricula, constant testing and an obsession with test scores, greater surveillance of their work, fewer opportunities for creativity, overcrowded schools, and the constant implementation of new policies, oft en through ballot initiatives.

For the most part, these students of mine were overachievers who were highly committed to their students. Most of them chose to work in low-income areas where their students' lack of access to social, cultural, and economic forms of capital made their work overwhelming but rewarding. Now it seemed that society was exclusively holding them accountable for low student performance. Th ey expected to be held accountable and wanted all mediocre teachers and principals to be held accountable as well. But this new system was not accountability in the authentic sense that any professional expects to be held accountable; rather it was a kind of accountability that was punitive and humiliating, like an angry mob searching for a scapegoat. How did school reform so effectively reach behind the classroom door, and with such problematic results?

Scapegoating School Professionals

Public schools for low-income kids have never been very good, and being a teacher or administrator in such schools was never easy. Teachers, principals, and superintendents are generally known for their resilience and their famous "high tolerance for ambiguity." Teachers survive a succession of principals—some good, some bad. They've seen many reforms and innovations come and go—some useful, most not. While some teachers are incompetent, even racist, and should be removed, the vast majority do the best they can under circumstances that are oft en less than ideal. In low-income neighborhoods, some of their students are homeless, have serious health problems, are recruited by gangs, or are victims of other forms of violence. Teachers in those schools oft en have children with special needs and English language learners in their classes. Even teachers in middle- and upper-class neighborhoods endure many privileged students and parents who treat teachers with disdain, and problems of drugs and stress-related illnesses are prevalent among students in these communities as well. In addition, teachers work under the anonymity of a profession with low status and low pay. While the range of good and not-so-good teachers is probably similar to the range of good and not-so-good doctors, nurses, CEOs, and lawyers, good teachers manage to do amazing things with children and youth in their classrooms.

Principals and superintendents are also resilient. They live in the crossfire of multiple constituencies, all with different needs and demands. They are expected to mediate these conflicting demands on a daily basis. They are middle managers, increasingly getting their marching orders from city, state, and federal-level mandates. In spite of layers of bureaucracy and limited autonomy, good principals have always somehow managed to create amenable work environments for teachers, a welcoming atmosphere for parents, and a safe and stimulating school culture for students.

But it has always been a given that this good work of teachers and administrators was done in spite of, not because of the largely problematic institutions they worked in. For decades reformers have decried "a grammar of schooling" that creates a dysfunctional workplace for teachers and administrators and a fragmented, monotonous, and tracked educational experience for students, especially in middle and high schools, and especially in low-income schools (Tyack & Cuban, 1997). Reforms that have attempted to "restructure" schools or target the inequities of the system through such policies as compensatory education, more equitable financing formulas, and desegregation plans have had only limited success.

Our best scholars and practitioners have worked long and hard to understand how to break open the grammar of schooling in ways that would create more effective and equitable public schools. Many critical scholars, including this author, have argued over the years that public schools not only could not ameliorate social inequalities, but that in fact, they may contribute to them though practices, such as tracking, that helped to reproduce an inequitable social order. But everyone, from Left to Right, from the academy to the school house, was optimistic that public schools could be made to work better for teachers and for children and that they could be changed. In fact, a whole new field of study, "educational change," was created to better understand how to break the code of the seemingly intractable grammar of schooling. But until recently, it was assumed that however we succeeded in improving schooling, it would be in the context of core values of a system of public schooling aimed at making opportunity available to all American children. Th ere were some groups that favored deschooling society, free schools, Afrocentric schools, and other experiments outside of the public bureaucracy, but none of those were pushing privatization per se. Whether you railed at the public schools from the left , the right, or the center, the core value of a rigorous, equitable, and *public* school system open to all was largely assumed.

During the 1980s and into the 1990s, school reforms continued along two parallel tracks that oft en coexisted in considerable tension; one harking back to John Dewey and the other to Edward Thorndike (Donmoyer, 2005). The Dewey track moved toward "authentic" reforms involving authentic assessments, participatory decision making, teaching the whole child, project methods, learning communities, small schools, and child-centered teaching. Reforms such as the Coalition of Essential Schools exemplified this approach. The Thorndike track found these reforms too unstructured and fragmented and sought more "systemic" change, relying on more centralized pressures for change, more standard-ized accountability systems, and more teacher directed learning.

Many scholars of color felt that neither the Deweyian nor the Thorndike approach was effective for low-income children and children of color. Delpit (1995) and others argued that so-called progressive reforms oft en failed to understand the needs of children who were not White or middle class. More importantly, these scholars of color felt left out of the school reform conversation.

Most teachers and administrators were also left out of these academic and policy conversations, or were having conversations of their own that were more focused on how they were coping with the day-to-day implications of school reform policies. But mostly, they didn't pay too much attention to these early debates over reform, since many were already suffering from policy overload. Teachers could usually hunker down and wait out the worst effects within the enclaves of their classrooms. Principals became experts at buffering good teachers from the latest innovation. They had seen so many reforms come and go that the skepticism was oft en palpable. They went to the workshops and retreats, used what they could, but were largely absorbed by the day-to-day work that anyone who has taught in or led a school knows is all consuming. Besides, teachers who work together all day need to get along, and many of these debates, particularly concerning teaching methods, were seen as divisive.

Then during the second half of the 1990s something changed. It's hard to pinpoint the exact moment. A few scholars and some practitioners had warned the change was coming, but because the changes were taking place largely over the heads and outside the typical education discourse, few people noticed. Early warnings came from a shift to outcomes-based assessment. This shift in focus from inputs to the statistical measurement of outputs, a concept borrowed from business management, became a centerpiece of the Goals 2000: Educate America Act passed in 1994. In Texas, there was some debate about the Texas accountability system before it was essentially transferred to Washington under former Texas governor, George W. Bush. This debate had more to do with how the TAAS test and the use of scores to punish schools were viewed (Anderson, 2001; McNeil, 2000, Skrla & Scheurich, 2004). Other early warnings came from British scholars' experiences under Thatcherism and the increasing marketization of schools under a neoliberal economic system (Gewirtz, Ball, & Bowe, 1995). There were rumblings about the Business Roundtable and local and national chambers of commerce taking a larger role in reform, but little of this made its way into a fragmented educational discourse. Some finance scholars had noticed that a new breed of school business managers with MBAs were shifting to outsourcing and privatizing of services, but again, few others were paying attention. There were debates over school vouchers, but vouchers didn't seem politically viable since the public had voted them down in ballot initiatives in several states. So there was a sense that as long as voucher legislation was held at bay, we were safe from a massive marketization of the public school system.

On January 8, 2002, George W. Bush signed the reauthorization of the Elementary and Secondary Education Act, known as No Child Left Behind, and did a photo op with liberal Senator Ted Kennedy. Even at that stage most educators were not too wary since it was a bipartisan bill, and George Bush was still seen as a moderate Republican in some education circles. Furthermore, the legislation had some seemingly progressive touches, like the disaggregation of test scores by race and socioeconomic status so that to be "high performing" a school had to be successful with all subgroups of students. And anyway, who could argue against schools being accountable to the public. Most educational researchers, teachers, and administrators went along without too much fuss. Nobody, including most politicians, knew what landmines lurked within the over 700 pages of dense legislation.

An accountability system that had only been experienced intensely in some states, such as Texas and North Carolina, was now a national phenomenon, and it soon became apparent that this reform was different. Aft er many false starts, the change experts had figured out how to get behind the classroom door, and they did it, through high-stakes testing. Seemingly overnight, teachers had scripted curricula, test preparation booklets, and instructional "coaches" to make sure they did it the right way. Based on studies using randomized assignment to experimental and control groups, these "evidence-based" instructional programs had to be implemented in a particular way, using all of the components that vendors made available at considerable cost. Principals were taught to do "walk throughs" of classrooms as yet another layer of surveillance.

On the positive side, some principals were able to use the leverage NCLB gave them to selectively implement some good programs. Others were able to protect those teachers whose students always did well from the worst excesses of the reform. And some newer teachers found the scripted lessons helpful, since they didn't have to prepare their own materials (or learn how to teach for that matter). Undoubtedly some bad teachers disliked the extra attention because now they actually had to do something. Many teachers—generally, not the bad ones—retired early in disgust; others persevered, finding ways to work in the interstices of the reform. Some good principals with good teachers were able to raise test scores without throwing out authentic teaching practices. But one thing was certain, teaching and administration in schools would never be the same.

Finally, change experts had succeeded, but teachers were not celebrating. The Harvard Civil Rights Project did a study in 2004 of teachers in Virginia and California and reported that.

> Teachers confirm that the NCLB accountability system is influencing the instructional and curricular practices of teachers, but it is producing unintended and possibly negative consequences. They reported that, in response to NCLB accountability, they ignored important aspects of the curriculum, de-emphasized or neglected untested topics, and focused instruction on the tested subjects, probably excessively. Teachers rejected the idea that the NCLB testing requirements would focus teacher's instruction or improve the curriculum. (Sunderman, Tracey, Kim, & Orfield, 2004, p. 2)

While many teachers were teaching to the tests, many principals were "leading to the tests." Abernathy (2007) quotes a principal in his study who discusses how the reform has reallocated his time and priorities away from authentic time with teachers and students.

> I would estimate that exploring data takes at least five extra days each year. Testing takes about ten days out of my year. Staff development issues consume another three days. Th e service time I spend and additional time writing the district Title grant add another ten days. Additional state reports, all in one way or another tying into AYP, add about thirty days time in total taken away from other duties I used to perform. Some do not get done; some are shortchanged, and some I do by adding on to my day or year. (p. 104)

But this reform also had an airtight discursive strategy. Anyone who voiced any criticism of the reform was accused of not believing that poor kids could learn. Poverty didn't seem to be the problem; the problem, we were told, were the teachers and administrators.

Is No Child Left Behind an Authentic Form of Advocacy?

Most scholars, even those critical of NCLB, praise the legislation for its insistence on, not just calling for equal access to quality schooling, but to equality of achievement outcomes. While researchers at the Civil Rights Project at Harvard University have taken NCLB to task for its results, they have praised the legislation for its "inspiring vision." (Sunderman & Kim, 2004) Many of these researchers see the limitations of NCLB, not in its goals, but rather as a lack of funding for its mandates, a flawed theory of implementation resulting in various unintended consequences, or its primitive top-down/bottom-up mix of sticks and carrots (Abernathy, 2007). While my argument in this book includes a critique of these limitations, I am much more skeptical about the authenticity of its espoused equity agenda.

NCLB had widespread support among both political parties, and many conservatives and progressives shared former Secretary of Education, Rod Paige's view that holding schools accountable through high-stakes testing and the disaggregation of test scores by race and SES is a way to advocate for children. In fact, the title No Child Left Behind was taken from a politically liberal child advocacy group, the Children's Defense Fund, headed by Marian Wright Edelman. Some, even now, view the act as a form of advocacy and part of the legacy of the Civil Rights Movement. They point out that before NCLB, the only thing that mattered in many American school districts was whether the high school football team was winning, not how low-income kids, English language learners, or kids of color were doing in school. With No Child Left Behind and the disaggregation of test scores, all subgroups had to achieve at a higher level. Suddenly, they argue, principals began to give a damn about kids of color and low-income kids—or at least their test scores (Anderson, 2001).

Besides, supporters argue, it would be one thing if we were going back to some better time, some panacea of the past, but they point out that public schools have never served poor students and students of color well. They characterize critics of NCLB as the *education establishment*—also a code word for unions—wanting to protect a system that serves their interests, not those of the children. In fact, they point out that many members of the public education establishment don't even send their own children to public schools, and certainly not the innercity schools many of them work in.

These are sincere arguments and on the surface appear reasonable, but they are fundamentally flawed for reasons I will outline in this book. For one thing, they fail to understand how progressive social change is accomplished through authentic forms of democratic participation, not top-down mandates, however well intended. These mandates, even when they have teeth, as they do in NCLB, usually fail, especially in education, because they create inauthentic reforms.

Their arguments also fail to locate NCLB in the larger context of a growing neoliberal, free market agenda, one broadly supported by Republicans and "new" Democrats. Increasingly public schools are known as "government schools" or "public monopolies," a page taken directly from neoliberal economist Milton Friedman's (1962) *Capitalism and Freedom*. Neoliberal or neoclassical economists advocate the marketization of all social sectors. While neoliberals did not succeed this time in getting vouchers included in the NCLB legislation, there are many routes to the same end.

Finally, if it is true that NCLB represents advocacy at the federal level for low-income children, as some supporters argue, then how do we explain why a federal government that claims to care for poor and disenfranchised families had not raised the minimum wage of $5.15 since 1996, while corporate profits skyrocketed, or why it has reallocated wealth upward to such an extent that the country is more unequal today than at any time since the 1920s? Or how do we explain the fact that roughly 50 million Americans, mostly low-income, have no health insurance, or that, as *Business Week* reports, the average American worker makes $33,000 a year, while the average chief executive officer (CEO) makes $9.6 million (Lavelle, 2005). It seems ingenuous to see an authentic concern for the poor in a policy surrounded by other social policies that maintain, rather than challenge, poverty (Children's Defense Fund, 2004).

Taking a page from institutional theory (Meyer & Rowan, 1977; W. R. Scott, 2001), I want to suggest that school reform itself has become a legitimating ritual for a larger restructuring of the state from a welfare state to a competition state characterized by neoliberal economic policies. We are headed into a period in which the use of school reform language becomes a way to introduce new forms of governance. At the level of the state, these new forms of governance mean that the state moves from being a provider of services, to becoming an overseer and regulator of nonprofit and for-profit private service providers. In the British context, Ball (2007) describes a complex merging of the public and private sectors that includes a growing education service industry, new forms of ideological philanthropy, new social entrepreneurs, and new privatizing discourses. Similar changes are occurring in the U.S. context. Regardless of what we think about these changes, they are moving forward with little public deliberation. This lack of authentic deliberation makes such changes less likely to respond to public needs and more likely to respond to bottom lines and special interests.

Perhaps the most devastating critique of NCLB comes from The National Council of Churches' (2003) Committee on Public Education which has felt a need to speak out from an ethical, moral, and social justice perspective, objecting to NCLB on the following grounds.

1. The law will discredit public education. Undermining support for public schooling threatens our democracy.
2. The annual yearly progress component fails to acknowledge significant improvements students have made, too many are labeled failures even when they are making strides. Those labeled failures are disproportionately poor children and children of color.
3. Schools are ranked by test scores of children in demographic subgroups, a "failing group of children" will know when they are the ones who made their school a "failing" school.
4. Children in special education are required to pass tests designated for children without disabilities.
5. English language learners are required to take tests in English before they learn English.
6. Schools and teachers are blamed for many challenges that are neither of their own making nor within their capacity to change.
7. An emphasis on testing basic skills obscures the role of the humanities, the arts, and child and adolescent development. Children are treated as products to be tested, measured, and made more uniform.
8. The law operates through sanctions, it takes Federal Title I funding away from educational programming in already overstressed schools and uses funds to bus students to other schools or to pay for private tutoring firms.
9. The law exacerbates racial and economic segregation in urban areas. Because urban schools have more subgroups and more complex demands, they are more likely to be labeled "in

need of improvement" than more affluent districts. This labeling of schools and districts encourages families with means to move to wealthy, homogeneous school districts.

10. Demands are made on states and school districts without fully funding those reforms to build the capacity to close achievement gaps. (pp. 2–3)

While we could debate some of these assertions, the fact that a national ecumenical Christian organization would endorse such a strong moral objection to NCLB, suggests that NCLB's claim to be advocacy for low-income students and students of color should be viewed with some skepticism. The National Council of Churches in their 1999 policy statement, *Churches and the Public Schools at the Close of the Twentieth Century*, contains a claim that is becoming ever more obvious to more and more Americans,

> Too oft en, criticism of the public schools fails to reflect our present societal complexity. At a moment when childhood poverty is shamefully widespread, when many families are under constant stress, when schools are oft en limited by lack of funds or resources, criticism of the public schools oft en ignores an essential truth: we cannot believe that we can improve public schools by concentrating on the schools alone. They alone can neither cause nor cure the problems we face. In this context, we must address with prayerful determination the issues of race and class, which threaten both public education and democracy in America.

But perhaps most importantly, politically negotiated policies that fail to include the views of those most affected tend to lack both internal coherence and congruence with the lived reality of teachers, principals, superintendents, parents, and especially that constituency that is never heard from—students. In a word, such policies lack authenticity. Th is lack of authenticity is due to a lack of congruence between espoused equity goals and the reality on the ground, but is also due to a failure to locate school reform in its larger context of social policies that increase social inequality.

Redefining the Role of School Leaders

While some advocacy leaders may find ways to use some of NCLB's mandates to advance an equity agenda, I believe that overall, the legislation makes it more diffi cult to do so. Some may balk at the idea that teachers and administrators should take on an advocacy role of any kind. After all, aren't teachers and administrators supposed to be apolitical? This has been a chronic misconception of the role of professionals generally. Many researchers have documented the many ways the cards in education and society at large are stacked in both overt and subtle ways against those with the least power (Anyon, 2005; Rothstein, 2004). Educators often have only two choices: collude with a status quo that leaves poor children and children of color behind or be an advocate for those very children. Not everyone may agree on the form advocacy for children should take, but the notion that educators should advocate for children is taken for granted among many educators who work with low-income children and families of color.

Many school leaders are effective politicians, building political bases and garnering resources for their schools. This is not what I mean by being an advocacy leader. Typically, leaders who are politically savvy use their political capital to get promoted out of their current position. Those who acquire extra resources for their schools are often not creating new resources for low-income kids, but rather successfully winning the resources away from other equally deserving schools. Here's a brief example of what I mean by calling for school professionals to see themselves as advocates for children in schools.

When our daughter was in the second grade, she attended an elementary school in New Mexico in an urban neighborhood in which roughly half of the students were from middle-class families and the other half were from largely Latino lower-income families. In August the school posted the class lists for the fall on one of the doors to the school, and children and parents would drop by to find out which class they were placed in. My daughter saw her name on one of the lists and remarked how relieved she was that she hadn't been placed in the "dumb" class. I was familiar with the notion of tracking in high schools, and knew that within-class tracking occurred in elementary schools through assignment to reading groups, special education, and gifted programs, but I was unaware that there were whole classes that were considered "dumb" or "smart" classes. I noticed that the "dumb" class also had a larger percentage of Spanish surname students than the "smart" classes.

Since I taught at the nearby university, I had a mole in the school, a student of mine that taught fourth grade. I asked her in confidence about this and without skipping a beat she explained how many middle class parents would negotiate with the teachers and principal to get their children into the classes they wanted. In fact, she implied that some teachers were proactive in this, assuring parents—mostly what she called "soccer moms"—that they would see to it that their child got the best teacher for the following year. She told me that there was a high track through the school, and that these high track teachers would pass certain children along through this track. In fact, she said, one year when one of the middle-class students graduated from elementary school, the high track teachers could be identified because they all wore orchids, gift s of the mother whose child had moved smoothly up through the high track classes.

This teacher's observations were later confirmed as I attended community parent meetings, in which parents openly discussed the ways they worked the teachers and principal on behalf of their kids. These "tracks" were not formally structured, but rather came about through the micropolitics among principals, teachers, and parents, with either the indifference or tacit approval of the administrator.

Of course, these teachers and principals didn't think they were doing anything wrong—nor did the parents for that matter. In fact, the parents likely felt they were "advocating" for their children, and the teachers perhaps saw their behavior as advocacy for their students and parents. After all, this tracking system had its rationales. The high track teachers were more skilled and could integrate the more gifted students we were told. The slower students wouldn't be able to keep up and would hold other students back. (Why these skilled teachers could integrate the "gifted" kids but not the "slower" ones was never explained.) The low track had more bilingual teachers and so bilingual students were better off there. However, what was generally not acknowledged was that the middle class parents and the largely middle class teachers shared a common view of the destiny of "their" children. And if a teacher or administrator didn't have such a tacit understanding, then middle class parents knew how to apply pressure all the way up the system.

Sometimes middle-class parents don't even have to advocate. Our own daughter did not go through the high track; There was a middle range track that was less academically driven, but, in our view, more holistic. The mere perception that we might complain though, likely kept our daughter out of the lowest track. The parents of students in the "dumb classes" were largely lower-income parents who were less likely to be aware of this tracking system, and even if they were, many would not have had the social networks or the cultural capital to effectively contest their child's placement (Lareau, 1989).

More recently in New York City, a local community organization called the Center for Immigrant Families (CIF) challenged a similar situation in the rapidly gentrifying Upper West Side of Manhattan. The *New York Times* reports a feverish growth in demand for private schools in Manhattan, with tuitions hovering around $30,000 a year for preschool through high school (Hu, 2008). For those without access to $400,000 per child for a private school education, there are other ways to get a privileged education for your child. CIF describes the subtle and not so subtle ways principals admitted middle class condo owners to their schools over the children of immigrant families who lived in the neighborhood, including asking for a financial contribution to the school. Th eir participatory action research with local immigrant families exposed the worst excesses of these schools, and they protested to the New York City Department of Education. Through their advocacy, they were able to get the DOE to allocate spaces at these schools through a lottery system.

While these are examples of advocacy leadership exercised by community groups or individuals, they represent missed opportunities for principals who may have seen their professional star hitched to the more powerful middle class parents. Unfortunately most parents see advocacy only as linked to self-interest. Parents rightly advocate for their children, and this is unlikely to change in our individualistic culture and school choice policy environment. But parents with more economic, social, and cultural capital will generally be more effective. So who advocates for those low track students who end up in the "dumb classes" or the left over schools, if not teachers, counselors, school social workers, school psychologists, principals, and superintendents. Unless school professionals see themselves as advocates for more equitable placement of children in classes or schools, they are colluding in a tracking system that is unjust.

This example of how educators can be advocates for equity is relevant to many schools in socioeconomically mixed, gentrifying, or middle class communities. Unfortunately, in too many American schools tracking occurs not within schools, but through neighborhoods sharply segregated by income and race. Ironically, racial segregation nationally has increased not decreased since the passing of desegregation laws. As Americans continue to become less equal in socioeconomic terms, segregation by class has also become more pronounced. Anyone who works in an urban school knows that it is not uncommon for schools to have well over 90% of their students on free and reduced lunch programs. Under these circumstances, how do administrators exercise advocacy in schools in which internal tracking by class and race is less relevant because all of their students are low-income students and more oft en students of color.

The policy response to this problem through NCLB has been largely limited to school choice policies and a call for higher expectations and higher test scores for everyone. There may be some truth in former secretary of education, Rod Paige's claim that the soft bigotry of school professionals' low expectations may be partly to blame for the underachievement of low-income children and children of color. No one escapes the subtle forms of classism and racism that circulate among us on a daily basis. But the solution is not to make teachers the enemy and subject them and their students to high-stakes testing and public humiliation as the policies Paige promoted do.

While raising expectations is necessary in specific cases, a broader solution involves a new way of conceptualizing the role of school professionals. While I will discuss this in more detail in chapter 4, it partly involves linking forms of advocacy within the school to forms of advocacy outside the school. Not all of the principals rebuffed the Center for Immigrant Families' attempt to open up schools to their children. Some principals were allies and supported their work. These principals were not merely concerned with getting more donations from parents, but were motivated by a sense of social justice. While calls for social justice have become far too abstract of late, social justice consists of the kinds of courageous and concrete decisions that some teachers and principals make everyday.

Advocacy principals and teachers attempt to build alliances with existing community groups to leverage power and foster public forms of accountability grounded in empowered communities (Gold, Simon, & Brown, 2004; Shirley, 1997). As school professionals more closely interact with communities, they develop a greater understanding of the constraints under which low-income parents operate on a daily basis. What leaves children behind is more than mediocre education. Children are successful in school to the extent that they have good teachers, but their success also depends on what they experience or don't experience outside of school. In a word, it depends on their economic welfare and their access to mainstream social and cultural capital.

Social inequities are primarily caused by social and economic policies—not school-related factors. Cuban (1990) in his classic article on why school reforms seem to recycle every few decades speculates on why Americans turn to schools for solutions in times of social turmoil. One of the reasons offered by historians, according to Cuban, is

> that elite classes or dominant groups in the society that set directions for major social policies charge the public schools with the responsibility for solving national ills. These elite groups do so because the sources of those ills are deeply rooted in the structures of the society and, if the major problems of poverty, racism, drug addictions, and environmental destruction were addressed directly, grave upheavals in economic, social, and political institutions would occur. (p. 2)

Anyon (2005) takes this observation a step further in arguing that if we really want to improve the lot of poor children, we need to give them the same access to economic resources that the middle class currently enjoys. This means more equitable redistribution of wealth, not merely educational opportunity, tutorial services, or cultural capital. Student achievement improves as family resources increase. Anyon cites various studies that show the many ways that poverty is the result of macroeconomic policies, not low academic achievement. Anyon writes, "I believe that in the long run we would do better to increase the access of the urban poor to economic resources so they, too, can afford the time, money, and inclination to prepare their children for school success" (p. 71).

Somehow, we have been convinced that teachers and administrators should not and cannot influence social policy. A brief example drawn from our professional colleagues in nursing may be instructive. In 2005 several ballot initiatives, propositions 86, 87, and 89 were defeated in California in spite of a heroic effort by the California Nurses Association to get them passed. Th e nurses supported Proposition 86, which would have added a tax to cigarettes to fund health care and Proposition 87, which would have more heavily taxed oil companies. Proposition 89, or the clean elections proposition, was sponsored by the nurses union, and was an attempt to curb the influence of corporate money in politics. Th e tobacco and oil industries, along with a long list of other corporations lined up against the initiatives to the tune of a record $190 million. In a press release, Rose Ann DeMoro, executive director of the California Nurses Association, said

> CNA will also step up efforts for reform on other critical issues facing Cali-fornians, "especially the growing collapse of our healthcare system and the disgrace of having 6.5 million uninsured and millions more underinsured residents. We will transform healthcare in California, soon." (California Nurses Association, 2006)

Among these health professionals, there is a growing realization that they cannot be effective in doing their job unless they are supported by social policies that redirect resources to public health.

Meanwhile, the California teachers unions, with the notable exception of United Teachers of Los Angeles (UTLA), the Los Angeles local, largely sat on the sidelines and even fought the nurses on one of the propositions. Ironically, nurses are trying to call attention to the crises of our already privatized health care system, while associations that represent educators seem largely unconcerned about the growing privatization of our educational system.

The year before in 2004, governor Schwarzenegger promoted proposition 75 that would have required public employee unions to obtain annual written consent from each member in order to use a portion of that member's dues for political activity. In case anyone doubts that this represents an ideological struggle, Milton Friedman, the father of neoliberal, free-market policies was a signatory on official ballot arguments supporting the initiative. This initiative, which already exists in some states, has drastically reduced the political power of labor with respect to corporate support of social policies.

Opponents pointed out that corporate shareholders do not have to sign off for permission of their corporations to support political issues and candidates. Furthermore union members can already opt out of having their dues used for political activity if they choose to do so. Thanks to massive union organizing statewide, the initiative was defeated and once again, the nurses were at the forefront, fighting political battles that transcended their important, but narrower issues, such as salaries and nurse–patient ratios.

While structural change is always achieved collectively, in the absence of universal health care, individual advocacy educators have found ways to use data on students eligible for free and reduced lunch programs to get their parents signed up for free or low cost health insurance through Medicaid (Cohen Ross, 1999). This reduces the number of uninsured students in the school and represents another way of linking to the community. So educators can support those "finger in the dike" local solutions until real universal and affordable health care is available to all Americans. But educators will have to be trained to operate on two levels; one micro and short term; the other macro and long term. This dual approach is the bread and butter of advocacy movements. What is certain is that when it comes to insuring our students, insurance and pharmaceutical company lobbyists will win the day unless professionals who care about the well-being of children and their families provide a countervailing force.

While America has changed many times throughout its history, we are today experiencing one of those epochal shifts on a grand scale. The country will look very different as technology continues to develop, capital flows through cyberspace in real time, and the dividing line between the public and the private continues to blur. Whether we can harness these changes in a way that preserves a sense of democratic principles, a common good, a public sphere, and an authentic self, remains to be seen. For now, these democratic ideals seem increasingly like quaint concepts from a distance past—noble ideas, but not realistic in the current climate of crisis. Neoliberal policies in education and other social sectors seem inevitable. How oft en do we hear the expressions, "That train has already left the station" or "That genie is already out of the bottle"? We are swept along in a current that seems too strong to resist. But there are signs that we are getting clearer about what the real implications are for our educational system if current trends continue. In the next chapter, I will focus in greater detail on one casualty of the new economy: authenticity.

Educational Equity

INTRODUCTION
BY KISHA R. CUNNINGHAM, PHD

> *"Inclusive, good-quality education is a foundation for dynamic and equitable societies."*
>
> —Desmond Tutu

Educational equity and equitable education both play a role in education, but have two totally different meanings. These two topics encompass *separate but equal.* There has been a big change from what it used to be and how it is now. One case that changed history was *Brown v. Board of Education.* Chapter 7 examines educational equity and equitable education in a multicultural society.

Equal Education versus Equitable Education in a Multicultural Society

ANDREA L. MOORE, PHD
SAVANNAH STATE UNIVERSITY

There are two dimensions related to equity: resource and access. Equal education refers to providing the same resources, while equitable education means the process that leads to an equal outcome (Nieto and Bode, 2012). Equal education provides the same teachers, same textbooks, and same school environment, whereas equitable education would provide alternate teaching methods or alternate textbooks to accommodate students. In US classrooms, individuals use cooperative learning to address the needs of students in academically and linguistically heterogeneous groups (Cohen et al., 1999). Students become peer teachers/coaches to help classmates gain greater access to the material. Cooperative learning and other instructional practices are used to meet the demand of the diversity of student needs in an attempt to provide equitable education.

Many court cases since *Brown v. Board of Education* have documented unequal policies or practices against individuals on the basis of immigrant status, language, and/or disability. In each of the three cases here, the courts ruled that these cases violated the Equal Protection Clause under the Fourteenth Amendment. In *Plyler v. Doe* (1982), the Tyler Independent School District in Texas cited §21.031 to ban illegal aliens from Texas schools, on the grounds that the students were a drain on the state's fiscal budget due to their special education needs (e.g., English-language proficiency). The US Supreme Court for the Eastern District of Texas ruled that banning those students was a violation of the Equal Protection Clause and that §21.031 demonstrated discrimination.

Lau v. Nichols (1974) came on the heels of integration in the San Francisco, California, school system in 1971. The school system had 2,854 students of Chinese ancestry who did not speak English. The school system provided English language courses to 1,000 of them, but neglected the other 1,800 students. This class action suit was brought by non–English speaking Chinese students against the San Francisco Unified School District. The students had the same teachers, textbooks, and technology as all other students; however, the US Supreme Court, Court of Appeals, ruled that "equal is not the same." The Court's ruling meant that by not providing accommodations to all the non–English speaking students so that students could learn the material and obtain basic skills, the Equal Protection Clause was violated; and further, 8573 of the Education Code, which mandates that no pupil shall receive a high school diploma who has not met English proficiency standards, was also violated.

Mills et al. v. Board of Education of District of Columbia et al. (1972) was a civil action brought on behalf of seven school-aged children who had been labeled as having behavioral problems, as mentally retarded, emotionally disturbed, or hyperactive. The public schools denied these children admission or excluded them from admission after acceptance with no provision for alternative educational placement or periodic review. The case ended in a US District Court District of Columbia a summary judgment, where these seven students—among countless thousands—would be provided adequate education with accommodations for "exceptional" children.

These three cases demonstrate the attitude of the *Brown v. Board of Education* conclusion:

> Today, education is perhaps the most important function of state and local governments. Compulsory school attendance laws and the great expenditures for education both demonstrate our recognition of the importance of education to our democratic society. It is required in the performance of our most basic public responsibilities, even service in the armed forces. It is the very foundation of good citizenship. Today it is a principal instrument in awakening the child to cultural values, in preparing him for later professional training, and in helping him to adjust normally to his environment. In these days, it is doubtful that any child may reasonably be expected to succeed in life if he is denied the opportunity of an education. *Such an opportunity, where the state has undertaken to provide it, is a right which must be made available to all on equal terms.* [emphasis supplied]

In all three cases, the schools offered the same teachers, resources, and school environment to all or most of the students. Yet, the accommodations were insufficient to meet the needs of the diverse learners. In the *Plyler v. Doe* (1972) document, the Court states,

> We have recognized "the public schools as a most vital civic institution for the preservation of a democratic system of government," and as the primary vehicle for transmitting "the values on which our society rests." … We cannot ignore the

significant social costs borne by our Nation when select groups are denied the means to absorb the values and skills upon which our social order rests. In addition to the pivotal role of education in *sustaining our political and cultural heritage, denial of education to some isolated group of children poses an affront to one of the goals of the Equal Protection Clause*: the abolition of governmental barriers presenting unreasonable obstacles to advancement on the basis of individual merit. Paradoxically, by depriving the children of any disfavored group of an education, we foreclose the means by which that group might raise the level of esteem in which it is held by the majority. ... The inestimable toll of that deprivation [of a basic education] on the social, economic, intellectual, and psychological well-being of the individual, and the obstacle it poses to individual achievement, make it most difficult to reconcile the cost or the principle of a status-based denial of basic education with *the framework of equality embodied in the Equal Protection Clause*. [emphases supplied]

The concept of multicultural education recognizes that differences exist among cultural groups. Culture is defined as the beliefs, actions, traditions, and customs of particular groups in a place at a particular time. A multicultural society is one that includes the cultures, beliefs, and traditions of many groups. Despite the efforts of *Brown v. Board of Education* to bring equality to public schools, the problem of equality in education today lies in diversity—the diversity of racial/ethnic groups, language, gender, age, sexual orientation, and religion. Thus, the framework of multicultural education must embrace those differences and use them to inform the way we educate students.

With a clear achievement gap between racial/ethnic groups, the promise of students obtaining the basic tools necessary to lead economically productive lives is true for some, but not for countless others. The most recent 2012 National Assessment of Educational Progress (NAEP) long-term trend assessment report of knowledge and skills in mathematics and reading comprehension for fourth grade and eighth grade students shows that 1) math and reading scores were higher in 2012 than previous years; 2) fourth and eighth grade students are proficient in both math and reading; 3) racial/ethnic minorities score lower on average on the reading assessment than do their white counterparts; 4) females score higher on average in reading than males; 5) white students continue to score higher on average than blacks and Hispanics on the mathematics assessment; and 6) there is no significant difference in mathematics scores between males and females in 2012. The multicultural education movement recognizes three goals to address the unique needs of different cultural groups and achieve uniform academic achievement: 1) to tackle inequality and promote access to an equal education, 2) to raise achievement for all students, and 3) to provide apprenticeships as critical and productive members of a democratic society (Nieto and Bode, 2012).

The issue of equal education opportunity continues in America, and with the increasing numbers of immigrants and interracial couples having children and the number of students with special needs, the distance to achieving equality lengthens. The Equal Education Opportunity Act of 1974 recognizes equal education for all children as a national goal and hinged on the Fourteenth Amendment's clause on equal protection under the law. But what does equal mean? In mathematics, the term equal means the same. However, many court cases conclude that equal is not the same. Since *Brown v. Board of Education*, the question is not whether education should be equal, but how equal education is achieved (the process), which requires schools to change the way they educate students.

References

Cohen, Elizabeth G., Rachel A. Lotan, Beth A. Scarloss, and Adele R. Arellano (1999). "Complex instruction: Equity in cooperative learning classrooms." *Theory into Practice* 38(2): 80–86.

Ferretti, Ralph P. and Laura T. Eisenman (2010). "Commentary: Delivering educational services that meet the needs of all students." *Exceptional Children* 76(3): 378–383.

Lau v. Nichols, 414 U.S. 573 (1974).

Mills v. Board of Education of District of Columbia, 348 F. Supp. 866 (D.C.1972).

NAEP 2012 Trends in Academic Progress: Reading 1971–2012, Mathematics 1973–2012. Institute of Education Sciences, National Center for Education Statistics, US Department of Education NCES 2013–2456.

Nieto, Sonia and Patty Bode (2012). Affirming Diversity: The sociopolitical context of multicultural education (6th edition). Boston: Pearson.

Plyler v. Doe, 457 U.S. 202 (1982). http://law2.umkc.edu/faculty/projects/ftrials/conlaw/plyler.html, last accessed July 20, 2015.

DISCUSSION QUESTIONS

1. In mathematics, the term equal means the same. However, the US Supreme Court's decisions have concluded that "equal is not the same". How can education be equal, but not equitable?

2. In the Lau v. Nichols case, the Court ruled that "equal is not the same." If equal is not the same, what impact would there be on how schools operate? Answer from the district level, school administrator level, and teacher level.

3. Ferretti and Eisenman (2010) state that "Conceptions of equity are complicated by an education system that was designed to provide a model education to large numbers of children as efficiently as possible while at the same time responding to the diverse and challenging educational needs of underserved students."

    a. What problems exist in implementing the latter, rather than the former, education system?

    b. How do you respond to the problems of implementing an education system that responds to the various needs of diverse and underserved students?

CHAPTER 8

School Finance

INTRODUCTION
BY KISHA R. CUNNINGHAM, PHD

"In a time of tight budgets, difficult choices have to be made. We must make sure our very limited resources are spent on priorities. I believe we should have no higher priority than investing in our children's classrooms and in their future."

—Bob Riley

School Finance

BY MICHAEL IMBER AND TYLL VAN GEEL
EDUCATION LAW

The federal government, state governments, county and other intermediate units of government, municipal governments, and local school boards all contribute to the funding of public education. Money is collected through a variety of mechanisms including federal and state income taxes, state lotteries, sales and property taxes, and the issuance of bonds. Money is in turn distributed from higher levels of government to local school boards in various ways including categorical grants (money given for a specific program or purpose), block grants (money that may be utilized for any of a number of specified purposes), general state aid (money that can be used for any legal purpose), state reimbursement for local expenditures, direct state provision of services, and transfers from municipal governments to local school boards. Local school boards themselves, in accordance with state law, must implement their own taxing authority. In addition, they must establish management systems for handling the money they have raised or received from other units of government. A system this complex and involving large amounts of public funds inevitably raises many legal issues. These issues can be divided into two categories:

1. **Pure finance issues** concern taxation and the utilization of funds for education generally. Litigation in this category has dealt with property tax assessments and exemptions; procedures for imposing a tax or adopting a budget; disposition of assets and liabilities when school district boundaries are altered or dissolved; school accounting procedures; administration of school funds; insurance, sale, and disposition of school property; the issuance and sale of bonds; limits on indebtedness; and procedures for bidding on contracts.
2. **Issues of educational equity and adequacy** concern constitutional and statutory mandates for the provision of services and equality of opportunity. Litigation in this category has challenged interdistrict as well as intradistrict inequalities in per pupil expenditures; fees charged to pupils for tuition, books, and extracurricular activities; the authority of local school boards to spend money for particular purposes; and the overall quality of education provided in a school, school district, or state.

This chapter focuses on finance issues of direct relevance to educational policy and practice. Most of these issues fall into the category of educational equity and adequacy, but many of the principles and cases presented also touch on questions of pure finance. The chapter begins by providing an overview of the school finance system necessary for understanding the legal issues discussed subsequently.

A Legal Perspective on School Finance

The starting point for understanding the legal framework of educational finance is that there is no federal constitutional right to an education. The U.S. Constitution imposes no obligation on either the federal or state government to operate a system of public education or to assist parents in financing private education. Thus, any government effort to establish a system of public schools is, in a legal sense, voluntary. However, once government does undertake to provide a system of public schools, its effort must conform to constitutional requirements.

Given that there is no government duty under the federal Constitution to fund education, the next question is whether government has the authority to provide money for schools. At one time, this was a controversial issue at least regarding the federal government. In theory, the federal government possesses only those powers specifically delegated to it by the people through the Constitution. But the Constitution contains no express delegation to Congress of authority to spend money or do anything else with regard to education.

Though Congress has provided some assistance to education since the Northwest Ordinance of 1787, its constitutional authority was not firmly grounded until 1936. In that year, the Supreme Court decided that Article I, Section 8, the General Welfare Clause, gave Congress the power to tax and spend for activities not specifically mentioned in the Constitution.[1] Thus, the General Welfare Clause justifies the many federal grant programs Congress has authorized for elementary and secondary schools. In total, these grants amount to about six percent of the funds expended for kindergarten through twelfth-grade (K–12) education. As discussed in previous chapters, Congress exercises considerable influence over certain facets of education through requirements that local districts must satisfy if they wish to receive federal funds.

The most extensive of the federal grant programs in terms of both the funds provided and the requirements attached are the Individuals with Disabilities Education Act (see sec. 7.3) and the

No Child Left Behind Act (NCLB) (see sec. 3.6). An issue that is pending in the courts at this writing is whether the federal government is violating the following provision of NCLB:

> Nothing in this [Act] shall be construed to authorize an officer or employee of the Federal Government to mandate, direct, or control a State, local educational agency, or school's curriculum, program of instruction, or allocation of State or local resources, or mandate a State or any subdivision thereof to spend any funds or incur any costs not paid for under this chapter.[2]

A consortium of school districts in three states, the NEA, and ten NEA affiliates brought suit against the Department of Education arguing that the Secretary of Education violated this provision "by requiring states and school districts to comply fully with all of the NCLB mandates even though states and school districts have not been provided with sufficient federal funds to pay for such compliance." The district court dismissed the complaint on the grounds that, although the statute prevented "an officer or employee" of the federal government from imposing an unfunded mandate, the statute did not bar Congress from doing so.[3] On appeal, the Sixth Circuit reversed the lower court and sent the case back to trial. Citing Supreme Court precedent, the Sixth Circuit said that while Congress has the power to attach conditions to its grants, when Congress does attach conditions to a state's acceptance of federal money, the conditions must be set out unambiguously: "Congress must express clearly its intent to impose conditions on the grant of federal funds so that the States can knowingly decide whether or not to accept those funds." Thus, the Sixth Circuit said, the issue before the court was "whether NCLB furnishes clear notice to the ... State [that], if it chooses to participate, [it] will have to pay for whatever additional costs of implementing the Act are not covered by the federal funding provided for under the Act." The court concluded that clear notice was not provided by the statute because it contains the provision that "[n]othing in this Act shall be construed" to require States and localities to "spend any funds or incur any costs not paid for under the Act." Based on this provision a state officer could "could plausibly contend that she understood ... that her State need not comply with NCLB requirements for which federal funding falls short."[4]

What about the states? Where do they obtain the authority to tax and spend on behalf of education? The answer begins with the Tenth Amendment to the Constitution: "The powers not delegated to the United States by the Constitution, nor prohibited by it to the States, are reserved to the States respectively, or to the people."

Because power over education is not specifically delegated to the federal government, education is one of the powers reserved to the states. Thus, states have inherent power to tax and spend for education, if they so choose. The people of all states, through their state constitutions, have in turn required their legislatures to exercise this power. For example, Article XII, Section 1 of the West Virginia Constitution provides: "The legislature shall provide, by general law, for a thorough and efficient system of free schools."

Although some state constitutions make brief mention of local school districts, most leave it entirely to the legislature to decide whether the state shall provide funds for education directly to parents, create and operate schools itself, or delegate this authority to local school boards. In any case, with the exception of Hawaii where the schools are state-run, all states have chosen to create local school districts as the primary mechanism for fulfilling their educational duty.

Having chosen this option, legislatures must next decide how these locally run school districts are to be funded. For historical and political reasons, most states have a multifaceted finance system involving the following features:

1. A statewide system of taxation, usually sales and income tax, for general revenue, some of which is used to fund schools. Some states also have a specialized mechanism for raising money for education such as a lottery.
2. A plan for the distribution of state funds to local school districts. These plans may include general financial aid distributed through formulas adopted by the legislature, grant and categorical aid programs, and reimbursement for the provision of state-mandated services.
3. Delegation to local government units, such as city councils, of the authority and duty to tax for education with the money raised to be turned over to local school boards.
4. Delegation to local school boards of the authority to tax and spend on behalf of their local schools usually through the mechanism of a local property tax.
5. Delegation of the authority to local school boards to borrow money, typically by issuing bonds, for construction projects.

Any authority local school boards enjoy to levy taxes for their schools is delegated by the state legislature. Any taxation by a local board must be based on expressly granted or implied authority and must conform to that authority.[5] In addition to the authority to tax, school boards may have a duty to tax for certain educational purposes. This duty can and must be exercised even against the wishes of the taxpayers.[6] Each state also has a detailed set of statutory requirements controlling the raising, management, allocation, and expenditure of money by local boards.

In sum, the U.S. school finance system operates in conjunction with a complex school governance system comprising fifty separate state systems of education. With the exception of Hawaii, these systems rely on local school districts with significant authority to raise and spend money. State legislatures supplement these local funds in a variety of ways—most important, through general aid distribution allocated on the basis of complex formulas. Local school districts also receive federal financial assistance, mostly in the form of categorical aid and block grants.

This complex system has resulted in significant interstate and, in most states, interdistrict disparities in per pupil funding. Funding disparities arise from varying capacities and desires to fund education in different states and districts. Federal financial assistance does nothing to equalize per pupil funding from state to state. In most states, interdistrict disparities result from heavy reliance on money raised by local school districts through the property tax. State aid generally has only a modest equalizing effect on per pupil expenditures.

The Federal Constitution and School Finance

Disparities in per pupil expenditures from state to state do not violate the U.S. Constitution. There is no constitutional provision that requires the states to adopt the same educational policies or that requires the federal government to counteract interstate inequalities in the provision of education or any other benefit or service. The Equal Protection Clause is not concerned with interstate inequalities or with anything the federal government does. Rather, the clause addresses only state action and intrastate inequalities (see sec. 6.1). Hence, unless Congress decides to address interstate inequalities or the states themselves voluntarily seek to adopt uniform educational finance policies, interstate differences in expenditures per pupil will remain.

By virtue of Article VI of the Constitution, state law and policy may not contradict federal law. Thus, in *Lawrence County v. Lead-Deadwood School District No. 40–1*,[7] the Supreme Court invalidated a state law directing local school boards to allocate certain federal funds according to state guidelines. The federal law granting the funds to local districts indicated that Congress intended them to be utilized at the discretion of the local board. Therefore, the state's attempt to control the funds was unconstitutional.

The most significant federal constitutional provisions affecting school finance are the First and Fourteenth Amendments. The implications of the First Amendment's religion clauses for state financing of education are discussed in Chapter 2. The Fourteenth Amendment's Equal Protection Clause prohibits intentional racial discrimination in taxation or the allocation of funds. Even under the old separate-but-equal standard, providing unequal educational services on the basis of race was unconstitutional (see chap. 6).

What about state systems of finance that result in interdistrict inequalities in the amount of money spent per pupil? Is it consistent with the Equal Protection Clause that the amount of money spent by a state on a child's public education varies dramatically depending on where in the state the child lives? The Supreme Court considered this issue in *San Antonio Independent School District v. Rodriguez*.[8]

Plaintiffs' argument in *Rodriguez* was lengthy and complex and only its major claims are summarized here. Plaintiffs first sought to show that interdistrict inequalities in per pupil spending were a direct result of state law and policy. Texas, like most states, had created local school districts with the authority and duty to raise taxes for their own schools. The primary revenue-raising mechanism delegated to the districts was the property tax. Different school districts had within their borders widely varying amounts of property wealth per pupil. Districts that were rich in terms of property value per pupil were able, with a given tax rate, to raise more money per pupil than districts that were poor. Property-poor districts could attempt to match the money raised by property-rich districts by adopting much higher tax rates, but this was politically and economically infeasible in most places. Thus, given that neither state nor federal aid compensated for differences in local property tax revenues, poor districts had significantly less to spend per pupil than wealthy districts.

Realizing that their chances of winning would be greatly enhanced if the Court employed strict scrutiny (see chap. 6) in evaluating their claim, plaintiffs next sought to establish that this was the appropriate standard. Two arguments supported their position. First, Texas's school finance system discriminated among students on the basis of the property wealth of their district of residence. This, plaintiffs claimed, was a form of wealth-based discrimination, which, like discrimination on the basis of race, ought to trigger the use of the strict scrutiny test. In support of this claim, they cited a body of cases that dealt with very different forms of wealth discrimination and argued that most of those disadvantaged by the system were members of minority groups.

Second, plaintiffs argued that education is a "fundamental interest" and that when public policy discriminates regarding a fundamental interest, the strict scrutiny test ought to be used. Even though not expressly mentioned in the Constitution, education, they said, is a fundamental right because of its social importance and because a good education is necessary to the effective exercise of other constitutional rights such as freedom of speech.

The next step in the argument was to show that the Texas system of finance could not survive strict scrutiny. Plaintiffs rejected Texas's claim that its finance system was necessary to achieve a compelling state interest, namely the provision of an effective, locally controlled system of education. They argued that the state's funding plan did not minimize administrative difficulties, did not maintain effective or meaningful local control, and did not foster an equitable distribution of educational services. In sum, they claimed, the system did not serve any purpose other than "to make wealth the basis for determining the allocation of education dollars." Neither did the state's funding plan assure all students a minimum education "unless one defines that minimum as simply the lowest level of expenditure in the State."

To be permissible under the Equal Protection Clause, argued the plaintiffs, a state system of educational finance had to meet a standard known as "fiscal neutrality." Fiscal neutrality requires that the quality of education in a school district as measured by per pupil expenditures may not be a function of the district's wealth but only of the total wealth of the state. Plaintiffs went on to suggest three possible finance systems that satisfied fiscal neutrality while preserving local control of education. First, the state could take over the raising of money for education and distribute equal amounts per pupil to the local districts. Local districts would then have the discretion of using this money according to their educational priorities. Second, local district boundaries could be changed to ensure that each school district had the same property wealth per pupil. Third, existing boundaries could be maintained, but the state could guarantee through a revised state aid formula that a given property tax rate would yield a specific amount of money regardless of a district's property values.

This last system is known as **power equalization**. In power equalization, if a district raises less money per pupil than guaranteed by the aid formula, the state provides the balance. If a district raises excess money, the state takes it for use in other districts. Districts would still be free to choose different tax rates, and there still would be interdistrict inequalities in the amount of money spent per pupil; however, these differences would be determined not by interdistrict differences in property wealth but only by the differences in the importance different districts placed on education.

Finally, plaintiffs' argument rested on the premise that differences in spending resulted in meaningful disparities in services, program quality, and, ultimately, educational achievement. In their brief, they urged the Court not to reserve application of the Equal Protection Clause to cases of complete denial of educational services but to apply it to relative deprivations as well:

> To be sure, a complete denial of all educational opportunity is more compelling than a relative denial. But in view of the magnitude of the differences in the capacity of state-created school districts in Texas to raise education dollars, and in light of the vast disparities in educational expenditures between districts, plaintiffs have surely been injured in a comparable way. A complete denial of all educational opportunity is not necessary to demonstrate an unconstitutional deprivation ... Can the State of Texas open its doors to the poor, compel their attendance ... and then effectively deprive them of an equal educational opportunity because of their economic status?

As the following excerpt shows, the Supreme Court answered plaintiffs' question in the affirmative: Relative deprivations of education, at least those arising from Texas's educational finance system, did not violate the Equal Protection Clause.

SAN ANTONIO INDEPENDENT SCHOOL DISTRICT V. RODRIGUEZ
SUPREME COURT OF THE UNITED STATES, 1973
411 U.S. 1

Mr. Justice Powell delivered the opinion of the Court.

I.

...We must decide, first, whether the Texas system of financing public education operates to the disadvantage of some suspect class or impinges upon a fundamental right explicitly or implicitly protected by the Constitution, thereby requiring strict judicial scrutiny. If so, the judgment of the District Court should be affirmed. If not, the Texas scheme must still be examined to determine whether it rationally furthers some legitimate, articulated state purpose and therefore does not constitute an invidious discrimination in violation of the Equal Protection Clause of the Fourteenth Amendment...

II.

A.

The wealth discrimination discovered by the District Court in this case, and by several other courts that have recently struck down school-financing laws in other States, is quite unlike any of the forms of wealth discrimination heretofore reviewed by this Court ... . The individuals, or groups of individuals, who constituted the class discriminated against in our prior cases shared two distinguishing characteristics: because of their impecunity they were completely unable to pay for some desired benefit, and as a consequence, they sustained an absolute deprivation of a meaningful opportunity to enjoy that benefit ... .

Even a cursory examination, however, demonstrates that neither of the two distinguishing characteristics of wealth classifications can be found here. First, in support of their charge that the system discriminates against the "poor," appellees have made no effort to demonstrate that it operates to the peculiar disadvantage of any class fairly definable as indigent, or as composed of persons whose incomes are beneath any designated poverty level. Indeed, there is reason to believe that the poorest families are not necessarily clustered in the poorest property districts. A recent and exhaustive study of school districts in Connecticut concluded that ... the poor were clustered around commercial and industrial areas—those same areas that provide the most attractive sources of property tax income for school districts. Whether a similar pattern would be discovered in Texas is not known, but there is no basis on the record in this case for assuming that the poorest people—defined by reference to any level of absolute impecunity—are concentrated in the poorest districts.

Second, neither appellees nor the District Court addressed the fact that, unlike each of the foregoing cases, lack of personal resources has not occasioned an absolute deprivation of the desired benefit. The argument here is not that the children in districts having relatively low assessable property values are receiving no public education; rather, it is that they are receiving a poorer quality education than that available to children in districts having more assessable wealth. Apart from the unsettled and disputed question whether the quality of education may be determined by the amount of money expended for it, a sufficient answer to appellees' argument is that, at least where wealth is involved, the Equal Protection Clause does not require absolute equality or precisely equal advantages. Nor, indeed, in view of the infinite variables affecting the educational process, can any system assure equal quality of education except in the most relative sense. Texas asserts that the Minimum Foundation Program provides an "adequate" education for all children in the

State. By providing 12 years of free public-school education, and by assuring teachers, books, transportation, and operating funds, the Texas Legislature has endeavored to "guarantee, for the welfare of the state as a whole, that all people shall have at least an adequate program of education. This is what is meant by 'A Minimum Foundation Program of Education.'" The State repeatedly asserted in its briefs in this Court that it has fulfilled this desire and that it now assures "every child in every school district an adequate education." No proof was offered at trial persuasively discrediting or refuting the State's assertion.

For these two reasons—the absence of any evidence that the financing system discriminates against any definable category of "poor" people or that it results in the absolute deprivation of education—the disadvantaged class is not susceptible of identification in traditional terms.[9] ...

This brings us, then, to the third way in which the classification scheme might be defined—district wealth discrimination. Since the only correlation indicated by the evidence is between district property wealth and expenditures, it may be argued that discrimination might be found without regard to the individual income characteristics of district residents. Assuming a perfect correlation between district property wealth and expenditures from top to bottom, the disadvantaged class might be viewed as encompassing every child in every district except the district that has the most assessable wealth and spends the most on education ... .

However described, it is clear that appellees' suit asks this Court to extend its most exacting scrutiny to review a system that allegedly discriminates against a large, diverse, and amorphous class, unified only by the common factor of residence in districts that happen to have less taxable wealth than other districts. The system of alleged discrimination and the class it defines have none of the traditional indicia of suspectness: the class is not saddled with such disabilities, or subjected to such a history of purposeful unequal treatment, or relegated to such a position of political powerlessness as to command extraordinary protection from the majoritarian political process.

We thus conclude that the Texas system does not operate to the peculiar disadvantage of any suspect class. But in recognition of the fact that this Court has never heretofore held that wealth discrimination alone provides an adequate basis for invoking strict scrutiny, appellees have not relied solely on this contention. They also assert that the State's system impermissibly interferes with the exercise of a "fundamental" right and that accordingly the prior decisions of this Court require the application of the strict standard of judicial review. It is this question—whether education is a fundamental right, in the sense that it is among the rights and liberties protected by the Constitution—which has so consumed the attention of courts and commentators in recent years.

B.

... Nothing this Court holds today in any way detracts from our historic dedication to public education. We are in complete agreement with the conclusion of the three-judge panel below that "the grave significance of education both to the individual and to our society" cannot be doubted. But the importance of a service performed by the State does not determine whether it must be regarded as fundamental for purposes of examination under the Equal Protection Clause ... .

It is not the province of this Court to create substantive constitutional rights in the name of guaranteeing equal protection of the laws. Thus, the key to discovering whether education is "fundamental" is not to be found in comparisons of the relative societal significance of education as opposed to subsistence or housing. Nor is it to be found by weighing whether education is as important as the right to travel. Rather, the answer lies in assessing whether there is a right to education explicitly or implicitly guaranteed by the Constitution.

Education, of course, is not among the rights afforded explicit protection under our Federal Constitution. Nor do we find any basis for saying it is implicitly so protected. As we have said, the undisputed importance of education will not alone cause this Court to depart from the usual standard for reviewing a State's social and economic legislation. It is appellees' contention, however, that education is distinguishable from other services and benefits provided by the State because it bears a peculiarly close relationship to other rights and liberties accorded protection under the Constitution. Specifically, they insist that education is itself a fundamental personal right because it is essential to the effective exercise of First Amendment freedoms and to intelligent utilization of the right to vote. In asserting a nexus between speech and education, appellees urge that the right to speak is meaningless unless the speaker is capable of articulating his thoughts intelligently and persuasively. The "marketplace of ideas" is an empty forum for those lacking basic communicative tools. Likewise, they argue that the corollary right to receive information becomes little more than a hollow privilege when the recipient has not been taught to read, assimilate, and utilize available knowledge.

A similar line of reasoning is pursued with respect to the right to vote. Exercise of the franchise, it is contended, cannot be divorced from the educational foundation of the voter. The electoral process, if reality is to conform to the democratic ideal, depends on an informed electorate: a voter cannot cast his ballot intelligently unless his reading skills and thought processes have been adequately developed.

We need not dispute any of these propositions. The Court has long afforded zealous protection against unjustifiable governmental interference with the individual's rights to speak and to vote. Yet we have never presumed to possess either the ability or the authority to guarantee to the citizenry the most *effective* speech or the most *informed* electoral choice. That these may be desirable goals of a system of freedom of expression and of a representative form of government is not to be doubted. These are indeed goals to be pursued by a people whose thoughts and beliefs are freed from governmental interference. But they are not values to be implemented by judicial intrusion into otherwise legitimate state activities.

Even if it were conceded that some identifiable quantum of education is a constitutionally protected prerequisite to the mean ingful exercise of either right, we have no indication that the present levels of educational expenditure in Texas provide an education that falls short. Whatever merit appellees' argument might have if a State's financing system occasioned an absolute denial of educational opportunities to any of its children, that argument provides no basis for finding an interference with fundamental rights where only relative differences in spending levels are involved and where—as is true in the present case—no charge fairly could be made that the system fails to provide each child with an opportunity to acquire the basic minimal skills necessary for the enjoyment of the rights of speech and of full participation in the political process.

Furthermore, the logical limitations on appellees' nexus theory are difficult to perceive. How, for instance, is education to be distinguished from the significant personal interests in the basics of decent food and shelter? Empirical examination might well buttress an assumption that the ill-fed, ill-clothed, and ill-housed are among the most ineffective participants in the political process, and that they derive the least enjoyment from the benefits of the First Amendment ... .

Every step leading to the establishment of the system Texas utilizes today—including the decisions permitting localities to tax and expend locally, and creating and continuously expanding state aid—was implemented in an effort to *extend* public education and to improve its quality. Of course, every reform that benefits some more than others may be criticized for what it fails to accomplish. But we think it plain that, in substance, the thrust of the Texas system is affirmative and reformatory and, therefore, should be scrutinized under judicial principles sensitive to the nature of the State's efforts and to the rights reserved to the States under the Constitution .... .

C.

We need not rest our decision, however, solely on the inappropriateness of the strict-scrutiny test. A century of Supreme Court adjudication under the Equal Protection Clause affirmatively supports the application of the traditional standard of review, which requires only that the State's system be shown to bear some rational relationship to legitimate state purposes. This case represents far more than a challenge to the manner in which Texas provides for the education of its children. We have here nothing less than a direct attack on the way in which Texas has chosen to raise and disburse state and local tax revenues. We are asked to condemn the State's judgment in conferring on political subdivisions the power to tax local property to supply revenues for local interests. In so doing, appellees would have the Court intrude in an area in which it has traditionally deferred to state legislatures. This Court has often admonished against such interferences with the State's fiscal policies under the Equal Protection Clause .... .

In such a complex arena in which no perfect alternatives exist, the Court does well not to impose too rigorous a standard of scrutiny lest all local fiscal schemes become subjects of criticism under the Equal Protection Clause.

In addition to matters of fiscal policy, this case also involves the most persistent and difficult questions of educational policy, another area in which this Court's lack of specialized knowledge and experience counsels against premature interference with the informed judgments made at the state and local levels. Education, perhaps even more than welfare assistance, presents a myriad of "intractable economic, social, and even philosophical problems." ... Indeed, one of the major sources of controversy concerns the extent to which there is a demonstrable correlation between educational expenditures and the quality of education—an assumed correlation underlying virtually every legal conclusion drawn by the District Court in this case. Related to the questioned relationship between cost and quality is the equally unsettled controversy as to the proper goals of a system of public education. And the question regarding the most effective relationship between state boards of education and local school boards, in terms of their respective responsibilities and degrees of control, is now undergoing searching re-examination .... .

The foregoing considerations buttress our conclusion that Texas' system of public school finance is an inappropriate candidate for strict judicial scrutiny. These same considerations are relevant to the determination whether that system, with its conceded imperfections, nevertheless bears some rational relationship to a legitimate state purpose. It is to this question that we next turn our attention ...

III.

Because of differences in expenditure levels occasioned by disparities in property tax income, appellees claim that children in less affluent districts have been made the subject of invidious discrimination. The District Court found that the State had failed even "to establish a reasonable basis" for a system that results in different levels of per-pupil expenditure. We disagree.

In its reliance on state as well as local resources, the Texas system is comparable to the systems employed in virtually every other State ... .

While assuring a basic education for every child in the State, it permits and encourages a large measure of participation in and control of each district's schools at the local level ... .

No area of social concern stands to profit more from a multiplicity of viewpoints and from a diversity of approaches than does public education.

Appellees do not question the propriety of Texas' dedication to local control of education. To the contrary, they attack the school-financing system precisely because, in their view, it does not provide the same level of local control and fiscal flexibility in all districts. Appellees suggest that local control could be preserved and promoted under other financing systems that resulted in more equality in educational expenditures. While it is no doubt true that reliance on local property taxation for school revenues provides less freedom of choice with respect to expenditures for some districts than for others, the existence of "some inequality" in the manner in which the State's rationale is achieved is not alone a sufficient basis for striking down the entire system ... Nor must the financing system fail because, as appellees suggest, other methods of satisfying the State's interest, which occasion "less drastic" disparities in expenditures, might be conceived. Only where state action impinges on the exercise of fundamental constitutional rights or liberties must it be found to have chosen the least restrictive alternative. It is also well to remember that even those districts that have reduced ability to make free decisions with respect to how much they spend on education still retain under the present system a large measure of authority as to how available funds will be allocated. They further enjoy the power to make numerous other decisions with respect to the operation of the schools. The people of Texas may be justified in believing that other systems of school financing, which place more of the financial responsibility in the hands of the State, will result in a comparable lessening of desired local autonomy. That is, they may believe that along with increased control of the purse strings at the state level will go increased control over local policies.

Appellees further urge that the Texas system is unconstitutionally arbitrary because it allows the availability of local taxable resources to turn on "happenstance." They see no justification for a system that allows, as they contend, the quality of education to fluctuate on the basis of the fortuitous positioning of the boundary lines of political subdivisions and the location of valuable commercial and industrial property. But any scheme of local taxation—indeed the very existence of identifiable local government units—requires the establishment of jurisdictional boundaries that are inevitably arbitrary. It is equally inevitable that some localities are going to be blessed with more taxable assets than others. Nor is local wealth a static quantity. Changes in the level of taxable wealth within any district may result from any number of events, some of which local residents can and do influence. For instance, commercial and industrial enterprises may be encouraged to locate within a district by various actions— public and private.

Moreover, if local taxation for local expenditures were an unconstitutional method of providing for education then it might be an equally impermissible means of providing other necessary services customarily financed largely from local property taxes, including local police and fire protection, public health and hospitals, and public utility facilities of various kinds ... .

In sum, to the extent that the Texas system of school financing results in unequal expenditures between children who happen to reside in different districts, we cannot say that such disparities are the product of a system that is so irrational as to be invidiously discriminatory ...

IV.

[A] cautionary postscript seems appropriate. It cannot be questioned that the constitutional judgment reached by the District Court and approved by our dissenting Brothers today would occasion in Texas and elsewhere an unprecedented upheaval in public education. Some commentators have concluded that, whatever the contours of the alternative financing programs that might be devised and approved, the result could not avoid being a beneficial one. But just as there is nothing simple about the constitutional issues involved in these cases, there is nothing simple or certain about predicting the consequences of massive change in the financing and control of public education ... .

The complexity of these problems is demonstrated by the lack of consensus with respect to whether it may be said with any assurance that the poor, the racial minorities, or the children in overburdened core-city school districts would be benefited by abrogation of traditional modes of financing education. Unless there is to be a substantial increase in state expenditures on education across the board—an event the likelihood of which is open to considerable question—these groups stand to realize gains in terms of increased per-pupil expenditures only if they reside in districts that presently spend at relatively low levels, i.e., in those districts that would benefit from the redistribution of existing resources. Yet, recent studies have indicated that the poorest families are not invariably clustered in the most impecunious school districts. Nor does it now appear that there is any more than a random chance that racial minorities are concentrated in property-poor districts. Additionally, several research projects have concluded that any financing alternative designed to achieve a greater equality of expenditures is likely to lead to higher taxation and lower educational expenditures in the major urban centers,

a result that would exacerbate rather than ameliorate existing conditions in those areas.

These practical considerations, of course, play no role in the adjudication of the constitutional issues presented here. But they serve to highlight the wisdom of the traditional limitations on this Court's function ... We hardly need add that this Court's action today is not to be viewed as placing its judicial imprimatur on the status quo. The need is apparent for reform in tax systems which may well have relied too long and too heavily on the local property tax. And certainly innovative thinking as to public education, its methods, and its funding is necessary to assure both a higher level of quality and greater uniformity of opportunity. These matters merit the continued attention of the scholars who already have contributed much by their challenges. But the ultimate solutions must come from the lawmakers and from the democratic pressures of those who elect them.

Reversed.

[Stewart filed a concurring opinion. Brennan, White, Douglas, and Marshall dissented in three separate opinions.]

As a practical matter, the *Rodriguez* decision brought to a close what has come to be known as the first wave of educational finance reform litigation. Reformers had hoped to use the federal courts to eliminate the significant disparities in per pupil funding that existed in almost every state. But, after *Rodriguez*, litigation to force states to more equitably redesign their educational finance systems could only be pursued in state courts (see sec. 8.3).

The next Supreme Court case concerning educational finance, *Plyler v. Doe*,[10] dealt not with disparities in per pupil funding but rather with a Texas law that totally excluded illegal alien children from obtaining a free public education. Although illegal alien status is not a suspect classification, the *Plyler* Court found that total denial of education to any child in the state's jurisdiction violated the Equal Protection Clause. However, the relationship of this decision to *Rodriguez* is a bit confusing. Although the *Rodriguez* Court suggested that an absolute denial of education would probably require the use of the strict scrutiny test, in *Plyler*, the Court said even an absolute denial did not call for strict scrutiny. Instead, the Court used a sort of middle-level test similar to the one used in gender discrimination cases.

The Court's next school finance decision, *Papasan v. Allain*,[11] involved a challenge to a Mississippi policy of distributing income from state-owned land only to school districts where the land was located. The opinion makes clear that this situation is distinguishable from *Rodriguez*. Whereas inequalities upheld in *Rodriguez* were a "necessary," adjunct of allowing meaningful local control over school funding," *Papasan* raised a problem of "a state decision to divide state resources unequally among school districts." The Court remanded the case to the lower courts to address the question of whether the state's policy of using income from these lands only in part of the state violated the Equal Protection Clause.

This decision adds to our uncertainty about constitutional doctrine in this area. The Court in *Papasan* announced that neither *Rodriguez* nor *Plyler* "definitively settled the questions whether a minimally adequate education was a fundamental right and whether a statute alleged to discriminatorily infringe that right should be accorded heightened equal protection review."

Two years later, in *Kadrmas v. Dickinson Public Schools*,[12] the Supreme Court considered the issue of whether a state scheme that permitted older "nonreorganized" school districts but not "reorganized" districts to charge a busing fee violated the Equal Protection Clause. Plaintiffs argued that the fee had the potential to result in a complete deprivation of education for children whose families were too poor to pay. Plaintiffs urged the Court to apply strict scrutiny or, at minimum, the "heightened" scrutiny used in *Plyler*. However, the Court saw the case as different from *Plyler*:

Unlike the children in that case, Sarita Kadrmas has not been penalized by the government—for illegal conduct by her parents. On the contrary, Sarita was denied access to the school bus only because her parents would not agree to pay the same user fee charged to all other families that took advantage of the service. Nor do we see any reason to suppose that this user fee will "promot[e] the creation and perpetuation of a subclass of illiterates within our boundaries, surely adding to the problems and costs of unemployment, welfare, and crime."

Nor did the Court view the busing fee as amounting to a complete denial of education for any child. Paying the fee was not a prerequisite for attending school because children were free to come to school by means other than riding the school bus. It did not matter that for children living far from school, the school bus was the only practical alternative available.

Having concluded that "the statute challenged in this case discriminates against no suspect class and interferes with no fundamental right," the Court applied the rational relation test to the claim that the busing fee was unconstitutional:

Applying the appropriate test—under which a statute is upheld if it bears a rational relation to a legitimate government objective—we think it is quite clear that a State's decision to allow local school boards the option of charging patrons a user fee for bus service is constitutionally permissible. The Constitution does not require that such service be provided at all, and it is difficult to imagine why choosing to offer the service should entail a constitutional obligation to offer it for free. No one denies that encouraging local school districts to provide school bus service is a legitimate state purpose or that such encouragement would be undermined by a rule requiring that general revenues be used to subsidize an optional service that will benefit a minority of the district's families. It is manifestly rational for the State to refrain from undermining its legitimate objective with such a rule.

The Court went on to consider the related claim that the statute violated the Equal Protection Clause because it permitted user fees for bus service only in nonreorganized school districts. Employing the rational basis test, the Court concluded that the appellants had failed to demonstrate that the challenged statute was arbitrary and irrational. The Court accepted the state's justification for the statute, that it was designed to encourage school district reorganization:

... it is evident that the legislature could conceivably have believed that such a policy would serve the legitimate purpose of fulfilling the reasonable expectations of those residing in districts with free busing arrangements imposed by reorganization plans. Because this purpose could have no application to nonreorganized districts, the legislature could just as rationally conclude that those districts should have the option of imposing user fees on those who take advantage of the service they are offered.

After *Rodriguez*, *Plyler*, and *Kadrmas*, federal constitutional doctrine concerning the status of education may be summarized as follows: Education is not a fundamental right under the U.S. Constitution. Neither interstate nor intrastate inequalities in educational opportunities (unless based on intentional racial or gender discrimination) nor policies that create economic obstacles for children wishing to exercise their legal right to attend school violate the Equal Protection Clause. However, any state scheme intentionally resulting in a total denial of education to any group of children within the jurisdiction of the state is unconstitutional.

State Constitutions and School Finance

Following the failure of the plaintiffs in *Rodriguez*, reformers seeking judicial mandates for change in state educational finance systems realized they must turn to state courts. There have been dozens of judicial proceedings involving the appellate courts of most states.[13] In many states, educational finance-reform litigation has resulted in several or more major judicial decisions; some of the cases have dragged on for decades. In about half the states, plaintiffs have succeeded in convincing the court to order the state legislature to change the educational finance system, but the resultant changes have not always been the ones plaintiffs had sought. In some states, reformers have won some cases and lost others. In some of the states where litigation failed, reformers, in some instances with judicial support, later convinced the legislature to change the system of educational finance even in the absence of a court order.

The arguments challenging state systems of educational finance have taken a number of different forms. The main issue in a New Hampshire case was taxpayer equity. The state constitution permitted the legislature to "impose and levy proportional and reasonable assessments, rates, and taxes ... ." The state's main mechanism for funding education was a locally imposed property tax, and the tax rates in various school districts around the state varied significantly.

The state's highest court found the taxing mechanism unconstitutional because it unreasonably placed a differential burden on taxpayers to carry out the responsibility of providing education throughout the state. Wrote the court, "There is nothing fair or just about taxing a home or other real estate in one town at four times the rate that similar property is taxed in another town to fulfill the same purpose of meeting the State's educational duty."[14]

A number of other cases have similarly raised constitutional challenges to differing levels of taxation as part of a broad assault on a state educational finance system. A Kansas case challenged the state's system of locally set property tax rates on the basis of the "uniform laws" clause of the state constitution.[15] An unsuccessful New York case was based on a principle known as "municipal overburden." Plaintiffs argued that the state finance system was inequitable to the students and taxpayers of urban areas because it did not account for the need for urban taxpayers to support a greater variety of public services, the need for urban schools to educate a disproportionate number of high-cost students, the higher costs in urban areas for educational goods and services, and the loss of revenues under attendance-based state aid formulas in urban areas because of high rates of student absenteeism.[16]

Most cases challenging state education funding systems are based on either the equal protection clause of the state constitution or on the education article of the state constitution. Most of the earlier cases, what has come to be known as the second wave of educational finance reform litigation, were based on state equal protection clauses. Like the first wave of finance-reform litigation (which attempted unsuccessfully to rely on the federal Equal Protection Clause), the primary goal of the second wave was to eliminate intrastate disparities in per-pupil funding for education. More recent cases, the third wave, rely primarily on education articles or on both. The third wave's goals are to ensure not only equity in state finance systems but also adequacy by increasing the level of per-pupil funding available to some or all of the school districts in the state.

Educational Equity

Second wave cases often parallel *Rodriguez* in arguing that under the state equal protection clause it is unconstitutional for a state to maintain a funding system that provides greater per pupil funding in some districts than others, or they may claim that the state equal protection clause prohibits a system that provides an "adequate" education to some children and an inadequate education to others.

Plaintiffs fail in these cases (and also in adequacy cases) if the court rules that decisions about how and at what level to fund education are solely a legislative matter, not subject to court review; that for a court to address questions of education funding would violate the principle of separation of powers between the branches of state government; that state education articles are so vague and ambiguous (requiring, for example, that the legislature provide for a "thorough and efficient" system of education) that no court can claim to determine specifically how they are to be applied; and that the issue of educational adequacy is "nonjusticible," that is, incapable of resolution by a court.[17]

Plaintiffs succeed in these cases if the court finds that education is a fundamental right under the state constitution, thereby requiring the use of strict scrutiny. The basis of this finding is that unlike the federal Constitution, state constitutions mandate that their legislatures provide an education to the state's children. However, a number of state courts have declined to view education as a fundamental right under the state constitution. That the state constitution designates education as a required state service does not make it a fundamental right, say these courts. The Georgia Supreme Court agreed with plaintiffs that education was "vital," but said the court, no more vital than police and fire protection, water, and public health services. None of these goods or services is a fundamental right that must be provided equally to all state residents. Applying the rational basis test, the court paralleled *Rodriguez* in finding that the state's funding system, despite significant disparities in per pupil funding across districts, was rationally related to the legitimate purpose of promoting local control of education.[18] However, even if education is not a fundamental state right, a state finance system may still violate the state equal protection clause if the funding disparities between rich and poor districts are completely irrational: "Even without deciding whether the right to a public education is fundamental," wrote the Arkansas Supreme Court, "we can find no constitutional basis for the present system, as it has no rational bearing on the educational needs of the districts."[19]

In one of the earliest educational finance reform cases, *Serrano v. Priest*, the California Supreme Court ruled that the state's children have a fundamental right to an education and that the state legislature had a duty to provide an equitable system of funding for the state's schools. A pre-*Rodriguez* case, *Serrano* is a link between the first and second waves of educational finance-reform litigation because it was based on both the federal and state Equal Protection Clauses.

SERRANO V. PRIEST (SERRANO I)
SUPREME COURT OF CALIFORNIA, 1971
487 P.2D 1241

Sullivan, Justice.

[Plaintiffs, Los Angeles County public school children and their parents, filed a complaint that set forth two central causes of action. First, the plaintiffs alleged that California's system of finance relied heavily on local property taxes resulting in substantial disparities in the amount of money spent per pupil among the districts of the state. Districts with smaller tax bases were not able to spend as much money per pupil as districts with larger assessed valuations. These disparities, claimed the plaintiffs, meant that children attending the property-poorer districts received a substantially inferior education in violation of the equal protection clauses of both the U.S. and California constitutions. Second, the plaintiffs alleged that as a result of this financing scheme they were required to pay a higher tax rate than taxpayers in many other districts in order to obtain for their children a similar or inferior education.

The defendants demurred claiming that none of the claims stated facts sufficient to constitute a cause of action. The trial court sustained the demurrer and dismissed the complaint; the plaintiffs appealed. On appeal the California Supreme Court assumed the facts alleged by the plaintiffs were correct for purposes of deciding whether the facts as alleged were legally sufficient to establish a violation of the two equal protection clauses. The court observed that the plaintiffs had alleged that the finance system of the state, with its heavy reliance on the local property tax, resulted in differences in the amount of money spent per pupil and that these differences were not equalized by the state aid flowing to the districts. The state aid consisted of both a "flat grant" and "equalization aid" provided in inverse proportion to the property wealth of the district. Another separate program provided "supplemental aid" to subsidize particularly poor school districts that were willing to make an extra local tax effort. These three sources of state aid did mitigate the disparities among the districts, yet the plaintiffs alleged vast disparities in the money available still persisted among the districts. The range in expenditures went from $577.49 to $1,231.72 per pupil.]

III.

[W]e now take up the chief contention underlying plaintiffs' complaint, namely that the California public school financing scheme violates the equal protection clause of the Fourteenth Amendment to the United States Constitution.

As recent decisions of this court have pointed out, the United States Supreme Court has employed a two-level test for measuring legislative classifications against the equal protection clause. "In the area of economic regulation, the high court has exercised restraint, investing legislation with a presumption of constitutionality and requiring merely that distinctions drawn by a challenged statute bear some rational relationship to a conceivable legitimate state purpose."

"On the other hand, in cases involving 'suspect classifications' or touching on 'fundamental interests,' the court has adopted an attitude of active and critical analysis, subjecting the classification to strict scrutiny. Under the strict standard applied in such cases, the state bears the burden of establishing not only that it has a *compelling* interest which justifies the law but that the distinctions drawn by the law are *necessary* to further its purpose."

A. Wealth as a Suspect Classification

In recent years, the United States Supreme Court has demonstrated a marked antipathy toward legislative classifications which discriminate on the basis of certain "suspect"

personal characteristics. One factor which has repeatedly come under the close scrutiny of the high court is wealth. "Lines drawn on the basis of wealth or property, like those of race are traditionally disfavored." ...

Plaintiffs contend that the school financing system classifies on the basis of wealth. We find this proposition irrefutable ... [O]ver half of all educational revenue is raised locally by levying taxes on real property in the individual school districts. Above the foundation program minimum ($355 per elementary student and $488 per high school student), the wealth of a school district, as measured by its assessed valuation, is the major determinant of educational expenditures. Although the amount of money raised locally is also a function of the rate at which the residents of a district are willing to tax themselves, as a practical matter districts with small tax bases simply cannot levy taxes at a rate sufficient to produce the revenue that more affluent districts reap with minimal tax efforts. For example, Baldwin Park citizens, who paid a school tax of $5.48 per $100 of assessed valuation in 1968–1969, were able to spend less than half as much on education as Beverly Hills residents, who were taxed only $2.38 per $100.

Defendants vigorously dispute the proposition that the financing scheme discriminates on the basis of wealth. Their first argument is essentially this: through *basic* aid, the state distributes school funds equally to all pupils; through *equalization* aid, it distributes funds in a manner beneficial to the poor districts. However, state funds constitute only one part of the entire school fiscal system. The foundation program partially alleviates the great disparities in local sources of revenue, but the system as a whole generates school revenue in proportion to the wealth of the individual district ... .

But, say defendants, the expenditure per child does not accurately reflect a district's wealth because that expenditure is partly determined by the district's tax rate. Thus, a district with a high total assessed valuation might levy a low school tax, and end up spending the same amount per pupil as a poorer district whose residents opt to pay higher taxes. This argument is also meritless. Obviously, the richer district is favored when it can provide the same educational quality for its children with less tax effort. Furthermore, as a statistical matter, the poorer districts are financially unable to raise their taxes high enough to match the educational offerings of wealthier districts. Thus, affluent districts can have their cake and eat it too: they can provide a high quality education for their children while paying lower taxes. Poor districts, by contrast, have no cake at all.

Finally, defendants suggest that the wealth of a school district does not necessarily reflect the wealth of the families who live there. The simple answer to this argument is that plaintiffs have alleged that there is a correlation between a district's per pupil assessed valuation and the wealth of its residents and we treat these material facts as admitted by the demurrers.

More basically, however, we reject defendants' underlying thesis that classification by wealth is constitutional so long as the wealth is that of the district, not the individual. We think that discrimination on the basis of district wealth is equally invalid. The commercial and industrial property which augments a district's tax base is distributed unevenly throughout the state. To allot more educational dollars to the children of one district than to those of another merely because of the fortuitous presence of such property is to make the quality of a child's education dependent upon the location of private commercial and industrial establishments. Surely, this is to rely on the most irrelevant of factors as the basis for educational financing ... .

B. Education as a Fundamental Interest

But plaintiffs' equal protection attack on the fiscal system has an additional dimension. They assert that the system not only draws lines on the basis of wealth but that it "touches upon," indeed has a direct and significant impact upon, a "fundamental interest," namely education. It is urged that these two grounds, particularly in combination, establish a demonstrable denial of equal protection of the laws. To this phase of the argument we now turn our attention.

Until the present time wealth classifications have been invalidated only in conjunction with a limited number of fundamental interests—rights of defendants in criminal cases. Plaintiffs' contention—that education is a fundamental interest which may not be conditioned on wealth—is not supported by any direct authority.

We, therefore, begin by examining the indispensable role which education plays in the modern industrial state. This role, we believe, has two significant aspects: first, education is a major determinant of an individual's chances for economic and social success in our competitive society; second, education is a unique influence on a child's development as a citizen and his participation in political and community life. "[T]he pivotal position of education to success in American society and its essential role in opening up to the individual the central experiences of our culture lend it an importance that is undeniable." Thus, education is the lifeline of both the individual and society.

The fundamental importance of education has been recognized in other contexts by the United States Supreme Court and by this court. These decisions—while not *legally*

controlling on the exact issue before us—are persuasive in their accurate factual description of the significance of learning ... .

It is illuminating to compare in importance the right to an education with the rights of defendants in criminal cases and the right to vote—two "fundamental interests" which the Supreme Court has already protected against discrimination based on wealth. Although an individual's interest in his freedom is unique, we think that from a larger perspective, education may have far greater social significance than a free transcript or a court-appointed lawyer. "[E]ducation not only affects directly a vastly greater number of persons than the criminal law, but it affects them in ways which—to the state—have an enormous and much more varied significance. Aside from reducing the crime rate (the inverse relation is strong), education also supports each and every other value of a democratic society— participation, communication, and social mobility, to name but a few."

The analogy between education and voting is much more direct: both are crucial to participation in, and the functioning of, a democracy. Voting has been regarded as a fundamental right because it is "preservative of other basic civil and political rights ... ."

The need for an educated populace assumes greater importance as the problems of our diverse society become increasingly complex. The United States Supreme Court has repeatedly recognized the role of public education as a unifying social force and the basic tool for shaping democratic values. The public school has been termed "the most powerful agency for promoting cohesion among a heterogeneous democratic people ... at once the symbol of our democracy and the most pervasive means for promoting our common destiny." ...

We are convinced that the distinctive and priceless function of education in our society warrants, indeed compels, our treating it as a "fundamental interest."

First, education is essential in maintaining what several commentators have termed "free enterprise democracy." ...

Second, education is universally relevant. "Not every person finds it necessary to call upon the fire department or even the police in an entire lifetime. Relatively few are on welfare. Every person, however, benefits from education ... ."

Third, public education continues over a lengthy period of life—between 10 and 13 years. Few other government services have such sustained, intensive contact with the recipient.

Fourth, education is unmatched in the extent to which it molds the personality of the youth of society. While police and fire protection, garbage collection and street lights are essentially neutral in their effect on the individual psyche, public education actively attempts to shape a child's personal development in a manner chosen not by the child or his parents but by the state.

Finally, education is so important that the state has made it compulsory—not only in the requirement of attendance but also by assignment to a particular district and school. Although a child of wealthy parents has the opportunity to attend a private school, this freedom is seldom available to the indigent. In this context, it has been suggested that "a child of the poor assigned willy-nilly to an inferior state school takes on the complexion of a prisoner, complete with a minimum sentence of 12 years."

C. The Financing System Is Not Necessary to Accomplish a Compelling State Interest

We now reach the final step in the application of the "strict scrutiny" equal protection standard—the determination of whether the California school financing system, as presently structured, is necessary to achieve a compelling state interest.

The state interest which defendants advance in support of the current fiscal scheme is California's policy "to strengthen and encourage local responsibility for control of public education." We treat separately the two possible aspects of this goal: first, the granting to local districts of effective decision-making power over the administration of their schools; and second, the promotion of local fiscal control over the amount of money to be spent on education.

The individual district may well be in the best position to decide whom to hire, how to schedule its educational offerings, and a host of other matters which are either of significant local impact or of such a detailed nature as to require decentralized determination. But even assuming arguendo that local administrative control may be a compelling state interest, the present financial system cannot be considered necessary to further this interest. No matter how the state decides to finance its system of public education, it can still leave this decision-making power in the hands of local districts.

The other asserted policy interest is that of a local district to choose how much it wishes to spend on the education of its children ... .

We need not decide whether such decentralized financial decision-making is a compelling state interest, since under the present financing system, such fiscal freewill is a cruel illusion for the poor school districts. We cannot agree that Baldwin Park residents care less about education than those in Beverly Hills solely because Baldwin Park spends less than $600 per child while Beverly Hills spends over $1,200. As defendants

themselves recognize, perhaps the most accurate reflection of a community's commitment to education is the rate at which its citizens are willing to tax themselves to support their schools. Yet by that standard, Baldwin Park should be deemed far more devoted to learning than Beverly Hills, for Baldwin Park citizens levied a school tax of well over $5 per $100 of assessed valuation, while residents of Beverly Hills paid only slightly more than $2.

In summary, so long as the assessed valuation within a district's boundaries is a major determinant of how much it can spend for its schools, only a district with a large tax base will be truly able to decide how much it really cares about education. The poor district cannot freely choose to tax itself into an excellence which its tax rolls cannot provide. Far from being necessary to promote local fiscal choice, the present financing system actually deprives the less wealthy districts of that option ... .

The judgment is reversed and the cause remanded to the trial court with directions to over rule the demurrers and to allow defendants a reasonable time within which to answer.

The California court's finding in *Serrano* that education is a fundamental right under the federal Equal Protection Clause was effectively overruled by *Rodriguez*; however, the ruling based on the California constitution still stands.[20] Recall that state high courts have the final say regarding the meaning of their state constitution.

Sixteen years after *Rodriguez*, the Texas Supreme Court, in *Edgewood Independent School District v. Kirby*,[21] considered a challenge to the state's educational finance system based on the state constitution. Like the *Serrano* court, the *Kirby* court objected to the state's educational finance system because wealthy school districts could raise more money with the same tax rate than poorer ones. However, unlike *Serrano*, which was based on the state equal protection clause, the Texas case was based on the education article of the Texas constitution. The Texas state constitution says that in order to promote a "general diffusion of knowledge," the legislature should make "suitable provision" for an "efficient" system of education. In finding the Texas system unconstitutional under this provision, the Texas Supreme Court said that the framers of the state constitution did not "intend a system with such vast disparities as now exist ... The present system ... provides not for a diffusion of knowledge that is general, but for one that is limited and unbalanced." Thus, said the court, "districts must have substantially equal access to similar revenues per pupil at similar levels of tax effort." That is, a given tax rate in a property-poor district should yield about the same revenues per pupil as would that tax rate in a property-rich district.

Educational Adequacy

Unlike state equal protection clauses, the education articles of state constitutions vary considerably: Some simply impose a duty on the state legislature to provide for a system of free public schools, some impose minimum quality standards such as the requirement that a state's school system be "thorough and efficient" or "suitable," some identify the goals of schooling (e.g., "a general diffusion of knowledge" or "promotion of intellectual, scientific, moral, and agricultural improvement"), and some declare that the provision of education is the primary or paramount duty of the state. Regardless of their specific wording, education articles may be the basis of a claim that a state's provision of funding for education fails to provide a minimally adequate education to some or all of the state's children. Some education articles may also support equity claims (e.g., a system of educational finance that provides much more money for some pupils than others is not "efficient" or "suitable"). Third-wave cases often make both these claims.

There appears to be no pattern to the outcome of third-wave cases either based on the wording of the education article or the specifics of the finance system under challenge. Given that no state's current system of finance is perfectly equitable and that any educational system can be viewed as inadequate in some ways, it simply appears that some courts are willing to try to improve educational finance systems through judicial activism and others are more inclined to defer to the legislature. Some state courts have simply said that funding inequities do not prove that the state's educational system is inadequate.[22] Pennsylvania's highest court strongly expressed its preference for judicial restraint in educational policy making, noting that it would be

> contrary to the "essence" of the Constitutional provision for this Court to bind future Legislatures and school boards to a present judicial view of a constitutionally required "normal" program of educational services. It is only through free experimentation that the best possible educational services can be achieved. Even were this Court to attempt to define the specific components of a "thorough and efficient education" in a manner which would foresee the needs of the future, the only judicially manageable standard that this Court could adopt would be the rigid rule that each pupil must receive the same dollar expenditures. Even appellants recognize, however, that expenditures are not the exclusive yardstick of educational quality ... The educational product is dependent upon many factors, including the wisdom of the expenditures as well as the efficiency and economy with which available resources are utilized.[23]

The Georgia Supreme Court, quoting from the *Rodriguez* decision, agreed with plaintiffs that "education must provide each child with an opportunity to acquire the basic minimum skills necessary for the enjoyment of the rights of speech and of full participation in the political process." Nevertheless, the court declined to second-guess the legislature: "While an 'adequate' education must be designed to produce individuals who can function in society, it is primarily the legislative branch of government which must give content to the term 'adequate.'"[24]

Unlike the Pennsylvania and Georgia cases, a number of state courts have been willing to tackle the issue of what constitutes an adequate education under the state constitution. The West Virginia Supreme Court interpreted its constitution's call for a "thorough and efficient" system of education as requiring every school to develop "the minds, bodies and social morality of its charges to prepare them for useful and happy occupations, recreation and citizenship, and to do so economically." The court expanded its ruling by listing the subjects and skills all children should receive including arithmetic, social ethics, and recreation.[25]

In striking down its state finance plan, the Supreme Court of Washington took a different approach to defining the concept of a legally adequate education. It suggested several ways for determining whether the educational program of the state met the state constitution's requirement for "ample provision." Ample provision could be measured in terms of the state board of education accreditation standards, or the adequacy of programs could be determined in terms of the "statewide aggregate per pupil deployment of certified and classified staff and nonsalary related costs for the maintenance and operation of a school program for the normal range of student." In other words, something close to the average level of educational services that school districts have chosen to provide is defined as adequate or ample. This measure was termed the "collective wisdom" criterion.[26]

A Kansas court reasoned that the state constitutional requirement that the legislature provide a "suitable" system of education requires an equitable distribution of educational funds. The mandate is not for equitable treatment of school districts such as by a system of power equalization, but to offer each Kansas child an "equal educational opportunity." This does not mean that the same amount of money needs to be spent on each child's education, but rather that any disparity in educational funding be justified by a "rational educational explanation." Although not questioning the adequacy of the current system, the court noted that if current levels of funding were reduced, the system might become inadequate. Thus, the Kansas court found that both equity and adequacy are necessary conditions of a suitable system of education.[27]

In the following excerpt from a very long opinion, the Kentucky Supreme Court provided a detailed analysis of the meaning of the state constitutional mandate to "provide an efficient system of common schools throughout the state." The analysis deals with issues of both equity and adequacy.

ROSE V. COUNCIL FOR BETTER EDUCATION, INC.
SUPREME COURT OF KENTUCKY, 1989
790 S.W.2D 186

Stephens, Chief Justice.

The issue we decide on this appeal is whether the Kentucky General Assembly has complied with its constitutional mandate to "provide an efficient system of common schools throughout the State" [Kentucky Constitution, Section 183].

In deciding that it has not, we intend no criticism of the substantial efforts made by the present General Assembly and by its predecessors, nor do we intend to substitute our judicial authority for the authority and discretion of the General Assembly. We are, rather, exercising our constitutional duty in declaring that, when we consider the evidence in the record, and when we apply the constitutional requirement of Section 183 to that evidence, it is crystal clear that the General Assembly has fallen short of its duty to enact legislation to provide for an efficient system of common schools throughout the state. In a word, the present system of common schools in Kentucky is not an "efficient" one in our view of the clear mandate of Section 183. The common school system in Kentucky is constitutionally deficient.

In reaching this decision, we are ever mindful of the immeasurable worth of education to our state and its citizens, especially to its young people. The framers of our constitution intended that each and every child in this state should receive a proper and an adequate education, *to be provided for by the General Assembly*. This opinion dutifully applies the constitutional test of Section 183 to the existing system of common schools. We do no more, nor may we do any less.

The goal of the framers of our constitution, and the polestar of this opinion, is eloquently and movingly stated in the landmark case of *Brown v. Board of Education*:

"*education is perhaps the most important function of state and local governments.* Compulsory school attendance laws and the great expenditures for education both demonstrate our recognition of the importance of education to our democratic society. It is required in the performance of our most basic public responsibilities, even service in the armed forces. It is the very foundation of good citizenship. Today it is a principal instrument in awakening the child to cultural values, in preparing him for later professional training, and in helping him to adjust normally to his environment. In these days, it is doubtful that any child may reasonably be expected to succeed in life if he is denied the opportunity of an education. *Such an opportunity, where the state has undertaken to provide it, is a right which must be made available to all on equal terms."*

These thoughts were as applicable in 1891 when Section 183 was adopted as they are today and the goals they express reflect the goals set out by the framers of our Kentucky Constitution ...

The complaint included allegations that the system of school financing provided for by the General Assembly is inadequate; place too much emphasis on local school board resources; and results in inadequacies, inequities and inequalities throughout the state so as to result in an inefficient system of common school education in violation of Kentucky Constitution, Sections 1, 3 and 183 and the equal protection clause and the due process of law clause of the 14th Amendment to the United States Constitution. Additionally the complaint maintains the entire system is not efficient under the mandate of Section 183 ... .

The trial court ... found Kentucky's common school finance system to be unconstitutional and discriminatory and held that the General Assembly had not produced an efficient system of common schools throughout the state ...

[The opinion next summarizes the history and current system of educational finance in Kentucky including its two primary mechanisms of state aid to local districts—a Minimum Foundation Program (MFP) and a Power Equalization Program (PEP). The MFP provided some aid to any district that met certain financial and educational standards. The PEP was designed to augment the taxing power of the property-poor districts but in practice had very little effect.]

THE EVIDENCE

As we proceed to summarize the evidence before us, the legal test we must apply is whether that evidence supports the conclusion of the trial court that the Kentucky system of common schools is not efficient ...

The evidence in this case consists of numerous depositions, volumes of oral evidence heard by the trial court, and a seemingly endless amount of statistical data, reports, etc. We will not unduly lengthen this opinion with an extensive discussion of that evidence. As a matter of fact, such is really not necessary. The overall effect of appellants' evidence is a virtual concession that Kentucky's system of common schools is underfunded and inadequate; is fraught with inequalities and inequities throughout the 177 local school districts; is ranked nationally in the lower 20–25% in virtually every category that is used to evaluate educational performance; and is not uniform among the districts in educational opportunities. When one considers the evidence presented by the appellants, there is little or no evidence to even begin to negate that of the appellees. The tidal wave of the appellees' evidence literally engulfs that of the appellants.

In spite of the Minimum Foundation Program and the Power Equalization Program, there are wide variations in financial resources and dispositions thereof which result in unequal educational opportunities throughout Kentucky. The local districts have large variances in taxable property per student. Even a total elimination of all mismanagement and waste in local school districts would not correct the situation as it now exists. A substantial difference in the curricula offered in the poorer districts contrasts with that of the richer districts, particularly in the areas of foreign language, science, mathematics, music and art.

The achievement test scores in the poorer districts are lower than those in the richer districts and expert opinion clearly established that there is a correlation between those scores and the wealth of the district. Student-teacher ratios are higher in the poorer districts. Moreover, although Kentucky's per capita income is low, it makes an even lower per capita effort to support the common schools.

Students in property poor districts receive inadequate and inferior educational opportunities as compared to those offered to those students in the more affluent districts.

That Kentucky's overall effort and resulting achievement in the area of primary and secondary education are comparatively low, nationally, is not in dispute. Thirty-five percent of our adult population are high school dropouts. Eighty percent of Kentucky's local school districts are identified as being "poor," in terms of taxable property. The other twenty percent are under the national average. Thirty percent of our local school districts are "functionally bankrupt."

Evidence relative to educational performance was introduced by appellees to make a comparison of Kentucky with its neighbors—Ohio, Indiana, Illinois, Missouri, Tennessee, Virginia, and West Virginia. It also ranked Kentucky, nationally in the same areas.

In the area of per pupil expenditures, Kentucky ranks 6th among the 8 states and ranks 40th nationally. With respect to the average annual salary of instructional staff, Kentucky again ranks 6th among its neighbors and 37th nationally. In the area of classroom teacher compensation, Kentucky is 7th and 37th. Our classroom teacher average salary is 84.68% of the national average and our per pupil expenditure is 78.20% of the national average.

When one considers the use of property taxes as a percent of sources of school revenue,

Kentucky is 7th among our neighboring states and 43rd nationally. The national average is 30.1% while Kentucky's rate is 18.2%. If any more evidence is needed to show the inadequacy of our overall effort, consider that only 68.2% of ninth grade students eventually graduate from high school in Kentucky. That ranks us 7th among our eight adjacent sister states. Among the 6 of our neighboring states that use the ACT scholastic achievement test, our high school graduates average score is 18.1, which ranks us 4th. Kentucky's ratio of pupil-teacher is 19.2, which ranks us 7th in this region. In spite of the appellants' claim, at both the trial level and on appeal, that appellees' statistics are not current, all the above figures are based on a 1986 study, which was published in 1987.

Numerous well-qualified educators and school administrators testified before the trial court and all described Kentucky's educational effort as being inadequate and well below the national effort.

With this background of Kentucky's overall effort with regard to education and its comparison to other states in the area, and nationally, we proceed to examine the trial court's finding relative to inequity and lack of uniformity in the overabundance of local school districts. We will discuss the educational opportunities offered and then address the disparity in financial effort and support.

EDUCATIONAL EFFORT

The numerous witnesses that testified before the trial court are recognized experts in the field of primary and secondary education. They have advanced college degrees, they have taught school, they have been school administrators, they have been participants at a local or state level in Kentucky's education system, and they have performed in-depth studies of Kentucky's system. Without exception, they testified that there is great disparity in the poor and the more affluent school districts with regard to classroom teachers' pay; provision of basic educational materials; student-teacher ratio; curriculum; quality of basic management; size, adequacy and condition of school physical plants; and per year expenditure per student. Kentucky's children, simply because of their place of residence, are offered a virtual hodgepodge of educational opportunities. The quality of education in the poorer local school districts is substantially less in most, if not all, of the above categories.

Can anyone seriously argue that these disparities do not affect the basic educational opportunities of those children in the poorer districts? To ask the question is to answer it. Children in 80% of local school districts in this Commonwealth are not as well-educated as those in the other 20%.

Moreover, most of the witnesses before the trial court testified that not only were the state's educational opportunities unequal and lacking in uniformity, but that *all* were inadequate. Testimony indicated that not only do the so-called poorer districts provide inadequate education to fulfill the needs of the students but the more affluent districts' efforts are inadequate as well, as judged by accepted national standards.

As stated, when one reads the record, and when one considers the argument of counsel for the appellants, one can find no proof, no statement that contradicts the evidence about the existing inequalities and lack of uniformity in the overall performance of Kentucky's system of common schools.

Summarizing appellants' argument, and without intending to give it short shrift, it is contended that over the years the General Assembly has continually enacted such programs as the MFP, the PEP, and other progressive programs during recent sessions of the General Assembly. Moreover, uncontroverted evidence is adduced to show that the overall amount of money appropriated for local schools has increased by a substantial amount. The argument seems to be to the effect that "we have done our best." However, it is significant that *all* the experts were keenly aware of the legislative history, including substantive legislation and increased funding and yet, all of them stated that inequalities still

exist, and indeed have been exacerbated by some of the legislation. Appellants conceded, the trial court found and we concur that in spite of legislative efforts, the total local and state effort in education in Kentucky's primary and secondary education is inadequate and is lacking in uniformity. It is discriminatory as to the children served in 80% of our local school districts.

FINANCIAL EFFORT

Uniform testimony of the expert witnesses at trial, corroborated by data, showed a definite correlation between the money spent per child on education and the quality of the education received. As we have previously stated in our discussion of the history of Kentucky's school finances, our system does not *require* a minimum local effort. The MFP, being based on average daily attendance, certainly infuses more money into each local district, but is not designed to correct problems of inequality and lack of uniformity between local school districts. The experts stated that the PEP, although a good idea, was and is underfunded.

The disparity in per pupil expenditure by the local school boards runs in the thousands of dollars per year. Moreover, between the extreme high allocation and the extreme low allocation lies a wide range of annual per pupil expenditures. In theory (and perhaps in actual practice) there could be 177 different per pupil expenditures, thus leading to 177 different educational efforts. The financing effort of local school districts is, figuratively speaking, a jigsaw puzzle.

It is argued by the appellants that the so-called permissive taxes are at least part of the solution to equalizing local financial efforts. There are two easy answers that dispose of this argument. First, the taxes are permissive. Responding to obvious voter resistance to the imposition of taxes, 89 districts have enacted the tax on gross utility receipts; 5 districts have enacted the occupational tax; 82 districts have also enacted a special building tax, normally for a specific project for one time only, and not affecting teacher pay, instructional equipment, or any of the specific needs of educational opportunity. As the nature of the taxes is permissive, in many districts they are not adopted and therefore do not produce one cent in additional local revenue.

Secondly, according to the testimony of the expert witnesses, even if all the permissive taxes were enacted, the financial effort would still be inadequate, and because the population of the districts is in direct proportion to the amount of money that could and is raised by these taxes, the overall problem of an unequal local effort would be exacerbated by such action. Clearly, the permissive taxes are not the solution to the problems. Rather,

they contribute to the disparity of per pupil expenditures.

Additionally, because the assessable and taxable real and personal property in the 177 districts is so varied, and because of a lack of uniformity in tax rates, the local school boards' tax effort is not only lacking in uniformity but is also lacking in adequate effort. The history of school financing in Kentucky, certainly corroborates the trial court's finding as to the lack of uniformity and the lack of adequacy of local and state funding of education in the state. Based on the record before us, it is beyond cavil that the trial court's finding was correct . . .

OPINIONS OF EXPERTS

Numerous well-qualified experts testified in this case. They were all well educated, experienced teachers, educators, or administrators; and all were familiar with the Kentucky system of common schools and with other states' and national school issues.

Dr. Richard Salmon testified that the concept of efficiency was a three part concept. First, the system should impose no financial hardship or advantage on any group of citizens. Further, local school districts must make comparable tax efforts. Second, resources provided by the system must be adequate and uniform throughout the state. Third, the system must not waste resources.

Dr. Kern Alexander opined that an efficient system is one which is unitary. It is one in which there is uniformity throughout the state. It is one in which equality is a hallmark and one in which students must be given equal educational opportunities, regardless of economic status, or place of residence. He also testified that "efficient" involves pay and training of teachers, school buildings, other teaching staff, materials, and adequacy of all educational resources. Moreover, he, like Dr. Salmon, believed that "efficient" also applies to the quality of management of schools. Summarizing Dr. Alexander's opinion, an efficient system is unitary, uniform, adequate and properly managed.

The definitions of "efficient" were documented and supported by numerous national and local studies, prepared and authorized by many of the giants of the education profession.

The primary expert for the appellees was a local school superintendent who felt that an efficient system is one which is operated as best as can be with the money that was provided. We reject such a definition which could result in a system of common schools, efficient only in the uniformly deplorable conditions it provides throughout the state.

In summary, the experts in this case believed that an "efficient" system of common schools should have several elements:

1. The system is the sole responsibility of the General Assembly.
2. The tax effort should be evenly spread. (3) The system must provide the necessary resources throughout the state—they must be uniform.
3. (The system must provide an adequate education.
4. The system must be properly managed.

DEFINITION OF "EFFICIENT"

We now home in on the heart of this litigation. In defining "efficient," we use all the tools that are made available to us. In spite of any protestations to the contrary, we do not engage in judicial legislating. We do not make policy. We do not substitute our judgment for that of the General Assembly. We simply take the plain directive of the Constitution, and, armed with its purpose, we decide what our General Assembly must achieve in complying with its solemn constitutional duty.

Any system of common schools must be created and maintained with the premise that education is absolutely vital to the present and to the future of our Commonwealth. As Herbert Spencer observed, "Education has for its object the formation of character." ... No tax proceeds have a more important position or purpose than those for education in the grand scheme of our government.

The importance of common schools and the education they provide Kentucky's children cannot be overemphasized or overstated.

The sole responsibility for providing the system of common schools is that of our General Assembly. It is a duty—it is a constitutional mandate placed by the people on the 138 members of that body who represent those selfsame people.

The General Assembly must not only establish the system, but it must monitor it on a continuing basis so that it will always be maintained in a constitutional manner. The General Assembly must carefully supervise it, so that there is no waste, no duplication, no mismanagement, at any level.

The system of common schools must be adequately funded to achieve its goals. The system of common schools must be substantially uniform throughout the state. Each child, *every child*, in this Commonwealth must be provided with an equal opportunity to have an adequate education. Equality is the key word here. The children of the poor and the children of the rich, the children who live in the poor districts and the children who live in the rich districts must be given the same opportunity and access to an adequate education. This obligation cannot be shifted to local counties and local school districts.

As we have indicated, Section 183 requires the General Assembly to establish a system of common schools that provides an equal opportunity for children to have an adequate education. In no way does this constitutional requirement act as a limitation on the General Assembly's power to create local school entities and to grant to those entities the authority to supplement the state system. Therefore, if the General Assembly decides to establish local school entities, it may also empower them to enact local revenue initiatives to supplement the uniform, equal educational effort that the General Assembly must provide. This includes not only revenue measures similar to the special taxes previously discussed, but also the power to assess local ad valorem taxes on real property and personal property at a rate over and above that set by the General Assembly to fund the statewide system of common schools. Such local efforts may not be used by the General Assembly as a substitute for providing an adequate, equal and substantially uniform educational system throughout this state.

Having declared the system of common schools to be constitutionally deficient, we have directed the General Assembly to recreate and redesign a new system that will comply with the standards we have set out. Such system will guarantee to all children the opportunity for an adequate education, through a *state* system. To allow local citizens and taxpayers to make a supplementary effort in no way reduces or negates the minimum quality of education required in the statewide system.

We do not instruct the General Assembly to enact any specific legislation. We do not direct the members of the General Assembly to raise taxes. It is their decision how best to achieve efficiency. We only decide the nature of the constitutional mandate. We only determine the intent of the framers. Carrying out that intent is the duty of the General Assembly.

A child's right to an adequate education is a fundamental one under our Constitution. The General Assembly must protect and advance that right. We concur with the trial court that an efficient system of education must have as its goal to provide each and every child with at least the seven following capacities: (i) sufficient oral and written communication skills to enable students to function in a complex and rapidly changing civilization; (ii) sufficient knowledge of economic, social, and political systems to enable the student to make informed choices; (iii) sufficient understanding of governmental processes to enable the student to understand the issues that affect his or her community, state, and nation; (iv) sufficient self-knowledge and knowledge of his or her mental and physical wellness; (v) sufficient grounding in the arts to enable each student to appreciate his or her cultural and historical heritage; (vi) sufficient training or preparation for advanced training in either academic or vocational fields so as to enable each child to choose and pursue life work intelligently; and (vii) sufficient levels of academic or vocational skills to enable public school students to compete favorably with their counterparts in surrounding states, in academics or in the job market.[28]

The essential, and minimal, characteristics of an "efficient" system of common schools, may be summarized as follows:

1. The establishment, maintenance and funding of common schools in Kentucky is the sole responsibility of the General Assembly.
2. Common schools shall be free to all.
3. Common schools shall be available to all Kentucky children.
4. Common schools shall be substantially uniform throughout the state.
5. Common schools shall provide equal educational opportunities to all Kentucky children, regardless of place of residence or economic circumstances.
6. Common schools shall be monitored by the General Assembly to assure that they are operated with no waste, no duplication, no mismanagement, and with no political influence.
7. The premise for the existence of common schools is that all children in Kentucky have a constitutional right to an adequate education.

8. The General Assembly shall provide funding which is sufficient to provide each child in Kentucky an adequate education.

9. An adequate education is one which has as its goal the development of the seven capacities recited previously.

SUMMARY/CONCLUSION

We have decided one legal issue—and one legal issue only—viz., that the General Assembly of the Commonwealth has failed to establish an efficient system of common schools throughout the Commonwealth.

Lest there be any doubt, the result of our decision is that Kentucky's *entire system* of common schools is unconstitutional. There is no allegation that only part of the common school system is invalid, and we find no such circumstance. This decision applies to the entire sweep of the system—all its parts and parcels. This decision applies to the statutes creating, implementing and financing the *system* and to all regulations, etc., pertaining thereto. This decision covers the creation of local school districts, school boards, and the Kentucky Department of Education to the

Minimum Foundation Program and Power Equalization Program. It covers school construction and maintenance, teacher certification—the whole gamut of the common school system in Kentucky.

While individual statutes are not herein addressed specifically or considered and declared to be facially unconstitutional, the statutory system as a whole and the inter-relationship of the parts therein are hereby declared to be in violation of Section 183 of the Kentucky Constitution. Just as the bricks and mortar used in the construction of a schoolhouse, while contributing to the building's facade, do not ensure the overall structural adequacy of the schoolhouse, particular statutes drafted by the legislature in crafting and designing the current school system are not unconstitutional in and of themselves. Like the crumbling schoolhouse which must be redesigned and revitalized for more efficient use, with some component parts found to be adequate, some found to be less than adequate, statutes relating to education may be reenacted as components of a constitutional system if they combine with other component statutes to form an efficient and thereby constitutional system ...

Rose amounts to a judicial order to the Kentucky legislature to devise and fund a system of education that is both equitable and adequate. The legislature has responded not only by significantly changing the way education is funded in Kentucky, but also by instituting reforms designed to improve student outcomes. Some of these changes have been politically and legally controversial.[29]

Rose is among the most influential of the third-wave cases. The highest courts in both New Hampshire and Massachusetts have embraced the seven outcome goals listed in *Rose* as constitutionally mandated in their states as well.[30] The Massachusetts court further declared that the legislature's "duty to educate ... will evolve together with our society. Our Constitution, and its education clause, must be interpreted in accordance with the demands of modern society or it will be in constant danger of becoming atrophied and, in fact, may even lose its original meaning." The implication of this statement is that the court will be open to continued reevaluation of the adequacy of the state's system of education.

In *Hoke County Board of Education v. North Carolina*,[31] student-plaintiffs claimed that they were being denied the opportunity to a constitutionally mandated "sound basic education." North Carolina's highest court based its analysis on this definition of an adequate education:

> 'an education that does not serve the purpose of preparing students to participate and compete in the society in which they live and work is devoid of substance and is constitutionally inadequate.' [A] sound basic education ... provides students with at least: (1) sufficient knowledge of fundamental mathematics and physical science to enable the student to function in a complex and rapidly changing society; (2) sufficient fundamental knowledge of geography, history, and basic economic and political systems to enable the student to make informed choices with regard to issues that affect the student personally or affect the student's community, state, and nation; (3) sufficient academic and vocational skills to enable the student to successfully engage in post-secondary education or vocational training; and (4) sufficient academic and vocational skills to enable the student to compete on an equal basis with others in formal education or gainful employment in contemporary society.

In applying this definition the court considered both outputs (student outcomes) and inputs (expenditures and resources). Regarding outputs, the court concluded that,

... over the past decade, an inordinate number of Hoke County students have consistently failed to match the academic performance of their statewide public school counterparts and that such failure, measured by their performance while attending Hoke County schools, their dropout rates, theirgraduation rates, their need for remedial help, their inability to compete in the job markets, and their inability to compete in collegiate ranks, constitute a clear showing that they have failed to obtain [an adequate education].

Regarding inputs, the court found that at least with regard to the district's at-risk pupils, the state had failed in its duty to allocate resources to give them an "equal opportunity to obtain a sound basic education." To correct the problem the state was ordered to ensure

that every classroom be staffed with a competent, certified, well-trained teacher; that every school be led by a well-trained competent principal; and that every school be provided, in the most cost effective manner, the resources necessary to support the effective instructional program within that school so that the educational needs of all children, including at-risk children, to have the equal opportunity to obtain a sound basic education, can be met.

The court also concluded that the state had a further obligation to provide pre-school, at-risk students the "assistance [they need] in order to avail themselves of their right to the opportunity for a sound basic education."

By contrast, the highest court in Rhode Island rejected the notion that the constitutional adequacy of educational funding could be determined by student outcomes. Wrote the court:

We are particularly troubled by a definition of "equity" that requires "a sufficient amount of money ... to achieve learner outcomes." As observed by the United States Supreme Court ... "numerous external factors beyond the control of the [school district] and the State affect ... student achievement."[32]

In *Campaign for Fiscal Equity* (CFE) *v. State*,[33] New York State's highest court based its decision on whether the state's system for financing the public schools of New York City met constitutional requirements on its finding that the state was constitutionally obligated to ensure the availability of a "sound basic education" to all children. The court equated a sound basic education with the "the basic literacy, calculating, and verbal skills necessary to enable children to eventually function productively as civic participants capable of voting and serving on a jury." The court found that productive citizenship requires more than an eighth-grade education, so the state is obligated to provide all students with a "meaningful high school education." In deciding that New York State had not met this standard with regard to New York City, the court examined a variety of inputs including teacher qualifications and class size and several measures of school outputs including dropout rates and test scores.

Another New York highest court case raised the issue of whether the state is in fact responsible for controlling some of the "external factors" that affect student achievement. In this case, plaintiffs did not focus on the adequacy of educational funding, but instead claimed that the state's "fault lies in practices and policies that have resulted in high concentrations of racial minorities and poverty in the [Rochester] school district, leading to abysmal student performance." Plaintiffs argued that in schools marked by high concentrations of students living in poverty and racial isolation, it was impossible to provide an education that met the state constitutionally required standard. As the court stated, "Plaintiffs say that no matter how well the State funds their schools, if plaintiffs and their classmates fail, it is the State's responsibility to change the school population until results improve." The court acknowledged that research did establish a correlation between concentrations of poverty and racial isolation, and poor educational performance. Nevertheless, the court concluded that "allegations of academic failure alone, without allegations that the State somehow fails in its obligation to provide minimally acceptable educational services, are insufficient" to support a finding that the state has failed to meet its obligation. Despite its focus on student outcomes in the *CFE* case, decided the same day, the court stated, "if the State truly puts adequate resources into the classroom, it satisfies its constitutional promise under the Education Article, even though student performance remains substandard."[34] In a prior ruling in the same case, the court dismissed the plaintiff's claim that the de facto segregation of the Rochester school district was a violation of Title VI of the Civil Rights Act of 1964 (see sec. 6.8). The dismissal was based on Supreme Court rulings that unintentional discrimination cannot be the basis of private lawsuits under Title VI.[35]

Legislatures in states whose courts view educational adequacy in terms of inputs face the daunting task of calculating the dollar cost of the court-defined adequate education. A variety of methods have been suggested for accomplishing this task, some based on an analysis of expenditures in districts judged to be adequate or exemplary and others relying on the opinions of experts. Wyoming, Kansas, Ohio, and Maryland are among the states that have undertaken these efforts, with varying results. States whose courts view adequacy in terms of outputs face an even more daunting task because, as the Rhode Island and New York courts quoted earlier recognize, desired educational outcomes may be impossible to achieve at any level of expenditure. The New Hampshire Supreme Court is involved in an ongoing process of monitoring whether the educational assessment and accountability system adopted by the legislature "ensure[s]" delivery of a constitutionally adequate education.[36] The federal No Child Left Behind Act (see sec. 3.6) may influence more state courts and legislatures to adopt an output approach to educational equity, and the state assessment plans mandated by the Act may become the basis of future litigation attacking the adequacy of the educational funding systems of some states.[37]

Whether more than three decades of educational finance litigation has resulted in greater equity or an overall improvement in educational quality is the subject of extensive continuing research and debate. Given the complexity of producing and assessing educational equity and quality, the educational results of educational finance litigation in individual states and overall may always remain uncertain. Nevertheless, an increasing number of state courts are embracing the principles that:

- State constitutions place the responsibility for provision of education directly on the state legislature.
- The legislature is responsible for funding all the state's public schools.
- If a state constitution mandates a "thorough and efficient" or "suitable" system of education, it means that the education provided by the state must be equitably distributed and at least minimally adequate.
- Even in the absence of such language, an education article may be interpreted to require equitable and adequate provision of education to all children within the jurisdiction of the state.
- The legislature cannot discharge its educational responsibilities simply by creating local school boards with the power to raise money at varying levels based on local wealth and desires.
- It is the role of state courts to ensure that the legislature lives up to its constitutional responsibilities for the provision of education.

Local School Board Authority to Raise and Spend Money

School boards have no inherent constitutional authority to tax, borrow, and spend. The authority to tax must be expressly granted and cannot be inferred from general grants of authority to operate schools.[38] Money earmarked by law for specific purposes cannot be spent for any other purpose.[39] State laws and state constitutional provisions sometimes limit year-to-year increases in local taxes and cap the total amount of money that may be raised and borrowed. School authority to tax and spend is also circumscribed by federal and state constitutional limitations that prohibit the establishment of religion, and by state constitutional provisions that limit expenditures to "public" purposes.

A mostly older, but still valid, body of case law explored the limitations on school boards' authority to spend. The general rule is that school boards may only spend money to operate schools and for related educational purposes unless specifically authorized by the legislature to perform other functions. Expenditures not specifically authorized by law are permitted if reasonably implied by the authority granted to the school board by the legislature or if necessary to carry out the school board's educational mandate. Three early-twentieth-century cases in Washington state challenging the authority of school boards to build and operate playgrounds, gymnasiums, and medical clinics illustrate these principles.[40] These cases were decided before organized physical activities and sports became a standard or required part of the curriculum in most states. Nevertheless, the courts found that expenditures for playgrounds and gymnasiums were permitted. The court in the medical clinic case explained why:

> Playgrounds in connection with public schools have for generations been so common that it must be presumed that the legislature, by giving the general power to maintain public schools, incidentally intended to also give the authority to provide such playgrounds in connection therewith; and while gymnasiums in connection with public schools have not been so common, the work and exercise of the students carried on therein is manifestly so intimately connected with the education of the pupil as to warrant the assumption that the legislature intended the school districts and their officers to possess the power providing the same as a proper public school equipment.

However, the same reasoning did not apply to medical clinics:

The rendering of medical, surgical and dental services to the pupils, however, is, and always has been, we think, so foreign to the powers to be exercised by a school district or its officers that such power cannot be held to exist in the absence of express legislative language so providing.

School boards must formulate and manage their budgets in accordance with state law. Statutes may limit the board's budgetary authority such as by putting a cap on the annual percentage increase or by prohibiting the annual budget from exceeding the amount of money anticipated to be available from tax levies and state aid.[41] In some states, local school boards must submit their budgets either to the voters or to a higher government authority for approval. In New York, if the voters fail to approve the proposed budget, the board must adopt an austerity budget that covers only teacher salaries and "ordinary contingent expenses."[42] In Arizona if a proposed budget exceeds the budget limit for the year, the district must hold an override election and simultaneously prepare an alternative budget in case the override fails.[43] In California, if a local district's proposed budget fails to win approval from the county and state, the county superintendent has authority to adopt a budget for the district and to control the district's expenditures to keep them within that budget.[44] School districts in Georgia are permitted to hold an election seeking a special-purpose local-option sales tax to be used "exclusively for the purpose or purposes specified in the resolution or ordinance calling for imposition of the tax."[45] In one case, plaintiffs successfully claimed the district's use of local-option sales-tax money to purchase laptop computers for all middle school students violated the resolution, which said the money would be used for capital outlay projects such as system-wide technological improvements.[46] State statutes generally authorize schools to charge fees for attending school activities such as sports and some specify how the money is to be used.[47]

State statutes place specific requirements and limitations on local school board procedures for dealing with financial exigency. Most states authorize districts wishing to initiate large-scale building or remodeling projects to finance them with bonds. Procedures for issuing bonds are often quite specific and may include limits on indebtedness and a requirement of local voter approval. Most states also authorize school boards to secure short-term loans when cash on hand is temporarily insufficient to cover expenses. Statutes may specify procedures for securing short-term loans and impose limitations such as maximum terms, rates of interest, and levels of indebtedness. Some states permit districts to maintain a "contingency fund" to deal with unexpected needs for cash. Some states also permit school boards to deal with unexpected needs by shifting funds from one category of expense to another[48] or to increase their budgets in the middle of a school year to deal with necessary expenses that could not reasonably have been foreseen at the time the budget was adopted.[49] School districts wishing to sell or lease unneeded school facilities must also comply with the requirements of state law.[50]

School districts sometimes wish to impose fees on students for admission to the school or to a particular class, for books and other supplies, for specific services, or for participation in extracurricular activities. The judicial opinions concerning the legality of school fees deal mostly with two issues: Is the fee consistent with the state constitution's guarantee of a free education and does the fee discriminate against the poor. The resolution of these issues depends on the precise language of the state constitution, the court's concept of education and what services are essential, and the court's notion of equity.

Because all state constitutions guarantee a free education or an education free of tuition, no cases permit public schools to charge district residents for access to the basic program during the regular school year. However, some rulings permit tuition for summer school[51] and for students defined by law as nonresidents of the district.[52] Courts are split on the question of fees for nonrequired courses: Some allow course fees, some forbid them, and some allow them unless the course can be used for credit toward graduation.[53] Courts are also split on the question of whether fees may be charged for the use of textbooks. Some courts permit the fee provided it is waived for poor children.[54] In general, textbook fees are allowed in states where the constitution requires a system of education "free of" or "without tuition," but are prohibited where the constitution mandates "free public schools."[55]

A majority of courts have upheld reasonable fees for school supplies or activities.[56] In some cases, the acceptability of fees depends on the availability of waivers in cases of economic hardship or whether the activity is required or closely related to the school's educational goals. The Supreme Court of Montana stated the latter principle as follows:

> Is a given course or activity reasonably related to a recognized academic and educational goal of the particular school system? If it is, it constitutes part of the free, public school system commanded by … the Montana Constitution and additional fees or charges cannot be levied, directly or indirectly, against the student or his parents. If it is not, reasonable fees or charges may be imposed.[57]

When money is tight, school districts may resort to cost-cutting measures such as deferred building maintenance or reduction in staff size. In addition to its educational consequences, deferred maintenance may have legal consequences if poorly maintained buildings pose a danger to health and safety (see sec. 12.6). Personnel may not be reduced beyond the level needed to satisfy legal mandates (e.g., state statutes specifying maximum class size and federal and state laws mandating services to students with disabilities). In addition, any reduction in certified personnel necessitated by financial exigency must comply with statutory and contractual mandates concerning reduction-in-force (see sec. 10.6) and constitutional and statutory antidiscrimination laws (see sec. 9.4).

In a few cases, school boards have decided to bring the school year to a premature conclusion because the school district ran out of funds. However, in *Butt v. State*,[58] the California Supreme Court refused on equal protection grounds to permit a school district that ran out of money to close its doors six weeks ahead of schedule. Finding that the early closing would "cause an extreme and unprecedented disparity in educational service and progress" to the district's pupils, the court ruled that the state was obliged to loan the school district the money necessary to allow the schools to remain open until the scheduled end of the year. If a school district runs out of money as a result of school board mismanagement, the board may be subject to removal from office by methods established in state law.[59] Some states' statutes also provide for state takeover of school districts whose funds are mismanaged by the local school board.[60]

Summary

All levels of government play a part in funding public education. Although not obliged by the Constitution, Congress has chosen to provide a modest level of funding to public schools. Most federal aid is in the form of categorical aid or block grants and is given on condition that certain programs be offered, certain procedures followed, and that there be no discrimination against specified groups.

In accordance with the mandates of their own constitutions, state legislatures are responsible for ensuring an adequate level of funding to the state's public schools. With some variation, legislatures have chosen to finance public schools by delegating to local school boards the authority to tax real property within their districts and supplementing local revenue with state funds allocated according to a complex formula. Depending on state and locality, school district funds may be further enhanced by direct transfers of funds from municipal or country governments as authorized and required by the state legislature.

This multifaceted, complex system has engendered a great variety of litigation. Much of this litigation, especially in the early years of public schooling, involved general issues of taxation and spending authority. It is now well settled that Congress has the authority to use tax money to aid schools, that state legislatures have the power to tax on behalf of schools, and that school boards have only as much taxing and spending authority as specifically delegated to them by the state legislature.

The primary focus of most significant recent litigation in the area of educational finance and of this chapter is on issues involving questions of equity and adequacy in education. In *San Antonio Independent School District v. Rodriguez*, the Supreme Court ruled that state systems of educational finance that result in significantly different levels of per pupil expenditures across districts do not violate the Equal Protection Clause. However, this ruling suggests and subsequent cases confirm that total denial of education to any child within the state's jurisdiction is unconstitutional.

Suits have also been brought in the courts of most states attacking the constitutionality of state educational finance systems. These suits have objected to interdistrict funding inequities or to the alleged inadequacy of the educational program offered in some or all of the state's schools. The suits have been based on the particular state's equal protection clause or education article in the state constitution. Regardless of their specific claims, these lawsuits have produced mixed results. Some state courts have ratified school funding plans despite wide disparities in school districts' power to raise money and in per pupil expenditures across districts and others have sought to equalize these financial indicators. Still other state courts have interpreted their state constitutions as requiring the state legislature to provide to every child in the state an educational opportunity that is both adequate and equivalent to the opportunity provided to other children. Some courts have even offered a detailed analysis of what constitutes an adequate education.

Endnotes

1. United States v. Butler, 297 U.S. 1 (1936).
2. 20 U.S.C. § 7907(a).
3. Sch. Dist. of City of Pontiac v. Spellings, 2005 WL 3149545 (E.D. Mich. 2005).
4. Sch. Dist. of City of Pontiac v. Sec. of U.S. Dept. of Educ., 512 F.3d 252 (6th Cir. 2008); *compare* State v. Spellings, 549 F. Supp. 2d 161 (D. Conn. 2008).

5. Manges v. Freer Indep. Sch. Dist., 653 S.W.2d 553 (Tex. App. 1983), *rev'd on other grounds*, 677 S.W.2d 488 (Tex. 1984).

6. State v. Bd. of Comm'rs of Elk County, 58 P.959 (Kan. 1899).

7. 469 U.S. 256 (1985).

8. 411 U.S. 1 (1973).

9. An educational financing system might be hypothesized, however, in which the analogy to the wealth discrimination cases would be considerably closer. If elementary and secondary education were made available by the State only to those able to pay a tuition assessed against each pupil, there would be a clearly defined class of "poor" people—definable in terms of their inability to pay the prescribed sum—who would be absolutely precluded from receiving an education. That case would present a far more compelling set of circumstances for judicial assistance than the case before us today. After all, Texas has undertaken to do a good deal more than provide an education to those who can afford it. It has provided what it considers to be an adequate base education for all children and has attempted, though imperfectly, to ameliorate by state funding and by the local assessment program the disparities in local tax resources.

10. 457 U.S. 202 (1982).

11. 478 U.S. 265 (1986).

12. 487 U.S. 450 (1988).

13. Successful cases: Idaho Sch. for Equal Educational Opportunity v. State of Idaho, 129 P.3d 1199 (Idaho 2005); Columbia Falls Elementary Sch. Dist. No. 6 v. State of Montana, 109 P.3d 257 (Mont. 2005); Hoke County Bd. of Educ. v. State of North Carolina, 599 S.E.2d 365 (N.C. 2004); Montoy v. State, 138 P.3d 755 (Kan. 2006); Neely v. West Orange-Cove Consol. Indep. Sch. Dist., 176 S.W.3d 746 (Tex. 2005); Lake View Sch. Dist. No. 25 v. Huckabee, 220 S.W.3d 645 (Ark. 2005); Brigham v. State, 2005 Vt. 105, 889 A.2d 715 (Vt. 2005); DuPree v. Alma Sch. Dist. No. 30, 651 S.W.2d 90 (Ark. 1983); Serrano v. Priest, 487 P.2d 1241 (Cal. 1971); Horton v. Meskill, 376 A.2d 359 (Conn. 1977); Idaho Schs. for Equal Educ., Opportunity v. Evans, 850 P.2d 724 (Idaho 1993); Rose v. Council for Better Educ., Inc., 790 S.W.2d 186 (Ky. 1989); McDuffy v. Sec'y of the Executive Office of Educ., 615 N.E.2d 516 (Mass. 1993); Leandro v. State, 468 S.E.2d 543 (N.C. App. 1996), *aff'd in part and rev'd in part*, 488 S.E.2d 249 (N.C. 1997); Claremont Sch. Dist. v. Governor, 703 A.2d 1353 (N.H. 1997); Bismarck Pub. Sch. Dist. No. 1 v. State, 511 N.W.2d 247 (N.D. 1994); Helena Elementary Sch. Dist. No. 1 v. State, 769 P.2d 684 (1989), *modified*, 784 P.2d 412 (Mont. 1990); Claremont Sch. Dist. v. Governor, 635 A.2d 1375 (N.H. 1993); Abbott v. Burke, 495 A.2d 376 (1985), 575 A.2d 359 (1990), 643 A.2d 575 (1994), and 693 A.2d 417 (N.J. 1997); Robinson v. Cahill, 303 A.2d 273 (N.J. 1973); Campaign for Fiscal Equity v. State, Slip Op. No. 15615 (N.Y. June 26, 2003); DeRolph v. State, 677 N.E.2d 733 (Ohio 1997); Abbeville County Sch. Dist. v. State, 515 S.E.2d 535 (S.C. 1999); Tenn. Small Sch. Sys. v. McWherter,

851 S.W.2d 139 (Tenn. 1993); Edgewood Indep. Sch. Dist. v. Meno, 893 S.W.2d 450 (Tex. 1995); Edgewood Indep. Sch. Dist. v. Kirby, 777 S.W.2d 391 (1989), and 804 S.W.2d 491 (Tex. 1991); Seattle Sch. Dist. No. 1 v. State, 585 P.2d 71 (Wash. 1978); State *ex rel.* Educ. for County of Randolph v. Bailey, 453 S.E.2d 368 (W. Va. 1994); Pauley v. Kelley, 255 S.E.2d 859 (W. Va. 1979); Washakie County Sch. Dist. No. 1 v. Herschler, 606 P.2d 310 (Wyo. 1980); Brigham v. State, 692 A.2d 384 (Vt. 1997); Campbell County Sch. Dist. v. Ohman, 907 P.2d 1238 (Wyo. 1995). Unsuccessful cases: Coalition for Educ. Equity v. Heineman, 731 N.W.2d 164 (Neb. 2007); OEA v. State *ex rel.* Oklahoma Legislature, 158 P.3d 1058 (Okla. 2007); Matanuska-Susitna Borough Sch. Dist. v. State, 931 P.2d 391 (Alaska 1997); Roosevelt Elementary Sch. Dist. v. Bishop, 877 P.2d 806 (Ariz. 1994); Shofstall v. Hollins, 515 P.2d 590 (Ariz. 1973); Lujan v. Colo. State Bd. of Educ., 649 P.2d 1005 (Colo. 1982); Coalition for Adequacy & Fairness in Sch. Funding v. Chiles, 680 So. 2d 400 (Fla. 1996); McDaniel v. Thomas, 285 S.E.2d 156 (Ga. 1981); Thompson v. Engelking, 537 P.2d 635 (Idaho 1975); Comm. for Educ. Rights v. Edgar, 672 N.E.2d 1178 (Ill. 1996); Blase v. State, 302 N.E.2d 46 (Ill. 1973); Unified Sch. Dist. 229 v. State, 885 P.2d 1170 (Kan. 1994); La. Ass'n of Educators v. Edwards, 521 So. 2d 390 (La. 1988), *superseded by* Louisiana Constitutional Amendment *in* Charlet v. Legislature of La., 713 So. 2d 11199 (La. 1998); Sch. Admin. Dist. No. 1 v. Comm'r, 659 A.2d 854 (Me. 1994); Hornbeck v. Somerset County Bd. of Educ., 458 A.2d 758 (Md. 1983); Skeen v. State, 505 N.W.2d 299 (Minn. 1993); Gould v. Orr, 506 N.W.2d 349 (Neb. 1993); Paynter v. New York, 765 N.Y.S.2d 819 (N.Y. 2003); Bd. of Educ., Levittown Union Free Sch. Dist. v. Nyquist, 439 N.E.2d 359 (N.Y. 1982); Reform Educ. Financing Inequities Today v. Cuomo, 606 N.Y.S.2d 44 (N.Y. App. Div. 1993); Britt v. N.C. State Bd. of Educ., 357 S.E.2d 432 (N.C. Ct. App.), *review denied by* 361 S.E.2d 71 (N.C. 1987); Bismarck Pub. Sch. Dist. No. 1 v. State, 511 N.W.2d 247 (N.D. 1994); Bd. of Educ. v. Walter, 390 N.E.2d 813 (Ohio 1979); Fair Sch. Fin. Council of Okla., Inc. v. Oklahoma, 746 P.2d 1135 (Okla. 1987); Coalition for Equitable Sch. Funding v. State, 811 P.2d 116 (Or. 1991); Olsen v. State, 554 P.2d 139 (Or. 1976); Withers v. State, 891 P.2d 675 (Or. Ct. App. 1995); Danson v. Casey, 399 A.2d 360 (Pa. 1979); City of Pawtucket v. Sundlun, 662 A.2d 40 (R.I. 1995); Richland County v. Campbell, 364 S.E.2d 470 (S.C. 1988); Scott v. Virginia, 443 S.E.2d 138 (Va. 1994); Vincent v. Voight, 614 N.W.2d 388 (Wis. 2000); Kukor v. Grover, 436 N.W.2d 568 (Wis. 1989). *See also* Londonderry School District v. State, 907 A.2d 988 (N.H. 2006).

14. Claremont Sch. Dist. v. Governor, 703 A.2d 1353 (N.H. 1997).

15. Mock v. Kansas, Case No. 91-CV-1009 (Shawnee County Dist. Ct., Kan. 1991).

16. Levittown Union Free Sch. Dist. v. Nyquist, 439 N.E.2d 359 (N.Y. 1982).

17. *See, for example,* Coalition for Educ. Equity v. Heineman, 731 N.W.2d 164 (Neb. 2007); Comm. for Educ. Rights v. Edgar, 672 N.E.2d 1178 (Ill. 1996); City of Pawtucket v. Sundlun, 662 A.2d 40 (R.I. 1995); Oklahoma Education Association v. State *ex rel.* Oklahoma Legislature, 158 P.3d 1058 (Okla. 2007).

18. McDaniel v. Thomas, 285 S.E.2d 15 (Ga. 1981); *see also* Lujan v. Colo. State Bd. of Educ., 649 P.2d 1005 (Colo. 1982); Bd. of Educ. of Cincinnati v. Walter, 390 N.E.2d 813 (Ohio 1979).

19. Dupree v. Alma Sch. Dist. No. 30, 651 S.W.2d 90 (Ark. 1983).

20. Serrano v. Priest (Serrano II), 557 P.2d 929 (Cal. 1976).

21. 21 777 S.W.2d 391 (Tex. 1989).

22. R.E.F.I.T. v. Cuomo, 655 N.E.2d 647 (N.Y. 1995); Gould v. Orr, 506 N.W.2d 349 (Neb. 1993); McDaniel v. Thomas, 285 S.E.2d 156 (Ga. 1981).

23. Danson v. Casey, 399 A.2d 360 (Pa. 1979).

24. McDaniel v. Thomas, 285 S.E.2d 156 (Ga. 1981).

25. Pauley v. Kelley, 255 S.E.2d 859 (W. Va. 1979).

26. Seattle Sch. Dist. No. 1 v. State, 585 P.2d 71 (Wash. 1978) (en banc).

27. Mock v. State, Case No. 91-CV-1009 (Shawnee County Dist. Ct., Kan. 1991); *see also* Montoy v. State, No. 99-C-1738 (Shawnee County Dist. Ct., Kan. December 2, 2003).

28. In recreating and redesigning the Kentucky system of common schools, these seven characteristics should be considered as *minimum* goals in providing an adequate education. Certainly, there is no prohibition against higher goals—whether such are implemented statewide by the General Assembly or through the efforts of any local education entities that the General Assembly may establish—so long as the General Assembly meets the standards set out in this Opinion.

29. *See* Bd. of Educ. v. Bushee, 889 S.W.2d 809 (Ky. 1994).

30. Claremont Sch. Dist. v. Governor, 703 A.2d 1353 (N.H. 1997); McDuffy v. Sec'y of the Executive Office of Educ., 615 N.E.2d 516 (Mass. 1993).

31. 599 S.E.2d 365 (N.C. 2004).

32. City of Pawtucket v. Sundlun, 662 A.2d 40 (R.I. 1995).

33. 801 N.E.2d 326 (N.Y. 2003).

34. Paynter v. New York, 797 N.E.2d 1225 (N.Y. 2003).

35. Alexander v. Sandoval, 532 U.S.275 (2001); Gonzaga Univ. v. Doe, 536 U.S. 273 (2002); *compare* Powell v. Ridge, 189 F.3d 387 (3d Cir. 1999).

36. Claremont Sch. Dist. v. Governor, 794 A.2d 744 (N.H. 2002).

37. *See* Montoy v. Kansas, No. 99-C-1738 (Shawnee County Dist. Ct., Kan. December 2, 2003).

38. Manges v. Freer Indep. Sch. Dist., 653 S.W.2d 533 (Tex. App. 1983), *rev'd on other grounds*, 677 S.W.2d 488 (Tex. 1984).

39. Barth v. Bd. of Educ., 322 N.W.2d 694 (Wis. Ct. App. 1982).

40. State *ex rel.* Sch. Dist. No. 56 v. Superior Court, 124 P. 484 (Wash. 1912) (playground); Sorenson v. Perkins & Co., 129 P. 577 (Wash. 1913) (gymnasium); McGilvra v. Seattle Sch. Dist. No. 1, 194 P. 817 (Wash. 1921) (medical clinic).

41. Marsh v. Erhard, 47 A.2d 713 (Pa. 1946).

42. N.Y. EDUC. LAW § 2023.

43. Ariz. Rev. Stat. Ann. § 15–481.

44. CAL. EDUC. CODE § 42127.3(b)(1).

45. O.C.G.A. § 48–8-111(a)(1).

46. Johnstone v. Thompson, 631 S.E.2d 650 (Ga. 2006).

47. Kan. Stat. Ann. § 72–8208a; Miss. Code Ann. § 37-7-301; Okla. Stat. § 5–129.

48. Isley v. Sch. Dist. No. 2, 305 P.2d 432 (Ariz. 1956).

49. Raffone v. Pearsall, 333 N.Y.S. 2d 316 (N.Y. App. Div. 1972).

50. Madachy v. Huntington Horse Show Ass'n, 192 S.E. 128 (W. Va. 1937).

51. Washington v. Salisbury, 306 S.E.2d 600 (S.C. 1983).

52. Oracle Sch. Dist. No. 2 v. Mammoth High Sch. Dist. No. 88, 633 P.2d 450 (Ariz. Ct. App. 1981).

53. Concerned Parents v. Caruthersville Sch. Dist. 18, 548 S.W.2d 554 (Mo. 1977) (en banc); Norton v. Bd. of Educ., 553 P.2d 1277 (N.M. 1976).

54. Vandevender v. Cassell, 208 S.E.2d 436 (W. Va. 1974).

55. 55 Cardiff v. Bismarck Pub. Sch. Dist., 263 N.W.2d 105 (N.D. 1978); Sneed v. Greenboro City Bd. of Educ., 264 S.E.2d 106 (N.C. 1980).

56. Hamer v. Bd. of Educ., 367 N.E.2d 739 (Ill. App. Ct. 1977); Paulson v. Minidoka County Sch. Dist. No. 331, 463 P.2d 935 (Idaho 1970); Kelley v. E. Jackson Pub. Sch., 372 N.W.2d 638 (Mich. Ct. App. 1985); *contra,* Hartzell v. Connell, 679 P.2d 35 (Cal. 1984).

57. Granger v. Cascade County Sch. Dist. No. 1, 499 P.2d 780 (Mont. 1972).

58. 842 P.2d 1240 (Cal. 1992).

59. Tautenhahn v. State, 334 S.W.2d 574 (Tex. App. 1960).

60. N.J. STAT. ANN. § 18A:7A-10.

PART FOUR

Curriculum and Instructional Foundations of Education

"I was going to teach them the meaning of life ... but it wasn't on the test."

Standards and Standardized Testing

INTRODUCTION
BY KISHA R. CUNNINGHAM, PHD

"Too often we give children answers to remember rather than problems to solve."

—Roger Lewin

Chapter 9 examines standardized assessments, standards, and accountability and how they affect different school systems. It is obviously important that education value standards, as they are important in being accountable. In dealing with assessments, there are many different views on the quality of assessments and the impact the accountability system has on curriculum and instruction about courses in the classroom. The effects of accountability in education can lead to different things. Adequate yearly progress (AYP) pressure and student achievement are two of them. Teachers find themselves more focused on improving students and pressuring them to make AYP. Many teachers admit to not understanding the accountability system rather than AYP specifically. The morale of teachers has declined due to the state's accountability system. This chapter discusses disconnects between a teacher's own beliefs and the approach being adopted into schools.

Educators' Opinions About Standards, Assessments, and Accountability

BY LAURA S. HAMILTON, BRIAN M. STECHER, AND JULIE A. MARSH

STANDARDS-BASED ACCOUNTABILITY UNDER NO CHILD LEFT BEHIND

Gathering information about educators' opinions about their state accountability systems is important for understanding the actions they take in response to the systems. The study probed educators' opinions about key components of NCLB, including academic content standards, annual assessments, and AYP determinations, as well as educators' responses to the pressures associated with accountability. In general, teachers and administrators were familiar with the components of NCLB accountability, had mixed opinions about the accuracy of test scores and AYP status determinations, and reported both positive and negative effects of accountability.

State Content Standards

Standards are at the core of the accountability system, so it is important that educators be knowledgeable about them. Almost all teachers and principals in California, Georgia, and Pennsylvania reported that they were familiar with their state standards in mathematics and science. Familiarity was especially high for mathematics; almost 95 percent of mathematics teachers and principals reported either having a thorough understanding of the mathematics standards or being familiar with the main points.[1] Responses were similar for science in California and Georgia; however, in Pennsylva-nia, only slightly more than half of the teachers were familiar with the state science standards. This result is likely because Pennsylvania had adopted science standards only in grades four, seven, eight, and 12 and did not administer a science assessment in 2004–2005.

USEFULNESS OF STATE CONTENT STANDARDS

Most teachers in California and Georgia agreed that the mathematics and science standards were useful for planning their lessons (see Figure 1). These responses suggest that the standards documents were not "left on the shelf" but that teachers used them for curriculum and lesson planning. As one elementary school teacher in California commented, "In both subjects [math and science] . . . teaching is based on the standards. So you have some place to start your teaching, and that has helped, rather than just doing random things. So it's helped me stay focused." Teachers in the case study schools generally noted that standards were useful for bringing focus and consistency of instruction within and across schools. For example, they reported that state standards made sure teachers were on the same page and prevented teachers from teaching simply what they knew and liked best.

Pennsylvania teachers were somewhat less likely to agree that the standards were useful for instructional planning in mathematics and were considerably less likely to agree in science. The reports from Pennsylvania science teachers were consistent with the fact that Pennsylvania had science standards only for selected grades and had not yet administered science tests.

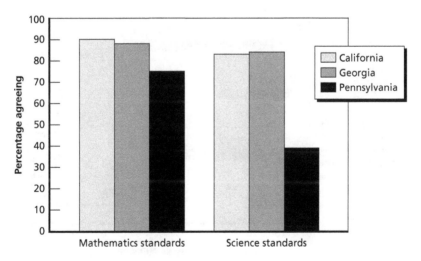

Figure 1. Elementary School Teachers Agreeing That Standards Are Useful for Planning Their Lessons, 2004–2005

Note: See Table B.5 in Appendix B for standard errors and additional information.

COVERAGE OF STATE CONTENT STANDARDS

Although teachers reported using the state standards to help plan their lessons, they also reported concerns about the breadth of the standards (see Figure 2). Most elementary school teachers in all three states agreed that the mathematics and science standards covered more content than they could address in a year. In such a situation, teachers must decide on their own whether to cover some standards fully and omit others or whether to cover all the standards incompletely. Pennsylvania had created assessment anchors to help teachers understand which aspects of the standards would be included in state assessments, and the responses reported here reflect teachers' opinions about the more focused anchors (not just the standards). Teachers were somewhat more likely to agree that the mathematics standards were too broad than to agree that the science standards were too broad.

In addition, about 20 percent of the elementary school math teachers and 20 to 30 percent of the science teachers in all three states thought the standards omitted important material in math or science (for similar results from middle school teacher, see Table B.5 in Appendix B).

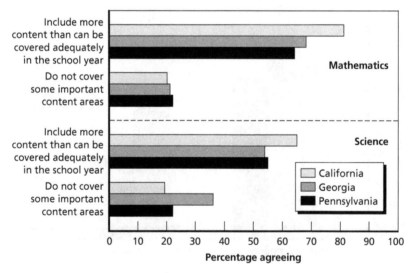

Figure 2. Elementary School Teachers Agreeing with Statements About Content Coverage of State Standards

Note: See Table B.5 in Appendix B for standard errors and additional information.

These teachers faced the dilemma of teaching the content though it was not included in the standards and would not be on the assessment or omitting the content though they believed it was important. Middle school science teachers, who generally have more training in science than do elementary school science teachers, were more likely to report omissions than elementary school science teachers were.

Taken together, these findings suggest somewhat of a mismatch remaining between the content described in state standards documents (and supplementary materials) and the curriculum that teachers believed that they should cover during a school year. Our surveys do not allow us to estimate the extent of the mismatch nor to say whether it reflects overly ambitious (or incorrectly focused) standards, undemanding (or misdirected) teachers, or underprepared students.

State Assessments

Teachers' and administrators' opinions about the accuracy and appropriateness of state assessments provide one indication of the quality of the assessments. In addition, their attitudes toward the assessments are likely to influence their use of test results as well as the impact that the accountability system has on curriculum and instruction. There were considerable differences of opinion among respondents on these issues.

ADMINISTRATORS' OPINIONS OF VALIDITY OF STATE TESTS

About two-thirds of the district superintendents in California and Georgia and about one-half in Pennsylvania agreed that the state tests accurately reflected the achievement of students in their districts (see Figure 3). Principals also had mixed responses to similar questions about the validity of the state test scores. Georgia principals were more likely to report that test results provided an accurate indication of student achievement than were principals in California and Pennsylvania. These attitudes are consistent with administrators' and teachers' reports concerning their use of test results (which will be discussed in Chapter Five).

However, it is important to point out that administrators in districts and schools that made AYP held more positive views about the validity of state tests than administrators in districts and schools that did not make AYP (see Figure 4). In all three states, superintendents who reported that their districts met AYP targets were far more likely to agree that test results

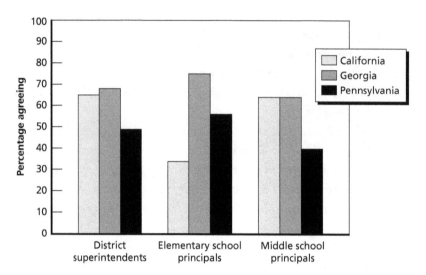

Figure 3. Administrators Agreeing That State Assessment Scores Accurately Reflect Student Achievement

Note: See Table B.6 in Appendix B for standard errors and additional information.

accurately reflected their students' achievements than were superintendents who reported that their districts did not make AYP. Principals' views on the validity of state tests follow a similar pattern, although the differences in attitudes toward the validity of tests between principals in schools that met AYP and those that did not were not as large as the differences between superintendents.

It is not surprising that administrators in schools and districts that were deemed more successful based on state test results would be more likely to have favorable views of the validity of the test scores than were administrators in schools and districts deemed less successful. However, for SBA to function most effectively, all stakeholders should endorse the measures of progress (the state assessments, in the case of NCLB). If they do not, it may undermine the functioning of the accountability system.

TEACHERS' OPINIONS OF VALIDITY OF STATE TESTS

Teachers were more critical than superintendents and principals in their views about the state assessments (see Table 4.1). Only about 40 percent of the teachers in California, about 50 percent

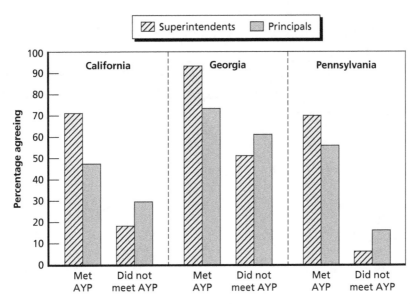

Figure 4. Administrators Agreeing That State Assessment Scores Accurately Reflect Student Achievement, by District or School AYP Status

Note: See Table B.7 in Appendix B for standard errors and additional information.

in Pennsylvania, and about 60 percent in Georgia agreed that the mathematics assessment was a good measure of students' mastery of the content standards. The percentages were even lower for the science assessments (Pennsylvania had not yet administered a science test in 2004–2005). Georgia teachers were more likely to agree that the assessments were good measures than were teachers in the other states, consistent with the opinions of Georgia administrators reported above.

DIFFICULTY AND CURRICULUM ALIGNMENT OF STATE TESTS

Teachers may have thought that state assessments were not good measures of students' mastery of content standards because they found the state assessments to be too difficult for the majority of their students. In California and Pennsylvania, two-thirds of middle school teachers reported that the tests were too difficult, as did almost half of Georgia middle school teachers. In all three states, middle school teachers were more likely than elementary school teachers to report that

Table 4.1. Teachers Agreeing with Statements Regarding State Assessments

Statement	California (%)		Georgia (%)		Pennsylvania (%)	
	Elem.	Middle	Elem.	Middle	Elem.	Middle
The mathematics assessment						
Is a good measure of students' mastery of content standards	42	38	60	57	45	50
Is too difficult for the majority of my students	47	65	31	46	47	64
Includes considerable content that is not in our curriculum	33	32	24	27	25	43
Omits considerable content that is in our curriculum	35	30	26	37	27	49
The science assessment						
Is a good measure of students' mastery of content standards	21	30	46	47	NA	NA
Is too difficult for the majority of my students	64	73	43	45	NA	NA
Includes considerable content that is not in our curriculum	44	54	34	39	NA	NA
Omits considerable content that is in our curriculum	36	28	28	45	NA	NA

Note: Reports percentages of teachers in tested grades. Response options included strongly disagree, disagree, agree, strongly agree, and don't know. Table entries are percentages responding agree or strongly agree. See Table B.8 in Appendix B for standard errors and additional information.

state assessments were too diffi-cult. From the teachers' perspective, the challenges associated with meeting the states' NCLB targets in mathematics and science appeared to be greater for older students than for younger ones.

In addition, many teachers believed that the assessments were misaligned with their curriculum—either by including considerable content that was not in the curriculum or by omitting important content that was in the curriculum. Figure 5 shows the percentage of mathematics teachers who reported that the mathematics assessment either omitted considerable content that was part of their curricula or included considerable content that was not in their curricula. In mathematics, majorities of middle school teachers reported considerable misalignment between the assessments and the curricula, as did a majority of elementary school teachers in California. The percentage of science teachers reporting such misalignment was a bit higher (71 percent of elementary school science teachers and 74 percent of middle school science teachers in California; 53 percent of elementary school science teachers and 63 percent of middle school science teachers in Georgia).

One Georgia eighth-grade mathematics teacher noted some specific problems with alignment: "With eighth grade, because we're teaching algebra, and the CRCT does not test algebra, it's testing eighth-grade math, which doesn't exist anymore in [this district]; then it's difficult because you're not getting tested on what you've been teaching all year. For all kids, they're tested on the basic skills, things that they should have mastered, but they haven't. And, because we have to follow the pacing chart, because we're doing Springboard, because we're doing this whole curriculum that isn't really aligned with the test, then it puts them at a disadvantage."

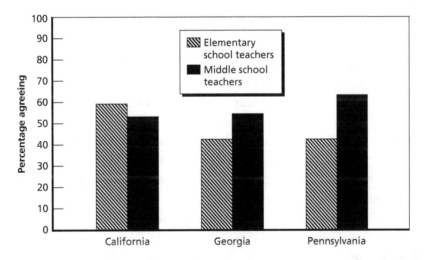

Figure 5. Math Teachers Reporting That State Assessment Omits Considerable Content in the Local Curriculum or Includes Considerable Content Not in the Local Curriculum
Note: See Table B.9 in Appendix B for standard errors and additional information.

193

For the accountability system to function effectively, the standards should be clear, appropriate, and well understood, the tests should align with the standards, and the curriculum should align with both. These results suggest that alignment among standards, assessments, and curriculum could be improved in all three states and in both subjects.

Adequate Yearly Progress

AYP is the metric that determines whether schools and districts meet their goals for student achievement or are identified for improvement and face interventions and sanctions. For the accountability system to promote improved student performance, teachers and administrations must understand AYP calculation and see a connection between the school's AYP status and their efforts on behalf of students.

UNDERSTANDING OF ACCOUNTABILITY SYSTEM

Despite the complexities of state AYP calculations, three-quarters or more of superintendents and principals in all three states agreed that they had a clear understanding of AYP criteria (see Figure 6).[2] In addition, about two-thirds of the principals in all three states reported receiving assistance to understand the state accountability system (see Table B.10 in Appendix B). Interviews with staff in the state departments of education confirmed that all three states had devoted resources to communicating AYP rules and regulations to administrators and teachers (e.g., via memos, email, or Web sites) and that much of each state's technical assistance to schools during the first few years of NCLB focused on clarifying NCLB requirements.

Teachers, who were asked about their understanding of the accountability system in general rather than about AYP specifically, tended to report a lack of understanding of the system (see Table B.10 in Appendix B). Approximately one-half of the elementary and middle school teachers in all three states agreed that the accountability system was so complicated that it was hard for them to understand.[3] Georgia teachers were slightly less likely than California and Pennsylvania teachers to agree that the system was difficult to understand. This result is consistent with previous findings about Georgia educators' reactions to accountability in their state. Responses to these questions did not change much between 2003–2004 (the first year of the study) and

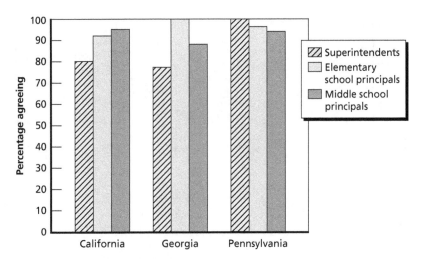

Figure 6. Administrators with Clear Understanding of AYP Criteria
Note: See Table B.10 in Appendix B for standard errors and additional information.

2004–2005, indicating that, despite an additional year of operating under NCLB, many teachers remained confused by the policy in their states.

In our case study visits, we encountered a number of teachers in schools or districts that had failed to make AYP, usually for the first time, who were misinformed about the reasons that the school or district had failed to make AYP. In these cases, it seemed like the principal or district administration had intentionally downplayed the results, focusing the blame on technicalities that they did not describe clearly to teachers. It appeared that this was the result of an attempt to keep up school morale and help the school community get past the stigma of failing.

CONFIDENCE IN ABILITY TO MEET AYP TARGETS

As noted in the introduction to this monograph, research suggests that incentives are most effective when the majority of people believe the goals can be attained with hard work (Kelley et al., 2000). School administrators in California, Georgia, and Pennsylvania were uncertain about meeting future AYP targets for their districts and schools. On the one hand, majorities of superintendents and principals in all three states believed that their schools or districts would meet their AYP targets for the following year (2005–2006) (see Figure 7).

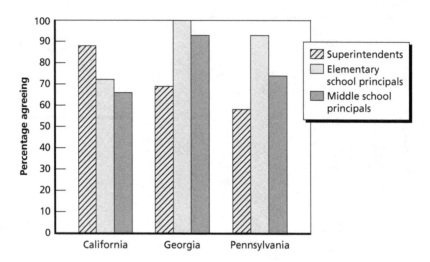

Figure 7. Superintendents and Principals Agreeing That Their Districts or Schools Would Meet AYP Targets for the Next School Year

Note: See Table B.11 in Appendix B for standard errors and additional information.

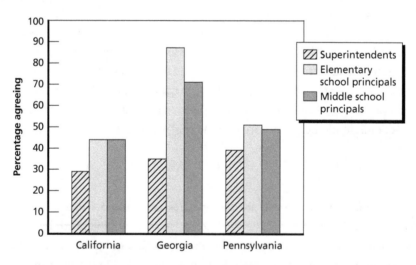

Figure 8. Superintendents and Principals Agreeing That Their Districts or Schools Would Meet AYP Targets for the Next Five School Years

Note: See Table B.11 in Appendix B for standard errors and additional information.

On the other hand, only about one-third of superintendents in all three states believed that their districts could attain their AYP targets for the next five years (see Figure 8). Similarly, a lower percentage of principals in all three states agreed that their schools could meet AYP targets for the next five years. The overall pattern of results is not surprising, given that all three states will increase the percentage of students required to be proficient in coming years (see Figures 3.1 and 3.2 in Chapter Three for state trajectories). Georgia principals were far more confident than principals in the other two states; 71 percent of elementary school principals and 87 percent of middle school principals agreed that their schools could meet AYP targets for the next five years. Georgia principals' higher expectations may be due to the facts that they face a more gradual trajectory than California schools and that a greater percentage of students in their state had already reached the proficient level. These attitudes deserve continued monitoring because it may be detrimental to NCLB accountability if future targets are perceived to be unattainable.

PERCEIVED VALIDITY OF AYP

About two-thirds of elementary school principals agreed that their school's AYP status accurately reflected the overall performance of their students; however, only half or fewer middle school principals agreed (see Figure 9). Superintendents' opinions varied across states, from 30 percent of Pennsylvania superintendents who agreed that their district's AYP status reflected the overall performance of students to 60 percent of California superintendents. As might be expected, since primarily test scores determine AYP status, the wide range of opinions regarding the validity of AYP status mirrors the wide range of opinions regarding the validity of test scores.

As was the case with test scores, administrators in districts and schools that made AYP held more positive views about the validity of AYP status than did administrators in districts and schools that did not make AYP (see Figure 10). The pattern was most dramatic in Georgia, where almost all administrators in districts and schools that made AYP thought the results reflected overall student performance compared with almost none of the administrators in districts that did not make AYP. The overall pattern was similar in California and Pennsylvania, although not as dramatic. In both states, about one-third or more of administrators in successful districts and schools did not agree that AYP status was an accurate reflection of school performance. California was especially interesting because, as described in Chapter Three, the state assigns its own accountability metric, the API, in addition to AYP. Although more than half of

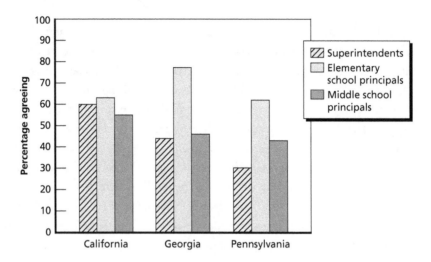

Figure 9. Superintendents and Principals Agreeing That District or School AYP Status Accurately Reflected Overall Student Performance

Note: See Table B.12 in Appendix B for standard errors and additional information.

administrators in California viewed AYP as valid, the administrators we interviewed in case studies explained why many preferred the API, which is based on growth over time. As one middle school principal stated,

> The thing with AYP that's so frustrating is that it didn't take into account where you started. Everybody had to hit an arbitrary mark no matter where you started, no matter what you were dealing with. Schools that have high special ed populations, high ESL [English as a second language] populations, are looked at the same as schools that have one ESL kid and one special ed kid, and that's not right. That's totally ridiculous if you look at it. We're dealing with situations much more difficult.

Further, many teachers in California reported that the differences between AYP and API caused confusion among parents and some staff, particularly when their schools were deemed to be performing well in terms of state API scores but failed to make federal AYP targets. This may explain, in part, why California administrators questioned the validity of AYP. In fact, the California State Superintendent of Public Instruction articulated this point in a public statement:

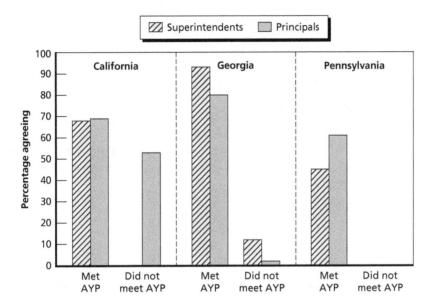

Figure 10. Superintendents and Principals Agreeing That District or School AYP Status Accurately Reflected Overall Student Performance, by AYP Status
Note: See Table B.13 in Appendix B for standard errors and additional information.

"The fact that 317 of our schools grew 30 points or more [on the API], yet failed to make the federal benchmark, illustrates why I believe a growth model of accountability such as we have here in California more accurately reflects actual student learning" (California Department of Education, 2004c). According to one report, 2,339 schools statewide met API but did not meet AYP in 2003–2004 (Education Trust—West, 2004). These views were reflected at the schools we visited as well. As one California principal put it, "So, being an API-7 school, and not making AYP in this one area, I mean, come on. They've got to look at this bigger picture here."

Teachers' responses suggested other ways in which AYP might not be an effective indicator of school performance (see Table B.40 in Appendix B). For example, approximately half the teachers reported that high-achieving students were not receiving appropriately challenging curriculum and instruction due to the state's accountability system. In addition, the vast majority of teachers in the states believed that the state system left little time to teach content not on state tests. (As we discuss further in Chapter Six, this tendency to focus on tested subjects raised concerns about possible narrowing of curriculum and instruction.)

The Effects of Accountability

Superintendents, principals, and teachers were asked about the pressure they felt as a result of the accountability system and the impact of accountability on the school's instructional program and their own attitudes.

AYP PRESSURE AND STUDENT ACHIEVEMENT EMPHASIS

Most educators at all levels in Georgia and Pennsylvania and most teachers in Cali-fornia agreed that staff were focusing more on improving student achievement as a result of pressure to make AYP (see Figure 11). We asked superintendents about principals' focus on student achievement and principals about teachers' focus, and teachers reported on their individual behaviors. Three-quarters of teachers agreed that they focused more on student achievement as a result of pressure to make AYP. Although we do not know exactly what behaviors teachers changed, the fact that a large proportion of teachers was attending more to student achievement is the sort of change that the accountability system was designed to promote. In addition, more than half of the principals in Georgia and Pennsylvania agreed that their staff were focusing more on student achievement, and more than two-thirds of the superintendents in these states agreed that principals were focused more on achievement, which represents a consistent pattern of change due to the accountability system. Less than half of the administrators in California agreed that their subordinates focused more on achievement as a result of AYP, perhaps because California had an accountability system that predated NCLB, which had already shifted staff attention to student performance or perhaps because they thought, as previously noted, that the API metric was more credible.

AYP PRESSURE AND INSTRUMENTAL IMPROVEMENT

Responses to other survey items suggested that accountability led to improvements in the academic rigor of the curriculum, staff focus on student learning, students' focus on schoolwork, and, perhaps as a consequence, student learning of important knowledge and skills. Figure 12

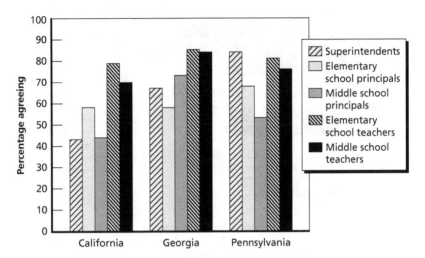

Figure 11. Educators Agreeing That Staff Were Focusing More on Improving Student Achievement as a Result of Pressure to Make AYP

Note: See Table B.14 in Appendix B for standard errors and additional information.

shows the percentage of superintendents, principals, and teachers reporting that the academic rigor of the curriculum changed for the better or changed for the worse as a result of the state's accountability system (the other results are displayed in Table B.15 in Appendix B). Majorities of superintendents and principals as well as about 40 percent of teachers in all three states reported that the academic rigor of the curriculum had changed for the better in the wake of state accountability. As one California elementary school teacher put it,

> I think standards are great. It keeps us on track as far as—you know something might be a really cute, fun project—but is there academic rigor in it, are they learning from it and how can we make it more rigorous for them so that they are learning?

Parents also seemed to notice the change: One parent in Georgia stated: "I think—as a parent— [NCLB is] extremely beneficial, because I see that the standards are not being lowered. Th e standards are actually—they're being raised, and children need to rise to that standard."

As a group, Pennsylvania teachers were less likely than others to report that academic rigor had changed for the better and more likely to report that it changed for the worse as a result

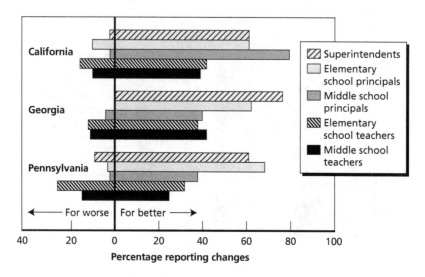

Figure 12. Educators Reporting Changes in the Academic Rigor of the Curriculum as a Result of the State's Accountability System

Note: See Table B.15 in Appendix B for standard errors and additional information.

of accountability. Teachers at one Pennsylvania case study school attributed the negative effect on rigor to the district's pacing guides and interim assessment systems, which they believed led to a lack of mastery of material. On one hand, teachers feel pressure to move on regardless of whether students have mastered content. For example, one teacher commented, "It says on the calendar, 'Today you're going to test cause and effect. Tomorrow, you're going to test double digit addition.' And you test, and you move on. And we do some remediation after we test, based on our test scores, and how our kids did, but I think the frustration is that a lot of us aren't sure that there is a lot of mastery." Several teachers described a phenomenon of coverage without mastery. In addition, some teachers at this school noted that the pace of the calendar was holding higher-level students back.

Two-thirds or more of superintendents and principals and 40 to 60 percent of teachers reported that staff focus on student learning had improved as a result of the accountability system (see Table B.15 in Appendix B). Case studies elaborated on this finding. For example, a middle school principal interviewed in Georgia believed that AYP forced teachers to examine their practices, identify weak areas, and improve their teaching strategies. Similarly, a middle school principal in Pennsylvania said accountability had led them to focus on curriculum and instruction:

> You've got to have a defined curriculum. It's caused us to look at the classroom methods, how you are teaching your classes and the idea of the constant lecture is not a good way to do it. You've got to have a variety of different things. All of that has been good.

Smaller percentages of principals and teachers reported changes for the better in terms of students' attention to their schoolwork; the majority reported no change. NCLB contains no direct incentives for students to change their behavior; they must be motivated to put more emphasis on schoolwork through the efforts of schools and communities. Yet, one-half to two-thirds of principals and about one-third of teachers reported changes for the better in student learning as a result of accountability. Teachers in Georgia were most likely to report a positive change in students' focus on schoolwork, perhaps because Georgia had adopted promotion testing for students (i.e., grades at which students must pass the state test to be promoted) so there were direct incentives for students. Teachers in Georgia case study schools mentioned this additional pressure, noting that it had both positive and negative effects on students.

In general, the perception that academic rigor, teachers' focus on student learning, and actual student learning had changed for the better was more prevalent among superintendents than principals and was more prevalent among principals than it was among teachers (see Table B.15 in Appendix B). Also, in almost every case, 10 percent or fewer of respondents reported that these features had changed for the worse as a result of the state's accountability system.

About half of the teachers reported that their own teaching practices had improved as a result of the state accountability system, while few reported a change for the worse (see Table B.16 in Appendix B). In addition, between 14 and 34 percent of teachers agreed that teachers' relationships with their students had changed for the better, while 5 to 14 percent reported that these relationships had changed for the worse. Georgia teachers were more likely to report changes for the better in both these aspects of teaching than Pennsylvania teachers, with California teachers in between.

Looking more broadly at curriculum, one-half to three-quarters of superintendents and principals reported that the pressure to make AYP had led to better coordination of the mathematics curriculum across grades (see Table B.17 in Appendix B). Similarly, 40 to 50 percent of superintendents and about one-third of principals reported improvements in coordination of the science curriculum across grade levels as a result of NCLB accountability pressures. Between 26 and 64 percent of principals also reported a change for the better in terms of the use of innovative curricular program and instructional approaches.

The vast majority of superintendents in all three states also reported that one impact of NCLB was higher expectations for subgroups of students: 98 percent of district leaders in Pennsylvania, 80 percent in California, and 78 percent in Georgia agreed or strongly agreed that they were increasing academic expectations for special education students or ELLs.[4]

Finally, between one-quarter and one-half of teachers reported that their principal's effectiveness as an instructional leader had improved as a result of accountability, while 19 percent or fewer reported that it had changed for the worse (see Table B.18 in Appendix B). Again, a higher percentage of Georgia teachers than Pennsylvania teachers reported positive changes, with California teacher reports falling in between. Reports from elementary school teachers and middle school teachers were comparable.

AYP PRESSURE AND MORALE

Three-quarters of superintendents and one-third or more of principals and teachers in all three states reported that staff morale had changed for the worse due to the state's accountability system (see Figure 13). Approximately 10 to 20 percent thought morale had changed for the better. (We asked superintendents about principals' morale and principals and teachers about school staff morale.) The most prevalent negative responses came from superintendents, who suggested that principals may be feeling the accountability pressures more strongly than teachers are. The reports of lower morale were most widespread in Pennsylvania, where majorities of teachers and principals reported that staff morale had changed for the worse and less than 10 percent reported a change for the better. Interestingly, across all three states, teachers in schools that made AYP were just as likely if not more likely as teachers in schools that did not make AYP to report this negative impact on morale.

One partial explanation for the reported decline in morale among teachers may be a disconnect between the approach to teaching being adopted in schools and teachers' own beliefs. Only 30 percent of teachers in Pennsylvania and 29 percent of teachers in California agreed that the state accountability system supported their personal approach to teaching. Slightly more than

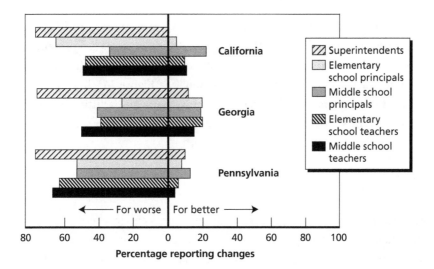

Figure 13. Educators Reporting Changes in Staff Morale as a Result of the State's Accountability System

Note: See Table B.16 in Appendix B for standard errors and additional information.

one-half of the teachers in Georgia (52 percent) reported that the accountability system in that state supported their personal approach to teaching. Thus, many teachers were experiencing some conflict between their own approach and the approach that their state was asking them to adopt as part of the NCLB initiatives. For example, one California teacher told us,

> I know that for teachers, it's this great big machinery that's hanging over your head. You know you've got to do this, you've got to do that, you've got to be this, you've got to be that, to the point where you sort of lose the focus of how about just exploring things for the kids.

PERCEIVED EFFECTS OF ACCOUNTABILITY SYSTEM ON STUDENTS

Despite concerns about morale, most principals and many teachers judged the overall effects of accountability to be positive. Principals were more positive than teachers about the overall impact of the accountability systems, and Georgia educators were more positive than educators in the other two states. More than half of principals in all three states (73 percent in California, 59 percent in Georgia, and 65 percent in Penn-sylvania) reported that the state accountability system had been beneficial for students in their school (see Figure 14). In comparison, approximately one-third of teachers in California and Pennsylvania and a little over half in Georgia agreed that, overall, the state's accountability system has benefited their students.

Summary

Results presented in this chapter suggest that administrators and teachers worked to implement SBA and that state accountability systems had positive effects, though some concerns remain.

- Looking first at broad trends across the three states, most educators were familiar with state content standards in mathematics, although science standards were not yet as well known. Furthermore, teachers found standards helpful for planning lessons, indicating that they were incorporating standards into regular instruction. However, about half of

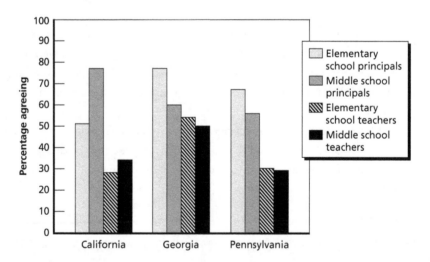

Figure 14. Teachers and Principals Agreeing That the State's Accountability System Has Benefited Students

Note: See Table B.17 in Appendix B for standard errors and additional information.

the teachers reported some mismatch between the standards and their curricula: The standards included too much content or omitted some important content or both.

- Teachers also reported a mismatch between state tests and their curricula. Most teachers reported that the state tests were not well aligned with their curriculum and were too difficult for their students. At the same time, most administrators and about half of the teachers thought that the assessments were a good indicator of student performance.

- Assessment results are used to make AYP determinations, and this process can be complicated. Yet, most administrators reported that they understood AYP rules, although about half the teachers found the overall accountability system to be difficult to understand. More importantly (in terms of accountability), the majority of elementary school principals thought that AYP status reflected their students' overall performance. However, the majority of middle school principals and superintendents did not share this opinion. Thus, there appear to be lingering concerns about school designation validity. Although administrators were optimistic that their districts and schools would meet their AYP targets for the following year, most did not believe they would meet AYP in five years, when the requirements would become more stringent. Widespread failure to meet targets coupled with doubts about the meaningfulness of AYP might pose a serious challenge for the accountability systems in the future.

- For the moment, however, the accountability systems appeared to have some positive effects on administrator and teacher behaviors. Reports indicated that schools were focusing more on student achievement, the curriculum was more rigorous, and student learning was improving. In addition, there was greater coordination of the curriculum across grades (potentially helping to address the alignment problems reported above), and teachers reported that principals' leadership had changed for the better. Despite these optimistic findings, some concerns remain. Both administrators and teachers reported declines in morale, and most teachers disagreed with the statement that the accountability system has benefited students (although most principals agreed).

There were few noteworthy differences between responses from elementary and middle schools, but there were some notable differences among the three states. In the area of science, the responses from the states reflected the varying status of science standards and assessments. Responses were more positive in Georgia, which had grade-level standards in place and was already testing science in grades three through eight. Most educators in Georgia were familiar with science standards, and about half thought that the assessments were a good measure of the standards (although about half thought that the tests were too difficult). Responses from teachers in the other states were consistent with the degree to which the state had implemented standards and assessments in science. There were also differences among the states in educators' opinions about accountability and their reports about its impact on curriculum and instruction. In some cases, Georgia educators were more positive than California or Pennsylvania educators. For example, Georgia teachers were more likely to agree that their state's accountability system had benefited students. We can only speculate about the reasons for these differences. Some cross-state differences probably stem from the choices made by states and districts in how to focus school improvement efforts, a topic we address in the next chapter.

Endnotes

1. At the time of the surveys, the Pennsylvania Academic Standards for Mathematics were being supplemented with the Pennsylvania Assessment Anchors and Eligible Content for Mathematics. The Georgia Quality Core Curriculum (QCC) for Mathematics (and for science) was being supplemented with the Georgia Performance Standards (GPS) for Mathematics (and for science). Three-quarters of the principals and two-thirds of the teachers in Georgia and Pennsylvania reported being familiar with the additional material, as well.
2. Superintendent responses to this item come from the first year of data collection (2003–2004) only.
3. Part of the difference in responses between teachers and administrators may have occurred because the question was phrased in a negative way for teachers whereas the administrator questions used positive wording.
4. Standard errors for these percentage estimates were 2, 9, and 12, respectively.

DISCUSSION QUESTIONS

1. Why is it important to value certain standards when dealing with education?
2. Discuss administrative results where AYP was met and why positive reviews were made on how valid the state exams were.
3. The state accountability system of Georgia had positive effects. What could be a positive concern?

Assessment and Evaluation

INTRODUCTION
BY KISHA R. CUNNINGHAM, PHD

"The illiterate of the 21st century will not be those who cannot read and write, but those who cannot learn, unlearn, and relearn."

—Alvin Toffler

Teachers are required to use different assessments to check the status of their students' learning. These assessments can be tests, quizzes, surveys, or anything that will check their continual grasp of concepts and learning. It is expected that they perform well on assessments. This is not always the case, as many students fall short on these assessments. Chapter 10 examines assessment, evaluation, and tools that promote deeper learning.

Classroom-Level Assessment: Aligning Pedagogical Practices to Enhance Student Learning

BY KATHRYNE DREZEK MCCONNELL AND PETER E. DOOLITTLE
HANDBOOK OF MEASUREMENT, ASSESSMENT, AND EVALUATION IN HIGHER EDUCATION

The classroom is an intuitive unit of analysis when it comes to measuring student learning. Ask a student or recent graduate about their most meaningful learning experience in college, and you will likely hear about a specific class or favorite professor. Inquire about faculty members' most successful teaching episodes, and they may regale you with tales of a memorable lecture, seminar, or in-class activity when students' eyes lit up with comprehension, or talk about how participation in an out-of-class experience, such as a service-learning project, showcased the students' abilities to put a course's theories into action. Given this pattern, classroom-level assessment holds the promise for most directly connecting the measurement of student learning outcomes to the actual teaching and learning process.

In *The Art and Science of Classroom Assessment*—aptly subtitled *The Missing Part of Pedagogy*—Susan Brookhart (1999) delineated the multiple purposes classroom assessment may serve, from giving students feedback in order to improve their learning and shape their future academic choices, to providing faculty with data to enhance their teaching and inform larger discussions of class content and curricula. She argued that "because important decisions are based on information derived from classroom assessments, it is imperative that the information be of high-quality: accurate, dependable, meaningful, and appropriate" (p. 1). This chapter aims to further the case for classroom-level assessment by making explicit its intimate connection to teaching and learning.

A caveat before we proceed: the term *classroom-level assessment*, while descriptive, might appear to exclude out-of-classroom learning opportunities from the discussion. In this chapter, we take a more expansive view of the "classroom" as encompassing any single purposeful, organized experience offered by the institution in which students engage in order to learn. Included in this broad interpretation are the learning opportunities empirically demonstrated to promote deeper learning and greater engagement among undergraduate students, collectively known as high-impact educational practices (Kuh, 2008). Such practices include first-year seminars and experiences, common intellectual experiences, learning communities, writing-intensive courses, collaborative assignments and projects, undergraduate research, diversity or global learning, service/community-based learning, internships, and capstone courses and projects (Kuh, 2008), which need not necessarily be housed within a traditional, credit-bearing course in order to capitalize upon classroom assessment techniques (Palomba & Banta, 1999). Furthermore, considering our expansive view of the classroom, "faculty" may include co-curricular professionals in either academic or student affairs units responsible for the teaching, learning, and assessment process for non-course based experiences like these high-impact practices. Our use of the terms *classroom* and *faculty* throughout the chapter should be understood to include such non-course based learning experiences and co-curricular professionals engaged in teaching and learning.

Foundational Principles of Classroom-Level Assessment

The assessment of student learning has been studied for decades and has included both broad examinations of assessment (e.g., Palomba & Banta, 1999; Walvoord, 2004) and specific recommendations for classroom assessment (e.g., Angelo & Cross, 1993; Huba & Freed, 2000). From this scholarship, four foundational principles have been constructed to frame further discussions.

Principle #1: Classroom assessment must be defined in terms of the improvement of student learning. A definition of classroom assessment must address its three components: process, evaluation, and purpose. First, the process of classroom assessment involves the gathering of information from multiple sources and perspectives and focuses on student performance; sources of information collected from teachers, peers, and professionals may include tests and quizzes, observations and writings, reflections on research and service, projects, and activities. Second, each of these sources yield information that must be evaluated and interpreted "in order to develop a deep understanding of what students know, understand, and can do with their knowledge as a result of their educational experiences" (Huba & Freed, 2000, p. 8). And, third, the purpose of classroom assessment is the improvement of student learning through modifications in the students' and the teachers' understanding, choice of strategy, or epistemological perspective. Therefore, if truly meant to improve student learning, classroom assessment needs to be a major component of sound pedagogical practice that explicitly addresses the instructional development process.

Principle #2: Classroom assessment is the purview of those most directly responsible for the construction of instructional environments—faculty. In their seminal book on classroom assessment, Angelo and Cross (1993) argue that, in contrast to programmatic and institutional assessment efforts, classroom assessment does not necessarily require a high level of training in psychometrics or the social science research methodologies utilized by assessment professionals. Instead, faculty, as arbiters of the instructional environment of a particular course and its larger place in the curriculum (e.g., instructional design, strategies, content, and assessment) are best suited to articulate appropriate learning outcomes, design opportunities for students to demonstrate mastery of these outcomes, evaluate student performance, and make any necessary changes based on their assessment of the overall success of the class in achieving the desired outcomes (see "Seven Basic Assumptions of Classroom Assessment", Angelo & Cross, 1993, pp. 7–11). The "active, continuous, and personal involvement" of faculty, and by extension their students, in the assessment of student learning is necessary "if assessment is ever to improve substantially the quality of student learning" (Angelo, 1994, p. 1).

Principle #3: Classroom assessment is implemented through the judicious use of course assignments. Valid course assignments are those that align directly with the course's learning outcomes, pedagogical practices, course content, and student characteristics. These assignments may be formative or sum-mative, qualitative or quantitative, and behavioral, cognitive, or affective. The nature of these assessments is limited only by the imagination of the instructor and the requirement that the assessment aligns with the course; thus, classroom assessments may include more traditional avenues (e.g., multiple-choice tests, true-false quizzes, written essays) or more alternative avenues (e.g., metacognitive reflections, service-learning projects, video essays). Each of these assignments provides information related to student learning and performance that may then be evaluated for the purpose of improving student learning.

Principle #4: Since classroom assessment is an essential element of institutional assessment, faculty members and institutional assessment administrators must collaborate. Faculty benefit from collaborating with others on campus who bring to bear empirically sound approaches to measuring student learning outcomes; moreover, those responsible for coordinating assessment at the college or university must seek out opportunities to collaborate with those on campus actively engaged in teaching and learning (Culver & Van Dyke, 2009). Faculty antipathy toward all things assessment is often taken as a truism, one reinforced by assessment efforts that emphasize accountability and accreditation over teaching and learning. Framing assessment efforts as teaching and learning efforts rather than accountability efforts helps to cultivate a culture of assessment on campuses (Suskie, 2004, p. 37). Culver and Van Dyke make the case that assessment conversations "invariably evolve into conversations about the importance of teaching" because "a stated strength of assessment is its ability to increase the transparency of teaching and learning and the educational experience" (p. 342).

Ultimately, Principles 1–4 focus on student learning through the construction of instructional environments containing embedded assignments that are used to improve both student learning and institutional effectiveness by *aligning* (a) course outcomes, content, and context; (b) students' prior knowledge and experience; (c) instructional strategies and resources; and (d) institutional improvement and accountability. It is this focus on alignment, often overlooked when considering assessment, that will serve as the backbone of this chapter. Specifically, we offer pragmatic strategies for connecting classroom assessment to the teaching and learning process through the appropriate alignment of pedagogical practices. We will address alignment issues concerning what, who, and how one teaches. Within each section, we will suggest strategies, tools, or technologies that facilitate the use of class activities and assignments—whatever the format—as measurable artifacts of learning.

The Importance of Alignment to Meaningful Classroom Assessment

In examining the essential role of alignment in creating an instructional environment focused on student learning, it is first necessary to express an assessment-based *mea culpa*. The assessment of student learning outcomes is often presented as a variation on the same cyclical theme, regardless of level (e.g., classroom, program, or institution). For the sake of clarity, we have intentionally simplified the visualization of the standard assessment cycle at Virginia Tech (see Figure 1). The standard cycle includes the following constituent parts: (a) identifying and articulating student learning outcomes, (b) gathering and analyzing information about the students' achievement of these outcomes, and (c) using the information that was gathered to improve student learning.

This simple description of the assessment cycle—with its arrows linking each step in a continuously spinning circle of activity—may promote conceptual understanding; however, we have found that it often belies the complexity that exists in the spaces between writing outcomes,

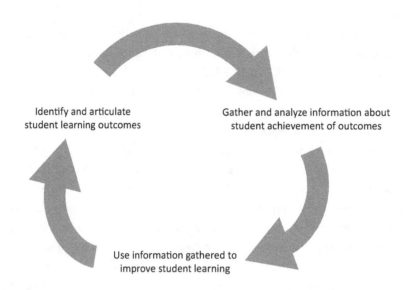

Figure 1. The assessment cycle

This figure is based on one developed by S. M. Culver & R. Van Dyke for use in workshops conducted by the Office of Academic Assessment (http://www.aap.vt.edu/index.html) at Virginia Polytechnic Institute and State University.

measuring student achievement, and making sense of the data. As professionals responsible for providing faculty development in the areas of outcomes assessment and effective pedagogy, we have been guilty of diluting its inherent complexity in order to help those with the least amount of assessment experience achieve the greatest possible level of understanding. In our estimation, less successful classroom-level initiatives suffer from a critical problem within the assessment cycle—a failure of alignment. While faculty may have learned that the measures they employ to assess student learning must correspond to the learning outcomes they have articulated, too often this is where efforts at alignment stop.

An illustrative example: Consider the well-respected academic department known for its high-quality classroom and program assessment work that decided to investigate first-year students' critical thinking skills. A group of faculty responsible for teaching multiple sections of the same first-year course decided to focus on student learning associated with critical thinking, using a course assignment—a persuasive essay—as the primary source of information related to student learning. The persuasive essay has been integrated into the course across multiple sections as a common assignment the previous semester. The faculty members spent a great deal of time developing a definition of critical thinking appropriate to their discipline and subsequently created a rubric that delineated the criteria against which students' essays would be judged that aligned with that definition. They followed appropriate procedures to establish inter-rater reliability and used multiple raters to judge essays sampled from across the previous semester's class sections. Once the scores were tallied, however, participating faculty were shocked to discover that the majority of the first-year students exhibited little to no critical thinking skills whatsoever.

Fortunately, this group's collective assessment wisdom prevented panic or angry denial from setting in; instead, they revisited their assessment process. They checked to see if their articulation of the student learning outcome (i.e., critical thinking) aligned with the measurement rubric that they had used. On the surface, their definition of critical thinking and the rubric for assessing students' critical thinking did indeed align; however, upon deeper investigation, they acknowledged several significant failures of alignment between the assignment and the rubric that provided an explanation for unexpectedly poor results. While the outcome and the criteria for assessing student achievement of the outcome aligned, they had failed to align other key elements in the teaching, learning, and assessment process. For example, they never considered whether the criteria for critical thinking that they had developed fitted the level of maturation and academic prowess of first-year college students. Additionally, there was a significant misalignment between the original directions and evaluation criteria for the persuasive essay and the subsequent rubric-based criteria for critical thinking. In other words, critical thinking as defined for the assessment process was neither communicated as a learning outcome to the students nor incorporated into the learning artifact used to judge students' skills and abilities. Faculty members were, in essence, using an assessment tool unrelated to the original assignment.

We believe that the missing links in this assessment of critical thinking were not measurement problems per se, but pedagogical problems that could have been mitigated through more sophisticated approaches to alignment. It is our contention that, for classroom assessment to generate meaningful information, all aspects of the classroom experience must align pedagogically. This alignment must take into consideration the course outcomes and content, the learners themselves, the instructional and performance contexts, and the pedagogical strategies used. In other words, assessment must be related to the *what*, *who*, and *how* of teaching and learning.

Outcomes and Content: What Are You Teaching?

Classroom assessment, as well as good pedagogical practice, "begins not with creating or implementing tests, assignments, or other assessment tools but by first deciding . . . what you want your students to learn" (Suskie, 2004, p. 73). Explicit articulation of learning outcomes is key to being successful in aligning the teaching, learning, and assessment processes. Well-crafted learning outcomes state the specific skills, abilities, knowledge, beliefs, attitudes, or dispositions that students are expected to develop as a result of completing a class. They should be ambitious, yet attainable by the students taking the course, and measurable. These outcomes answer the question, "To what end?" To what end are students writing papers, engaging in group work, or giving oral presentations before the class? Course syllabi often focus on the operational (e.g., due dates, grading policy, schedules) rather than aspirational components of a class (Doolittle & Siudzinski, 2010). Faculty sometimes confuse objectives and outcomes on a syllabus, labeling objectives like "By the end of this course, students will complete a research paper" or "By the end of the semester, students will participate in a group project" as learning outcomes. Such statements may delineate expected actions or behaviors of students, but they fail to specify the *ends* for which students are engaging in this work. Are students developing information literacy and research skills? Are the students enhancing their ability to work as part of a diverse team? Considering all the factors that learning outcomes must address, writing outcomes can be a daunting process. Fortunately, there are ample resources available to faculty to assist them in writing realistic learning outcomes. A simple Web search of peer academic departments at other institutions is a useful first stop in the search for discipline-specific learning outcomes. Disciplinary associations are another potential source for learning outcomes (Suskie, 2004). Regardless of whether they accredit programs in their field, professional associations as diverse as the American Political Science Association (APSA) and the Accreditation Board for Engineering and Technology (ABET) have begun to delineate program-level disciplinary learning outcomes that can be modified to fit individual courses. In addition to resources provided by academic associations, NASPA—Student Affairs Administrators in Higher Education—has a knowledge community dedicated to assessment, evaluation, and research that serves as a resource for those assessing co-curricular student learning (www.naspa.org/kc/saaer/default.cfm). Beyond discipline-specific or content-specific outcomes, the Association of American Colleges and Universities (AAC&U) has delineated 14 learning outcomes—from critical thinking and communication skills to ethical reasoning and integrative learning—deemed essential to undergraduate education. These Essential Learning

Outcomes were articulated and further refined for assessment purposes by two of the AAC&U's most well-regarded initiatives, the Liberal Education and America's Promise (LEAP) and the Valid Assessment of Learning in Undergraduate Education (VALUE) projects (AAC&U, 2007; Rhodes, 2010). Though originally conceived to facilitate program-level assessment, the language provided in AAC&U's Web resources and many publications is an excellent starting point for developing learning outcomes for classroom-level assessment.

A final tool of note is the commercially available "critical thinking wheel" developed by Michael L. Lujan from www.MentoringMinds.com. Based on both the original Bloom's Taxonomy (1956) and the revised version (Anderson & Krathwohl, 2001), the wheel provides faculty with succinct definitions for the six levels of the taxonomy (knowledge/remember, comprehension/understand, application/apply, analysis/analyze, evaluation/evaluate, and synthesis/create), along with a bank of "power words" and questioning prompts designed to elicit student learning and engagement at each level. More convenient than a thesaurus, this tool not only helps faculty craft language for learning outcomes, but helps facilitate the alignment between outcomes, content, and sequence by reminding faculty that, if they desire learning outcomes that require higher-order thinking like synthesis or evaluation, the content they address and the sequence in which they engage the material needs to correspond to the appropriate type of learning outcomes. In other words, faculty would be hard-pressed to see student learning at the upper levels of Bloom's taxonomy if the content and sequence of the course only demanded memorization of facts and figures.

It is likely that learning outcomes will not be perfect in their first iteration; they will probably require tweaking from one semester to the next, even for the same class. Rather than focusing on linguistic perfection, however, it is more important to ensure that the outcomes reflect the expected and desired end-result of the faculty member and align with the content addressed by the class and the sequencing of content for the students. If the faculty teaching the course cannot draw a direct connection between the expected learning outcomes and the content of the class, then one or both need to be revisited.

As stated previously, course content—which includes not only the relevant knowledge, skills, and attitudes, but also the assignments required of students—must align with the learning outcomes. Thinking back to the critical thinking example: student coursework did not demonstrate critical thinking because it was not a required component of the assignment given to them. If the assignment did not explicitly include critical thinking, one expects that explicit instruction related to the development of specific critical thinking skills was lacking as well. Some may dispute the necessity of explicit instruction in the belief that, by simply engaging in certain activities, students will naturally develop desired skills and abilities. While that may be true for some students, such an approach to teaching is inherently risky and begs the question of whether individual faculty members are needed as expert guides in the learning process. Explicit instruction is not synonymous with a didactic approach to teaching either. It can be accommodated within any number of active, learner-centered pedagogical practices. Whatever the content, it must reflect the articulated learning outcomes and be part of the intellectual framework for the student assignments if it is to be meaningful for classroom assessment.

Learners and Learner Characteristics: Who Are You Teaching?

The educational psychologist David Ausubel (1968) asserted, "the most important single factor influencing learning is what the learner already knows. Ascertain this and teach . . . accordingly" (p. 18). Yet often we develop outcomes, determine content, establish expectations, and begin to teach a class without first assessing the students' prior knowledge and discovering where our students are as learners. Aligning learning outcomes, content, and strategies is unworkable if the entire alignment is not in concert with the learner. Prior knowledge includes not only content knowledge specific to the class, but also the students' beliefs, experiences, study strategies, and non-academic knowledge. All of students' prior knowledge—academic and non-academic, declarative and procedural, cognitive and metacognitive—influences how and what they learn in a course.

Faculty members have several methods available to them for getting to know their students. On the first day of class, many faculty ask students to share a bit about themselves. Are they first-year students or seniors? Are they taking the class as a major requirement or an elective? Are they traditional in age (ages 18–24) or students returning to the classroom after accumulating a range of life experiences beyond schooling? What, if anything, do students already know about the content of the class? This type of sharing may take place as a class conversation with students introducing themselves to the professor and each other, or more formally by having students fill out an index card or submit information electronically through e-mail or a short online survey. These activities not only serve to foster a learner-centered environment in a classroom (Weimer, 2002), they can also provide an opportunity for collecting data about your students' prior knowledge that may be relevant to classroom assessment. By incorporating some more detailed questions about students' academic, co-curricular, and/or professional interests, their reasons for enrolling in the course, their initial comfort level with the material, and what they hope to gain from the class, faculty gain useful insights into what their students bring to the first day of class. This information can help faculty contextualize course material to make it relevant to the specific students enrolled in the class by tapping into the interests of the students. Aligning course content to this knowledge of the students promotes the acquisition, processing, and retention of course material, including the skills of problem-solving, critical thinking, and the transferral of knowledge.

Simply structuring opportunities for students to tell you about themselves is the easiest and least costly method of data collection in terms of faculty time, effort, and resources. That said, students' prior knowledge may be directly and perhaps more accurately assessed by administering a pre-test of the material you intend to cover in the course in order to determine what students already know. Pre-tests can also be used to evaluate students' mastery of content and skills considered prerequisites for the successful completion of the class. Pre-tests, like any assignment, can take a variety of forms (e.g., multiple choice tests, open-ended reflection prompts, peer-to-peer interviews). The format of the pre-test should make sense as part of the overall course design and material to be covered. Pre-test data can help faculty both identify specific strengths and deficiencies in students' prior knowledge and respond appropriately in the design and delivery of class content. For example, the information provided by a pre-test may lead faculty to present more in-depth treatment of a topic in which students in the class demonstrated the greatest deficiencies. Topics that the students have already mastered may receive lighter treatment in the course, thereby freeing up more time for alternate content to be introduced. Data generated by pre-tests may also help faculty to adjust their expectations and reframe appropriate learning outcomes for the class. This type of adjustment in response to deficiencies need not be seen as a lowering of standards or expectations, but a sensible recalibration of what is possible within the context of a single class.

Understanding one's students as learners is not limited to measuring class content knowledge alone. Other factors may impact the students' ability to achieve the desired learning outcomes of a class. Faculty can also explore cognitive and affective characteristics early on in order to shape the direction, depth, and design of the course. One example of a potentially useful diagnostic is the *Motivated Strategies for Learning Questionnaire*, or MSLQ (McKeachie, Pintrich, & Lin, 1985; Pintrich, McK-eachie, & Lin, 1987). The MSLQ was designed to assess motivation and use of learning strategies by college students (Pintrich, Smith, García, & McKeachie, 1991). Specifically designed for use at the course or class level (Duncan & McKeachie, 2005), this

81-item, self-report instrument is available at no cost in the literature and can be modified to fit the context of a specific course or subject-matter. Used as a self-diagnostic for students and in educational psychology research (Duncan & McKeachie, 2005), students rate statements from *not at all true of me* (1) to *very true of me* (7). Statements include, "If I don't understand the course material, it is because I didn't try hard enough," "I find it hard to stick to a study schedule," and "When a theory, interpretation, or conclusion is presented in the class or in the readings, I try to decide if there is good supporting evidence." Items like these form the basis of six subscales that measure the students' motivation, and nine subscales measuring students' use of learning strategies. Why should we worry about such characteristics of learners? It is the premise of the MSLQ that, in any course, the student is "an active processor of information whose beliefs and cognitions mediate important instructional input and task characteristics" (Duncan & McKeachie, 2005, p. 117). In other words, student motivation and approaches to studying effectively serve as filters for course content, helping to determine what and how students learn in any given class. Using the MSLQ, faculty can develop a profile of the students in a class and teach accordingly—playing to students' strengths, tapping into aspects of their motivation, even stretching students by explicitly offering content related to the employment of more sophisticated learning strategies.

Understanding the learners who make up a class is key to successful teaching and assessment, and provides a basis for pedagogical decisions about what and how one teaches. If instructional design is not contextualized to accommodate the actual students enrolled in the class, faculty may be setting students up to fail in the task of learning the course material. As in the case of the assessment of critical thinking described earlier, classroom assessment activities may note this failure, but the lack of alignment between characteristics of the learners and course outcomes, content, and instructional strategies may lead faculty to draw incorrect conclusions from the data. Incorrect conclusions make the improvement of student learning through assessment nearly impossible and defeat the purpose of classroom assessment.

Instructional Context and Strategies: How Are You Teaching?

As noted in the rationale for explaining the critical thinking assessment example and evident in Figure 1, alignment often focuses on outcomes and assessments. Focusing on alignment, however, requires that each instructional element be examined and carefully constructed. Two such elements, often overlooked, are instructional contexts and instructional strategy. Like learner characteristics, instructional contexts and strategies in the classroom serve to mediate and shape what students learn. Thus, faculty need to be as mindful of how they are teaching as they are of who and what they are teaching.

The importance of instructional contexts and instructional strategies, in relation to alignment, can be generalized within the *encoding-specificity principle* (Tulving, 1983). The encoding-specificity principle states that when, where, how, and why knowledge, skills, and attitudes are learned affects how those knowledge, skills, and attitudes will be recalled and applied. In short, this principle states that learning and performance are intricately related. The research on encoding specificity clearly indicates that, when the learning context and the performance context align, performance is enhanced (Godden & Baddeley, 1975; Ucros, 1989); moreover, when the cognitive processes employed during learning and the cognitive processes employed during performance align, performance is also enhanced (Lockhart, 2002; Tulving & Thompson, 1973). Thus, it is essential for faculty to proactively examine instructional contexts and strategies in order to align desired outcomes (learning) and learner assessments (performance).

Instructional contexts refer to the physical and affective states of the instructional environment. The physical states of instructional context include the general approach to instruction (e.g., face-to-face, online, hybrid) and the specific artifacts of instruction (e.g., location, instruments, technology). The affective states of instructional context include the physiological states (e.g., anxiety, pharmacology, stress) and emotional states (e.g., happy, sad, mood) of the learner. It has been demonstrated that misalignments in physical and emotional states between learning and performance episodes have an adverse impact on performance (see Eich, 1980; Overton, 1991, for reviews); for example, misalignments between learning and performance episodes in location (Gooden & Baddeley, 1975), instrumentation (Rosen, 2008), technology use (Doolittle & Mariano, 2008), alcohol use (Weissen-born & Duka, 2000), marijuana use (Darley, Tinklenberg, Roth, & Atkinson, 1974), nicotine use (Lowe, 1986), anxiety (Morissette, Spiegel, & Barlow, 2008), and mood (Teasdale & Russell, 1983) have all resulted in poorer performance.

Just as context has been demonstrated to be an important factor in instructional alignment, so have instructional strategies. Instructional strategies refer to the design of instructional activity and the cognitive processing that occurs during the instructional activity. It should be noted that the value of the designed instructional activity lies in its ability to motivate relevant cognitive processing, not in the mere completion of the activity; that is, a critical thinking activity is only beneficial if the learner actually thinks critically during the execution of the activity. This focus on cognitive processing plays a central role within the encoding-specificity principle in that the nature and depth of processing that occurs during learning affects the nature and degree of recall, application, and transfer of knowledge at the time of performance (Craik, 2002; Lockhart, 2002). Specifically, research into how "deeply" one processes information during a learning episode (Craik & Lockhart, 1972) and how congruent the cognitive processing is between the learning and performance episodes (Morris, Bransford, & Franks, 1977) has determined that both depth and congruence—*alignment*—are essential to learning and performance. Thus, unless instructional strategies, which motivate cognitive processing, are in alignment with both outcomes and assessments, significant learning and performance are not likely to occur.

Leveraging Technology for Classroom-Level Assessment

Alignment between what, who, and how one teaches is essential to ensuring the meaningfulness of the data collected as part of classroom-level assessment. That said, collecting information on all three dimensions of the alignment equation can be challenging. Fortunately, educational technologies exist that can support and promote a learner-centered approach to classroom-level assessment by helping faculty to collect evidence about what, who, and how they are teaching. What follows is a discussion of two very different—but equally useful—tools that hold great promise for gathering classroom assessment data.

CLICKERS

Student or personal response systems, colloquially known as "clickers," represent a technological innovation to the traditional in-class quiz that is particularly useful within larger classrooms (Boyle & Nichol, 2003; Mayer et al., 2009). Commercially available from a number of vendors, clickers conjure images of the gameshow *Jeopardy*, in which contestants furiously click a hand-held device in order to be the first to buzz in to answer the quiz show's questions. Rather than a tool for competition between students, however, clickers allow for mass student participation in large lecture-based courses. Clicker in hand, students respond electronically to questions posed by the instructor. Clickers have been used to monitor class attendance and more actively engage students in a given lecture; increasingly, clickers are also being recognized as a powerful tool for facilitating the assessment of student learning outcomes (Kolikant, Drane, & Calkins, 2010).

Specifically, clickers offer a more convenient and adaptable in-class tool for quizzing students on more facets of a course than either pen-and-paper or Web-based questionnaires, the former requiring greater faculty time to score and the latter requiring universal computer access for enrolled students.

While the clicker allows students anonymity when they respond to questions in class, each clicker also has an assigned number that can be linked to an individual student's responses and that generate data that faculty may use later for grading and classroom assessment purposes. Faculty can directly assess student comprehension of assigned readings or concepts presented in a previous class meeting by quizzing them with three or five short multiple-choice questions at the beginning of the lecture. Students use the clickers to respond to the questions and, instantaneously, the faculty member has quantitative data to analyze and use to improve student learning. Since the instructor and students can immediately see how the majority responded to each question, the faculty member has the ability to respond to student misunderstandings in real time, while the system quietly records individual responses in a database.

From an assessment perspective, faculty can conduct clicker quizzes over the course of a semester and track student responses in order to determine what content presented more of a challenge and what content was most easily mastered. Faculty can also create questionnaires that ask students questions related to the class's instructional context and strategies, thus providing feedback on a faculty's teaching at any point during the semester and not just summatively with the traditional course evaluation form presented to students at the end of the semester. While the power of the clicker to improve student learning is still not settled (Mayer et al, 2009; Martyn, 2007), scholars note the need for faculty to take into consideration the relationship between learner characteristics, the instructional context, and the content covered as they introduce clickers as a pedagogical practice (Kolikant, Drane, and Calkins, 2010), mirroring the case made in this chapter for assuring alignment between these elements in order to promote sound classroom assessment practices.

ePORTFOLIOS

Another popular technological innovation for classroom assessment is ePortfolio. When effectively integrated into a class, it can simultaneously serve as a powerful teaching tool and a useful mechanism for assessment (Cambridge, 2010). Traditionally associated with programs in the creative arts, architecture, and teacher education (Chen & Light, 2010; Lombardi, 2008), portfolios have been used to assess student learning for decades, either showcasing a student's best work or documenting a student's learning process (Lombardi, 2008). Portfolios also provide students with an important opportunity to demonstrate both their in-class learning and the non-course based learning that they experience through the co-curriculum. As an assessment tool, the portfolio "is unique insofar as it captures evidence of student learning over time—in multiple formats and contexts—documents practice, and includes a student's own reflection on his or her learning" (Chen & Light, 2010, p. 1). Today's electronic iteration of this tool—the "e" in ePortfolio—not only taps into contemporary students' comfort with technology, but facilitates the collection and archiving of extensive samples of student work without the inconvenience of the bulky paper versions of the past.

Like the clicker, ePortfolio technology is commercially available from multiple vendors, as well as from such open source communities as Sakai. In contrast to the clicker, which is best suited to gathering quantitative data quickly through short quizzes or student questionnaires, the ePortfolio serves to organize and archive more qualitative evidence of student learning. Best practice with ePortfolios emphasizes the student reflection component, or "folio thinking" (Chen & Mazlow, 2002), with the student engaging in meaning-making and the integration of class content with his or her own knowledge and perspective. Specifically, ePortfolios can be a beneficial technology for teaching and learning in any discipline as they help promote students' ability to: (a) integrate theory and practice; (b) be explicit in their focus on the reflective purpose of an ePortfolio; (c) provide authentic, direct links between assignments and classroom practice; and (d) think critically (Parks & Kajder, 2010, p. 220). Reflections most often take written form, but need not be limited to a traditional essay; ePortfolio systems can include a student's wiki or a blog. Increasingly, faculty ask students to leverage new technologies and include digital voice or video reflections such as video logs, or Vlogs (Parks & Kajder, 2010). Regardless of ePortfolio format, opportunities to reflect upon one's learning generate cognitive benefits for students, improving their ability to engage in metacognition and synthesis (Suskie, 2004).

While there is no magic button to press that will evaluate students' work for evidence of their attainment of the desired learning outcomes, rubrics serve as a popular tool for making sense of the collection of student work assembled within an ePortfolio (Chen & Light, 2010). Rubrics are scoring tools that provide specific performance criteria and well-defined levels of achievement for each criterion (Stevens & Levi, 2005). Rubrics have long been used to grade student assignments and have multiple pedagogical benefits, including providing timely feedback, preparing students to use detailed feedback, encouraging critical thinking, facilitating communication, and helping faculty refine their teaching skills (Stevens & Levi, 2005, pp. 17–25). Using rubrics, faculty have aligned learning outcomes with specific assignments and clearly communicated the expected performance criteria to students. The same rubrics used to grade student work on an individual basis can be used to generate data for classroom-level assessment.

Developing rubrics from scratch is a difficult task. Fortunately, many rubrics are available to serve as starting points for assessing a variety of learning outcomes. Perhaps the most comprehensive rubric development project to date, the aforementioned AAC&U VALUE project has generated 15 rubrics—one for each of the 14 original essential learning outcomes, plus one to evaluate students' reading skills (http://www.aacu.org/value/index.cfm). Developed by teams of faculty and co-curricular professionals at colleges and universities around the nation, the rubrics and accompanying documentation define and operationalize essential learning outcomes, present criteria and levels of performance for learning, and provide framing language and a glossary of terms. In fact, the VALUE project made explicit the connection between using ePortfolios as a powerful mechanism for student reflection and the VALUE rubrics as useful tools for translating those reflections into assessment data (Chen & Light, 2010). Though designed initially to further program-level assessment, faculty can tweak the VALUE rubrics in order to assess learning within a single class.

Clickers and ePortfolios—while not silver bullets for assessment efforts—represent two powerful tools for faculty to use. Once faculty become adept at using these technologies, clickers and ePortfolios can help simplify the logistics of capturing evidence of student learning in class and shift faculty's focus back to the intellectual aspects of assessment and the alignment of outcomes, content, and course sequence. Though on very different scales, both clickers and ePortfolios help promote learner-centeredness by providing students with a voice and an opportunity to demonstrate learning in a meaningful way, regardless of class size. Assessment professionals can help faculty use these scalable teaching and learning technologies for data collection and provide guidance on how to make sense of the data in order to improve their students' learning. Faculty and assessment professionals can work together to determine how best to use clickers and ePortfolios and how best to ensure that the tools support, rather than drive, the teaching and learning process.

Aligning Pedagogical Practice: How Do You Pull It All Together?

Other chapters as well as entire books exist that address how to design and implement assignments and activities with the potential to serve as powerful tools for classroom-level assessment (e.g., Angelo & Cross, 1993; Banta, Lund, Black, & Oblander, 1996; Huba & Freed, 2000; Palomba & Banta, 1999; Suskie, 2004). These resources provide a much more comprehensive treatment of the range of possible classroom-level assessment techniques than is possible here, and we recommend these works as excellent references for everyone embarking upon classroom-level assessment. What follows instead is an illustrative example of "pulling it all together" to achieve the desired alignment of pedagogical practices. Embedded in this discussion are descriptions of a number of assignments we have found to elicit particularly useful data for classroom-level assessment efforts.

Imagine for a moment that you are a faculty member designing the syllabus for the first required course in your major, and you have just completed a multi-day workshop on classroom-level assessment jointly sponsored by your institution's center for teaching and learning and academic assessment office. Your head is swimming with new information, so you pull out your workshop notes to help organize your thoughts. Down the left hand side of your notes you have drafted several possible learning goals for the class under the heading *The Students Will Be Able To*, including:

- Demonstrate disciplinary content knowledge;
- Improve oral communication skills; and
- Understand research.

Down the right hand side of your notes, you have listed several types of assignments you are considering for your class instead of the traditional objective test or final essay exam:

- 25-word summaries—clear, concise statements of the main idea of a chapter, lecture, or other instructional activity (Doolittle & Sherman, 2011).
- Video logs, or "Vlogs"—a video recording of a student orally reflecting upon what she had learned related to a specific lesson/aspect of a course, usually less formal in tone (Parks & Kajder, 2010).

- Oral explanations —a clear, coherently organized 10-minute, video-recorded scholarly oral presentation constructed to: (a) explain a concept to an audience that is unfamiliar with the concept; and (b) apply the addressed concept appropriately to a problem, situation, or issue in the discipline (Doolittle, 2011b).
- Extended abstracts—a short paper (no more than three pages) reflecting the student's understanding of an empirical article addressing the article's reference information, summary of the literature/background, research question(s)/purpose of the research, research design, results, implications, and any questions or concerns the student has about the reading (Doolittle, 2011a).

Finally, at the bottom of your notes, you have written "Clickers" and "ePortfolios," technologies that interest you but have not yet integrated into any of your courses. With the mantra "align, align, align" running through your head, you begin to organize and link the what, who and how of your course.

FIRST, CONTENT

Students in your course are expected to develop disciplinary content knowledge; a tall order to be sure, but easily contextualized after considering the introductory nature of the course. As you are responsible for establishing a basis for students' further academic study in the major, you decide to focus on a finite number of key concepts that students must master by the end of the semester related to disciplinary content. You also want students to improve their oral communication skills, and want students to have multiple opportunities for practicing these skills without sacrificing too much in-class time. Upon further reflection, you realize that your final goal to have students "understand research" is a bit vague. You decide that you first need to introduce students to research in your discipline, which means students will need to be exposed to empirical articles in peer-reviewed journals. As such, you revise your third learning outcome to focus more specifically on having students learn how to read and evaluate empirical articles.

Considering these outcomes, you now turn to your bank of potential assignments to see what might match up with what you want the students to learn. You recognize that the objective tests from years past may not foster the development of conceptual understanding as much as they provide evidence of the existence of such understanding after it is learned. As such, you decide to have students complete 25-word summaries (Doolittle & Sherman, 2011) of the readings you assign for each key disciplinary concept you address in the class. Not only will this help ensure students take the time to read out of class, but it will also help them learn to focus on the main idea or premise behind each key disciplinary concept. Through this very short format, you hope to be able identify both students' understanding and *mis*understanding of concepts, and track the development of students' disciplinary content knowledge across the semester.

From your list of assignments, two—the Vlog (Parks & Kajder, 2010) and the oral explanation (Doolittle, 2011b)—have potential as classroom assessment techniques for oral communication. While both may help students improve their presentation skills, you are interested in more formal modes of presentation versus the more free-form reflection of the Vlog format. Additionally, you believe the requirement that students not only define but apply disciplinary concepts through illustrative examples will also promote understanding of key disciplinary concepts. Also, the requirement that oral explanations be geared toward a novice (e.g., disciplinary non-expert) audience will force students to put the disciplinary concepts into their own words, rather simply parroting the language of their professor or their texts. Finally, you decide to require your students to complete the extended abstract (Doolittle, 2011a) as it seems to be the best way to structure what is often students' first experience with empirical research in your major.

NEXT, STUDENTS

You begin the process of connecting the course outcomes and content to your specific students by thinking through what you already know about them, and identifying what else you need to ascertain about them as learners. Based on their high school records, you know the students in your major are academically strong, highly motivated, and performance-oriented. While there are no pre-requisites for your course and the content you address is introductory, you recognize students do come in with prior knowledge related to the discipline, but that knowledge varies greatly from student to student and year to year. You decide to use a test from a previous semester as a short objective pre-test the first day of class to get a sense of what students know so you can better shape your teaching. Despite your students' strong academic backgrounds, over the years you have noticed that many seem to struggle with moving beyond issues of knowledge and comprehension to application of disciplinary concepts. You want to begin to prepare them for upper level work in the major by giving them a bit of practice applying disciplinary concepts, even at the introductory level. Thinking back, you decide that both the 25-word summary assignment and the oral explanation assignment will help push students toward thinking more critically about disciplinary concepts. You have also heard from alumni and employers that many graduates of your program struggle while attempting to communicate complex technical information to a lay audience, a shortcoming you will begin to address through the oral explanation assignment. Lastly, over the years you have noticed that many of your students double major in a wide range of disciplines, and this has always intrigued you. You decide to ask them to respond to a few open-ended questions at the end of the pre-test regarding their motivation for choosing this major, and how it connects to other fields and disciplines, so that you can begin to incorporate relevant examples from other disciplines that may hold some intrinsic interest for your students as you help to build their conceptual understanding.

LASTLY, INSTRUCTION

You turn your attention to the specific instructional context of and strategies used for your class. The class is taught in a traditional classroom that seats your 40 students comfortably. You plan to punctuate lecture-based instruction with more active learning strategies designed to get students to interact in class. Though the desks in the theater-style classroom are fixed to the floor, you intend to have students break into groups for both general discussion activities as well as peer learning groups responsible for components of the assignments delineated on the syllabus. For example, you decide to dedicate an entire class to discussing the extended abstract assignment. Knowing your students are just beginning to delve into the discipline through this course, you believe that they will benefit from some structured scaffolding for the assignment. As such, you decide to have students submit not one but two extended abstracts. The first will be on a common article assigned to all students in the class, one they will have the opportunity to dissect in class with their peers, using you as an expert resource. The second extended abstract students will complete independently on an article of their choice selected from among a list of peer-reviewed journals that you provide.

You decide students will complete three oral explanations, but allow them to choose which three disciplinary concepts from among all those covered in class to address in the assignment. This allows students to exercise some choice and autonomy within the class, while helping to alleviate some of your grading load. Furthermore, you plan to modify and use the AAC&U VALUE rubric for "oral communication" to provide feedback and score students' work for classroom assessment data. With only 40 students, you do not think the clicker will be a useful technology for the class, but you are intrigued by the possibilities for student reflection and assessment offered by the ePortfolio. You decide to have students submit their assignments through the ePortfolio, and will require them to reflect upon the development of their disciplinary content knowledge, oral communication skills, and ability to read and analyze empirical studies to help students synthesize a semester's worth of learning. You plan to reach out to your assessment and teaching and learning colleagues to secure their assistance in developing instructions for the new assignments that will frame them appropriately for the students and connect them to the course's learning outcomes so that the data generated can be used for classroom-level assessment.

Though certainly not exhaustive, the example provided demonstrates how one can meaningfully connect the course outcome, content—including assignments—students, and instructional strategies and context in the pedagogical alignment process. Outcomes, assignments, students, and instructional contexts and strategies will vary greatly; the process of alignment requires faculty to think purposefully and strategically about the best way to organize and link teaching, learning, and assessment activities at the classroom level.

Conclusion

In order to be effective and generate data that is valuable for a decision-making process, classroom assessment must exhibit alignment between the desired course outcomes, its content, the learners enrolled in the class, and the instructional contexts and strategies employed. Alignment of these pedagogical elements promotes the four foundational principles identified in this chapter. Faculty are empowered as the leaders of the process as they not only select which course assignments best represent student learning, but also as they work to align what they know about their students as learners, the instructional contexts they create, and the teaching strategies they employ. Furthermore, by grounding assessment work in the classroom as a unit of analysis, assessment professionals can create assessment opportunities that are connected to learning environments that have meaning to students and faculty. Alignment between what, who, and how we are teaching helps to ensure that classroom assessment works toward the improvement of student learning as its primary goal. By focusing on the alignment of what, who, and how we teach, faculty and their assessment professional partners will go a long way toward ensuring that the classroom is not only an intuitive unit of analysis for student learning, but—more importantly—a valid one.

References

Anderson, L. W., & Krathwohl, D. R. (Eds.). (2001). *A taxonomy for learning, teaching, and assessing: A revision of Bloom's Taxonomy of educational objectives.* New York, NY: Longman.

Angelo, T. A. (1994). Classroom assessment: Involving faculty and students where it matters most. *Assessment Update, 6* (4), p. 1–10.

Angelo, T. A., & Cross, K. P. (1993). *Classroom assessment techniques: A handbook for college teachers.* San Francisco, CA: Jossey-Bass.

Association of American Colleges and Universities. (2007). *College learning for the new global century.* Washington, DC: Author.

Ausubel, D. P. (1968). *Educational psychology: A cognitive view.* New York, NY: Holt, Rinehart & Winston.

Banta, T. W., Lund, J. P., Black, K. E., & Oblander, F. W. (1996). *Assessment in practice: Putting principles to work on college campuses.* San Francisco, CA: Jossey-Bass.

Bloom, B. (Ed.) (1956). *Taxonomy of educational objectives: The classification of educational goals (Handbook I: Cognitive Domain).* New York, NY: David McKay.

Boyle, J. T., & Nichol, D. J. (2003). Using classroom communication systems to increase interaction and discussion in large class settings. *Studies in Higher Education, 28,* 457–473.

Brookhart, S. M. (1999). *The art and science of classroom assessment: The missing part of pedagogy.* San Francisco, CA: Jossey-Bass.

Cambridge, D. (2010). *Eportfolios for lifelong learning and assessment.* San Francisco, CA: Jossey-Bass.

Chen, H., & Light, P. (2010). *Electronic portfolios and student success: Effectiveness, efficiency, and learning.* Washing-ton, DC: Association of American Colleges and Universities.

Chen, H. L., & Mazlow, C. (2002). Electronic learning portfolios and student affairs. *Net Results.* Retrieved April 6, 2009, from www.naspa.org/netresults/PrinterFriendly.cfm?ID=825 (NASPA membership required for access.)

Craik, F. M. I. (2002). Levels of processing: Past, present … and future? *Memory, 10*(5/6), 305–318.

Craik, F. M. I., & Lockhart, R. S. (1972). Levels of processing: A framework for memory research. *Journal of Verbal Learning and Verbal Behavior, 11,* 671–684.

Culver, S. M., & Van Dyke, R. (2009). Developing a receptive and faculty-focused environment for assessment. In C. Schreiner (Ed.), *Handbook of research on assessment technologies, methods, and applications in higher education* (pp. 337–347). Hershey, PA: Information Science Reference.

Darley, C. F., Tinklenberg, J. R., Roth, W. T., & Atkinson, R. C. (1997). The nature of storage deficits and state-dependent retrieval under marijuana, *Psychopharmacologia, 37*, 139–149.

Doolittle, P. E. (2011a). College teaching course materials: Extended abstracts. Blacksburg, VA: Author.

Doolittle, P. E. (2011b). College teaching course materials: Oral explanations. Blacksburg, VA: Author.

Doolittle, P. E., & Mariano, G. J. (2008). Working memory capacity and mobile multimedia learning environments: Is mobile learning from portable digital media players for everyone? *Journal of Educational Multimedia and Hypermedia, 17*(4), 511–530.

Doolittle, P. E., & Sherman, T. (2011). College teaching course materials: 25 word summaries. Blacksburg, VA: Authors.

Doolittle, P. E., & Siudzinski, R. (2010). Recommended syllabus components: What do higher education faculty include on their syllabi? *Journal on Excellence in College Teaching, 21*(3), 29–60.

Duncan, T. G., & McKeachie, W. J. (2005). The making of the Motivated Strategies for Learning Questionnaire. *Educational Psychologist, 40*, 117–128.

Eich, J. E. (1980). The cue-dependent nature of state-dependent retrieval. *Memory & Cognition, 8*, 157–173. Godden, D. R. & Baddeley, A. D. (1975). Context-dependent memory in two natural environments: On land and underwater. *British Journal of Psychology, 66*(3), 325–331.

Huba, M. E., & Freed, J. E. (2000). *Learner-centered assessment on college campuses: Shifting the focus from teaching to learning.* Boston, MA: Allyn & Bacon.

Kolikant, Y. B.-D., Drane, D., & Calkins, S. (2010). "Clickers" as Catalysts for Transformation of Teachers. *College Teaching, 58*(4), 127–135.

Kuh, G. D. (2008). *High-impact educational practices: What they are, who has access to them, and why they matter.* Washington, DC: Association of American Colleges and Universities.

Lockhart, R. S. (2002). Levels of processing, transfer-appropriate processing, and the concept of robust encoding. *Memory, 19*(5/6), 397–403.

Lombardi, J. (2008). To portfolio or not to portfolio. *College Teaching, 56*(1), 7–10.

Lowe, G. (1986). State-dependent learning effects with a combination of alcohol and nicotine. *Psychopharma-cology, 89*, 105–107.

Martyn, M. (2007). Clickers in the classroom: An active learning approach. *Educause Quarterly, 2*, 71–74.

Mayer, R. E., Stull, A., DeLeeuw, K., Almeroth, K., Bimber, B., Chun, D., . . . Zhang, H. (2009). Clickers in college classrooms: Fostering learning with questioning methods in large lecture classes. *Contemporary Educational Psychology, 34*(1), 51–57.

McKeachie, W. J., Pintrich, P. R., & Lin, Y.-G. (1985). Teaching learning strategies. *Educational Psychologist, 20*(3), 153–160.

Morissette, S. B., Spiegel, D. A., & Barlow, D. H. (2008). Combining exposure and pharmaco-therapy in the treatment of social anxiety disorder: A preliminary study of state dependent learning. *Journal of Psychopathology and Behavioral Assessment, 30*, 211–219.

Morris, C. D., Bransford, J. D., & Franks, J. J. (1977). Levels of processing versus transfer appro-priate processing. *Journal of Verbal Learning and Verbal Behavior, 16*, 519–533.

Palomba, C., & Banta, T. (1999). *Assessment essentials: Planning, implementing, and improving assessment in higher education.* San Francisco, CA: Jossey-Bass.

Parkes, K., & Kajder, S. (2010). Eliciting and assessing reflective practice: Best practices. *International Journal of Teaching and Learning in Higher Education, 22*(2), 218–228.

Pintrich, P. R., McKeachie, W. J., & Lin, Y. G. (1987). Teaching a course in learning to learn. *Teaching of Psychology, 14*, 81–86.

Pintrich, P. R., Smith, D. A. F., García, T., & McKeachie, W. J. (1991). *A manual for the use of the Motivated Strategies for Learning Questionnaire (MSLQ).* (Technical Report No. 91-B-004). Ann Arbor, MI: University of Michigan, National Center for Research to Improve Postsecondary Teaching and Learning. Retrieved from http://www.eric.ed.gov/ERICWebPortal/detail?accno=ED338122

Rhodes, T. L. (2010). *Assessing outcomes and improving achievement: Tips and tools for using rubrics.* Washington, DC: Association of American Colleges and Universities.

Rosen, K. R. (2008). The history of medical simulation. *Journal of Critical Care, 23*, 157–166.

Stevens, D. D., & Levi, A. J. (2005). *Introduction to rubrics: An assessment tool to save grading time, convey effective feedback and promote student learning.* Sterling, VA: Stylus.

Suskie, L. (2004). *Assessing student learning: A common sense guide.* Bolton, MA: Anker.

Teasdale, J. D., & Russell, M. L. (1983). Differential effects of induced mood on the recall of positive, negative and neutral words. *British Journal of Clinical Psychology, 22*, 163–171.

Tulving, E. (1983). *Elements of episodic memory.* Oxford, UK: Clarendon Press.

Tulving, E., & Thomson, D. M. (1973). Encoding specificity and retrieval processes in episodic memory.*Psychological Review, 80,* 352–373.

Ucros, C. G. (1989). Mood state-dependent memory: A meta-analysis. *Cognition and Emotion, 3,* 139–167.

Walvoord, B. E. (2004). *Assessment clear and simple: A practical guide for institutions, department, and general education.* San Francisco, CA: Jossey-Bass.

Weimer, M. G. (2002). *Learner-centered teaching: Five key changes to practice.* San Francisco, CA: Jossey-Bass.

Weissenborn, R., & Duka, T. (2000). State-dependent effects of alcohol on explicit memory: The role of semantic associations. *Psychopharmacology, 149,* 98–106.

Exceptionalities

INTRODUCTION
BY KISHA R. CUNNINGHAM, PHD

"The teacher must derive not only the capacity, but the desire, to observe natural phenomena. The teacher must understand and feel her position of observer: the activity must lie in the phenomenon."

—Maria Montessori

Society today has a way of teaching us through certain treatments on our differences, even when they haven't been categorized as exceptionalities. Exceptionalities can define students, from the gifted and talented learner to special education students. Each requires differences to be noted in how they are observed and evaluated. Chapter 11 examines exceptionalities and how society views and influences them. It also discusses how to identify exceptionalities and how to engage those students in the classroom.

Addressing Exceptional Learners

KEENYA G. MOSLEY, PHD
SCHOOL OF TEACHER EDUCATION
SAVANNAH STATE UNIVERSITY

Society's View of Exceptionalities

A lot of focus tends to be on what is normal—or better yet, *who* is normal. Merriam-Webster defines normal as usual or ordinary; not strange; mentally and physically healthy. However, being usual, ordinary, or not strange can be subjective. Individuals who are differently abled are quite capable of performing regular duties in such a way that is different from what some people may consider normal. For example, students who have physical limitations can access door entrances and multiple level floors through accommodations designed to address individuals with wheelchairs or those who utilize walking devices. According to Mercer & Mercer (2001), students who learn differently are able to meet learning objectives with specific learning support that specifically address their learning needs. Furthermore, the large majority who have agreed or determined that normal is something that a select group can identify with is exactly how the group being judged views their differences: as normal.

Parents of newborn babies often have desires for the newest member of the family. Parents typically express their interest in a specific gender, characteristics, and a positive health prognosis for their child. Is it not fair to say that a child who is breathing with a heartbeat is healthy? Some would say that child is alive, but other factors would determine if the child is healthy. Within the first few years after birth, children are provided various medical examinations as well as administered different vaccinations. As a result, some of the medical challenges children face can be detected in those early years while others may not be identified until later in their young lives. Upon learning a child is differently abled, parents become consumed with ensuring their child/children are provided the means to live a normal and healthy life (Hallahan, Kauffman & Pullen, 2011). However, many assume life will never be normal for individuals with different needs. On the contrary, parents of children who are differently abled have a contrasting view of what is healthy for their loved one when society has determined their differences make them less than perfect, good, or desired (Reid, 1996). Although these differences are called exceptionalities, they are viewed as characteristics so different that society have isolated and provided treatment not always desired by many.

Society's Influences on Exceptionalities

Exceptional learners have been placed in isolation in our education systems, homes, and public places. Society has decided that being different needs to be identified and then emphasized, which negates how we treat the owners of the exceptionality. Individuals with exceptionalities are quite capable or exceling at many tasks in spite of their differences. However, their differences are not widely celebrated, but instead separated, making the owners less enthusiastic about the differences until confronted with opposition to this view. The "Individuals with Disabilities Education Act (IDEA) born out of Public Law 94-142 ..." (Hallahan, Kauffman, & Pullen, 2011) has brought exceptionalities to a new place; making what was once misunderstood a phenomenon. Today, exceptional learners are celebrated for their abilities, provided proper services and support are made available (Council for Exceptional Children, 2015). Many are advocating for exceptional individuals rights and more services, exposing their successes and pushing for greater legislation to support their needs. Organizations such as the Council for Exceptional Children (CEC) have created a forum to address individuals with special needs. The forum provides a large network of individuals in every state who are dedicated to research in the field while enhancing the lives of individuals who are differently abled. More so, exceptional learners are celebrated now more than before for how they share many similarities, as opposed to focusing on what they do differently.

Children understand the world to be pure and simple until they are taught differently. Society has a way of teaching us through specific treatment about our differences, even when our differences have not been categorized as exceptionalities. Once students have been identified as having an exceptionality, society makes certain decisions that influence the treatment of these individuals and their relevance, or as someone believed to not be a contributing member of society. This treatment whether intended or not can affect how the exceptional learner perceives his/her abilities in the classroom and beyond (Slavin, 2012).

Identifying Exceptionalities

Exceptionalities range from special education to gifted and talented. However, both spectrums of exceptionality require these differences to be recognized, where a student is observed, identified, evaluated, and accommodated with services and support. There is a team of people responsible for identifying exceptionalities in students. In most cases, parents are normally the first to identify a difference in their child. The identification can be made based on their experience with the child's siblings, what they have observed in other children, or their instinct about how the child should respond or behave in certain situations. Additionally, the medical professional, educators, counselors, and educational administrators are all involved in the identification process of a child with an exceptionality. Sometimes, the order of those involved in the identification process can be different, but all parties have a vested interest in the development and well-being of the child. Identifying an exceptionality can be an emotional journey for parents. Being identified as different can carry a lot of challenges, which complicates the possibility of a normal life (Taylor, Hume, & Welsh, 2010). For instance, a child who has been identified as being exceptional can still enjoy the love, affection, and attention from parents, friends, and community members if the identification does not have an affiliation with being good or bad. Some exceptionality categories include learning/intellectual, mental, emotional, physical, health, or gifted and talented. In addition, teachers play a significant role with students who are exceptional.

Teachers serve as facilitators in the classroom. In working with students, teachers plan and prepare for each student's academic success in their classroom. As a part of the academic preparation for teachers, they are prepared to work with all students in a general education classroom with enough information to make referrals if students show signs of needing additional support. In some cases, a student may not have needs that warrant special education services but for those who do the teacher has to make daily decisions about the student's academic environment until further action is taken (Mercer & Mercer, 2001). Proper evaluation is essential for adequate preparation of a student who has special needs. However, until the student has been evaluated, the teacher is left to his/her own resources to assist the students. More often than not the teacher seeks alternatives in assisting the student meet the requirements of the objectives, lessons and assignments. Then the teacher is involved in the process by providing critical information for the evaluation (Hallahan, Kauffman & Pullen, 2011).

Meeting Exceptionalities in the Classroom

Students with exceptionalities need special services. These services can be found as part of a student's Individual Education Program, also known as an IEP (Slavin, 2012). These services are conditions to ensure the student is successful based on the goals that were established for him or her as they relate to the exceptionality identified. According to the National Center for Learning Disabilities (NCLD), when a child is considered for special education services, the following steps are involved in the process:

- Identification
- Evaluation
- Eligibility determination
- Qualification for services
- IEP meeting scheduled and held
- IEP established
- Services rendered
- Progress measured
- Meeting with parents and progress reported
- Review of IEP
- Reevaluation performed

The IEP is essential in the academic progress of students with special needs. However, a student with special needs will require an annual academic assessment based on progress made in the previous year. The IEP provides an in-depth look at requirements needed for the student's success. Specific skills are targeted for specific subjects and it is mandated that the teacher adheres to the accommodations for the student in which the IEP is designed for (Hallahan, Kauffman & Pullen, 2011).

In severe cases, students can be placed and taught in self-contained, special residential schools or even at home or hospitalized for their special needs (Mercer & Mercer, 2001). For gifted students, their gifts and talents must be nurtured in order for them to continue to develop properly into adulthood (Hallahan, Kauffman, & Pullen, 2011). These students are often ostracized for their exceptionality. This can cause a negative perception of being strangely intelligent, unexplainably smart, or even being referred to as a nerd. None of these descriptions reflects a positive side of being exceptional and having abilities that are extraordinary and warranting special treatment and services, causing one to embrace their differences. Therefore, it becomes the role of the teacher to establish the classroom environment that is conducive to the special abilities of all students. This can be accomplished through leadership roles in learning activities or group activities of mixed abilities that permit various levels for learners in completing assignments.

Employing Effective Teaching Practices

Educators must become creative in their teaching methodologies to address exceptionalities. In order to increase success for exceptional learners, educators must design assignments that meet the needs of the exceptionality. They must find ways to teach academic skills and expose students to various ways to be successful using identified accommodations (Milsom, 2006). Assessments of their teaching practices should include the following:

- Identification of the student's needs
- Determination of effective approaches to the needs identified
- Planning for educationally relevant and needs-specific approaches to instruction
- Monitoring of the student's progress
- Evaluation of their process and outcomes

Response to Intervention (RTI) is a multi-tiered approach in an early-identification process for students with exceptional needs. Although this process doesn't always lead to students being identified for special services, it does aid the educator in making instructional adaptions that can benefit students with and without exceptionalities (RTI Action Network, 2011). Making the appropriate adjustments early in the academic process can make a major difference for students needing special services. When modifications are made, educators must be consistent and reflective in their practice to determine when to make adjustments in their instructional strategies. Effective teaching practices can be reflected in students' progress based on their IEPs. Once the progress is noted, the educator can then build on those tasks while identifying when to make further adjustments based on skills needed for the various assignments. Educators can also employ modality instruction, taking into consideration cultural diversity and language differences that may also play a role in the challenges students face in the classroom, in addition to their exceptionality. Furthermore, including students with exceptionalities in a general education environment increases their potential for individual success (Bennett, 2009). For example, exceptional students with exposure to general education students observe appropriate decorum such as sitting in the desk, asking questions when allowed as well as behavior that is culturally acceptable in the classroom setting.

Creating Responsive Learning Environments

In order to create responsive environments, educators need to use effective communication to support the needs of exceptional students (Polloway & Smith, 2000). In doing so, they provide a bridge between the social and emotional gaps that can exist among exceptional students and their teachers. Communication being a major factor in responding to the needs of exceptional learners, it is unequivocally necessary to ensure all parties involved with supporting exceptional students are clear and lucid in their communication to include but not limited to the parents, teachers, counselors, principals and psychologist. Since early intervention increases the chances of success in children with emotional and behavior disorders, it is believed that these efforts serve as a preventive measure in assisting students with exceptionalities (Hallahan, Kauffman, & Pullen, 2011). Teachers can begin a dialogue with students by learning about their interests and/or hobbies. Learning activities that align to exceptional students' IEP goals and objectives can include those interests. Parents are a great resource for communicating the needs of exceptional students that may not have been observed in the classroom. This type of communication can ensure the connection between what happens at home and what should be occurring in school.

Addressing Exceptional Learners

When addressing exceptional learners, educators should provide a caring attitude that fosters a nurturing environment. Students with special needs are individuals with capabilities who learn and function independently with the appropriate accommodations. Some cases can be more severe than others, but each individual is capable of learning to the maximum of his or her potential. Some students require specific learning environments, while others can be successful in general classrooms with occasional to regular one-on-one assistance (Mercer & Mercer, 2001). Working with special-needs and gifted students requires educators to be flexible in their lesson plans and overall teaching strategies. Furthermore, unique assignments can unlock the true potential of exceptional students and the particular learning needs of that student. An educator who is open-minded and adaptable in the education process can be a great reward to an exceptional learner. It is through patience, thorough planning, and finding the right balance between the teacher and student that makes the experience exceptional for students who are differently abled.

DISCUSSION QUESTIONS

1. What influence does society have on the treatment of exceptional students?
2. Explain the challenges faced in the classroom when exceptional students are not accommodated.
3. What role do parents play in the learning process for exceptional students?
4. Describe the teacher's responsibility in the evaluation process.
5. When does it become necessary to implement an IEP?
6. When should RTI be implemented?
7. What non-academic personnel are involved in the evaluation process?
8. Describe ways to address exceptional learners.
9. Explain how society influences the perception of exceptional learners.
10. What is a critical element in responding to the needs of exceptional learners?

References

Bennett, S. (2009). Including Students with Exceptionalities. *What Works? Research Into Practice*, ISSN 913-1100. Retrieved from www.edu.gov.on.ca.

Council for Exceptional Students. (2015). Retrieved from www.cec.sped.org.

Hoover J. J., Klingner, J. K., Baca, L. M. & Patton, J. R. (2008). *Methods for Teaching Culturally and Linguistically Diverse Exceptional Learners*. Upper Saddle River, NJ: Pearson Education.

Hallahan, D. P., Kauffman, J. M. & Pullen, P. C. (2011). *Exceptional Learners: An Introduction to Special Education* (12th ed.). Boston: Allyn & Bacon.

Lyon, G. R. (1996). Learning Disabilities. *The Future of Children*, 6(1), pp. 54-76.

Mercer, C. D. & Mercer, A. R. (2001). *Teaching Students with Learning Problems* (6th ed.). Upper Saddle River, NJ: Prentice Hall.

Milsom, A. (2006). Creating Positive School Experiences for Students with Disabilities. *Professional School Counseling* 10(1), pp.66-72.

Polloway, E. A. & Smith, T.E.C. (2000). *Language Instruction for Students with Disabilities,* (2nd ed.). Denver, CO: Love.

Reid, R. (1996) Three faces of attention-deficit hyperactivity disorder. *Journal of Child and Family Studies,* 5(3), 249-265. Retrieved from EBSCOhost.

RTI Action Network. (2011). Retrieved from www.rtinetwork.org

Slavin, R. (2012). *Educational Psychology: Theory and Practice* (10th ed.). Upper Saddle River, NJ: Pearson Education.

Taylor, L., Hume, I. & Welsh, N. (2010). Labelling and Self-Esteem: The impact of using specific vs. generic labels. *Educational Psychology,* 30 (2), 191-202.

PART FIVE

Classroom Management in Teaching and Learning

Bullying

INTRODUCTION
BY KISHA R. CUNNINGHAM, PHD

"For too long, our society has shrugged off bullying by labeling it a 'rite of passage' and by asking students to simply 'get over it.' Those attitudes need to change. Every day, students are bullied into silence and are afraid to speak up. Let's break this silence and end school bullying."

—Linda Sanchez

Bullying is still an ongoing problem in school systems across the nation. When we think of bullying, we often think of a big kid taking someone's lunch money. Because of technological advances, bullying today has several faces. Verbal abuse, cyberbullying, and online shaming have led to suicides and violent retaliations. Chapter 12 examines the many facets of bullying as well as how to deal with it.

The Many Faces of Bullying

BY JEROME S. ALLENDER AND DONNA SCLAROW ALLENDER
ETHICS FOR THE YOUNG MIND: A GUIDE FOR TEACHERS AND PARENTS OF
CHILDREN BECOMING ADOLESCENTS

When bullying becomes news, we already know two things: (1) there has been an unattended history of bullying, and (2) inadequate attention has been paid to the context in which the bullying is occurring. When there was an outbreak of bullying in the junior high at the Project Learn School, we immediately knew that multiple social dynamics required examination, beginning with the roles that both children and adults play. Everyone involved, including bystanders—the community as a whole—needed to be held accountable.

But first, caveat emptor. Much of what has been written about bullying conveys something akin to a misplaced fascination with bullies and their victims. This is why it is news. However, we must not shy away from placing blame if it is clear where it belongs. It is essential to pinpoint responsibility—or, more accurately, irresponsibility. And it is essential to redress wrongs done to victims.

Bullying entails more than one big child threatening or acting violently with one or more smaller children. Someone who is blustering, quarrelsome, and overbearing and who badgers and intimidates weaker people is without doubt a bully. But intimidation has many forms: teasing, taunting, slandering, exclusion from a rightful place in the community, othering with racial and sexual slurs, and threats of all kinds are part of the problem. Anything meant to hurt or intimidate another, done by one person or many, counts. Sometimes this is true even when intent is missing. And most often, what looks simply like bullying is more complex than it appears (Allender and Allender 2001; Coloroso 2008; Rigby 2008; Sullivan 2000).

There are many ways to hurt others, but the predominant tactic of the bully is to instill fear. There are other ways to infringe on the rights of others, but fear puts young people on a worse footing for learning how to get along. Clear leadership is necessary to alleviate the fear and to guide the victim and the bully to an equitable reconciliation. This chapter aims to provide teachers with sufficient information to create a curriculum that ameliorates and helps prevent bullying.

An Outbreak of Bullying

At dinner one evening, early in the school year, Donna talked about an outbreak of bullying in the junior high at the Project Learn School. This was shocking. We appreciated that there was no physical violence involved. But this small school, with fewer than one hundred students in any given year, is known in Philadelphia, around the country, and in other places in the world for a humanistic philosophy that captures the hearts of the parents who run the school, the teachers who are delighted for the opportunity to teach there, and the children who love coming

to school every morning. Though problems found in schools everywhere arise there, an "outbreak of bullying" was unusual and disturbing.

Project Learn is a community where members of all ages are expected to work together cooperatively. The breakdown of respect is everyone's business. No one is excused—including the two of us. Among the founders of Project Learn forty years ago, Donna, along with Fran Fox and Nancy Bailey, were teacher-parents who led this parent-cooperative K–8 school. Our children graduated, and then came the grandchildren. Donna retired in the early 1990s to become a psychotherapist, but in recent years, with our own grandson enrolled, she began helping out as an assistant

Text Box 12.1 I Was a Bully

"Gestalt Theory for Teachers" by Jerome S. Allender and Donna Sclarow Allender (2001)

Soon after we were married (in 1958), Jerry told me one night at dinner about how his teaching had gone that day. Two junior high students had been so incorrigible, he had pressed one against the blackboard with his knee and squeezed the other in a tight grip. I imagine he glared at them. For him, there was a truce. But not for me. Out of my depths came, "Don't you ever do that again." Sometimes a strong authoritative voice makes a difference. Leadership comes in many forms. "OK," Jerry said, and then we talked.

We learned a lot that evening. A fine theoretician and a good enough teacher, Jerry had a lot to discover about practice. His anger came from his own fear that he was unable to control these boys. Forty years later, we had more confidence and a better understanding: "An awareness of fears makes them less figural, gives teachers more creative self-control, and supports an openness for contact" (Allender and Allender 2001, 135). Contact means a connection with another individual that engenders change in both people.

Were you ever a bully?

Were you ever bullied?

Maybe not. Find someone who was—it's not hard.

Deep knowledge of bullying begins with these experiences.

teacher and serving on the administrative committee. Jerry did staff development and worked as an assistant teacher.

We witnessed none of the instances. We were bystanders with a history of active involvement. Teachers talked of slurs about homosexuality, text messages with inappropriate sexual content ostensibly sent by a child who didn't send them, and an assigned Halloween paper for English that detailed how each teacher in the school would die. This all began with a misguided democratic process for choosing who would stay in which bunk during an overnight end-of-school camping trip, one that would have left one child to sleep in a cabin alone. It was nice to know that a classmate stepped up and changed his choice. Both were ostracized and pelted with homophobic slurs by the biggest bully.

For some time before the bullying incident, we had been witnessing ruder behavior between children and adults than we had seen before. We worried about a lack of the structure that young people should be expected to live and learn within. There needs to be leeway, but not so loose that critical behaviors are excused. We talked. Donna met with the junior high teachers, Jerry met with one of the teachers who despaired most, and out of these talks we planned an ethics course for the two junior high classes.

Taking Charge

Jerry met with the junior high students to introduce the course. They didn't object to the plan, except for the fact that the ethics class would meet during the special times during the week reserved for a promised course based on their own interests. It was to be a special kind of "elective." They complained bitterly about this. "Why couldn't one of our regular courses be canceled to make time?" Jerry calmly and firmly told them that they were not required to like it, just to participate and do the work. The students challenged his ethics, because the course had arbitrarily been imposed in a school where the child's needs are professed to come first. "You temporarily lost your right to choose."

They are good kids. They saw that there was a job to be done—to learn more about ethics and to put into practice a more complete understanding. They recognized that this was not punishment and that these were reasonable consequences. We recognize the gift of such a beginning. Most kids are not bad. A lot has to do with their sense of safety and their needs being met sufficiently. There has to be a level of respect for each individual; no one expects to get everything he or she wants. We are thankful that daily classroom behavior at Project Learn has never come close to the terrors we know others experience. We don't know exactly what we would do in extreme circumstances. But what happened at the school is how most kinds of bullying begin. We must not wait until it gets worse. This is more than bad enough.

Ken Rigby, in his book *Children and Bullying* (2008), distinguishes between nonmalign and malign bullying. Sometimes kids horse around. Sometimes there can be a middle ground. And then there is outright bullying. He lists what we have to watch out for: the use of greater, aggressive power; when kids want to hurt someone or do; when threats are made; when actions taken are not provoked in any way; and when there are feelings of oppression or perpetrators announce how they enjoy domination. Gestures, words, and physical force all count. It is a good list—not perfect, but helpful.

At Project Learn, the teachers differed in their perceptions of the severity of the problem of the bullying. Ironically, the children agreed on the value of an ethics course, if not with what it would replace in the weekly schedule. Our call was based on what had transpired over several months—coupled with incidences of overt malign bullying.

The two of us asked a single question: Were teachers and students primarily working together or against each other? Against, we agreed, and decided that a community intervention was needed. No one was entirely happy with our offer to teach an ethics course, but on different levels, all agreed to cooperate. Good enough.

Leadership

The story must include the actions of someone in charge (Shulman 2004). A response must not be hindered by waiting for full exploration of the circumstances. The story must immediately be interrupted and changed. Guided by intuitive knowledge, someone has to respond in a way that demonstrates firm and responsive leadership. It would be great if a child were to do this. But there has to be a public display of concern, clarity, and belief that consequences will follow.

The tension between reflection and action is not resolvable. This tension underlies the meaning of leadership. An environment that implicitly condones bullying, or even the appearance of bullying that turns out to be benign, is lined with potholes at best; it is a minefield at worst. It is not as if adults have all the answers. At stake is the ability to cope with ambiguity and the competence to model for young people what they need to learn. A story of bullying can look less like bad behavior, with successful leadership, and more like an opportunity. Bullying can be turned around in the process of the confrontation. What looks like bullying doesn't have to harden into a sensational event that becomes an item of bad news for a newspaper.

There are the elements of successful confrontation: employing the power of authority, speaking out strongly, using techniques of mediation, and transforming injustices into a community problem (Swearer, Espelage, and Napolitano 2009). Sometimes it is most useful for adults to work individually with bullies with the aim of substantially changing their behavior. A bully might be capable of and ready for this transformation. With sensitivity, victims can become smarter and more confident in handling difficulties that confront them. There are possibilities for helping a victim and a bully to resolve injustice on their own. There is always more to learn that can broaden our understanding of what has happened and what might be done to address and redress the situation. Importantly, a community that learns to resolve problems on its own, not necessarily with adult involvement, can best bring all of this together. In the process, everyone has something at stake and something to learn.

A sense of the larger context must take into account that adult life is rife with unethical behavior (Lichtenberg 1990; Lichtenberg, van Beusekom, and Gibbons 1997). This is a significant component of the model the adult world sets for children. Only blinders could possibly let us forget that a large part of life includes cruelty. Every child on earth inherits this legacy. From time immemorial, humans, more than any other species, have treated each other in cruel ways. Nothing we do can hide this from young people. Every day, much of what we speak about, publish in the newspaper, show on television, and post online teaches the young that expectations of them differ from what they read, hear, and see. Demanding that children be holier than we are—less tolerant of their mistakes than our own—will likely exacerbate problems and diminish the desire to demonstrate cooperative social behavior. We have to be humbled by the big picture and not expect more of children than we can model in our own lives.

The smart strategy for adults, teachers, parents, and anyone else is to interweave kindness with the firm requirement for acceptable behavior. The details of this smaller local context can become a story of change that leads to an improved life for the community. As problems get more complex, the goal is to simplify them and get on with the productive and fun part of being a community. We paint this kind of rosy picture because it represents the best of our experience and the hope we maintain for the lives of children growing up. Contrary to imagining that zero tolerance and holding to hard lines are the best ways to teach children ethics, we see the real world as more nuanced for people of all ages. There even exist national and international rights for children that support the opportunity to learn how to live ethically (Wall 2010). In the long run, an open attitude is in their interest and ours. Standards of cooperative social behavior can be maintained, along with a mutual awareness of room for negotiating differences of opinion.

The Anti-bullying Handbook by Keith Sullivan argues how often studies "tend to generalize about the components of the bullying dynamic, to make judgments about the individuals involved, and to deal more with the components [roles] than the whole system" (2000, 4). In contrast, his "perspective recognizes that bullying is a serious problem, and it aims to work hard to find solutions that improve everyone's chances, both the bully and the bullied" (Sullivan 2000, 4). In her book *The Bully, the Bullied, and the Bystander* (2008), Barbara Coloroso uses the roles of the bully, the bullied, and the bystander "to identify only a role that a child is performing at that moment, in that one scene of one act in a longer play. It is not intended to define or permanently label a child. The goal is to gain a clearer understanding of these roles and how the interactions involved in such role playing . . . are not healthy, not normal, and certainly not necessary and in fact can be devastating to children playing any of the three characters" (4–5).

We found children and adults who remembered both bullying and being bullied, as well as bystanders who today carry regrets for not having acted to protect a friend. There are children who have acted and succeeded in helping. There are also those who feel otherwise about what happened. A sense of agency can change and turn around the meaning of a bad event, because it is within the power of the players to complain, to change, and to learn how to get along better.

However much we discuss the big picture and its nuances, however much we need to develop methods for coping with bullying and the introduction of antibullying programs, something must be done first to immediately stop the behavior. This is the zero tolerance. Acts of bullying must stop now! Then the consequences for the bully or the bullies are subject to discussion, and these discussions must eschew zero tolerance so that workable solutions can be found. The bully must suffer consequences, if possible without exclusion from the community.

Discussions about preventing bullying, problem solving, and exploring and demanding responsibility must take place in an emotional and intellectual climate where the bullying has first been stopped. This is where adults have to take charge or find someone with the social or physical power to halt the hurtful actions. The most powerful response in the long run is found in the use of words that command. Earning this power is what becoming a responsible adult is about in an important way. This is how we model thinking about and practicing ethics.

Text Box 12.2 How Little We Know

Bullying Prevention and Intervention by Susan Swearer, Dorothy Espelage, and Scott Napolitano (2009)

Swearer, Espelage, and Napolitano ask, "Is there a need for another book about bullying?" They answer that despite a huge increase in writing and research about bullying over the last thirty years, "we still don't have very good solutions about what to do about bullying, how to stop bullying, or more realistically, how to reduce bullying behavior among school-age children" (ix).

In response to their worries, they have written a thorough report that can serve as a starting point in a wide range of contexts. They cover children of all ages and pay attention to the individual, peer group, school, family, and community. The report heightens awareness of social conditions that aggravate day-to-day relationships and includes a variety of case studies, strategies for developing policy, attention to legal issues, and realistic plans to reduce bullying. It also considers the impact of technology on bullying and ways to think about evaluation. The report is an excellent resource that itself points to many other resources.

Swearer, Espelage, and Napolitano clarify that for all they have learned, each unique sphere within which bullying appears requires careful attention. With their knowledge and so many other resources that have served us in our work, we have created, and continue to create, ever-new possibilities for guiding the children, teachers, and parents we encounter.

Bullying 101

As teachers, we have to help our children figure out strategies for responding creatively (Ludwig 2010; Palacio 2012). Are there ways to undermine bullying before it escalates dangerously? What might be options for confronting a bully? What can one do as an observer of bullying? How might a bully learn to have and apply some self-awareness?

The introduction to the unit on bullying was a lecture based on a shortened version of this discussion so far. Students were invited to share their thoughts, reactions, and creative possibilities. As a counterpoint, Susan Deutsch, a parent at Project Learn and a movement educator, was asked to introduce a bullying exercise where talking was ruled out. During this exercise, no conversation and no touching were allowed.

The activity began with students in pairs seated face to face, not talking, not touching, with their feet on the floor. With only the upper part of the body, they were to move their hands, arms, torso, and heads—using body language to communicate—with a special emphasis on using bold and creative facial expressions as much as possible. They were even allowed to threaten physical violence. The task was to create a problem between the two of them and resolve it in the space of five minutes. Students were drawn in by the craziness of the task and its obvious poignancy. It was funny and instructive. The students' experiences demonstrated how creative behaviors could possibly de-escalate tensions. We all knew they were not sure bets, but our minds were opened to searching for such moves.

A high-spirited and insightful discussion followed the experience. The students understood that this was not what would happen in real life, but the activity elevated the talk to a thoughtful ethical conversation about possibilities that they hadn't thought of before this class. They realized the difference between actions that created (or expressed) fear and those that created contact. These possibilities were within their grasp.

Role-Playing

Role-playing also has the potential for shifting children's minds (Allender 2001). There are various ways to set it up. Situations can be based on personal experience, where students have the opportunity to replay what didn't work—to say what they wish they had said. They can be based on stories that children have heard or on readings that stimulate experimental possibilities. And they can be creative adventures into behaviors that at first seem outside their repertoire. Children can experiment with expressing anger in a controlled way, or they might not use words at all and instead stare into the aggressor's eyes, reflecting a hidden power. This creativity brings a larger range of behaviors into view.

Asking children to act out different ways of reacting in a situation with a bully evokes a variety of feelings. These can be queried and coached. Playing the victim, a student is instructed to acquiesce to the bully who says, "Give me your lunch money." How does that feel? In a replay, students might engage the bully in talk. "What's up? Are you hungry?" "No money for lunch?" What is that like? Again, students can imagine deceiving a bully. "I've got money in my locker." The intention is to move the bully to a place where the victim can get help. Another is to resist. "I am going to tell my parents or my teacher if I give you money. Even if you threaten me or hurt me, someone still is going to know." We believe this will give students a sense of strength.

Another set of alternatives for role-playing can respond to the more typical ways in which girls bully. One can search for a variety of responses to statements intended to humiliate, such as, "Your skirt is really ugly." Without the context in which behaviors like these actually unfold, responses in the role-playing can border on or become a farce. Yet all of this play, as it can be called, does loosen up potentially useful responses in the event of a real confrontation. Subtleties abound. Maybe the confrontation is nothing more than "That skirt's out of style," and yet the comment hurts. Certainly, all the little plays are grist for serious conversation.

Bottom line, protecting oneself from violence is key. It's a good thing to measure the risk involved. Children who are studying karate have a better shot. It is helpful that their discipline comes with a strong emphasis on avoiding violence. It gets toughest when a bully is only out to hurt someone. Truth be told, there might not be a role-playing situation to anticipate the worst; there might be opportunities for learning, though, in replaying a bad experience with both a hardened bully and a badly hurt victim. Sometimes the scenario is too hard to imagine, and role-playing is not the answer.

Art

A mix of writing and drawing opens another world to the deepening of understanding; this mode of expression can teach us how to communicate peacefully and powerfully. However much one might mistakenly disregard art as less than central to children's learning, it has been poignantly significant in our teaching. One activity began with the question, What is a bully? We used the answers to construct a web of words on a four-by-eight-foot poster. The web is a kind of picture that represents a thorough definition, even if not derived from academic considerations, of a bully. Then, each student illustrated his or her contribution to the web on a smaller poster.

Shayma offered, "Closed in." She drew, with a set of marking pens, a colorful young man with outrageous hair, not quite realistic but in your face. His chest exposed his heart in bright red—trapped behind a black iron grate that one might find on the window of a prison cell. Though Shayma recognized that the drawing accurately conveyed what she knew and felt, the primitive artwork embarrassed her. It was not up to the standards she had developed with her art teacher. A discussion of the valued role of primitive artists in the art world convinced her to allow us to show it here.

What Can Parents Do?

When trouble surfaces and a child says something to an adult outside school, and the school is not doing enough, what options empower us as adults and empower children? Make time and think creatively. Begin by listening empathetically, not only to a victim or a bystander but even to a culprit. Hear the story, enter into it, and become a character who changes its course. Optimally, confronting bullying will turn into a conversation that responds to the needs and wants of everyone involved—in the classroom, in the home, or in the street. The reality is often hard and painful (Coloroso 2008; Rigby 2008; Sullivan 2000).

An effective response has to break a lot of mind-sets. A relevant question is, How do we change negative behaviors into those that nurture positive social behavior? We hope to find allies among other parents, teachers, administrators, and our children's friends. Our friend, Kathe Telingator, did take action as a parent when she discovered that her daughter was the target of cyberbullying. She contacted the parents of the bullies and organized a meeting of all the children and their parents. Together they sorted out what had happened, sincere apologies were made, and the bullying behavior stopped (Telingator 2007).

It doesn't always happen that way. Sometimes potential friends turn out to be enemies. Start by being more connected with your youngsters. Have regular connections with other parents. Be helpful to teachers. Gather allies. Generate conversation. Amass some political power. On a larger scale, it is like making peace instead of war. Work together, and hope for the best.

Activities involving movement exercises, role-playing, and art could take place, with a bit of pushiness and humor, at home. From the example above, we see that it may not be so difficult to bring together children in a setting outside school. This can help level the playing ground and get at problems without

Figure 1. Draw a Bully

Text Box 12.3 Two Stories

Confessions of a Former Bully by Trudy Ludwig (2010)
Wonder by R. J. Palacio (2012)

In *Confessions*, Katie the bully narrates. In *Wonder*, August is bullied, and often he is the narrator. Sometimes it is Jack, his best friend, who betrays him, or Summer, a steadfast, trusted friend, or Olivia, or Justin.

Katie tells her story like a curriculum. Roles are clarified: there are the bully, teachers, parents, bystanders, and a counselor. Katie changes. Big values are emphasized: caring, friendship, listening, and practical advice.

Wonder is dramatic. At one point, August says, "Rat boy. Freak. Freddy Krueger. E.T. Gross-out. Lizard face. Mutant. I know the names they call me. I've been in enough playgrounds to know kids can be mean. I know, I know, I know" (Palacio 2012, 79). August's face is badly deformed. Children and adults recoil. Be vulnerable, and the story will touch your heart.

As August and Jack whisper about a mix of slug juice and dog pee to spray at bullies, the teacher reprimands them for disturbing the class. Then Jack whispers, "Are you always going to look this way, August? I mean, can't you get plastic surgery or something?" August smiles and points to his face. "Hello? This is after plastic surgery!" Jack claps his hand over his forehead and starts laughing hysterically. "Dude, you should sue your doctor!" (64).

Older children can teach *Confessions* to younger ones. *Wonder* can connect children with adults. Both books are winners.

the complication of having teachers about. In a bullying incident, remember that it is valuable for all children involved to be gathered together to talk. Assess whether you have the skills to lead such a discussion. Be aware that ineffective leadership can make things worse.

When each child tells her or his take on what happened, it might be possible to establish a sense of responsibility. The adult needs to confront publicly the child who has been bullying for the sake of the bullied child or children. This establishes a path for potentially making amends. Bullying most often happens in secret with threats of revenge for disclosure. The gathering of the children with a responsible adult undermines the secrecy.

The advantage of working with children before they are fully adolescent is that they are likely to be less guarded and less entrenched in new habits that are forming. There may be little spaces where vulnerability makes for more openness. As adults, we need to rise to the personal challenge by matching our own vulnerability with theirs. As always, this in no way means we give up our proper authority as adults. We just don't let our self-importance make us think we are smarter than we really are. It's a matter of modeling openness as a way of connecting. If a problem turns out not to be bullying, likely something else is troublesome. Breakdowns in the social fabric need to be addressed. Social environments of every kind are like mobiles with their rods, wires, and artistic objects; when one part moves, everything else in the system moves.

THE KARATE KID

Sometimes children younger than junior high age have thoughtful answers to questions too. Donna asked Dylan, our grandson, then nine, "What makes someone a bully?" He answered, "They have mean parents." This is not the only answer, but it strikes at the heart.

Another time, he and I were talking on the way to his karate class. We were comparing the two kinds of sensei portrayed in the movie *The Karate Kid*. It was clear to us that his own sensei was all about "peace and friendship," as they say regularly in each lesson, not winning by cheating.

"What about bullying?" I asked. He was clear: "First, I would try to find an adult. If I didn't, I'd think about my chances, and then I would deck him." I have to admit, I felt proud. As a grandfather, I was clear. As a teacher and once a parent of more than one nine-year-old, I still have some thinking to do. My pride aside, I also know that violence does not resolve violence.

DISCUSSION QUESTIONS

1. What are some ways to prevent bullying in school systems today?
2. What is the role of teachers in dealing with and preventing bullying?
3. What is the parents' role in dealing with and preventing bullying?

CHAPTER 13

Violence and Zero Tolerance

INTRODUCTION
BY KISHA R. CUNNINGHAM, PHD

"Nothing good ever comes from violence."

—Martin Luther

School Violence

BY ANNE GREGORY AND ELISE CAPPELLA

HANDBOOK OF SCHOOL COUNSELING

Introduction

In the past 10 years, many communities were shaken by well-publicized shootings that resulted in multiple student deaths. Discussions about the problem of school violence increased. Fears of students as "super predators" were on the rise. While the events were certainly tragic, heightened concerns have not been grounded in the reality of declining violent crime in school settings over the past decade (National Center for Education Statistics [NCES], 2004). The chances of serious violent crime occurring in school are statistically quite low. During the school year 1999–2000, 16 of the 2,124 homicide victims who were school-aged children occurred in the school setting (NCES).

While violent crime may be rare, low-level aggression in schools is not uncommon. Thus, this chapter addresses prevalent behavior, to which many school staff are faced with on a daily basis. We define *aggression* as an intent or action to harm through verbal or physical force. A broad definition of aggression allows for a consideration of how delinquency in adolescents and young adults unfolds. For a group of serious offenders, aggressive actions begin early in life, gain momentum across the school years, and take on multiple and increasingly serious forms (Loeber, Burke, Lahey, Winters, & Zera, 2000). A preventive approach is called for in light of the escalation of aggressive behaviors across the school years.

Violence and Aggression in Schools

Rates of violence vary by the characteristics of the school. Violent crimes, including those against teachers, are more likely to happen in high schools than elementary or middle schools (NCES, 2004). Overall, urban schools have higher rates of vio lence than suburban and rural communities (NCES). Teachers in urban schools are more likely to be victims than those teaching in rural or suburban schools (NCES). Negative gang activities are particularly common in city schools, such that, in 1999, one third of city schools reported this as a problem (NCES, 1999). While urban schools have a particular confluence of poverty and violence, some evidence is suggestive that rural schools also have contextually specific patterns of violence. In 2003, students from rural areas, compared with urban and suburban areas, reported higher rates of bullying (NCES, 2004). A more in-depth study of three rural schools with students in grades three to eight also found high rates of bullying (Dulmus, Theriot, & Sowers, 2004). With greater residential stability and smaller populations in rural settings (Osgood & Chambers, 2003), perhaps rural students are more likely to attend years of schooling as a stable cohort leaving little room for reputations as victims or bullies to shift across the years.

Even with the variation in rates of violence across schools, there has been an overall downward trend in violence. A recent report issued by the U.S. Department of Education declared that school-based violent crimes against adolescents from 1992 to 2002 dropped by half (NCES, 2004). By 2003, 13% of high school students reported having been in a fight on school grounds—down from 16% in 2003. Similarly, students' reports of carrying weapons to school within the past month dropped from 12% to 6%.

Serious violent crime might be an infrequent occurrence, but low-level aggression appears to be more prevalent. The 1999 national school survey on crime and safety found that almost 30% of schools reported frequent bullying and almost 20% of schools reported frequent student acts of disrespect for teachers (NCES, 1999). In 2000, 3 million suspensions and 97,000 expulsions were reported. In some states, such as Delaware and South Carolina, between 14% and 19% of the male students had been suspended (NCES, 2000). A study of 1992–1993 data from a random sample of disciplined 6th through 12th graders in 67 Florida school districts found that 47% of in- and out-of-school suspensions, corporal punishment, and expulsions were given for disruptive behavior in class, defiance of authority, or disrespectful behavior. The next largest offense, fighting, accounted for 9.5% of the disciplinary consequences (Florida Department of Education [DOE], 1995). The frequency of suspensions and expulsions and the reasons for such sanctions suggest that schools and counselors are faced with a serious problem of aggressive behavior.

Current Developments

"Get tough approach." Sociopolitical and historical developments affect how school violence and aggression is conceptualized and addressed. School counselors may have to navigate the tensions between a punishment orientation and a support orientation toward aggressive behavior.

In response to increased public fear of school violence, many schools have taken an increasingly punitive, "get tough" approach. In the 1990s, zero tolerance policies were implemented across the states with a federal mandate passed in 1994, which called for a minimum 1-year expulsion for bringing a weapon to school (Gun-Free Schools Act). Critics of such policies argue that a mandate for expulsions does not take into account extenuating or contextual circumstances, which results in superfluous and overly punitive sanctions. The Harvard Civil Rights Project (2000) compiled case examples of children suspended or expelled for carrying sparklers, a Boy Scout pocketknife, a toenail clipper, and a toy ax for Halloween. They argued that punitive approaches to discipline may differentially affect African American and Latino students, who are overrepresented in suspensions and expulsions. In 1999, a survey showed that in grades 7 to 12, 20% of Hispanic students, 35% of African American students, and 15% of White students had ever been suspended or expelled (NCES, 2003). In light of the increasing numbers of students, particularly African American students, being suspended or expelled and with heightened fears of school violence, educational researchers (e.g., Devine, 1996) have documented the prison-like school environments that rely on video surveillance, metal detectors, and harsh sanctions.

Recognition of the complex needs of students provides a counterweight to the popularity of increased surveillance and harsh sanctions to reduce school violence. Some states and school districts are acknowledging the importance of addressing social and emotional develop ment in school (Shriver & Weissberg, 2005), with states in every region across the United States man-dating the teaching of social and emotional development alongside academic learning (National Association of State Boards of Education, 2005). In the mid-1990s, federal school safety funds spawned preventive interventions. Antibul-lying programs (e.g., Olweus, 1999), conflict mediation interventions (Johnson & Johnson, 1996), and on-campus suspension programs have become widespread. Concerns about the punitive approach of zero tolerance policies have gener-ated new programs, such as a systematic school-based threat assessment to lower overreaction to a *perception* of student threat (Cornell et al., 2004). This may be helpful in addressing the problem of crimi-nalizing youth, particularly youth of color.

Research-based interventions. Increasingly, school coun-selors may be asked to show the results of their interventions with evidence of decreased aggressive behavior and increased prosocial behavior. At the same time, counsel-ors may be faced with the pressure to continue programs that are familiar to school staff, despite a lack of rigorous evidence that suggests they are helping. Currently, there is a federal push toward the use of evidence-based practice in schools, as seen in the establishment of the Institute for Education Sciences whose mission is to understand the effectiveness of education programs and improve academic achievement and access to educational opportunities for students. Efficacy and effectiveness research that uti-lizes experimental designs—randomly assigning schools, classrooms, or students to interventions—is prioritized in funding.

Faced with the pressure to show results, counselors may be called upon to ask critical questions of the research on interventions. This chapter aims to provide counselors with a knowledge base from which to raise such questions. It begins with an outline of the current research on the predictors of child and adolescent aggression. A theoretical understanding of how environmental factors interact with individual student characteristics to predict aggressive behavior will help counselors target risk factors specific to developmental stage and identify the reasons the intervention may help reduce aggressive behavior. With its focus on the prevention of serious school violence, the chapter then describes a range of research-based interventions. Several of the interventions focus on supporting students already identified as aggressive; others involve supporting individuals in the students' lives, namely teachers, parents, and peers. Also described are multilevel programs that intervene systematically across a range of settings and with different types of participants. Finally, the chapter provides counselors with concrete strategies to consider when selecting and developing interventions.

Aggressive Behavior in School
INDIVIDUAL STUDENT CHARACTERISTICS

Individual students differ in many ways—in their approach to social situations, in their struggles or successes with academic schoolwork, and in the ways their bodies are made up. These differences have been hypothesized to contribute to the behaviors students are likely to use in school. Researchers have isolated each of these individual characteristics to examine their relative contribution to the development and use of overt aggression in school settings. However, none of these factors operates separately from one another or outside the contexts of family, school, and community. We will outline the theory and evidence for the biological, cognitive, and academic differences associated with overt aggression, while keeping in mind the complex and interactive pathways through which aggression develops in students in school.

Biological factors. Possible biological contributors to overt aggression include genetic inheritance, temperament differences, neurotransmitter effects, and hormonal influences. This literature has been reviewed thoroughly elsewhere and will be summarized only briefly here (see Berman, Kavoussi, & Coccaro, 1997; Brain & Susman, 1997; Coie & Dodge, 1998).

Behavior-geneticists have postulated that a *tendency* toward aggressive behavior can be inherited, but aggressive behavior itself cannot (see Coie & Dodge, 1998). For example, biological genotypes passed down from parent to child may affect physiological processes, which influence a child's behavioral or cognitive style, which then interact with environmental factors to lead to behaviors. Twin and adoption studies from around the world support the theory. Genetic factors influence individual characteristics such as impulsivity and reactivity, and these may lead to a *disposition* toward externalizing behavior (e.g., Matheny, 1989), but there appears to be no relationship between genes and *actual* physical aggression or violence (Mednick, Gabrielli, & Hutchings, 1984; Raine, 1993).

Children's temperament has been hypothesized to relate to future behavior, in part through the stability of personality characteristics and in part through an interaction with environmental influences such as relationships with parents and peers. Early demonstrations of emotional regulation—for example, ability to inhibit inappropriate behaviors, cope with arousal, and organize for goal-oriented behavior when experiencing strong emotions—have been thought critical to children's later use of aggression (Dishion & Patterson, 1997). Research has demonstrated qualified support for these hypotheses: tem peramental characteristics in preschool are stable over time (Bates, Bayles, Bennett, Ridge, & Brown, 1991), but a "difficult" temperament does not necessarily predict future delinquency (Caspi, Henry, McGee, Moffitt, & Silva, 1995; Earls & Jung, 1987). In addition, associations between early temperament and later aggression tend to be weak, confounded by use of maternal reports, and linked with parent—child attachment (Bates, Maslin, & Frankel, 1985) and the home environment (Earls & Jung). That said, *connections* between disposition and cognition (discussed next) may help to explain *some* children's aggressive responses to environmental stimuli (Dodge, 1991).

The framework for understanding the role of neurotransmitters in aggressive behavior is Gray's (1987) theory of brain function; in particular, his description of the behavioral facilitation and behavioral inhibition systems within the brain that launch or halt interactions with the environment. Although engagement or inhibition of activity is related to multiple neurotransmitters, concentration of *serotonin* metabolites in the cerebrospinal fluid is critical, such that low concentrations may lead to an increase in stress reactivity (Berman et al., 1997; Spoont,

1992). Studies of serotonin in children indicate that lower concentrations are, in fact, related to conduct disorder in adolescents (Pliszka, Rogeness, Renner, Sherman, & Broussard, 1988) and disruptive behavior disorders among children (Kruesi et al., 1992). However, investigators and theorists postulate a reciprocal transaction, such that the levels of neurotransmitters not only are genetically determined, but also respond to early environmental influences and socialization (see Rogeness, Javors, & Pliszka, 1992).

Finally, testosterone has been suggested to play an orga-nizing or activating role in physically aggressive behavior, the former occurring during the perinatal period and the latter occurring during puberty (Brain & Susman, 1997). Study results have been conflicting (Inoff-Germain et al., 1988; Olweus, Mattsson, Schalling, & Low, 1988; Susman et al., 1987), and Archer (1994) attempted to explain the differences in theory and research in a dynamic model that posits early gender differences due to hormonally driven activity levels that lead boys and girls toward different play subcultures with a different need for physical aggression. These subcultures then interact with broader societal influences, individual temperaments, and baseline levels of testosterone. Later in adolescence, when testosterone levels are rising, a child's established patterns of aggression interact with hormones to produce more or less aggression, which fuels future testosterone if the aggression induces feelings of dominance and success. Although not empirically tested, this model is a compelling explanation of the role of testosterone as an *interacting* agent across time influencing children's aggression.

Social cognition. Beyond biological factors, individuals bring particular cognitive styles to social interactions (Dishion & Patterson, 1997). One of the most studied cognitive theories, social information processing, suggests that a social situation triggers a succession of cognitive and emotional operations that first represent, then interpret, the situation (Dodge & Schwartz, 1997). When these operations are effective and accurate, the social behavior is adaptive; when the operations are biased, the behavior is often maladaptive. A set of conscious and unconscious steps are hypothesized to occur repeatedly; however, children may develop patterns that simplify the steps and create relatively stable behavioral responses to situations over time (Huesmann, 1988; Schneider, 1991).

Researchers have used correlational studies with hypothetical social scenarios to examine the links between different aspects of the social cognitive processing model and children's aggressive behavior. For the most part, these studies have verified the connection between social information processing skills—for example, attending to and recalling social cues, requesting additional information, interpreting others' intentions, generating responses to the situation—and aggressive behavior (see Dodge & Frame, 1982; Dodge, Pettit, McClaskey, & Brown, 1986; Guerra & Slaby, 1989; Quiggle, Garber, Panak, & Dodge, 1992; Slaby & Guerra, 1988; Spivak & Shure, 1980). In addition, several studies indicate that aggressive children evaluate aggressive actions in a more positive light than do their nonaggressive peers (Guerra & Slaby), value the results of aggression more highly (Boldizar, Perry, & Perry, 1989), and have positive efficacy beliefs for the use of aggression (Crick & Dodge, 1989). However, the defi-cits in social information processing have been shown to differ based on the child's use of a particular subtype of aggression, in par-ticular, reactive aggression (retaliation based in anger and frustration) and proactive aggression (unprovoked and goal-directed behavior; Dodge & Coie, 1987). Use of reactive aggression has been linked with hostile attributional biases, whereas use of proactive aggression is related to positive evaluations of aggressive behaviors and instrumental goals for social situations (Crick & Dodge, 1996).

Academic skills. An extensive body of research demonstrates a strong relationship between externalizing behavior problems and academic underachievement, with comorbidity up to 50% when including a broad set of externalizing syndromes and indications of school fail-ure (Barkley, Fischer, Edelbrock, & Smallish, 1990; Hinshaw, 1992). A recent meta-analysis demonstrated that students with emotional behavior disorders (EBD) performed significantly worse across settings and subject areas than their nondiagnosed peers (R. Reid, Gonzalez, Nordness, Trout, & Epstein, 2004). A meta-analysis of the link between underachievement and delinquency revealed that academic difficulties were related to the onset, level, frequency, and persistence of delinquency in both males and females (Maguin & Loeber, 1996). Early in schooling, the link can be explained primarily by inattention and hyperactivity (Frick et al., 1991); in adolescence, the association grows increasingly robust (Hinshaw).

Paths between underachievement and delinquency have been hypothesized to be unidirec-tional (problems in one domain cause problems in the other; e.g., Hirs-chi, 1969; Rutter & Giller, 1983) or cyclical (bidirectional influences between domains). Deficits in academic skills may lead to aggressive behavior through task frustration, lack of motivation, low academic self-concept, and school disengagement (see Arnold et al., 1999). For example, continued academic problems may produce a negative association with schooling, thus increasing the likelihood of hostility, disobedience, and aggression in school (McEvoy & Welker, 2000). High levels of exter-nalizing, on the other hand, have been thought to lead to academic problems through reduced time on task related to social skills deficits, inattention, or noncompliance (Arnold et al., 1999; McEvoy & Welker). Acting out in the classroom may help an underperforming student avoid academic tasks or may distract the teacher from the student's academic problems (Carr, Taylor, & Robinson, 1991).

Despite methodological problems, studies have provided some evidence of predictive, if not causal, pathways between academic skills and aggression. A subset of children with reading failure but no behavior problems in childhood has been shown to grow into adolescents with antisocial tendencies (Maughan, Gray, & Rutter, 1985). A delay in the onset of reading relates to later externalizing problems (e.g., McGee & Share, 1988), and aggression in middle childhood predicts low academic achievement in adulthood after controlling for early intelligence test scores (Huesmann & Eron, 1986). Finally, through such mechanisms as speech delay, familial adversity, and neurodevel-opmental immaturity (e.g., Howlin & Rutter, 1987; Richman, Stevenson, & Graham, 1982; Tallal, Dukette, & Curtiss, 1989), aggression and learning are linked even before a child begins school (see Hinshaw, 1992). This provides additional support that the connection between aggression and achievement is complex and multifaceted, beginning early in development and interacting across contexts and domains to reinforce the relationship.

Final issues. The research summarized briefly provides theory and evidence of individual student factors within the biological, social—cognitive, and academic domains related to the use of aggression in schools. This extensive body of research has limitations. First, male students tend to be overrepresented and female students underrepresented in the study samples. This leads to a lack of complete knowledge about possible gender differences in the development of aggression, particularly as related to hormonal influences (e.g., Inoff-Germain et al., 1988; Susman et al., 1987) and links to achievement. A second and related limitation is that studies define aggression as overt or direct, rather than covert or indirect. An emerging area of interest among researchers and school personnel alike is the development and use of subtle forms of aggression in schools (see Crick, 1996; Underwood, 2003), but the pathways toward the use of social or relational aggression are less understood (see Kaukianinen et al., 1999; Xie, Swift, Cairns, & Cairns, 2002). Finally, although researchers have isolated these areas to study the development of aggression, most models are dynamic and comprehensive, linking biological, social–cognitive, and academic domains, as well as the multiple social contexts in which students live, work, and play.

Characteristics of the Social Context

Children traverse multiple social contexts as they develop across their years of schooling. The primacy of the home context shifts as they enter schooling and interact with peers. They encounter new adults in classrooms and are asked to abide by the structures of the daily school routines and rules. They draw on multiple communities outside of school and the home while being exposed to mass media and entertainment. In interaction with a child's attitudes and attributes, these social contexts provide key experiences that shape development, including acerbating or escalating aggressive or violent behavior. A review of the literature suggests that family, peers, neighborhoods, mass media, schools, and classrooms should be considered when examining the ecology of the developing child.

Family. Children can transfer negative behaviors learned with family members into the school setting (e.g., Earls, 1981). Family research has identified two areas of the home context that have been linked to children's and adolescents' aggressive and violent behavior: (a) parent—child interactions and (b) parenting practices. Focused on the patterned exchanges between parents and their children, Patterson and his colleagues have investigated a social interactional theory of the development of aggressive behavior (J. B. Reid, Patterson, & Snyder, 2002). Drawing on principles of operant conditioning, they have documented coercive cycles between parents and young children whereby a child's whining or tantrums are rewarded when a parent gives in to the child's request. These interlocking reinforcement patterns repeat themselves daily and children learn that aggressive behavior ushers in positive results. Inves tigators have also studied how children learn from adult modeling of aggression (Bandura, 1973), especially related to parents' discipline practices. From a social learning theory perspective, if an adult expresses anger by physically punishing the child, then the child may learn to do the same. Longitudinal studies have linked physical punishment to later aggression and delinquency (Eron, Huesmann, & Zelli, 1991; Farrington & Hawkins, 1991). Supervision during adolescence has also been studied as a parenting practice linked to aggression. Providing structure and adult guidance for adolescents has been posited as developmentally appropriate, even during a stage when needs for autonomy increase (Connell, 1990). Several longitudinal studies have shown that a lack of parent supervision is one of the strongest predictors of adolescent conduct disorder and delinquency (e.g., Hawkins, Herrenkohl, & Farrington, 1998).

Increasingly, scholars recognize that parenting prac-tices should be considered within cultural context (Baum-rind, 1991). Generalizations about the detrimental effects of particular parenting practices can be hard to make when for some families in certain neighborhood contexts such practices may be protective. For instance, Lansford, Deater-Deckard, Dodge, Bates, and Pettit (2004) showed that for African Americans, unlike for White adolescents, physical discipline such as spanking was linked to lower externalizing problems. A similar cultural specificity may be considered when examining the role of parental supervision and adolescent aggression. While some evidence shows that authoritative parenting may be linked to positive outcomes for adolescents from diverse groups (Gregory & Weinstein, 2004), culturally specific findings (Gonzales, Cauce, & Friedman, 1996; Steinberg, Lamborn, & Darling, 1994) present a more complex picture. Strict monitoring was adaptive for adolescents living in high-crime neigh-borhoods (Eamon, 2001; Gonzales et al., 1996), suggestive of the benefits of an authoritarian parenting style.

Peers. As early as 1939, Sutherland theorized that peers make up a crucial social context in which aggressive and violent norms are transmitted. Since then, empirical research has firmly established the reciprocal relationship between friendship networks and behavior (e.g., Dishion, French, & Patterson, 1995). Negative peer experiences (both peer rejection and "deviant" peer affiliation) have been cited as "on-ramps" to adolescent aggression (Laird, Jordan, Dodge, Pettit, & Bates, 2001). Aggressive children are more likely to be rejected by their classmates, which then increases the risk for later antisocial behavior (Asher & Coie, 1990). In fact, research has shown that the link between peer rejection and antisocial behavior is mediated by affiliation among aggressive peers (Dishion, Patterson, Stoolmiller, & Skinner, 1991). In the early years of schooling, a pattern of negative interactions with peers can become relatively stable across the school year for aggressive children (Snyder, 2002). These children are reinforced for their behavior, but often rejected by other peers. Seeking social niches that will hold them in high regard, they develop relationships with other aggressive children (Thornberry & Krohn, 1997). Longitudinal studies have shown that affiliation with an aggressive peer group is a powerful predictor of the persistence and progression of antisocial behavior (Moffit & Caspi, 2001; Patterson, Dishion, & Yoerger, 2000).

Within peer networks, friends may support and encourage each other's aggressive behavior through positive reinforcement and modeling. In observational studies of adolescents, researchers have shown that peers reinforce each other's aggressive talk and behavior through both verbal and nonverbal behavior (Buehler, Patterson, & Furniss, 1966; Dishion, Andrews, & Crosby, 1995; Dishion, Spracklen, Andrews, & Patterson, 1996). Moreover, displays of toughness and power can help an adolescent gain status and, for males, reinforce a type of masculine identity

(Fagan & Wilkson, 1998). The processes of impression management, peer reinforced aggressive behavior, and expected gender roles need further examination. That said, research has firmly established that it is important to consider a teenager's friendship group to understand heightened aggression, especially during the adolescent years.

Neighborhood and media influences. A review of studies showed that differences in neighborhoods have a small to moderate effect on delinquency and violence (Leventhal & Brooks-Gunn, 2000). The mechanisms through which neighborhoods affect children's development include institutional resources, relationships, and the norms and collective efficacy in neighborhoods (Jencks & Mayer, 1990; Leventhal & Brooks-Gunn). For instance, access to high-quality childcare, with low adult-to-child ratios, is limited in poor neighborhoods (Fuller, Coonerty, Kipnis, & Choong, 1997); this resource is linked to positive behavioral outcomes (e.g., Benasich, Brooks-Gunn, & Clewell, 1992). Protective relationships may also be lacking or compromised in low-income communities. Economic hardship has been thought to increase parents' social isolation, stress, and depression, which then compromises their ability to provide monitoring (Conger et al., 2002). Lower monitoring predicts higher rates of delinquency (Hawkins, Herrenkohl, & Farrington, 1998). The benefits of watchful community members may also be compromised in low-income neigh-borhoods with high residential turnover. These neighbor-hoods have been shown to have weak norms to control aggressive behavior and low collective efficacy to change the neighborhood (Sampson, Morenoff, & Earls, 1999). Cut out from mainstream economic opportunities, key pathways out of poverty may be lost, which leaves generations trapped in poverty and exposed to violent neighborhoods (Hill, Fernando, Chen, & LaFrombois, 1994). Such exposure has been prospectively linked to greater aggressive behavior (Gorman-Smith & Tolan, 1998).

Increasing evidence has established a link between exposure to media violence and aggressive behavior (Ander-son & Bushman, 2001). The link is robust and replicable, although not statistically large (Huesmann, Moise, & Podo-loski, 1997). Experimental conditions in the lab have shown that exposure to violent media increases the likelihood of physical assault (see Anderson, Berkowitz, & Donnerstein, 2003, for a review). Longitudinal studies support the laboratory findings. For instance, in a study spanning over 25 years, Huesmann (1988) found that criminal convictions at age 30 were linked with preference for violent television in the third grade. Substantial evidence supports theories of observational learning of behaviors and cognitions to help explain why media exposure predicts aggression. Children replicate the behavior of admired television characters (Huesmann & Eron, 1986) who receive rewards for their acts of violence (Bandura, 1973). Via the media, children learn cognitive scripts for aggressive behavior and develop beliefs about the acceptability of aggression as a means to a goal (Huesmann et al., 1997).

Schools. Schools have been shown to differ in their rates of aggression and violence even when taking into account the characteristics of the enrolled students (Rutter, Maughan, Mortiore, & Ouston, 1979). Such differences have prompted inquiry into school policies, procedures, and structures that distinguish low from high aggressive schools. Three underlying theoretical approaches differentiate research in this area. The first approach implies that there is a developmental mismatch between students and the way schooling is organized such that the school either lacks appropriate monitoring or lacks appropriate autonomy. Said differently, schools are seen as under or over-controlling. The second approach posits that students are not given the opportunity to bond with school whereby they do not become personally invested in the rules and in the community. The third approach suggests that schools' organization of students results in reinforcing maladaptive behavior. Research with these approaches has been conducted primarily at the elementary school level, yet evidence is suggestive that they may be helpful in understanding middle and high school effects on aggression.

Mismatched with young children's developmental needs, some schools may lack consistent, schoolwide expectations for behavior (Horner, Sugai, Lewis-Palmer, & Todd, 2001) or adequate supervision throughout the school grounds. Specific settings in the school may be particularly conducive to aggressive behavior. Using naturalistic observations of elementary students, Craig, Pepler, and Atlas (2000) found that, compared with behavior in classroom settings, children exhibited more aggression on the playground, where very little teacher intervention occurred. J. B. Reid and colleagues (1999) also showed that less supervision during recess was linked with higher levels of aggression. Additional settings such as hallways and lunchrooms may also need to be examined for their lack of appropriate supervision. Behavioral regulation, while underemployed in certain settings in the elementary school grades, may be implemented in a counterproductive manner in later grades without consideration for adolescents' increasing need for autonomy. Hyman and Perone (1998) argued that police presence, metal detectors, and locker searchers are displays of control and disrespect. Zero-tolerance and punitive suspension policies may also contribute to a culture of threat and control (Ayers, Dohrn, & Ayers, 2001). In repressive school environments, students may respond with moral indignation and active resistance (Giroux, 1983). Correlational research has shown that students' perceptions of feeling respected and perceiving clear and fair rules are linked to lower rates of discipline (Gottfred-son,

273

Gottfredson, & Hybl, 1993; Hollingsworth, Lufler, & Clune, 1984). Additional research on students' responses to school cultures of threat and surveillance is needed.

Schools may vary in the degree to which they offer the conditions that promote school bonding, which has been theorized as a factor that can lower aggression and violence. Combining social control theory (Hirschi, 1969) and developmental theory, Hawkins, Smith, and Catalano, (2004) have conceptualized school bonding as a commitment to doing well in school and an attachment to those at school, characterized by close emotional relationships. They posit that a strong social bond asserts an informal control on a student's behavior. Evidence to support their theory has accrued. Lowered school bonding has been linked to escalating aggression during the teen years (Hawkins, Guo, & Hill 2001). Relatedly, Battistich, Solomon, Watson, & Schaps (1997), in a longitudinal study across elementary grades, found that students' sense of community predicted lower delinquency.

School policies on tracking and ability grouping may also be linked to the problem of aggression. The drawbacks of homogenous grouping have been examined from the perspective of operant conditioning principles such that students who behave similarly reinforce each other's behavior and, by doing so, strengthen it. Some evidence is suggestive that classroom placement can have long-term effects on the escalation of aggression. Kellam, Ling, and Merisca (1998) found that first graders perceived as high in aggression had higher rates of aggression in sixth grade if they were placed in first-grade classrooms with high mean levels of aggression. They concluded that tracking aggressive children with similar children can have detrimen tal effects. Similarly, grouping lower achieving students together has been linked to increasing behavior difficulties over time (Werthamer-Larsson, Kellam, & Wheeler, 1991). In fact, some scholars have described the sorting of students as "structural violence." They argue that the monitoring of African American students as "behavior disordered" in special education serves to colonize and control this population of students, which leads to stigmatizing labels (Watts & Erevelles, 2004).

Classrooms. Classrooms in the early grades and the later grades have been shown to differ in levels of discipline problems (Baerveldt, 1992; Gregory, Nygreen, & Moran, 2006). Inquiry into what differentiates classrooms with higher levels of aggression and disruptive behavior can be grouped into three approaches. The first approach emphasizes the teachers' abilities to manage the classroom as a whole. Of importance are teachers' skills in engaging the students in academic tasks without being sidetracked by disruption. The second approach empha-sizes the quality of teachers' relationships and interactions with individual students. The third approach focuses on teachers' attitudes and expectations that are brought into the classroom. While most of this research has been conducted at the elementary school level in single classrooms, some middle- and high-school-level research has sought to understand divergent behavior across classrooms (e.g., Gregory & Weinstein, in press).

The findings of Jacob Kounin (1970) are relevant today in understanding the importance of group management for well-run classrooms. Kounin found that more important than their specific discipline techniques, teachers with less aggression in their rooms were skilled at keeping the whole classroom on task and, thus, prevented escalating problems with aggression. Using systematic coding of videotaped elementary schools classrooms, Kounin found five skills that were linked with lower disruptions. "Withitness" is a teacher's preemptive actions and heightened awareness of behavior in the classroom. With quick and subtle interventions, a skilled teacher intervenes early to keep students engaged in the academic tasks. "Overlapping" is a teacher's ability to multitask with a focus on keeping the academic lesson going. He or she is able to address off-task behavior without derailing the lesson. "Momentum" helps transitions occur quickly with little time for losing students' motivation. "Smoothness" keeps the lessons focused with minimal deviations from the task at hand. "Group alerting" uses skills to keep each student engaged without letting some drift off. Overall, these teachers are able to anticipate problems with a focus on the antecedents of misbehavior (Emmer, Evertson, & Worsham, 2003; Evertson, Emmer, & Worhsam, 2003).

Indicators of well-run classrooms include how teachers interact with individual students. Reviews of research on classroom discipline have shown consistently that frequency of positive reinforcement is linked with orderly classrooms and low levels of misbehavior (see Doyle, 1985). The importance of positive feedback supports theories of operant conditioning, whereby behavior is strengthened when it is reinforced. The quality of interactions has also been examined from a relational standpoint. Close teacher relationships have been shown to serve as protective factors for young children at risk of negative discipline trajectories (Pianta, 1999). Evidence suggests that students' experience of teachers as nurturing with high academic expectations are linked to positive social and behavioral outcomes for middle school (Wentzel, 2002) and high school students (Gregory, 2004). Teachers, like parents, may help establish positive emotional climates with children (Davis, 2002). Within this climate, teachers may develop trust with students that enables them to effectively prevent or deescalate aggressive behavior (Gregory). Or, teachers may develop effective regulatory processes with their students (via the relationship) to help students identify and control their emotions (Pianta & Weinstein, in press).

Teacher attitudes and expectations may exacerbate or prevent escalating aggression in the classroom. Research in this area asserts that teachers enter classrooms with preconceived notions of students, which affect their teaching practices. Though conducted mostly at the elementary school grade levels, research on teacher perceptions suggests that, on average, teachers are more likely to hold negative judgments of students of color than of White students (Weinstein, 2002). For instance, compared with teachers of color, White kindergarten teachers were more likely to report having conflict with their students of color (Saft & Pianta, 2001) and report overall higher rates of student difficulty in following directions (Rimm-Kaufman, Pianta, & Cox, 2000). From her ethnographic study of an elementary school, Ferguson (2000) argued that White teachers draw on stereotypes and their own fears of difference when they perceive "defiance" in African American students. In their large study of urban middle schools in the Midwest, Skiba and colleagues (2002) identified reasons for suspension given to African American students as more subjective compared with reasons for suspensions given to White students. In a path analysis explaining the disproportionate sanctioning of Black students, McCarthy and Hoge (1987) found that, despite Black and White students' similar self-reports of misconduct, teachers' evaluation of the students' demeanor explained a significant amount of the association between race and sanctions received. Additional research is needed to examine students' behavioral response to differential treatment.

Final issues. The social contextual effects on aggression often have small to moderate effect sizes, with meaningful implications for the escalation of aggressive behavior across schooling. That said, limitations of the empirical understanding of social contextual effects need to be highlighted. While it is helpful to pinpoint a given setting's particular effects on aggression, the reality of interacting settings is far more complex. Ecologically grounded research that accounts for the interacting influences encountered in a given day and across developmental stages is needed. The field is only beginning to address the generalizability and the cultural specificity of particular processes. Differences related to gender, social class, race and ethnicity, and region may influence how and why some social forces have more or less impact on some children's behavior.

Continuous and Reciprocal Interactions Between Individuals and Contexts

Individual attitudes and attributes interact with social contextual influences in a dynamic and reinforcing fashion (Rutter & Sroufe, 2000). Thus, across a child's life, genetic, neural, behavioral, and environmental systems likely interplay in a bidirectional manner (Gottlieb & Halpern, 2002). A life-course developmental model of aggressive behavior points to critical windows when particular risk factors play a greater or lesser role (J. B. Reid & Eddy, 1997). Longitudinal research has helped to identify when such risk factors set in motion negative developmental trajectories within particular subgroups of children. Confirmed by other studies, Patterson (1995) and Moffitt and Caspi (2001) delineated between early childhood onset of aggression, which is more likely to be life-course persistent, and adolescent onset of aggression, which is more likely to desist in early adulthood. These early-onset children often exhibit aggressive behavior outside the normative developmental levels before they start formal schooling. An interplay between individual factors (e.g., attentional problems, low verbal IQ, or irritable temperament) and family factors (e.g., disrupted inconsistent parenting, parents with a history of antisocial behavior, or coercive parenting) has been shown to be a strong predictor of such early onset. Thus, in these early years between infancy and 5 years of age, family and individual risks factors are particularly salient (J. B. Reid & Eddy).

When the "early-onset" children enter formal schooling, another set of risk factors exacerbate the aggressive behavior. School and peer factors such as a lack of positive teacher attention, academic underachievement, and rejection by peers, contribute to the "snowballing" of the problem. In high school, these children with histories of aggressive behavior are matched by another subgroup of later onset youth (Moffit and Caspi, 2001). For both groups of teens, a lack of adequate monitoring by parents accompanied by affiliation with high-risk peers exacerbates the aggressive behavior. Equipped with a developmental perspective that considers multiple pathways and risk factors that co-occur between individuals and their social contexts, school counselors can better understand how aggressive behaviors can become more wide-ranging in scope and seriousness across children's years in schooling.

Counseling Practice to Reduce School Violence
CURRENT PRACTICE IN SCHOOLS

Recent efforts abound to study the effectiveness of school-based interventions to prevent violence and aggression (see Durlak & Wells, 1997; Henrich, Brown, & Aber, 1999; Johnson & Johnson, 1996; Leff, Power, Manz, Costigan, & Nabors, 2001; Wilson, Lipsey, & Derzon, 2003).

Based in theory and research, most programs with evidence of effectiveness have been designed and evaluated by university researchers. These demonstration programs focus on building competence and/or addressing deficits within the individual student (e.g., cognitive processing skills, academic achievement), supporting and/or changing one or more social contexts (e.g., playground, classroom), or both. Prevention programs have been found to have the largest effects on the highest risk populations (Wilson, Gottfredson, & Najaka, 2001). Unlike demonstration programs, "routine practice programs"—those that currently exist in schools—generally have not been studied, have been shown to be minimally effective, or are evidence-based programs being inadequately implemented (see Wilson et al., 2003). In the following sections, we will outline some common routine practice programs and several effective demonstration programs to prevent and/or reduce aggression and violence in schools.

Routine practice programs. One common practice to reduce school violence involves the removal of disruptive students from the situation (e.g., detention or suspension) either alone or in combination with a parent–teacher conference (Gottfredson et al., 1993; Tolan & Guerra, 1994). Although research has demonstrated the importance of consistent consequences for violation of clear school rules (e.g., Colvin, Sugai, Good, & Lee, 1997), the long-term effectiveness of punitive disciplinary measures in reducing or preventing violence is not evident (see Skiba, Peterson, & Williams, 1997; Mayer, 1995). Similarly, when parent– teacher conferences are oriented toward problem solving and establishing consistent policies and communication across home and school, they may be helpful. However, when they occur only after negative events and empha-size punishment, their helpfulness in reducing the problem behavior is questionable.

A second widespread practice involves providing psychological testing and/or supportive counseling for individual students. Although an educational and psychological assessment may be a reasonable first step for the most disruptive students, it is not a realistic preventive or treatment solution given the tremendous resources needed to carry out this approach for all whose behavior and achievement may suggest it. In addition, supportive counseling (noncog-nitive behavioral therapy) has not been demonstrated to be effective in reducing aggression in the contexts in which disruptive children and youth act out (Wilson et al., 2001). Finally, even when school personnel try to implement evidence-based demonstration programs, for many reasons, the implementation of these interventions is often inadequate, thus reducing the likelihood of effectiveness. In a recent review, Gottfredson and colleagues (2004) found that only 57% of delinquency prevention activities in schools were implemented to a satisfactory level in terms of duration, intensity, and frequency of activities; content of programming; method of delivery; and participation among staff and students.

Demonstration programs. Many preventive and treatment programs designed and supported by a university-based research team have been the subject of rigorous examination documenting at least moderate effectiveness within particular school—community contexts when implemented with fidelity. The intervention programs are based in theory and research, and focus on the students (e.g., as individuals or groups), the social context (e.g., classroom, playground), or both (e.g., multilevel and whole school). A recent meta-analysis of school-based intervention effects on aggressive behavior indicates that well-implemented, intensive, teacher-administrated, behavioral/academic/social competence programs can have a sizeable impact on student aggression (Wilson et al., 2003). We will discuss several of these programs next. In addition, we will describe some well-studied multimodal programs that may have smaller effects on aggressive behavior (see Wilson et al., 2003) but may have an impact *across* domains of student development such as social competence and academic learning. Given the differences in program effectiveness when programs are supported by a research team versus implemented without support, recommendations will be provided to coun-selors interested in utilizing an evidence-based approach in their schools to maximize the possibility of a positive impact on student aggression and violence.

Indicated or Treatment Programs

Typically, counselors intervene with individual students who already have demonstrated aggressive behavior with the aim of preventing the unfolding of a full-scale disorder. A recent meta-analysis showed that school-based programs that aim to prevent the escalation of aggression are most effective with students who already have exhibited aggressive behavior (Wilson et al., 2003). School interventions may be individual, parent, or group focused; however, the configuration of interventions with identified students is under strict scrutiny. With cost effectiveness a priority, schools often place aggressive children in group interventions, where students with similar difficulties interact in weekly meetings. Recent research on the negative peer influences in groups has raised questions about the unintended iatrogenic effects of group-format interventions at the elementary and middle schools (Boxer, Guerra, Huesmann, & Morales, 2005) and the high school level (Cho, Hallfors, & Sanchez, 2005). At this point, additional research is needed to understand whether mixed student groups are more or less beneficial than homogenous groups and whether high-aggressive or low-aggressive peers undermine or enhance intervention goals (Dishion & Dodge, 2005). With caution in mind, a well-studied group-based intervention follows. Then, we will describe a school-based parenting intervention, followed by a well-established individually focused intervention.

Anger Coping Program. The Anger Coping Program was designed as an 18-session, small—group format intervention with aggressive children (Lochman, Barry, & Pardini, 2003). The program draws on a social—cognitive approach, which emphasizes that children's perceptions of conflicts, encoding of relevant details, and interpretation of others' intentions are linked with their behavioral response (Crick & Dodge, 1996). Using a curriculum, group leaders address the following topics: anger management, perspective taking, socials skills training, goal setting, coping with peer pressure, emotional identification, problem solving, and relaxation training (Lochman et al., 2003). Sessions vary with a range of interactive tasks such as practicing calming self-talk while being teased, role-playing conflicts from different perspectives, and videotaping the negative consequences of an aggressive action.

The Anger Coping Program has been administered primarily in middle schools for boys identified as exhibiting aggressive behavior. It has been run as a single intervention (e.g., Lochman, 1992) and in combination with a parenting intervention (e.g., Lochman & Wells, 2004). Chorpita and his colleagues (2002) concluded in their review of three relevant studies that the intervention has a modest effect size in reducing aggressive behavior. In one study, only those who received a booster intervention the next school year showed significant reductions in classroom, off-task behavior (Lochman, 1992). The most recent published evaluation showed more promising results. The program was aimed at fifth- and sixth-grade boys who had relatively high aggressive ratings by parents and teachers (Loch-man & Wells). Small groups of 4 to 6 boys participated in 32 sessions across 2 school years. The year after the intervention was completed, teachers rated the boys as improved in behavioral problems, anger management, and problem solving. No moderating effects of race were found such that the intervention effects held for the sample of White and African American boys. While the Anger Coping Program is a promising intervention, as mentioned previously, care should be taken when grouping aggressive children and adolescents in sustained "pull-out" programs (Dishion & Dodge, 2005).

Functional behavioral assessment and intervention. The 1997 and 2004 reauthorizations of the Individuals with Disabilities Education Act require schools to address discipline problems with students in special education using functional behavioral assessment and intervention. Grounded in behaviorist and social learning theory, functional analysis and intervention is frequently conducted with students exhibiting aggressive or disruptive behavior (Quinn et al., 2001). Crone and Horner (2003) described the procedures in detail. A teacher and counselor gather data about environmental factors that precede and follow the behavior. Hypotheses about the predictors and function of the behavior are developed. For instance, students may engage in problematic behaviors to obtain or escape something in the classroom (Ervin et al., 2001). Once hypotheses are formed about what drives the behavior, interventions are then designed to make the behavior irrelevant, inefficient, and ineffective (Crone & Horner, 2003). Interventions can include teaching a child an appropriate replacement behav-ior to obtain the desired goals or eliminating the reinforcers that strengthen the negative behavior (Ervin et al., 2001).

The functional approach to changing individual behavior in the classroom seems to be ahead of the research supporting its widespread use. While examination of 100 studies using functional behavioral assessment and intervention with 278 students showed positive short-term gains, most of the studies have been conducted with preschool and elementary students with disabilities (Ervin et al., 2001). Research with older students and those without disabilities is scarce. Moreover, long-term follow up to ascertain if the gains are sustained is rare. In addition, this approach can be quite time intensive and requires anywhere from 1 week to 30 days (Quinn et al., 2001). Thus, whether it is a cost-effective use of teacher and counselor time in comparison with classroom-wide interventions remains open to question. That said, a recent meta-analysis concluded that interventions based on learning principles and behavioral theory are most effective compared with other interventions such as mentoring or supportive counseling (Wilson et al., 2001). Thus, despite the fact the research on functional behavioral assessment and intervention is lagging, it is a promising approach that has become expected professional practice.

Parenting—The incredible years. For the past 20 years, Carolyn Webster-Stratton and her colleagues at the University of Washington Clinic have been developing interventions with young children to prevent the onset and escalation of conduct problems. After fine-tuning a parenting intervention, they developed child and teacher components (Webster-Strat-ton, 2005). Their program theory uses cognitive social learning principles with a focus on relationships. Using Patterson's interactional model (1982), they aimed to interrupt the coercive patterns that can become established between children and parents, which have been predictive of aggressive behavior. They also emphasized the importance of the emotional climate between parents and children with the goal of reducing harsh and inconsistent parenting and increasing warmth and positive interactions. Their programs relied heavily on videotaped parenting vignettes to model effective and ineffective parenting (see Webster-Stratton). The BASIC training program has 13 to 14 weekly 2-hour sessions and teaches parents of 2- to 7-year-olds how to positively engage, use praise and rewards effectively, set limits, and deal with noncompliance. The ADVANCE program aims to maintain treatment effects by lowering the detrimental effects of relationship distress and divorce, which were found to be predictors of treatment relapse. The program attempts to strengthen interpersonal skills in coping, communication, problem solving, social support, and self-care. They also offer four to six additional sessions that address how parents can promote their children's learning.

The BASIC parenting intervention has been studied extensively and summarized in more detail elsewhere (Webster-Stratton, 2005). The bulk of the research was with White middle-class families and children aged 2 to 6 years. However, they have extended their scope to include more diverse populations and children up to 10 years old. In brief, six randomized controlled trials have shown that the intervention improves parent–child interaction and reduces child conduct problems. The intervention has resulted in sustained gains for half to three quarters of the participants. A 3-year follow-up study showed that children with single parents or parents with relationship difficulties or negative life stress were less likely to sustain benefits. The intervention has also been successfully implemented with a low-income, Head Start population (M. J. Reid, Webster-Stratton, & Baydar, 2004). Children and their mothers with more difficulties benefited the most. The parent training has shown that behavioral improvements can generalize to the school setting. A recent study showed that the children of the parents in the intervention sustained improved classroom behavior across one school year, as rated by teachers (Webster-Stratton, Reid, & Hammond, 2004).

Universal or Single Context Programs

Beyond programs focused on students who already have demonstrated some aggressive behaviors, several setting-wide programs have evidence of effectiveness. Some of these are curricula with the primary goal of building skills and competencies within individual children, such as the Promoting Alternative THinking Strategies (PATHS) curriculum or classwide peer tutoring. These programs have the potential benefit of impacting both those students who may be at risk of developing aggressive tendencies, as well as those who already use aggression in school. Others are interventions whose primary goal is to alter the functioning of a setting, such as teacher consultation and playground restructuring. In this case, addressing environmental or structural characteristics related to the promotion of aggression may be especially critical, particularly for children in elementary school (e.g., J. B. Reid, Eddy, & Fetrow, 1999).

PATHS. The Promoting Alternative THinking Strategies program is a 60-lesson curriculum taught by the elementary school classroom teacher over one school year and integrated into the classroom curriculum with an emphasis on both changing the environment and educating the child (Greenberg, Kusche, & Mihalic, 1998). In particular, the program is designed to increase student self-control, emotion understanding, positive communication, prosocial behavior, and interpersonal problem solving. This theory-based program derives from the ABCD model of development (affective—behavioral–cognitive—dynamic) in which children's internal and external coping arises from their combined emotion awareness, cognitive understanding, and behavioral skills, with the affective component preceding the cognitive and behavioral functions (see Greenberg et al., 1998). Teaching methods for the 20- to 30-minute lessons include direct instruction, discussion, role plays, modeling, and reinforcement. Lessons focus on labeling and managing feelings, delaying gratification and controlling impulses, reading and interpreting social cues, using a procedure for problem solving and decision making, and developing nonverbal and verbal communication skills. Teachers are trained in a 3-day workshop at the beginning of the year, with ongoing support and consultation.

The PATHS curriculum is unusual in the rigor of the research base and its demonstrated effectiveness in both regular and special education classrooms (Greenberg & Kusche, 1993; Greenberg, Kusche, Cook, & Quamma, 1995). It has been tested in randomized, longitudinal studies with classroom observation components in Seattle-area first- to third-grade classrooms with approximately 60% White and 40% African American students and mainly low- to middle-income families. Positive outcomes include increased fluency and comfort in discussing basic feelings, as well as positive efficacy beliefs around managing and changing feelings. Among students at behavioral risk, teachers noted significant improvements in frustration, tolerance, social skills, task orientation, peer relations, and internalizing behaviors. Investigators mentioned significant variation regarding the level at which the teacher modeled cognitive and behavioral skills, shared emotions, and established an atmosphere of respect for varying beliefs and feelings (Greenberg et al., 1998). However, no outcomes were reported regarding differences by teacher ability or ways in which support staff attempted to bolster teacher skills. Finally, although the program includes generalization activities to be used outside the classroom and materials for families, outcomes generally have not been reported on the impact of nonclassroom and parent materials.

Peer tutoring. Peer tutoring, also called peer-assisted learning, has been used as a classroom-wide intervention aimed at raising achievement and increasing prosocial behaviors. Students are paired in fixed or reciprocal tutor—tutee roles. Primarily implemented in the elementary and middle schools, programs have addressed reading (Fuchs, Fuchs, & Burish, 2000) and mathematics (Fantuzzo, King, & Heller, 1992). Student tutors are trained to structure the tutoring time and use immediate corrective feedback with their tutee. Goals and rewards are built into the tutoring time to help the pair work efficiently and foster mutual motivation. The theoretical basis of peer tutoring is derived from research on the influence of classroom peers on behav-ior and motivation. It has been argued that in successful tutoring programs, students teach academic skills, model on-task behavior (Topping & Ehly, 2001), and foster academic and social motivation for learning (Rohrbeck, Gins-burg-Block, Fantuzzo, & Miller, 2003).

Given that academically targeted programs have been shown to reduce aggressive behavior (Wilson et al., 2003), the effectiveness of peer tutoring at raising academic outcomes shows promise for improving overall classroom behavior. A meta-analytic review that looked across effect sizes in 90 studies found that, on average, students in peer tutoring made moderate achievement gains (Rohrbeck et al., 2003). The programs were particularly beneficial for younger elementary students, low-income students, and urban students. While much of the research has focused on achievement gains, several studies have shown that peer tutoring is linked with improved behavior (Pigott, Fan-tuzzo, & Clement, 1986; Wolfe, Fantuzzo, & Wolfe, 1986). For instance, in a study with urban African American peer tutors, groups that were given rewards contingent on academic success were perceived by the teacher as showing lower negative classroom conduct (Fantuzzo et al., 1992).

Teacher consultation (Good behavior game). It has been argued that school counselors' roles should be expanded to include teacher consultation with the aim of increasing teacher capacity in classroom management (e.g., Adelman & Taylor, 2002). Drawing on behavioral consultation models, a counselor identifies the teacher's concern, gathers information about antecedents and consequences of the concern, develops a plan of intervention with the teacher, and determines the outcome of the intervention (Sladeczek, Kratochwill, Steinback, Kumke, & Hagermoser, 2003). A counselor may consult with a teacher to help implement specific programmatic interventions designed to improve classroom behavior. One such program is the Good Behavior Game (Barrish, Saunders, & Wolf, 1969), which draws on the premise that group-based rewards increase the likelihood that peers will be motivated to inhibit negative behavior. To implement the program, the teacher identifies a specific block of time when the game likely will have initial success. Then, the teacher, in consultation with the students, selects negative behaviors to decrease and chooses "activity rewards," such as extra time for free-choice reading. The teacher divides the students into teams, which receive points when they exhibit the predetermined negative behaviors. All the teams can win if they have fewer than the predetermined number of points (Embry & Straatemeier, 2001). The intervention has been found to be well liked by teachers (Tingstrom, 1994).

Embry (2002) offered a thorough review of the Good Behavior Game and its proven effectiveness in diverse classrooms. In short, implementation of the game lowered a range of negative behaviors across grades levels, in multiple settings in the school, and with at-risk populations. For instance, the program was associated with lowered disruptions with fourth graders (Barrish et al., 1969), elementary-age special education students (Darveaux, 1984; Grandy, Madsen, & De Mersseman, 1973), and adolescents (Salend, Reynolds, & Coyle, 1989). In a randomized trial in Baltimore with first graders, the game had the largest effect in reducing the aggressive behavior of students rated as high on aggression prior to the intervention (Dolan, Kel-lam, & Brown, 1993). Long-term effects of the classroom-centered intervention found that by sixth grade, the first graders who had played the game, relative to the control group, had fewer conduct problems and fewer suspensions (Ialongo, Poduska, Werthamer, & Kellam, 2001). A key ingredient appears to be peer pressure, such that positive peer norms are set and disruptive behavior is discouraged (see Hegerle, Kesecker, & Couch, 1979).

Playground interventions. Aggressive behavior in schools occurs most frequently in unstructured settings such as the lunchroom and playground (Craig & Pepler, 2000; Craig et al., 2000). Recent attention has been paid to the characteristics of safe and productive playgrounds, and programs targeting these characteristics have been shown to reduce aggression and violence among elementary school students. The characteristics include access to structured activities and an organized space (Bay-Hinitz, Peterson, & Quilitch, 1994), clear communication of rules and expectations (Colvin et al., 1997), sufficient and active supervision (Olweus, 1999), and incentives and consequences for positive and negative behavior (Eddy, Reid, & Fetrow, 2000). Although playground interventions may be imbedded in more comprehensive programs, research demonstrates that targeting these characteristics can reduce aggressive behav-ior. In one low-income, predominantly African American, urban elementary school, structured and organized games on the playground were associated with higher cooperative play and lower rough physical play over the school year, while active supervision by parent volunteers was associated with higher intercultural interaction (Leff, Costi-gan, & Power, 2004).

Another research team included a playground intervention in a multicomponent program (Linking the Interests of Families and Teachers; LIFT) in high juvenile crime neighborhoods within a small and majority Caucasian city. Researchers modified the Good Behavior Game (previously described) so students earned armbands from playground staff for clearly identified positive behaviors (toward a whole class reward) and negative behaviors were logged and subtracted from "good faith" points (adding to small group rewards; Eddy et al., 2000). The comprehensive program had a 3-year positive effect on elementary school children with high initial levels of aggression. Younger students had reduced playground aggression and hyperactive/inattentive behaviors, and older students had reduced arrests, delinquency, and drug use (J. B. Reid et al., 1999).

Finally, related to the peer tutoring program previously described, older peers have been trained to mediate conflicts on the playground as a supplement to the supervision by adults. In one well-implemented and evaluated program, older peers received 15 hours of training in rec-ognizing and resolving conflicts, as well as ongoing support from a mediation team and playground supervisors. When eight trained and supported peer mediators were present on elementary school playgrounds in a middle-income, suburban community, there was an abrupt and sustained reduction in physical aggression that lasted for 2 years (Cunningham et al., 1998). Taken together, these intervention studies indicate the effectiveness of a strategy to target the *contexts* in which aggressive behaviors occur, not only the aggressive *individuals*.

Multilevel Programs

Programs designed to target multiple levels at which aggression develops and is impacted have been shown to be somewhat effective in preventing and reducing aggressive behavior in schools. These generally require more resources to implement, as well as more "buy-in" among school personnel, but the trade-off may be benefits across domains of development (e.g., reducing aggression *and* enhancing achievement).

Fast track. Based on research indicating that external-izing problems are multiply determined, the Conduct Problems Prevention Research Group (1999a, 1999b) designed, implemented, and studied a comprehensive school-based program to target risk and protective factors across universal and high-risk groups of first-grade students. The universal aspect of the program included the classroom-based PATHS curriculum addressing emotions, social behaviors, and social problem solving (described earlier), along with basic parent education and skills groups. The targeted program included student social skills groups, academic tutoring, parent—child pair work, peer pair work, and home visits for students identified as behaviorally disruptive (Conduct Problems Prevention Research Group). The universal program was delivered mainly by teachers after an intensive workshop and with regular consultation; the selective program was delivered by family/educational coordinators and paraprofessionals who received extensive and ongoing training and supervision.

This intervention study was unique in its scope and rigor. Researchers matched and randomly assigned 54 schools in diverse communities across the United States to intervention or control conditions, and studied the impact of the universal and high-risk components with classroom observations, as well as teacher, student, and parent reports, over a 3-year period. Initial positive effects were found for classroom climate, on-task behavior, and rule following among the universal population of students, and among parenting, aggressive behavior at school, coping skills, language arts grades, and peer acceptance for high-risk students across four sites (Conduct Problems Prevention Research Group, 1999a, 1999b). Differences were not found by site or student background (gender or race). Limitations to this intervention study include a lack of knowledge of program sustainability over time, the dosage necessary for a positive effect, the reasons why some students do not respond, and the role of school/classroom context in intervention impact. In addition, recent studies indicate that the long-term consequences for school behav-ior of this intensive and comprehensive program were less strong than anticipated (Conduct Problems Prevention Research Group, 2004).

Child Development Project. The Child Development Project aims to build "caring communities of learners" in elementary schools (Battistich, Schaps, Watson, & Solomon, 1996). Like the programs just described, the Child Development Project includes activities across multiple levels: (a) the school—principal leadership, schoolwide activities; (b) the classroom—developmental discipline; cooperative learning; values-rich, literature-based reading and language arts curricula, and a phonics-based reading program for struggling readers and, (c) the family—home activities to build home—school communication as well as understanding of family culture. Unlike these programs, however, the Child Development Project is designed not only to address the problem of aggressive behavior in school, but also to create a school *community* that more generally enhances student learning, cooperation, and respect.

Quasi-experimental studies with video observation of implementation quality and a range of student socio-demographic characteristics (ethnicity, income) showed short- and long-term positive results. In high implementation elementary schools, third- to sixth-grade students had lower rates of truancy, theft, substance use, and weapon carrying, and reported more sense of positive school community (Battistich et al., 1996). Follow-up studies indicated that when students in high-implementation elementary schools attend middle school, they had higher achievement and educational expectations, as well as lower misconduct and delinquent behavior than comparison students (Solomon, Battistich, Watson, Schaps, & Lewis, 2000). In addition, the phonics-based reading curriculum alone increased reading achievement for all students, but particularly for non-native English speakers (Battistich, 2000). A significant limitation of this program was that less than half of the schools that implemented the program did so to a high degree of fidelity. However, when implemented well, results indicated the potential importance of a universal emphasis on both academic learning and classroom/school culture as a means toward reducing behavioral problems among all students.

Positive Behavioral Interventions and Supports. Based on a public health model, Positive Behavioral Interventions and Supports (PBIS) emphasizes a three-tiered approach to preventing and addressing disruptive behaviors (Lewis & Sugai, 1999). The first tier (universal) targets all children and adults across the school setting with the idea that that every student needs clear instruction, support, and reinforcement regarding appropriate and inappropri ate behaviors in and around the school building (Horner et al., 2001). The second tier (targeted) is geared toward children at risk for disruptive behavior, meaning they have engaged in problem behaviors in the past and have minimal access to protective supports. They are seen as unlikely to respond to universal interventions and in need of secondary-level interventions (e.g., daily report card, functional behavioral assessment) to move them in a more positive direction (Hawken & Horner, 2003; March & Horner, 2002). The third tier (intensive) is designed to provide team-based individualized and comprehensive services for those children with more severe behavioral problems who respond to neither universal nor targeted interventions (see Eber & Nelson, 1997). Across the three tiers, PBIS emphasizes the importance of measuring outcomes and using data for decision making, using practices with evidence of effectiveness, and attending to systems within the school to sustain the program.

The implementation and research data on PBIS is promising. Elementary and middle schools in primarily suburban, middle-income communities have been able to incorporate PBIS into their schools to high standards (e.g., Lewis, Sugai, & Colvin, 1998; Taylor-Greene & Kartub, 2000). Research studies with a pre/post design indicate a 20% to 60% reduction in discipline referrals and suspensions between the year before and the year after full implementation of PBIS

(Lohrman-O'Rourke et al., 2000; Luiselli, Putnam, & Sunderland, 2002). These effects have been sustained over 6 years in schools that have continued to implement the program (Taylor-Greene & Kartub). Observational methods demonstrate that lower rates of discipline referrals are related to changes in disruptive behaviors in unstructured school settings such as the playground and hallway (Cushing, in press). What is not known is the ability of PBIS to be implemented to the same degree of fidelity and with the same effectiveness in urban low-income schools where the behavioral issues and school systems may be both qualitatively and quantitatively different from their suburban counterparts.

Final Issues

Although this section demonstrates the range of evidence-based interventions to prevent and reduce aggression in schools, there are several final issues to consider. First, intervention research tends to focus on overt forms of aggression and boys, rather than more subtle forms of aggression or girls. Recent efforts have been made to address the problem of relational or social aggression among girls (see Cap-pella & Weinstein, 2006; Leff, 2005), but these efforts are preliminary and must be linked with more comprehensive programs. Second, demonstration programs—in particular, those that operate at multiple levels—demand considerable resources. There is conflicting evidence regarding the importance of single- versus multiple-level approaches to addressing violence in schools, but research is clear regarding the importance of quality implementation. That said, few intervention studies describe implementation efforts, leaving gaps in understanding of methods for increasing implementation quality with school and community resources. Third, demonstration programs are developed and implemented most frequently in elementary schools, with middle and high schools receiving minimal attention. Although prevention with younger students is critical, given that aggression continues to develop through adolescence, older students deserve systematic efforts to create classroom and school environments in which prosocial behaviors are the norm. Fourth, with some exceptions, these interventions are largely a-contextual without consideration for peer and cultural norms—which may be critical to the effectiveness of a program. Finally, the evidence-based practice movement relies on a process that moves from highly controlled trials to wider dissemination within schools. A more ecologically valid approach to developing an understanding of what works may be an *iterative* process of research and development based not only in theory and research, but also within the school and community context in which the efforts exist.

Recommendations

The school counselor can play an integral role in assisting the school to prevent or address the problem of school violence by providing information and support around the use of evidence-based practices in their schools. However, given the multiple and complex realities of different school communities, there are several steps to consider prior to and during the process of implementing one of the previously discussed programs to maximize the potential benefit. From the research and theory on the development, prevention, and management of aggression in schools, we recommend the following guidelines when attempting to address school violence:

1. Collect and analyze data to understand where, when, and with whom aggression occurs.
   - Use existing datasets (e.g., discipline referrals) or gather new data (e.g., conversations or surveys with school staff).
   - Assess multiple forms of aggression, including physical, verbal, and relational aggression (Leff et al., 2001).
2. Coalesce key personnel and the school organization around the need for intervention within particular settings and/or groups of students.
   - Promote a supportive school climate around the prevention and reduction of aggression (Gottfredson et al., 2004).
   - Build school capacity to initiate and sustain an innovation (e.g., infrastructure and support, resources, and leadership; Sherman et al., 1997).
   - Prepare to integrate elements of the intervention into the structure of the school or setting (e.g., classroom, playground; Heller, 1990; Gottfred-son et al., 2004).
3. Help school personnel select empirically supported activities with particular attention to the population with which and context within which the services have been tested.
   - Consider interventions designed to promote change within the individual child, as well as within the social context (e.g., universal, targeted, and indicated levels; Weissberg & Green-berg, 1998).

- Multiple level programs accompanied by a clarification and communication of norms about behaviors are promising; however, it is more important to implement a less-resource heavy program well than a more-resource heavy program poorly (Durlak & Wells, 1997; Gottfred-son et al., 2004; Sherman et al., 1997).
- Intervene at the appropriate stage of development (e.g., early in the onset of problems for a student or setting) and during sensitive periods, such as transitions during the school day (Tolan, Guerra, & Kendall, 1995; Weissberg & Greenberg, 1998).

4. Monitor the implementation and/or adaptation of those programs or practices.
   - Adapt program content to ethnic and sociode-mographic characteristics of students to maxi-mize the potential that it has meaning in their lives, in particular if the program was tested in a demographically different school community than the one in which it will be implemented (Heller, 1990).
   - Provide extensive, quality training of personnel who deliver services, and provide supervision and support for ongoing delivery of services (Gottfredson et al., 2004).

5. Collect data to evaluate the progress of the intervention strategies and make adjustments as needed.
   - Think about the multiple outcomes that may be important to the school and collect data on those outcomes (e.g., different types of aggression, academic achievement, attendance) from multiple sources (e.g., teachers, students, school data).
   - Allow sufficient time for the activities to work before making major adjustments to the intervention strategies; anticipate that the strongest results will be for the students and settings exhibiting the most problems at the start.

References

Adelman, H. S., & Taylor, L. (2002). School counselors and school reform: New directions. *Professional School Counseling, 5*(4), 235–248.

Anderson, C. A., & Bushman, B. J. (2001). Effects of violent video games on aggressive behavior, aggressive cognition, aggressive affect, physiological arousal, and pro-social behavior: A meta-analytic review of the scientific literature. *Psychological Science, 12*(5), 353–359.

Anderson, C. A., Berkowitz, L., & Donnerstein, E. (2003). The influence of media violence on youth. *Psychological Science in the Public Interest, 4*(3), 81–110.

Archer, J. (1994). Testosterone and aggression: A theoretical review. *Journal of Offender Rehabilitation, 21,* 3–39. Arnold, D. H., Ortiz, C., Curry, J. C., Stowe, R. M., Goldstein, N. E., Fisher, P. H., et al. (1999). Promoting academic success and preventing disruptive behavior disorders through community partnership. *Journal of Community Psychology, 27*(5), 589–598.

Asher, S. R., & Coie, J. D. (1990). *Peer rejection in childhood.* New York: Cambridge University Press.

Ayers, W., Dohrn, B., & Ayers, R. (2001). *Zero tolerance: Resisting the drive for punishment in schools.* New York: The New Press.

Baerveldt, C. (1992). Schools and the prevention of petty crime: Search for a missing link. *Journal of Quantitative Criminology, 8,* 79–94.

Bandura, A. (1973). *Aggression: A social learning analysis.* Englewood Cliffs, NJ: Prentice Hall.

Barkley, R. A., Fischer, M., Edelbrock, C. S., & Smallish, L. (1990). The adolescent outcome of hyperactive children diagnosed by research criteria: An 8-year prospective follow-up study. *Journal of the American Academy of Child and Adolescent Psychiatry, 29,* 546–557.

Barrish, H. H., Saunders, M., & Wolf, M. M. (1969). Good behavior game: Effects of individual contingencies for group consequences on disruptive behavior in a classroom. *Journal of Applied Behavior Analysis, 2,* 119–124.

Bates, J. E., Bayles, K., Bennett, D. S., Ridge, B., & Brown, N. M. (1991). Origins of externalizing behavior problems at eight years of age. In D. J. Pepler & K. H. Rugin (Eds.), *The development and treatment of childhood aggression* (pp. 93–120). Hillsdale, NJ: Erlbaum.

Bates, J. E.; Maslin, C. A., & Frankel, K. A. (1985). Attachment security, mother–child interaction, and temperament as predictors of behavior-problem ratings at age three years. *Monographs of the Society for Research in Child Development, Vol. 50,* 167–193.

Battistich, V. (2000). *Summary of evaluation findings on the Child Development Project.* Oakland, CA: Developmental Studies Center.

Battistich, V., Schaps, E., Watson, M., & Solomon, D. (1996). Prevention effects of the Child Development Project: Early findings from an ongoing multisite demonstration trial. *Journal of Adolescent Research, 11,* 12–35.

Battistich, V., Solomon, V., Watson, M., & Schaps, E. (1997). Caring school communities. *Educational Psychologist, 32*(3), 137–151.

Baumrind, D. (1991). The influence of parenting style on adolescent competence and substance use. *Journal of Early Adolescence, 11*(1), 56–95.

Bay-Hinitz, A. K., Peterson, R. F., & Quilitch, H. R. (1994). Cooperative games: A way to modify aggressive and cooperative behaviors in young children. *Journal of Applied Behavior Analysis, 27,* 435–446.

Benasich, A. A., Brooks-Gunn, J., & Clewell, B. C. (1992). How do mothers benefit from early intervention programs? *Journal of Applied Developmental Psychology, 13,* 311–362.

Berman, M. E., Kavoussi, R. J., & Coccaro, E. F. (1997). Neurotransmitter correlates of human aggression. In D. M. Stoff, J. Breiling, & J. D. Maser (Eds.), *Handbook of antisocial behavior* (pp. 305–313). New York: John Wiley & Sons, Inc.

Boldizar, J. P., Perry, D. G., & Perry, L. C. (1989). Outcome values and aggression. *Child Development, 60,* 571–579.

Boxer, P., Guerra, N. G., Huesmann, L. R., & Morales, J. (2005). Proximal peer-level effects of a small-group selected prevention on aggression in elementary school children: An investigation of the peer contagion hypothesis. *Journal of Abnormal Child Psychology, 33*(3), 325–338.

Brain, P. F., & Susman, E. J. (1997). Hormonal aspects of aggression and violence. In D. M. Stoff, J. Breiling, & J. D. Maser (Eds.), *Handbook of antisocial behavior* (pp. 314–323). New York: John Wiley & Sons, Inc.

Buehler, R. E., Patterson, G. R., & Furniss, J. M. (1966). The reinforcement of behavior in institutional settings. *Behaviour Research and Therapy, 4,* 157–167.

Cappella, E., & Weinstein, R. S. (2006). The prevention of social aggression among girls. *Social Development.*

Carr, E. G., Taylor, J. G., & Robinson, S. (1991). The effects of severe behavior problems in children on the teaching behavior of adults. *Journal of Applied Behavior Analysis, 24,* 523–535.

Caspi, A., Henry, B., McGee, R. O., Moffitt, T. E., & Silva, P. A. (1995). Temperamental origins of child and adolescent behavior problems: From age 3 to age 15. *Child Development, 66,* 55–68.

Cho, H., Hallfors, D. D., & Sanchez, V. (2005). Evaluation of a high school peer group intervention for at-risk youth. *Journal of Abnormal Psychology, 33*(3), 363–374.

Chorpita, B. F., Yim, L. M., Donkervoet, J. C., Arensdorf, A., Amundsen, M. J., McGee, C., et al. (2002). Toward large-scale implementation of empirically supported treatments for children: A review and observations by the Hawaii Empirical Basis to Services Task Force. *Clinical Psychology: Science & Practice, 9*(2), 165–190.

Coie, J. D., & Dodge, K. A. (1998). Aggression and antisocial behavior. In W. Damon & N. Eisenberg (Eds.), *Handbook of child psychology: Vol. 3: Social, emotional, and personality development* (5th ed., pp. 779–862). New York: John Wiley & Sons, Inc.

Colvin, G., Sugai, G., Good, R. H., III., & Lee, Y. (1997). Using active supervision and precorrection to improve transition behaviors in an elementary school. *School Psychology Quarterly, 12,* 344–363.

Conduct Problems Prevention Research Group. (1999a). Initial impact of the Fast Track prevention trial for conduct problems: I. The high-risk sample. *Journal of Consulting and Clinical Psychology, 67,* 631–647.

Conduct Problems Prevention Research Group. (1999b). Initial impact of the Fast Track prevention trial for conduct problems: II. Classroom effects. *Journal of Consulting and Clinical Psychology, 67,* 648–657.

Conduct Problems Prevention Research Group (2004). The effects of the Fast Track Program on serious problem outcomes at the end of elementary school. *Journal of Clinical Child and Adolescent Psychology, 33,* 650–661.

Conger, R. D., Wallace, L. E., Sun, Y., Simons, R. L., McLoyd, V. C., & Brody, H. H. (2002). Economic pressure in Afri-can American families: A replication and extension of the family stress model. *Developmental Psychology, 38*(2), 179–193.

Connell, J. P. (1990). Context, self, and action: A motivational analysis of self-system processes across the life-span. In D. C. M. Beeghly (Ed.), *The self in transaction: Infancy to childhood* (pp. 61–97). Chicago: University of Chicago Press.

Cornell, D. G., Sheras, P. L., Kaplan, S., McConville, D., Dou-glass, J., Elkon, A., et al. (2004). Guidelines for student threat assessment: Field-test findings. *School Psychology Review, 33*(4), 527–546.

Craig, W. M., & Pepler, D. (2000). Observations of bullying and victimization in the school yard. In W. Craig (Ed.), *Childhood social development: The essential readings* (pp. 116–138). Malden, MA: Blackwell Publishers Inc.

Craig, W. M., Pepler, D., & Atlas, R. (2000). Observations of bullying in the playground and in the classroom. *School Psychology International, 21*(1), 22–36.

Crick, N. R. (1996). The role of overt aggression, relational aggression, and prosocial behavior in the prediction of children's future social adjustment. *Child Development, 67,* 2317–2327.

Crick, N. R., & Dodge, K. A. (1989). Children's evaluations of peer entry and conflict situations: Social strategies, goals, and outcome expectations. In B. Schneider, J. Nadel, G. Attili, & R.

Weissberg (Eds.), *Social competence in developmental perspective* (pp. 396–399). Dordrecht, The Netherlands: Kluwer.

Crick, N. R., & Dodge, K. A. (1996). Social information processing mechanisms in reactive and proactive aggression. *Child Development, 67,* 993–1002.

Crone, D. A., & Horner, R. H. (2003). *Building positive behav-ior support systems in schools: Functional behavioral assessment.* New York: Guilford Press.

Cunningham, C. E., Cunningham, L. J., Martorelli, V., Tran, A., Young, J., & Zacharias, R. (1998). The effects of primary division, student-mediated conflict resolution programs on playground aggression. *Journal of Child Psychology & Psychiatry, 39*(5), 653–662.

Cushing, L. S. (in press). Validation and congruent validity of a direct observation tool to assess student social climate at school. *Journal of Positive Interventions.*

Darveaux, D. X. (1984). The Good Behavior Game plus merit: Controlling disruptive behavior and improving student motivation. *School Psychology Review, 13,* 510–514.

Davis, H. A. (2002). Conceptualizing the role and influence of student-teacher relationships on children's social and cognitive development. *Educational Psychologist, 38*(4), 207–234.

Devine, J. (1996). Maximum security: *The culture of violence in inner-city schools.* Chicago: University of Chicago Press.

Dishion, T. J., Andrews, D. W., & Crosby, L. (1995). Antisocial boys and their friends in early adolescence: Relationship characteristics, quality, and interactional process. *Child Development, 66,* 139–151.

Dishion, T. J., & Dodge, K. A. (2005). Peer contagion in interventions for children and adolescents: Moving towards an understanding of the ecology and dynamics of change. *Journal of Abnormal Child Psychology, 33*(3), 395–400.

Dishion, T. J., French, D. C., & Patterson, G. R. (1995). The development and ecology of antisocial behavior. In D. Cicchetti & D. Cohen (Eds.), *Manual of developmental psychopathology: Vol 2: Risk, disorder, and adaptation* (pp. 421–471). New York: Wiley.

Dishion, T. J., & Patterson, G. R. (1997). The timing and severity of antisocial behavior: Three hypotheses within an ecological framework. In D. M. Stoff, J. Breiling, & J. D. Maser (Eds.), *Handbook of antisocial behavior* (pp. 205–217). New York: John Wiley & Sons, Inc.

Dishion, T. J., Patterson, G. R., Stoolmiller, M., & Skinner, M. S. (1991). Family, school, and behavioral antecedents to early adolescent involvement with antisocial peers. *Developmental psychology, 27,* 172–180.

Dishion, T. J., Spracklen, K. M., Andrews, D. W., & Patterson, G. R. (1996) Deviancy training in male adolescent friendships. *Behavior Therapy, 27,* 373–390.

Dodge, K. A. (1991). The structure and function of proactive and reactive aggression. In D. J. Pepler & K. H. Rubin (Eds.), *The development and treatment of childhood aggression* (pp. 201–218). Hillsdale, NJ: Erlbaum.

Dodge, K. A., & Coie, J. D. (1987). Social information-processing factors in reactive and proactive aggression in children's playgroups. *Journal of Personality and Social Psychology, 53,* 1146–1158.

Dodge, K. A., & Frame, C. L. (1982). Social-cognitive biases and deficits in aggressive boys. *Child Development, 53,* 620–635.

Dodge, K. A., Pettit, G. S., McClaskey, C. L., & Brown, M. M. (1986). Social competence in children. *Monographs of the Society for Research in Child Development, 51*(2, Serial No. 213), 1–85.

Dodge, K. A., & Schwartz, D. (1997). Social information processing mechanisms in aggressive behavior. In D. M. Stoff, J. Breiling, & J. D. Maser (Eds.), *Handbook of antisocial behavior* (pp. 171–180). New York: John Wiley & Sons.

Dolan, L. J., Kellam, S. G., & Brown, C. H. (1993). The short-term impact of two classroom-based preventive interventions on aggressive and shy behaviors and poor achievement. *Journal of Applied Developmental Psychology, 14*(3), 317–345.

Doyle, W. (1985). Classroom organization and management. In M. C. Wittrock (Ed.), *Handbook of research on teaching* (3rd ed., pp. 392–431). New York: MacMillan.

Dulmus, K., Theriot, M. T., & Sowers, K. M. (2004). Student report of peer bullying victimization in a rural school. *Stress, Trauma, and Crisis: An International Journal, 7*(1), 1–16.

Durlak, J. A., & Wells, A. M. (1997). Primary prevention mental health programs for children and adolescents: A meta-analytic review. *American Journal of Community Psychology, 25*(2), 115–152.

Eamon, M. K. (2001). Poverty, parenting, peer, and neighbor-hood influences on young adolescent antisocial behav-ior. *Journal of Social Service Research, 28*(1), 1–23.

Earls, F. (1981). Epidemiological child psychiatry: An Ameri-can perspective. In E. F. Purcell (Ed.), *Psychopathology of children and youth: A cross cultural perspective* (pp. 3–28). New York: Josial Macy Jr. Foundation.

Earls, F., & Jung, K. G. (1987). Temperament and home environment characteristics as causal factors in the early development of childhood psychopathology. *Journal of the American Academy of Child and Adolescent Psychiatry, 26,* 491–498.

Eber, L., & Nelson, C. M. (1997). School-based wraparound planning: Integrating services for students with emotional and behavioral needs. *American Journal of Ortho-psychiatry, 67,* 385–395.

Eddy, M. J., Reid, J. B., & Fetrow, R. A. (2000). An elementary school-based prevention program targeting modifiable antecedents of youth delinquency and violence: Linking the interests of families and teachers (LIFT). *Journal of Emotional & Behavioral Disorders, 8*(3), 165–176.

Embry, D. D. (2002). The Good Behavior Game: A best prac-tice candidate as a universal behavioral vaccine. *Clinical Child and Family Psychology Review, 5*(4), 273–297.

Embry, D. D., & Straatemeier, G. (2001). *The Pax acts game manual: How to apply the Good Behavior Game.* Tuscon, AZ: PAXIS Institute.

Emmer, E. T., Evertson, C. M., & Worsham, M. E. (2003). *Classroom management for secondary teachers* (6th ed.). Boston: Allyn and Bacon.

Eron, L. D., Huesmann, L. R., & Zelli, A. (1991). The role of parental variables in the learning of aggression. In D. J. Pepler & K. H Rubin (Eds.), *Development and treatment of childhood aggression* (pp. 169–188). Hillsdale, NJ, England: Lawrence Erlbaum Associates.

Ervin, R. A., Radford, P. M., Bertsch, K., Piper, A. L., Ehrhardt, K. E., & Poling, A. (2001). A descriptive analysis and critique of the empirical literature on school-based functional assessment. *School Psychology Review, 30*(2), 193–210.

Evertson, C. M., Emmer, E. T., & Worhsam, M. E. (2003). *Classroom management for elementary teachers* (6th ed.). Boston: Allyn and Bacon.

Fagan, J., & Wilkson, D. L. (1998). Social contexts and functions of adolescent violence. In D. S. Elliott, B. A. Hambrug, & K. R. Williams (Eds.), *Violence in American schools* (pp. 55–93). Cambridge, UK: Cambridge University Press.

Fantuzzo, J. W., King, J. A., & Heller, L. R. (1992). Effects of reciprocal tutoring on mathemat-ics and school adjustment: A component analysis. *Journal of Educational Psychology, 84*(3), 331–339.

Farrington, D. P., & Hawkins, J. D. (1991). Predicting participation, early onset, and later per-sistence in officially recorded offending. *Criminal Behaviour & Mental Health, 1*(1), 1–33.

Ferguson, A. A. (2000). *Bad boys: Public school and the making of black masculinity.* Ann Arbor: University of Michi-gan Press.

Florida Department of Education. (1995). *Florida school discipline study.* Tallahassee, FL: Office of Policy Research. (ED384981)

Frick, P., Kamphaus, R. W., Lahey, B. B., Loeber, R., Christ, M. G., Hart, E., et al. (1991). Academic underachievement and the disruptive behavior disorders. *Journal of Consulting and Clinical Psychology, 59,* 289–294.

Fuchs, D., Fuchs, L. S., & Burish, P. (2000). Peer-assisted learning strategies: An evidence-based practice to promote reading achievement. *Learning Disabilities Research and Practice, 15*(2), 85–91.

Fuller, B., Coonerty, C., Kipnis, F. M., & Choong, Y. (1997). An unfair headstart: California families face gaps in preschool and child care availability. Berkeley, CA: Berkeley-Stanford PACE Center, Yale University, and the California Child Care Resource and Referral Network's Growing Up in Poverty Project.

Giroux, H. A. (1983). Theories of reproduction and resistance in the new sociology of education: A critical analysis. *Harvard Educational Review, 53*(3), 257–293.

Gonzales, N. A., Cauce, A. M., & Friedman, R. J. (1996). Family, peer, and neighborhood influences on academic achievement among African-American adolescents: One-year prospective effects. *American Journal of Community Psychology, 24*(3), 365–387.

Gorman-Smith, D., & Tolan, P. (1998). The role of exposure to community violence and developmental problems among inner-city youth. *Development & Psychopathology, 10*(1), 101–116.

Gottfredson, D. G., Gottfredson, D. C., Czeh, E. R., Cantor, D., Crosse, S. B., & Hantman, I. (2004) Toward safe and orderly schools: National study of delinquency prevention in schools. *U.S. Department of Justice.* September 15, 2005, from http://www.ncjrs.gov/pdf-files1/nij/205005.pdf Gottfredson, D. C., Gottfredson, G. D., & Hybl, L. G. (1993).

Managing adolescent behavior: A multiyear, multischool study. *American Educational Research Journal, 30*(1), 179–215.

Gottlieb, G., & Halpern, C. T. (2002). A relational view of causality in normal and abnormal development. *Development and Psychopathology, 14,* 421–435.

Grandy, G. S., Madsen, C. H., & De Mersseman, L. M. (1973). The effects of individual and interdependent contingencies on inappropriate classroom behavior. *Psychology in the Schools, 10,* 488–493.

Gray, J. A. (1987). *The psychology of fear and stress.* Cam-bridge, UK: Cambridge University Press.

Greenberg, M. T., & Kusche, C. A. (1993). *Promoting social and emotional development in deaf children: The PATHS project.* Seattle, WA: University of Washington Press.

Greenberg, M. T., Kusche, C. A., Cook, E. T., & Quamma, J. P. (1995). Promoting emotional competence in school-aged children: The effects of the PATHS curriculum. *Development and Psychopathology, 7,* 117–136.

Greenberg, M. T., Kusche, C., & Mihalic, S. F. (1998). *Blueprints for violence prevention, book ten: Promoting alternative thinking strategies (PATHS).* Boulder, CO: Center for the Study and Prevention of Violence.

Gregory, A. (2004). *A window on the discipline gap: Cooperation or defiance in the high school classroom.* Doctoral dissertation, University of California, Berkeley.

Gregory, A., & Weinstein, S. R. (in press). A window on the discipline gap: Defiance or cooperation in the high school classroom. *Journal of School Psychology.*

Gregory, A., & Weinstein, R. S. (2004). Connection and regulation at home and in school: Predicting growth in achievement for adolescents. *Journal of Adolescent Research, 19*(4), 405–427.

Gregory, A., Nygreen, K., & Moran, D. (2006). The Discipline gap and the normalization of failure. In P. Noguera and J. Wing, (Eds.). *Unfinished business; Closing the racial achievement gap in our schools.* (pp. 121–150) John Wiley & Sons: CA.

Guerra, N. G., & Slaby, R. C. (1989). Evaluative factors in social problem solving by aggressive boys. *Journal of Abnormal Child Psychology, 17,* 277–289.

Gun–Free Schools Act of 1990, Crime Control Act of 1990, Pub. L. 101–647, 18 U.S.C. ₵ 922.

Harvard Civil Rights Project. (2000). *Opportunity suspended: The devastating consequence of zero-tolerance and school discipline policy.* Retrieved September 10, 2005, from http://www.civilrightsproject.harvard.edu/convenings/ zerotolerance/synopsis.php

Hawken, L. S., & Horner, R. H. (2003). Evaluation of a targeted intervention within a school-wide system of behavior support. *Journal of Behavioral Education, 12*(3), 225–240.

Hawkins, J. D., Guo, J., & Hill, K. G. (2001). Long-term effects of the Seattle Social Development Intervention on school bonding trajectories. *Applied Developmental Science, 5,* 225–236.

Hawkins, J. D., Herrenkohl, T., & Farrington, D. P. (1998). A review of predictors of youth violence. In R. Loeber & D. P. Farrington (Eds.), *Serious & violent juvenile offenders: Risk factors and successful interventions* (pp. 106– 146). Thousand Oaks, CA: Sage Publications, Inc.

Hawkins, J. D., Smith, B. H., & Catalano, R. F. (2004). Social development and social and emotional learning. In J. E. Zins, R. P. Weissberg, M. C. Wang, & H. J. Walberg (Eds.), *Building academic success on social and emotional learning: What does the research say?* (pp. 135–150). New York: Teachers College Press.

Hegerle, D. R., Kesecker, M. P., & Couch, J. V. (1979). A behav-ior game for the reduction of inappropriate classroom behaviors. *School Psychology Review, 8*, 339–343.

Heller, K. (1990). Social and community intervention. *Annual Review of Psychology, 41*, 141–168.

Henrich, C. C., Brown, J. L., & Aber, J. L. (1999). Evaluating the effectiveness of school-based violence prevention: Developmental approaches. *Social Policy Report, 13*, 1–16.

Hill, H. M., Fernando, I. S., Chen, S. A., & LaFrombois, T. D. (1994). Sociocultural factors in the etiology and prevention of violence among ethnic minority. In L. D. Eron, J. H. Gentry, P. Schlegel (Eds.), *Reason to hope. A psychosocial perspective on violence and youth* (pp. 59–98). Washington, DC: American Psychological Association.

Hinshaw, S. P. (1992). Academic underachievement, attention deficits, and aggression: Comorbidity and implications for intervention. *Journal of Consulting and Clinical Psychology, 60*(6), 893–903.

Hirschi, T. (1969). *Causes of delinquency*. Berkeley: University of California Press.

Hollingsworth, E. J., Lufler, H. S., & Clune, W. H. (1984). *School discipline: Order and autonomy*. New York: Praeger. Horner, R. H., Sugai, G., Lewis-Palmer, T., & Todd, A. W. (2001). Teaching school-wide behavioral expectations. *Report on Emotional & Behavioral Disorders in Youth, 1*(4), 77–79.

Howlin, P., & Rutter, M. (1987). The consequences of language delay for other aspects of development. In W. Yule & M. Rutter (Eds.), *Language development and disorders* (pp. 271–294). Oxford, UK: MacKeith.

Huesmann, L. R. (1988). An information processing model for the development of aggression. *Aggressive Behavior, 14*, 13–24.

Huesmann, L. R. & Eron, L. D (1984). Cognitive processes and the persistence of aggressive behavior. *Aggressive Behavior, 10*, 243–251.

Huesmann, L. R., & Eron, L. D. (Eds.). (1986). *Television and the aggressive child: A cross-national comparison*. Hills-dale, NJ: Erlbaum.

Huesmann, L. R., Moise, J. F., & Podoloski, C. (1997). The effects of media violence on the development of antisocial behavior. In D. M. Stoff, J. Breiling, & J. D. Maser (Eds.), *Handbook of antisocial behavior* (pp. 181–193). New York: John Wiley & Sons, Inc.

Hyman, I. A., & Perone, D. C. (1998). The other side of school violence: Educator policies and practices that may contribute to student misbehavior. *Journal of School Psychology, 36*(1), 7–27.

Ialongo, N., Poduska, J., Werthamer, L., & Kellam, S. (2001). The distal impact of two first-grade preventive interventions on conduct problems and disorder in early adolescence. *Journal of Emotional & Behavioral Disorders, 9*(3), 146–160.

Inoff-Germain, G., Arnold, G. S., Nottelmann, E. D., Susman, E. J., Cutler, G. B., & Chrousos, G. P. (1988). Relations between hormone levels and observational measures of aggressive behavior of young adolescents in family interactions. *Developmental Psychology, 24,* 129–139.

Jencks, C., & Mayer, S. (1990). The social consequence of growing up in a poor neighborhood. In L. E. Lynn & M. F. H. McGeary (Eds.), *Inner-city poverty in the United States* (pp. 111–186). Washington, DC: National Academy Press.

Johnson, D. W., & Johnson, R. T. (1996). Conflict resolution and peer mediation programs in elementary and secondary schools: A review of the research. *Review of Educational Research, 66*(4), 459–506.

Kaukianinen, A., Bjorkqvist, K., Lagerspetz, K., Osterman, K., Salmivalli, C., Rothberg, S., et al. (1999). The relationships between social intelligence, empathy, and three types of aggression. *Aggressive Behavior, 25,* 81–89.

Kellam, S. G., Ling, X., & Merisca, R. (1998). The effect of the level of aggression in the first grade classroom on the course and malleability of aggressive behavior into middle school. *Development & Psychopathology, 10*(2), 165–185.

Kounin, J. S. (1970). *Discipline and group management in classrooms.* Oxford, UK: Holt, Rinehart, & Winston.

Kruesi, M. J. P., Hibbs, E. D., Zahn, T. P., Keysor, C. S., Hamburger, S. D., Bartko, F. F., et al. (1992). A 2-year prospective follow-up study of children and adolescents with disruptive behavior disorders. *Archives of General Psychiatry, 49,* 429–435.

Laird, R. D., Jordan, K. Y., Dodge, K. A., Pettit, G. S., & Bates, J. E. (2001) Peer rejection in childhood, involvement with antisocial peers in early adolescence, and the development of externalizing problems. *Development and Psychopathology, 13,* 337–354.

Lansford, J. E., Deater-Deckard, K., Dodge, K. A., Bates, J. E., & Pettit, G. S. (2004). Ethnic differences in the link between physical discipline and later adolescent exter-nalizing behaviors. *Journal of Child Psychology and Psychiatry, 45*(4), 801–812.

Leff, S. S. (2005, July). *Joining with stakeholders to design a relational aggression program.* Poster presented at the Eighteenth NIMH Conference on Mental Health Services Research, Bethesda, MD.

Leff, S. S., Costigan, T., & Power, T. J. (2004). Using participatory research to develop a playground-based prevention program. *Journal of School Psychology, 42*(1), 3–21.

Leff, S. S., Power, T. J., Manz, P. H., Costigan, T. E., & Nabors, L. A. (2001). School-based aggression prevention programs for young children: Current status and implications for violence prevention. *School Psychology Review, 30*, 343–360.

Leventhal, T., & Brooks-Gunn, J. (2000). The neighborhood could live in: The effects of neighborhood residents on child and adolescent outcomes. *Psychological Bulletin, 126* (2), 309–337.

Lewis, T. J., & Sugai, G. (1999). Effective behavior support: A systems approach to proactive school-wide management. *Effective School Practices, 17*(4), 47–53.

Lewis, T. J., Sugai, G., & Colvin, G. (1998). Reducing problem behavior through a school-wide system of effective behavioral support: Investigation of a school-wide social skills training program and contextual interventions. *School Psychology Review, 27*, 446–459.

Lochman, J. E. (1992). Cognitive-behavioral intervention with aggressive boys: Three-year follow-up and preventive effects. *Journal of Consulting and Clinical Psychology, 60*(3), 426–432.

Lochman, J. E., Barry, T. D., & Pardini, D. A. (2003). Anger control training for aggressive youth. In A. E. Kazdin & J. R. Weisz (Eds.), *Evidence-based psychotherapies for children and adolescents* (pp. 263–281). New York: Guil-ford Press.

Lochman, J. E., & Wells, K. C. (2004). The Coping Power Program for preadolescent aggressive boys and their parents: Outcome effects at the 1-year follow-up. *Journal of Consulting & Clinical Psychology, 72*(4), 571–578.

Loeber, R., Burke, J. D., Lahey, B. B., Winters, A., & Zera, M. (2000). Oppositional defiant and conduct disorder: A review of the past 10 years, Part I. *Journal of the Ameri-can Academy of Child & Adolescent Psychiatry, 39*(12), 1468–1484.

Lohrman-O'Rourke, S., Knoster, T., Sabatine, K., Smith, D., Horvath, B., & Llewellyn, G. (2000). School-wide application of positive behavior support in the Bangor Area School District. *Journal of Positive Behavior Interventions, 2*, 238–240.

Luiselli, J. K., Putnam, R. F., & Sunderland, M. (2002). Longitudinal evaluation of behavior support intervention in a public middle school. *Journal of Positive Behavioral Interventions, 4*(3), 182–188.

Maguin, E., & Loeber, R. (1996). Academic performance and delinquency. In M. Tonry (Ed.), *Crime and justice: A review of research* (Vol. 20, pp. 145–264). Chicago: University of Chicago Press.

March, R. E., & Horner, R. H. (2002). Feasibility and contributions of functional behavior assessment in schools. *Journal of Emotional and Behavioral Disorders, 10*(3), 158–170.

Matheny, A. P. (1989). Children's behavioral inhibition over age and across situations: Genetic similarity for a trait during change. *Journal of Personality, 57,* 215–226.

Maughan, B., Gray, G., & Rutter, M. (1985). Reading retardation and antisocial behavior: A follow-up into employment. *Journal of Child Psychology and Psychiatry, 26,* 741–758.

Mayer, G. R. (1995). Preventing antisocial behavior in the schools. *Journal of Applied Behavior Analysis, 28,* 467–478.

McCarthy, J. D., & Hoge, D. R. (1987). Social construction of school punishment. *Social Forces, 65*(4), 1101–1120.

McEvoy, A., & Welker, R. (2000). Antisocial behavior, academic failure, and school climate: A critical review. *Journal of Emotional and Behavioral Disorders, 8*(3), 130–140.

McGee, R., & Share, D. L. (1988). Attention deficit disorder hyperactivity and academic failure: Which comes first and which should be treated? *Journal of the American Academy of Child and Adolescent Psychiatry, 27,* 318–325.

Mednick, S. A., Gabrielli, W. F., Jr., & Hutchings, B. (1984). Genetic influences in criminal convictions: Evidence from an adoption cohort. *Science, 224,* 891–894.

Moffitt, T. E., & Caspi, A. (2001). Childhood predictors differentiate life-course persistent and adolescence-limited antisocial pathways among males and females. *Development & Psychopathology, 13*(2), 355–375.

National Association of State Boards of Education. (2005). *State-by-state emotional and social health education.* Retrieved October 1, 2005, from http://www.nasbe.org/

National Center for Education Statistics. (1999). *School survey on crime and safety.* Retrieved October 1, 2005, from http://www.nces.ed.gov/

National Center for Education Statistics. (2000). *OCR Elementary and Secondary Survey.* Retrieved October 1, 2005, from http://www.nces.ed.gov/

National Center for Education Statistics (2003). *Status and trends in the education of Hispanic students.* Retrieved October 1, 2005, from http"//www.nces.ed.gov/

National Center for Education Statistics. (2004) *Indicators of school crime and safety.* Retrieved October 1, 2005, from http://www.nces.ed.gov/

Olweus, D. (1999). Sweden. In P. K. Smith, Y. Morita, J. Junger-Tas, D. Olweus, R. Catalano, & P. Slee (Eds.), *The nature of school bullying: A cross-national perspective* (pp. 7–27). London: Routledge.

Olweus, D., Mattsson, A., Schalling, D., & Low, H. (1988). Circulating testosterone levels and aggression in adolescent males: A causal analysis. *Psychosomatic Medicine, 50,* 261–272.

Osgood, D. W., & Chambers, J. M. (2003). *Community correlates of rural youth violence.* Washington DC: U.S. Department of Justice, Juvenile Justice Bulletin.

Patterson, G. R. (1982). *Coercive family process.* Eugene, OR: Castalia.

Patterson, G. R. (1995). Coercion as a basis for early age of onset for arrest. (pp. 81¬105). In J. McCord (Ed.) *Coercion and punishment in long-term perspectives.* New York: Cambridge University Press.

Patterson, G. R., Dishion, T. J., & Yoerger, K. (2000). Adolescent growth in new forms of problem behavior: Macro- and micro-peer dynamics. *Prevention Science, 1*(1), 3–13.

Pianta, R. C. (1999). *Enhancing relationships between children and teachers.* Washington, DC: American Psychological Association.

Pigott, H. E., Fantuzzo, J. W., & Clement, P. (1986). The effects of reciprocal peer tutoring and group contingencies on the academic performance of elementary school children. *Journal of Applied Behavior Analysis, 19,* 93–98.

Pliszka, S. R., Rogeness, G. A., Renner, P., Sherman, J., & Broussard, T. (1988). Plasma neurochemistry in juvenile offenders. *Journal of the American Academy of Child and Adolescent Psychiatry, 27,* 588–594.

Quiggle, N., Garber, J., Panak, W. F., & Dodge, K. A. (1992). Social-information processing in aggressive and depressed children. *Child Development, 63,* 1305–1320.

Quinn, M. M., Gable, R. A., Fox, J., Rutherford, R. B., Jr., Van Acker, R., Conroy, M., et al. (2001). Putting quality functional assessment into practice in schools: A research agenda on behalf of E/BD students. *Education & Treatment of Children, 24*(3), 261–275.

Raine, A. (1993). *The psychopathology of crime: Criminal behav-ior as a clinical disorder.* New York: Academic Press.

Reid, J. B., & Eddy, J. M. (1997). The prevention of antisocial behavior; Some considerations in the search for effective interventions. In D. M. Stoff, J. Breiling, & J. D. Maser (Eds.), *Handbook of antisocial behavior* (pp. 343–355). New York: John Wiley & Sons.

Reid, J. B., Eddy, J. M. & Fetrow, R. A. (1999). Description and immediate impacts of a preventive intervention for conduct problems. *American Journal of Community Psychology, 27*(4), 483–517.

Reid, R., Gonzalez, J. E., Nordness, P. D., Trout, A., & Epstein, M. H. (2004). A meta-analysis of the academic status of students with emotional/behavioral disturbance. *The Journal of Special Education, 38*(3), 130–143.

Reid, J. B., Patterson, G. R., & Snyder, J. (2002). *Antisocial behavior in children and adolescents: A developmental analysis and model for intervention.* Washington, DC: American Psychological Association.

Reid, M. J., Webster-Stratton, C., & Baydar, N. (2004). Halting the development of conduct problems in Head Start children: The effects of parent training. *Journal of Clinical Child & Adolescent Psychology, 33*(2), 279–291.

Richman, N., Stevenson, J., & Graham, P. (1982). *Preschool to school: A behavioral study.* San Diego, CA: Academic Press.

Rimm-Kaufman, S. E., Pianta, R. C., & Cox, M. J. (2000). Teachers' judgments of problems in the transition to kindergarten. *Early Childhood Research Quarterly, 15*(2), 147–166.

Rogeness, G. A., Javors, M. A., & Pliszka, S. R. (1992). Neuro-chemistry and child and adolescent psychiatry. *Journal of the American Academic of Child and Adolescent Psychiatry, 31,* 765–781.

Rohrbeck, C. A., Ginsburg-Block, M. D., Fantuzzo, J. W., & Miller, T. R. (2003). Peer-assisted learning interventions with elementary school students: A meta-analytic review. *Journal of Educational Psychology, 95*(2), 240–257.

Rutter, M., & Giller, H. (1983). *Juvenile delinquency: Trends and perspectives.* Harmondsworth, U.K.: Penguin Books.

Rutter, M., Maughan, B., Mortiore, P., & Ouston, J. (1979). *Fifteen thousand hours.* Cambridge, MA: Harvard University Press.

Rutter, M., & Sroufe, L. A. (2000). Developmental psychopathology: Concepts and challenges. *Development and Psychopathology, 12,* 265–296.

Saft, E. W., & Pianta, R. C. (2001). Teachers' perceptions of their relationships with students: Effects of child age, gender, and ethnicity of teachers and students. *School Psychology Quarterly, 16*(7), 125–140.

Salend, S. J., Reynolds, C. J., & Coyle, E. M. (1989). Individual-izing the good behavior game across type and frequency of behavior with emotionally disturbed adolescents. *Be-havior Modification, 13*(1), 108–126.

Sampson, R. J., Morenoff, J. D., & Earls, F. (1999). Beyond social capital: Spatial dynamics of collective efficacy for children. *American Sociological Review, 64*(5), 633–660.

Schneider, D. J. (1991). Social cognition. *Annual Review of Psychology, 42*, 527–561.

Sherman, L. W., Gottfredson, D., MacKenzie, D., Eck, J., Reuter, P., & Bushway, S. (1997). *Preventing crime: What works, what doesn't, what's promising. A report to the United States Congress.* Washington, DC: National Institute of Justice.

Shriver, T. P., & Weissberg, R. P. (2005, August 16). No emotion left behind. *New York Times,* p. A15.

Slaby, R. C., & Guerra, N. G. (1988). Cognitive mediators of aggression in adolescent offenders: I. Assessment. *Developmental Psychology, 24*, 580–588.

Sladeczek, I., Kratochwill, T. R., Steinback, C. L., Kumke, P., & Hagermoser, L. (2003). Problem-solving consultation in the new millennium. In E. Cole, J. A. Ester, Siegel, & A. Jane (Eds.), *Effective consultation in school psychology* (pp. 60–86). Ashland, OH: Hogrefe & Huber Publishers.

Skiba, R., Michael, R. S., Nardo, A. C., & Peterson, R. (2002). The color of discipline: Sources of racial and gender disproportionality in school punishment. *The Urban Review, 34*(4), 317–342.

Skiba, R. J., Peterson, R. L., & Williams, T. (1997). Office referrals and suspension: Disciplinary intervention in middle schools. *Education & Treatment of Children, 20*(3), 295–313.

Snyder, J. (2002). Reinforcement and coercion mechanisms in the development of antisocial behavior: Peer relationships. In J. B Reid, G. R. Patterson, & J. Snyder (Eds.), *Antisocial behavior and children in adolescence: The developmental analysis on model for intervention* (pp. 101–122). Washington, DC: American Psychological Association.

Solomon, D., Battistich, V., Watson, M., Schaps, E., & Lewis, C. (2000). A six-district study of educational change: Direct and mediated effects of the Child Development Project. *Social Psychology of Education, 4*, 3–51.

Spivak, G., & Shure, M. B. (1980). Interpersonal problem-solving as a mediator of behavioral adjustment in preschool and kindergarten children. *Journal of Developmental Psychology, 1*, 29–44.

Spoont, M. R. (1992). Modulatory role of serotonin in neural information processing: Implications for human psychopathology. *Psychological Bulletin, 112,* 330–350.

Steinberg, L., Lamborn, S. D., & Darling, N. (1994). Over-time changes in adjustment and competence among adolescents from authoritative, authoritarian, indulgent, and neglectful families. *Child Development, 65*(3), 754–770.

Susman, E. J., Inoff-Germain, G., Nottelmann, E. D., Loriaux, L., Cutler, G. B., & Chrousos, G. P. (1987). Hormones, emotional dispositions, and aggressive attributes in young adolescents. *Child Development, 58,* 1114–1134.

Sutherland, E. H. (1939). *Principles of criminology* (3rd ed.). Philadelphis: Lippincott. Reid, Eddy, & Fetrow, 1999.

Tallal, P., Dukette, D., & Curtiss, S. (1989). Behavioral/emotional profiles of preschool language-impaired children. *Development and Psychopathology, 1,* 51–67.

Taylor-Greene, S. J., & Kartub, D. T. (2000). Durable implementation of school-wide behavior support: The high five program. *Journal of Positive Behavior Interventions, 2,* 233–245.

Thornberrry, T. P., & Krohn, M. D. (1997). Peers, drug use, and delinquency. In D. M. Stoff, J. Breiling, & J. D. Maser (Eds.), *Handbook of antisocial behavior* (pp. 218–233). New York: John Wiley & Sons.

Tingstrom, D. H. (1994) The good behavior game: An investigation of teachers' acceptance. *Psychology in the Schools, 31,* 57–65.

Tolan, P. H., & Guerra, N. G. (1994). Prevention of delinquency: Current status and issues. *Applied & Preventive Psychology, 3*(4), 251–273.

Tolan, P. H., Guerra, N. G., & Kendall, P. C. (1995). A developmental-ecological perspective on antisocial behavior in children and adolescents: Toward a unified risk and intervention framework. *Journal of Consulting and Clinical Psychology, 63*(4), 579–584.

Topping, K. J., & Ehly, S. W. (2001). Peer assisted learning: A framework for consultations. *Journal of Educational and Psychological Consultation, 12*(2), 113–132.

Underwood, M. K. (2003). *Social aggression among girls.* New York: Guilford Press.

Watts, I. E., & Erevelles, N. (2004). These deadly times: Recon-ceptualizing school violence. *American Educational Research Journal, 41*(2), 271–299.

Webster-Stratton, C. (2005). The incredible years: A training series for the prevention and treatment of conduct problems in young children. In E. D. Hibbs & P. S. Jensen (Eds.), *Psychosocial treatments for child and adolescent disorders: Empirically based strategies for clinical prac-tice* (2nd ed., pp. 507–555). Washington, DC: American Psychological Association.

Webster-Stratton, C., Reid, M. J., & Hammond, M. (2004). Treating children with early onset conduct problems: Intervention outcomes for parent, child, teacher training. *Journal of Clinical Child and Adolescent Psychology, 33*(1), 105–124.

Weinstein, R. S. (2002). *Reaching higher: The power of expectations in schooling.* Cambridge, MA: Harvard University Press.

Weissberg, R. P., & Greenberg, M. T. (1998). School and community competence-enhancement and prevention programs. In W. Damon, I. E. Sigel, & K. A. Renninger (Eds.), *Handbook of child psychology: Vol. 4: Child psychology in prac-tice* (5th ed., pp. 877–954). New York: John Wiley & Sons,.

Wentzel, K. R. (2002). Are effective teachers like good parents? Teaching styles and student adjustment in early adolescence. *Child Development, 73*(1), 287–301.

Werthamer-Larsson, L., Kellam, S. G., & Wheeler, L. (1991). Effect of first-grade classroom environment on shy behavior, aggressive behavior, and concentration problems. *American Journal of Community Psychology, 19*(4), 585–602.

Wilson, D. B., Gottfredson, D. C., & Najaka, S. S. (2001). School-based prevention of problem behaviors: A meta-analysis. *Journal of Quantitative Criminology, 17*(3), 247–272.

Wilson, S. J., Lipsey, M. W., & Derzon, J. H. (2003). The effects of school-based intervention programs on aggressive behavior: A meta-analysis. *Journal of Consulting & Clinical Psychology, 71*(1), 136–149.

Wolfe, J. A., Fantuzzo, J. W., & Wolfe, P. K. (1986). The effects of reciprocal peer management on the arithmetic proficiency of underachieving students. *Behavior Therapy, 17,* 253–265.

Xie, H., Swift, D. J., Cairns, B., & Cairns, R. B. (2002). Aggressive behaviors in social interaction and developmental adaptation: A narrative analysis of interpersonal conflicts during early adolescence. *Social Development, 11*(2), 205–224.

CHAPTER 14

Classroom Management

INTRODUCTION
BY KISHA R. CUNNINGHAM, PHD

"A schoolmaster should have an atmosphere of awe, and walk wonderingly, as if he was amazed at being himself."

—Newton D. Baker

Many teachers often arrange classrooms or create routines such as flicking classroom lights on and off or creating chants that keep the class orderly. It is critical that all teachers keep their classrooms safe and manageable at the same time. Distractions are a constant in today's classrooms. Teachers must develop a policy that details the management plan. This can be difficult for teachers because most must make sacrifices to ensure that every student is learning to the best of their ability at all times. Teachers use management not to control student behavior, but to influence and direct it in a constructive manner to set the stage for instruction. Effective teachers know that student behavior is not only about rules and consequences, but that the development of a classroom climate influences how students perceive their environment and how they behave. Chapter 14 examines classroom management and the art of making the most out of the time allotted in the classroom.

Classroom Management

CORA THOMPSON, EDD

THE SCHOOL OF TEACHER EDUCATION, SAVANNAH STATE UNIVERSITY

One challenge that educators at all levels often face is that of classroom management. Whether you are just learning to teach, experiencing the first several years of your teaching career, or working as a veteran teacher with a rapidly changing student population, your classroom management skills will be a major factor in how your students learn and how satisfied you are with your role as a teacher.

Classroom management involves the effective use of the teacher's time in the classroom to be as productive as possible to facilitate and nurture a productive learning experience. As teachers face larger class sizes and an increasing number of students with special behavioral and learning needs, skills in classroom management will become the absolute foundation for creating classroom learning environments in which all students can achieve academic success. Regardless of how effectively schools implement school-wide methods for teaching and reinforcing desirable school behavior, because students spend the vast majority of their school day and virtually all of their academic learning time in classroom settings, teachers' classroom management skills will continue to be a key factor in students' academic success (Jones, 2011).

Concerns about student behavior and classroom management do more than create stress for teachers and affect the number of teachers who enter or remain in teaching for an extended duration. In addition, these concerns often cause teachers to limit their use of instructional methods that actively engage students in the learning process (Wong and Wong, 1991). If teachers are to implement engaging, meaningful instructional activities that enhance student motivation and higher-level thinking skills, teachers must become comfortable and effective with their classroom management skills.

The lack of classroom management undeniably interrupts the learning process. Research shows that teachers' actions in their classrooms have twice the impact on student achievement (Marzano, 2003). Therefore, the classroom teacher's most important job is managing the classroom effectively. Implementing a few basic classroom management strategies can help the teacher effectively organize his or her time and provide opportunities to explore learning.

Research not only supports the importance of classroom management, but it also sheds light on the dynamics of classroom management. There must be a balance between teacher actions that provide clear consequences for unacceptable behavior and teacher actions that recognize and reward acceptable behavior (Stage and Quiroz, 1997). According to Emmer, Evertson, and Worsham (2003), there are several important components of classroom management: room arrangement, routines and procedures, positive teacher-student relationship, and clear instructions.

Component One (Room Arrangement)

The physical aspect of the classroom is the first thing that students perceive when they step inside the classroom. It can influence their attitude toward learning, even without them being aware of it. According to Guillaume (2008), the design of the classroom must be productive and efficient and provide students with all the resources necessary to learn and do well. There are several ways to set up a classroom to enhance learning. Some teachers prefer a "hospital"-type environment that is very organized, efficient, neat, and clean. Others prefer more homelike surroundings that are cozy, warm, and personalized. The type of classroom design a teacher chooses is based on his or her own classroom needs, goals, and personality.

A disorganized classroom does not provide a lot of structure. If the layout of the classroom is not well organized, then it is hard for the teacher to get to the students. It is also hard for the students to get to each other and the materials necessary for them to learn. A messy classroom also makes it hard for the teacher to properly manage the class and monitor the students, which can make the classroom unsafe. A classroom should be designed in a way that is productive, so that it provides balance. The students need to be able to see and hear each other as well as the teacher. An organized classroom makes it easier for students to focus on the task at hand and for them to stay organized.

Successful classrooms make use of the space provided and provide freedom of movement. According to the *Classroom Teacher's Survival Guide*, "The physical arrangement of the classroom can influence students' behavior and learning. Classroom design should be carefully mapped out prior to the first day of school. The teacher should consider the placement of desk, bookshelves, supplies, and work stations so that students can interact with each other and be productive learners" (Partin, 2005).

Some things Guillaume (2008) says to think about when providing an academically rich and safe learning environment are:

- Will the students feel comfortable?
- Is the classroom arrangement conducive to learning?
- Is the classroom safe?
- Can I monitor all the students at once?
- Can my students hear me?
- Do the students know what is expected of them?
- Is my classroom free of traffic jams?
- Is there flexibility in my seating?
- Are there enough work stations and special-interest sites?
- Are the classroom rules posted where the class can see them?
- Do I have all the materials and supplies needed to effectively teach?

Component Two (Routines and Procedures)

Evertson and Weinstein (2006) identify appropriate dominance as an important characteristic of classroom management. The way the teacher manages the day-to-day operations of the classroom and discipline of the students directly affects the learning environment. Effective classroom teachers spend more of their time in the first few weeks of the year teaching classroom routines and procedures as opposed to academic content because routines and procedures are key to a well-managed, organized classroom. Research shows that most behavior problems result from a lack of classroom routines and procedures. Moreover, the number of interruptions to academic instruction are reduced, and things flows more smoothly (Jones, 2011).

Points to remember:

- Have a copy of your routines and procedures to hand to each of your students on the first day of school. Keep extra copies on hand for new students arriving later in the year.
- Discuss each routine and procedure to the fullest and be sure to monitor and reinforce when necessary.
  - Explain the rationale behind the routine or procedure

- Model the routine or procedure for the students
- Have the students model the procedures
- Assess the students on routines and class procedures (skits, role play, games, etc.)
- Be consistent. The time spent teaching, monitoring, and reinforcing routines and procedures during the first weeks will pay off tremendously. If the routines and procedures are established at the beginning of the year, the rest of the year will be more enjoyable and productive for both you and the students.
- Here are some items to make sure students understand the procedures for

  - Entering and leaving the classroom
  - Getting and working into groups
  - Working at a learning center station
  - Procedures for using/carrying/handling equipment
  - Sharpening pencils
  - Teacher's attention signal
  - Restroom
  - Finishing work early
  - Makeup work
  - Getting help and asking questions
  - Heading paper, passing in classwork and homework
  - Responding to fire drills or other emergency alerts
  - Cell phones
  - Visitor in the classroom

But before choosing any technique, it is crucial to understand the demographics of the classroom and then choose age-appropriate techniques. The teacher should also be sure to understand what behaviors are culturally and age-appropriate. Regardless of the demographics of the classroom and the technique the teacher chooses, the teacher must be consistent in his or her responses and actions to misbehavior. The students should not receive mixed messages and that the teacher favors some students over others. In addition, it is a great idea to get parents involved by drafting a document for them to discuss with their child at home and have both parent and student sign, indicating their acknowledgment of classroom routines and procedures.

Regardless of what grade level a teacher teaches, he or she deals with transitions on a daily basis. Transitions include any time the teacher stops one activity and goes to another. Taking control of transitions means the teacher will spend less time organizing the students so the teacher can get right to the activities. Transitions from one activity to another can also be the cause of many classroom behavioral problems. If the transitions are unstructured, teachers can guarantee themselves an increase in classroom management issues. Here are some simple but effective classroom management tips for transitioning:

- Have a respond signal—teachers must have some type of signal to bring students to a halt (hand clap, timer, song, chat, music, light flickering, etc.)
- Have students free-write in response to a topic
- Put a scrambled word on the board and allow students to create as many words as possible from the scrambled word
- Do some physical exercises

Component Three (Teacher-Student Relationship)

Research shows that the quality of the teacher-student relationship is the keystone for effective productive classroom management. It also shows that teachers who have high-quality relationships with their students have fewer discipline problems and rule violations than those who do not have high-quality relationships (Marzano, 2003). Based on extensive review of the literature, Evertson and Weinstein (2006) found that students preferred and responded best to teachers who (1) established caring relationships with students; (2) set limits and created a safe environment without being rigid, threatening, or punitive; and (3) made learning fun.

All students appreciate personal attention from the teacher. Although busy teachers, particularly those at the secondary level, do not have the time for extensive interaction with all students, some teacher actions can communicate personal interest and concern without taking up much time. Teachers can

- Talk informally with students before, during, and after class about their interests.
- Greet students outside of school, for instance, at extracurricular events.
- Single out a few students each day in the lunchroom and talk with them.

- Be aware of and comment on important events in students' lives such as participation in sports, drama, or other extracurricular activities.
- Compliment students on important achievements in and outside of school.
- Meet students at the door as they come into class and greet each one by name (Marzano, 2003).

On the whole, while many teachers may attribute students' academic and behavioral struggles to factors outside the classroom and school, research consistently shows that teachers and schools make a dramatic difference in the lives of many children, regardless of age (Jones, 2011). Effective classroom management is first and foremost about creating classroom environments in which all students feel safe and valued. Only in this type of environment are students able to maximize their learning of important social and academic skills. When students and teachers create these types of classroom settings, students make better choices, and their learning is enhanced. Effective classroom management involves thoughtful planning and focused professional growth. It is both a very personal and a very professional activity that requires integrating one's own professional knowledge and skills with careful attention to their own personal beliefs and values and students' wants and needs, including their developmental and learning needs and their cultural values. Responding to student behavior that disrupts the student's own learning and/or the learning of others in a way that treats students respectfully and helps them develop skills for working effectively in the classroom and school settings is crucial.

Dealing with disruptive behaviors in class is a skill that teachers must learn. Before attempting one of several strategies to manage bad behavior, teachers must understand what triggers it. There are multiple causes for students' misbehavior: curricular variables (tasks are too difficult, easy, boring, or unstructured); social variables (positive or negative interactions between students); and setting variables (time of day, personal problems at home, student feeling sick, hungry, or tired). When the causes are clear, teachers can take appropriate measures to handle inappropriate behavior.

Teachers who value students' opinions and feelings and are genuinely interested in their progress seldom have classroom management issues (Evertson and Weinstein, 2006). Treating students equally, yet trying to meet each and every one's needs as individuals with different learning styles, creates a positive learning climate in the classroom. Teacher-student relationships based on mutual trust and respect can contribute to students' successful acquisition of knowledge and lead to good academic results.

Have high expectations for each student. Students want to please and be accepted. If the teacher gives students structure and support, they will rise to the teacher's expectations.

Component Four (Clear Instructions)

Jones (2011) states that a key step in presenting a lesson is providing clear instructions for the activities in which students will be engaged. A significant amount of disruptive student behavior stems from student confusion about how to proceed or what they are to do when they require assistance or complete their work. Taking the time to plan creative lessons prevents classroom disruptions.

A lesson is meant to be an engaging and interactive learning experience for the students. When students do not find the lesson interesting, behavior and management issues might arise. Lessons should be planned in a creative manner that incorporates culture references, activities employing differentiated instruction, and bell-to-bell activities. When students are actively engaged, behavior problems disappear. Teachers must be clear when giving directions for daily activities in the classroom. Clearly state or write on a visual the steps the student needs to follow to complete the stated task. A lot of misbehavior comes from students simply not knowing what to do. Also, giving students the opportunity to set their own objectives at the beginning of a unit or asking students what they would like to learn conveys a sense of cooperation (Partin, 2005).

In addition, teachers must give clear, specific, descriptive feedback that helps students take responsibility for their successes. Research indicates that when teachers increase their rate of specific praise, there is a reduction in disruptive student behavior, the number of negative statements teachers make to students, and an increase in students' on-task behavior (Jones, 2011).

In conclusion, there are many ways to achieve successful classroom management. The ways the teacher manages the day-to-day operations of the classroom and discipline of the students directly affects the learning environment for the student. There is no one style of classroom management that is effective; usually, a combination of many different strategies must be used to achieve an optimal classroom environment. You have to find your own style. Find what works for you. Just because a method works for another teacher doesn't mean it will work for you. To sum it all up, strong classroom management is essential to effective teaching. Regardless of how wonderful a teacher might be, without classroom management, the students are simply unable to learn. As it is such a crucial part of teaching, there are many different opinions and views as to what the best classroom management techniques are. While these techniques may vary from teacher to teacher, there are a few guiding principles that distinguish effective classroom management from ineffective.

References

Emmer, E., C. Evertson, and M. Worsham (2003). *Classroom Management for Elementary Teachers*, 6th ed. Boston: Allyn & Bacon.

Evertson, C., and C. Weinstein (2006). *Handbook of Classroom Management: Research, Practice, and Contemporary Issues*. Mahwah, NJ: Lawrence Erlbaum.

Guillaume, A. (2008). *K–12 Classroom Teaching: A Primer for New Professionals*, 3rd ed. New York: Pearson.

Jones, V. (2011). *Practical Classroom Management*, 2nd ed. New York: Pearson. Marzano, R. (2003). *Classroom Management That Works*. Alexandria, VA: ASCD.

Partin, R. (2005). *Classroom Teacher's Survival Guide: Practical Strategies, Management Techniques, and Reproducibles for New and Experienced Teachers*, 2nd ed. NJ: John Wiley & Sons.

Stage, S., and D. Quiroz (1997). "A meta-analysis of interventions to decrease disruptive classroom behavior in public education settings." *School Psychology Review* 26(3), 333–368.

Wong, H., and R. Wong (1991). *First Day of School: How to Be an Effective Teacher*. CA: Wong Publishing.

REFLECTIONS

1. Write a brief statement on how your beliefs about discipline have been developed and how they relate to your own upbringing and personal values.

2. Try to remember a teacher you had in elementary, middle, or high school you felt created a safe, supportive environment and whom you admired as an educator.

What were the characteristics this teacher possessed that enabled him or her to be successful and to be remembered by you as an excellent teacher?

3. Create a list of what you or a teacher with whom you are working or observing has done to get to know students.

4. Consider a class you are currently teaching, one you have observed or one in which you are working. Create a list of five to ten procedures you believe are among the most important for facilitating a smooth, calm flow in the classroom.

5. Compare and contrast effective classroom management at the middle and high school levels. Which classroom management approach would be the most effective at the grade level you expect to teach?

CHAPTER 15

Math Between Creativity and Facts

INTRODUCTION
BY KISHA R. CUNNINGHAM, PHD

"The principle goal of education is to create men who are capable of doing new things, not simply of repeating what other generations have done—men who are creative, inventive and discoverers."

—Jean Piaget

Math Between Creativity and Facts

MIHAELA MUNDAY, PHD
SAVANNAH STATE UNIVERSITY

Broadly speaking, creativity is a concept that refers to the *potential* that a person has to take a *creative activity*. Creative activity is one of the fundamental forms of human activity (other forms are playing, learning, work, and communication). It differs from other forms of human activity by the characteristics of *products*, one of them being the *processuality*. The *products* meet a range of creative activity–specific attributes: *innovation, originality, ingenuity, practicality,* and *social value*. From the psychological viewpoint of the structures involved, creativity is an *integral dimension of personality*. Topics: Requires imagination, but not limited to imaginative processes; involving intelligence, but not every intelligent person is smart and creative; requires motivation and willpower, but cannot be explained only by these issues, etc.

As a process, creativity is related to solving problems, but the creative person is one who *discovers* new problems for which there was a previous resolution strategy, since the problem cannot be classified in a class of problems known.

Facts

"The Creativity Crisis: The Decrease in Creative Thinking Scores on the Torrance Tests of Creative Thinking," published in *Creativity Research Journal* (2011), discusses the decline of creativity among children in the United States. Mentioned in that article was the work of Kyung Hee Kim, an associate professor of educational psychology at the College of William & Mary in Williamsburg, Virginia. Kim has performed analyses of a creativity measure known as the Torrance test for almost 300,000 American adults and children. Her findings, that Americans' creativity has plummeted in recent years, caught the attention of teachers and psychologists across the country.

Dr. E. Paul Torrance developed the Torrance Tests of Creative Thinking (TTCT) in 1966; the test has been updated five times, in 1974, 1984, 1990, 1998, and 2008. The TTCT appears in almost 40 different languages. Educators and corporate entities use and reference the TTCT more than any other creativity test in the world.

TTCT measures the following subscales of creative potential: Fluency, Originality, 13 Checklists of Creative Strengths, Elaboration, Abstractness of Titles, and Resistance to Premature Closure. The above subscales can be grouped together into three main concepts of creative potential:

1. *Lateral/Innovative thinking factor* (Fluency and Originality): Fluency measures an ability to produce a number of relevant ideas. Originality measures an ability to produce a number of statistically infrequent ideas and shows how unique and unusual the ideas are.

2. *Vertical/Adaptive thinking factor* (Elaboration and Abstractness of Titles): Elaboration measures an ability to develop and elaborate upon ideas and detailed and reflective thinking, but it also indicates motivation to be creative. Abstractness of Titles measures an ability to produce the thinking processes of synthesis and organization; further, it measures an ability to capture the essence of the information involved and to know what is important. This is based on the idea that creativity requires an abstraction of thought. Abstractness of Titles is also related to verbal intelligence.

3. *Creative Personality factor* (Resistance to Premature Closure and 13 Checklists of Creative Strengths): Resistance to Premature Closure measures intellectual curiosity as well as open-mindedness. Open-mindedness predicts both IQ and creativity, and it is also found to be the most influential factor on intelligence. Finally, for the Creativity Personality factor, 13 Creative Strengths include creative personality traits such as being emotionally expressive (Emotional Expressiveness); energetic (Movement or Action); talkative or verbally expressive (Storytelling Articulateness, or Expressiveness of Titles); humorous (Humor); imaginative (Fantasy); unconventional (Extending or Breaking Boundaries); lively or passionate (Richness of Imagery); perceptive (Colorfulness of Imagery); connecting seemingly irrelevant things together (Synthesis of Incomplete Figures); synthesizing (Synthesis of Lines or Circles); and seeing things from a different angle (Unusual Visualization or Internal Visualization).

Creativity has decreased over the last 20 years. The results indicate that all of the scores of the Lateral/Innovative thinking factor, Vertical/Adaptive thinking factor, and Creative personality factor have significantly decreased or have started decreasing significantly. The decrease has been stronger in recent years than earlier years. The results of each subscale of the TTCT are below:

- Decrease in Fluency after 1990: Fluency scores (quantity of the ideas: ability to produce a number of ideas) decreased by 4.68 percent from 1990 to 1998 and by 7.00 percent from 1990 to 2008.

- Decrease in Originality after 1990: Originality scores (quality of the ideas: ability to produce a number of statistically infrequent ideas that shows how unique and unusual the ideas are) decreased by 3.74 percent from 1990 to 1998 and remained static from 1998 to 2008. Originality scores have actually significantly decreased, but the decrease has been deflated through the use of outdated scoring lists.

- Decrease in Creative Strengths after 1990: Creative Strengths scores (creative personality traits, including being emotionally expressive, energetic, talkative or verbally expressive, humorous, imaginative, unconventional, lively or passionate, perceptive, connecting seemingly irrelevant things together, synthesizing, and seeing things from a different angle) decreased by 3.16 percent from 1990 to 1998 and by 5.75 percent from 1990 to 2008.

- Decrease in Elaboration after 1984: Elaboration scores (ability to develop and elaborate upon ideas and detailed and reflective thinking and motivation to be creative) decreased more than other subscales of the TTCT. Elaboration scores decreased by 19.41 percent from 1984 to 1990, by 24.62 percent from 1984 to 1998, and by 36.80 percent from 1984 to 2008.

- Decrease in Abstractness of Titles after 1998: Titles scores (ability to produce the thinking processes of synthesis and organization, to capture the essence of the information involved, and to know what is important) increased until 1998, but decreased by 7.41 percent from 1998 to 2008.

- Decrease in Resistance to Premature Closure after 1998: Closure scores (intellectual curiosity and open-mindedness) decreased from 1984 to 1990, increased from 1990 to 1998, and decreased by 1.84 percent from 1998 to 2008.

How Might Decreased Creativity Impact Individuals and Society?

A world without creativity or with markedly reduced creativity would be less interesting and less satisfying in general, like eating dry cereal out of the box to the exclusion of other foods. The world would be more predictable, less exciting, and boring without creativity. Productivity and development would diminish.

The heart of the American spirit is American ingenuity, the ability to create novel solutions. The United States has provided an environment that fostered creativity, provided opportunities for creative individuals, and rewarded creative achievements.

The United States can expect its international status to slide if the new generation is less prepared to deal with the future challenges that await them and if innovation and free thinking are discouraged so the United States is unable to meet these challenges. Global competition will rush in to offer solutions to perceived problems. Future leaders will not be ready to accept risks, even though the population may expect the rewards that the previous generations enjoyed as their legacy. US productivity (compared with other countries) and the standard of living may slip, and this will lead to frustration and possibly to more insular thinking, increased nationalism, and to a jealous population.

The study of creativity is a creative exercise in and of itself. *It starts with our children. Our children start with us.*

What Can Parents and Teachers Use to Encourage Children to Be More Creative?

Individuals are born creative—some more so, some less. Creativity is quashed first by parents (especially parents who are perfectionists), then later by teachers, schools, society, cultures, and the like. So, before we worry about encouraging creativity, we should learn to preserve it. Research has determined that there are many ways to preserve creativity in our children.

Preserve curiosity: To preserve creativity, children's curiosity should be satisfied and encouraged. Most children go through a period when they ask a lot of questions to parents, teachers, adults, anyone where they can get answers. Parents take the brunt of this questioning, and at times this gets annoying. However, instead of getting annoyed and discouraging this curiosity, parents should take the time to try to find the answers, and probably more importantly, to demonstrate to their curious children how to find the answers.

Focus on ideas: The teachers might not emphasize spelling, for example, in an English test, but could emphasize original ideas in the essays. Thus, parents and teachers may not want to always stress getting the "right" answers and/or even the correct spelling; they should instead peek into a world of child fantasy, imagination, and inventiveness and encourage that ability. They can always help children prepare for being wrong or making mistakes and correcting those mistakes.

Raise nonconformists: Creative individuals do not like to follow the rules; they tend to follow their own rules. They tend to question and rebel against established norms. Perceptual and mental sets, well-learned and habitual ways of thinking, and rules and traditions that restrict the individual's behavior stifle creativity. Thus, parents and teachers should welcome unorthodox views and accept when children have different ideas or want to be different.

Raise girl-like boys and boy-like girls: Creative individuals show integration of feminine and masculine components. In our culture, however, sensitivity is viewed as feminine and independence as masculine. Creative children tend to sacrifice their creativity to maintain gender role expectations that parents and teachers impose upon them. Parents and teachers should welcome girl-like boys or boy-like girls.

Be playful: Creative individuals tend to have a sense of humor and demonstrate flexibility and playful thinking. Parents and teachers should not force children to think and act maturely and should provide opportunities for spontaneity and play, playfully engaging students, and encouraging childlike or even silly approaches to problems.

Be ready for drama: Creative individuals tend to be restless and energetic. They can be very talkative and have stronger needs for self-expression and a fuller range of emotional expression than other children. They are spontaneous and even impulsive. Highly creative individuals may be hard to live with. Research shows that many children diagnosed with ADHD are creative, and many creative children are misdiagnosed as having ADHD. The very qualities that facilitate individuals' creative accomplishments can be the same ones that may cause them to have problems. Research shows creativity is punished and discouraged by parents and teachers who perceive creative behavior as inconvenient and difficult to manage. Parents and teachers need to be patient and understanding of the characteristics of creative children, and there are many books and research articles on the subject that may help.

Be less protective: Creative people tend to have a somewhat marginalized family background, which means that they tend to be a member of a minority group in some ways (e.g., ethnicity, culture, language, geography, sexual orientation, religion, etc.). This could be because experiencing difficulties psychologically and emotionally may foster resilience, which allows them to become stronger and more persistent than those who are not experiencing such difficulties. Thus, having a perfectly happy and protected childhood can be worse than having an unhappy childhood in terms of fostering a child's creativity. Parents and teachers should not be overly protective of children and prevent them from having difficulties. Instead, parents and teachers should observe and understand the difficulties and be ready to discuss issues with a child.

Foster independence: Mild parental rejection is necessary for encouraging a child's creativity because a slightly rebellious attitude leads to more independent thinking. Enjoying experiences separately from the family and less encouragement of all family members doing all things together can encourage creativity. Thus, parents should let their children sleep over or camp out without their parents, under adult supervision, but not overly close.

Travel: Creative people tend to be well traveled. Traveling and experiencing places with different scenery or different cultures can encourage open-mindedness and seeing from different perspectives. Living in more than one culture or speaking more than one language can also foster creativity. Parents and teachers should be able to introduce children to different experiences, including different places, cultures, food, languages, and different people.

Give time alone: Most creative people have needs for privacy or time alone so that they can incubate their creative ideas. It is important for parents to let their children explore their interests by exposing them to different subjects, topics, programs, and areas. However, it is more important for those parents to give their children time alone. In addition, parents who nurture creativity tend not to rely on the use of premature and excessive worksheets and academic material.

Teach in unconventional ways: Creative individuals do not like competitive situations or restricted-choice situations. Thus, allowing choice of topics and variety of assignments is important to encourage creativity. Creative individuals do not like rote recitation, precise performance under time pressure, completion of familiar and repetitive procedures, or classes in a formal manner. Parents and teachers should give children open-ended assignments or components, encouraging brainstorming and intellectual risk taking, encouraging intrinsic (not extrinsic, because these children will perform when they like to) motivation and persistence, and delaying gratification.

Be less clean and organized: Parents of highly intelligent children focus on visible qualities such as right answers, cleanliness, and good manners, whereas parents of highly creative children focus on less-visible qualities such as openness to experience, interests, imagination, and enthusiasm.

Very organized and clean home environments can stifle children's creativity. A mother built an experiment room in the basement of her house for her fourth-grade son, who liked taking things apart and doing all kinds of experiments. The floor and walls of the room were made of tile to make for easy cleaning. Teaching children how to clean and organize is a good life skill, but it should not limit the child's freedom to explore or satisfy their curiosity. When there is no space for an additional room, then parents and teachers can designate a corner or space in which children can draw or build whatever they want and can make a mess.

Find a friend: Creative individuals tend to have imaginary childhood playmates. Talking to visible or invisible, non–human being objects should not be discouraged. Creative individuals tend to have friends who are younger or older than themselves. Parents tend to welcome older friends for their children compared to younger friends. However, not only does being friends with older children foster a child's maturity and resourcefulness, but also being friends with younger children can nurture a child's leadership skills. Being friends with non–peer group members can foster an ability to see from different perspectives than their peer group.

Find a mentor: Torrance's 40-year longitudinal study and other studies found that individuals who are creatively successful have at least one significant mentor in their lives. Introducing children to creative adults, especially those with similar interests as the children, is necessary to inspire creativity. Books, DVDs, and movies (especially good with guided viewing) that depict creative individuals are helpful for creative children with regard to their self-understanding and self-acceptance and for their identity issues and social and emotional needs.

Be educated: Teachers who claim to value creativity often display a preference for noncreative personality traits over creative personality traits in the classroom. Parents and teachers often say that they enjoy working with creative children; however, when they are questioned about the qualities of the ideal child, these qualities rarely include characteristics of highly creative children. Not only do parents and teachers often fail to recognize the talents of the creatively gifted, but these children are often treated with contempt.

Teaching Strategies to Stimulate Students' Creativity

Teachers have the responsibility to act to stimulate the creative potential of students in the following directions:

1. An identification of the creative potential of students;
2. Gnoseological (gnoseology is the philosophy of knowledge and the human faculties for learning) creation of premises of creative activity;
3. Develop individual communication capabilities;
4. Dynamic individual creative potential; adequate capitalization for the purposes of the cultivation of talents and creative attitude, in particular the main factors of creativity vectors;
5. May provide creative support ethical behavior.

For a long time, the act of creation was considered a hereditary privilege acquired by a minority, and schools did not deal specifically with this issue, although indeed, here and there special classes were created for the gifted children. The way in which the typical class session is carried today is beginning to resemble more and more with a factory and carried on in a typical mundane assembly line system. Like workers in a factory teacher feel like they are constricted by district standards and state tastes which allow only unitary view of education. Now more than ever, there is a paramount need for cultivation of innovative thinking in public schools. In addition to traditional efforts, teaching critical thinking and stimulating imagination appear to be a major objective. This involves major changes in both the mind-set of teachers, but also in terms of education and training methods.

Teaching methods must require *participation* and *student initiative* (active learning). Finally, fantasy must be properly appreciated, along with the merits of knowledge, *rigorous reasoning*, and *critical thinking*. Some methods that can be used in math classes for developing creativity are brainstorming, the mosaic method, the cube method, and the gallery tour.

Brainstorming is a method that helps create innovative ideas and creative concepts. To brainstorm effectively, one must do away with inhibitions and unhealthy criticism. There will be free expression, and participants in the process of brainstorming ideas and opinions will say what they wish without fear of being rejected or criticized. A brainstorming session lasts about half an hour; each session consists on average of ten students, or groups of a minimum of ten students. It exposes a concept, an idea, or an issue on which everyone can freely debate. A variation of brainstorming is brain writing. A good brainstorming session is directed to give everyone the opportunity to express their opinion on the matter having the end goal of giving the participants a constructive method by which they can improve their creativity.

The **jigsaw**, or "interdependent group method," is a strategy based on team learning. Each student has the learning task of becoming an *expert*. Each group receives an assignment. The teacher sets a topic of study divided into four or five sub-themes or tasks. Optionally, the teacher may determine for each sub-theme the main elements that should be emphasized by the student when studying the material independently or in an *expert* group. Each student from each group receives one task or sub-theme. The next phase is to regroup the students that have the same task in an *expert* group. After solving their task the students will go back at their initial groups and will finalize the assignments by explaining and summarizing their findings.

In this method, the teacher's role is greatly diminished. This diminished role occurs at the beginning of the lesson when the students are divided into groups and the tasks are set out, and at the end of the activity when the teacher will draw the final conclusions of the exercise.

The *cube method* involves exploring a topic, a situation from multiple perspectives, allowing a holistic approach and themes. The following steps are recommended: assembling a cube which has written on each side the words *describe, compare, analyze, associates, apply,* and *motivate*. Announce the theme and the subject under discussion. Divide the class into six groups, each examining the topic from one of the perspectives.

The *gallery tour*, an interactive learning method, is based on collaboration among students who are placed in a position to find solutions to solve problems. This method involves deeply interactive and formative assessment products created by groups of students.

Although it is a simple variant of brainstorming, the *cluster* is a method that involves the identification of logical connections between ideas that can be successfully used, both at the start of a previously taught lesson for updating knowledge, as well as lessons for synthesis and systematization of the knowledge.

The cluster is an introspection technique that gives the teacher access to outline how the students use their own knowledge to understand a topic or a certain content. This technique is effective for teaching and learning, and it encourages students to think freely and openly.

Each of us is a creative person with creative sides. Often, an idea is killed even by its creator, by a fellow critic, by fear of confrontation, and fear of embarrassment. It destroys self-criticism when a creative idea is wasted before it comes alive. Creative strategies work on the principle that quantity and quality assurance aim to eliminate the inconvenience caused by this very criticism.

References

Cropley, Arthur (emeritus professor of psychology, University of Hamburg–Germany) (2001). *Creativity in Education & Learning*. Routledge,434–473.

Kim, Kyung Hee (2011). "The creativity crisis: The decrease in creative thinking scores on the Torrance Tests of Creative Thinking." *Creativity Research Journal* 23, no. 4.

Lytton, Hugh (2014). *Creativity and Education*, 1st ed. Routledge.

Robinson, Ken (2011). *Out of Our Minds: Learning to Be Creative*. Capstone.

Torrance Test Practice: *www.testingmom.com/Torrance-Test*

DISCUSSION QUESTIONS

1. What can parents and teachers use to encourage children to be more creative?
2. What teaching strategies can stimulate students' creativity?
3. How might decreased creativity impact individuals and society?

The Teaching Profession

CHAPTER 16

Today's Teacher

INTRODUCTION

BY KISHA R. CUNNINGHAM, PHD

"A teacher who is attempting to teach without inspiring the pupil with a desire to learn is hammering on cold iron."

—Horace Mann

Becoming the Best Teacher in You: A Process, Not a Destination

BY ROBERT E. QUINN, KATHERINE HEYNOSKI,
AND MIKE THOMAS
THE BEST TEACHER IN YOU: HOW TO ACCELERATE LEARNING AND CHANGE LIVES

> No punishment anyone lays on you could possibly be worse than the punishment you lay on yourself by conspiring in your own diminishment. With that insight comes the ability to open cell doors that were never locked in the first place.
>
> —Parker Palmer
> *The Courage to Teach*

In our interview with Kelli, a veteran teacher with 24 years of experience, she told us about her goal of "reaching every student." While this sentiment is laudable, it also sounded unrealistic, so one of our interviewers decided to push back. He took on the persona of a skeptical colleague and argued that it is unreasonable and unrealistic to expect that a teacher can be successful with every child. Kelli quickly got into the role-play, becoming more passionate as she spoke. She confronted the interviewer: "Why do you have such a negative outlook? It is about you and your expectations for them. You have lowered your expectations. You have given up hope in those kids. What did you think your job was in the first place? It is not about teaching math. It is about getting them to want to learn."

Kelli's intensity and commitment brought about a transformation in the conversation. We were no longer in a role-play. We were having the kind of conversation that causes people to listen deeply, reflect, and see differently—the kind of conversation Kelli creates on a regular basis with her third-grade students.

Chapter Overview

Becoming the Best Teacher in You

In this chapter Kelli shares her story of becoming a highly effective teacher (HET). Her journey produced an expanded view of herself, her students, and what it means to be a teacher. With this expanded view came the capacity to do things she could not do before. Based on Kelli's story and the stories we have heard from more than 350 other exceptional teachers, we lay out two overarching perspectives of teaching: one we call the directive perspective and the other we call the co-creative perspective. The first is foundational. The second is elusive, but it paves the way for a teacher to accelerate learning and to change lives.

In the exchange above, two things became immediately clear about Kelli. First, she is a person who does not tolerate low expectations. She expects a lot of herself and a lot from others, even interviewers. This also extends to her students. She expects them to do things they do not believe they can do.

Second, while Kelli is a master of her content, she does not believe that her job is only to transfer mathematical information to students. Math is simply a reason to be with her students. She believes that her real job is to create a desire, a hunger, and a love for learning. She expects that her students will leave her with an expanded sense of themselves. They will leave as empowered people, able to learn in any situation.

While Kelli places great emphasis on growth and achievement, she balances it with an equally intense focus on forming and maintaining relationships. Within a few minutes of being with Kelli, we felt like our conversation mattered a great deal and that we also mattered a great deal. We felt both valued and stretched by this woman whom we had just met. She told us that when she was a student, school was a place where you went to "have things done to you." In contrast, Kelli places greater emphasis on doing things *with* her students.

The Year from Hell

Kelli believes that her ability to engage her students is a function of her own development. She speaks of a particularly important episode in which her assumptions about teaching were challenged and ultimately transformed. She came away from the episode with a new view of herself, her students, and what it means to teach.

She told us that her first year of teaching was "stellar." Her second year was "the year from hell." She had many children who were challenging. One was a "belligerent, mouthy, holy terror." On a particularly bad day, she saw him crawling on his belly at the door of her classroom. She lost her temper and moved toward him in anger. As he scurried out of her way, she turned away from him, slammed the door shut, and walked to the principal's o ce. She told her principal that she could no longer deal with this student, so the student was subsequently removed from her classroom.

This event was deeply troubling to Kelli, so she went to some experienced colleagues for advice. Their advice led to a turning point in Kelli's career. They said, "You have to realize early on that you are not the key to every door."

As Kelli recounted that conversation, she became visibly upset. She fought to compose herself and then looked up and said with conviction, "I hated that." She went on to tell us of a vow she took that day: "I told myself, *I'm not taking that. I'm going to figure out how to meet the needs of those kids.*"

A VOW TO LEARN

This vow represents a pivotal moment in Kelli's professional life. She could have taken the words of her colleagues to heart and become disenchanted, but she did not. Instead this painful event became an opportunity. It was the beginning of a lifelong journey of learning. In choosing to take this journey, Kelli has developed the ability to work more effectively with difficult students. "I've had other kids like that, but I never had another one of those moments." She described the work she had to do along the way:

> I needed to pay more attention to [struggling students]. I had to figure out what works for them, how to have respect for them, how to use humor to diffuse explosive situations. I learned how to make those kinds of kids feel safe in my room, and I learned how to teach them social skills so the other students would feel safe in the room with such a child. And then I learned that I have to be very parent-savvy. I have to sit down

and get the parents on my side very early on. So I learned those techniques, and I've never had another year like that. Those seem to be the kids that I'm most drawn to ... . I always get those kids now, the most unruly kid, the most disruptive kid, the bully.

Kelli told us that when a difficult child shows up in the school, her administrator says, "Let's put him in Kelli's room because Kelli will know what to do with him."

Teacher's Tip

Kelli: Do not be afraid to engage in new learning. Transformative learning begins to take shape when you engage in your own learning.

- Read qualified authors, observe exemplary teachers, view videos, and meet with other teachers who seem to have mastered what you are struggling with.
- Be willing to forgive yourself for your shortcomings and failures. Vow to make a change and stick with it.
- Seek a partnership with colleagues who will give you encouragement and guidance.

Deep Change

As she pursued her vow, Kelli learned to feel, think, and behave in new ways. She gained new capacity. She went through a learning process that transformed her understanding and aptitude. Robert Quinn, in his work with organizational leaders around the world, has identified two kinds of change that individuals experience: incremental change and deep change.[1] In our lives and in our work, we frequently make *incremental changes:* We make adjustments, we elaborate on a practice, we try harder, and we exert a greater degree of control. In other words, we attempt to solve the problem using the assumptions we currently hold.

Deep change is more demanding because it requires the surrender of control. It tends to be larger in scope, discontinuous with the past, and irreversible. It involves embracing a purpose and then moving forward by trial and error while attending to real-time feedback. Quinn often refers to the process of deep change as building the bridge as you walk on it.

Kelli knew she wanted to go to another level of performance. She wanted to flourish even with difficult students in the room. To acquire this capacity, she had to first reach for a higher standard and not compromise on that standard as her colleagues advised. Then she had to make a vow to engage in deep change. She moved forward in real-time, experiential learning.

When people move forward in this way, old assumptions are challenged and new ones are constructed. When the new assumptions lead to success, learning often becomes exhilarating. People feel empowered by their success and believe that they can do what Parker Palmer refers to in the epigraph as the ability to "open cell doors that were never locked in the first place."[2]

SLOW DEATH

We often avoid deep change because it can be difficult and unsettling. Ultimately, this avoidance can lead to disengagement, or what Quinn calls "slow death." When Kelli's colleagues told her that she could not expect to be the key to every door, they were unwittingly inviting her to "conspire" in her "own diminishment." They were inviting her to become an active participant in her own slow death.

What these well-meaning colleagues were doing was understandable. They were trying to comfort Kelli in a time of distress. This pattern is a common dynamic among friends and in organizations of all kinds. When people like Kelli aspire to excellence, they often meet adversity and become frustrated. To relieve her distress, Kelli's peers advised her to lower her aspirations. In education, as in all the other industries, this response is a phenomenon that can turn armies of idealistic young professionals into disenchanted victims of the system.

As you think about this dynamic, it is also worthwhile to consider your students' aspirations. Many of them may already travel the path to slow death. Sometimes an entire community of students can be locked into assumptions that prevent them from empowering themselves. What they believe about their ability to learn greatly hinders their own development. Their experiences and the assumptions that result from them can become "cell doors." They may "know," for example, that the act of trying will result in embarrassment and failure. Students who make such assumptions may show little interest in learning. In every industry and in every organization, there are personal and cultural assumptions that lead people away from deep change and toward slow death. Daily conversations that reflect a victim mentality regularly invite us all to the path of slow death.

THE BEST TEACHER IN YOU

Kelli's story illustrates an important point about deep change. Because she engaged in transformative learning, she grew in self-efficacy, or the belief that she could succeed in a demanding situation or activity.[3] More specifically, she is now con dent that she can learn to teach any child in any situation. Addressing an imaginary problem child, Kelli told us, "If you are de ant, I will get you. I will figure out what makes you work. I might not get tremendous growth and I might not get engagement every day, but I'm going to get something out of you. I'm going to be your new best friend."

While the statement suggests that Kelli is an empowered person, it also suggests that she is an empowering person. She subjects her students to high expectations, and she also partners with them to help them grow into more-effective versions of themselves. Because she has experienced the realization of her own potential, Kelli sees potential in all of her students and feels compelled to help them change the limiting assumptions that they make about themselves.

When a teacher is with students in a way that is empowering to them, the students can transform. When this begins to happen, the transformation in the students loops back to the teacher and another transformation takes place. The work of teaching becomes the joy of teaching because they are in a mutually empowering relationship. Teachers experience the most powerful of all rewards in this kind of relationship—the realization of their best self, or the best teacher in them. Kelli explains it as follows: "I breathe students. They are my life's blood. I am not whole without them. They bring me joy. They make me frustrated. They make me cry. They give me hope. When I invest in them, I become the best me."

Teacher's Tip

Kelli: Ask yourself, *Do I believe that student growth starts with me?* Be strategic about how you make the learning happen in your classroom. As you prepare your lessons and instruction, consider how you can incorporate formative instructional practices.

- Make the learning intentions clear to students.
- Be sure students understand what you want them to know and be able to do.
- Align assessments with the intended learning and allow students to partner with you on collecting that data.
- Ensure that the feedback you give around the learning is effective. Teach students how to use and give feedback to you and their peers. This strengthens classrooms.
- Allow for opportunities for strong student engagement and ownership of learning. Teach students how to self-assess and set goals. When the vision is clear for students, they can and will join you on the teaching and learning journey.

Transformational Influence

Kelli told us that teaching is about "helping children grow." Kelli said that she can teach a child to read or do math, but that is not what her kind of teaching is about. Her kind of teaching is about helping each child internalize the desire and the ability to learn. With re in her eyes and conviction in her voice, Kelli stated, "I am the key to every door."

In other fields, such as business or government, the few people with this kind of confidence, passion, and capacity are called *transformational leaders*. They know how to engage people in learning that alters their assumptions and mindsets. They help individuals and groups grow into more-effective versions of themselves. They know how to release potential that is unrecognized and unrealized.

In telling us that she is "the key to every door," Kelli is not claiming that she moves every child forward every minute that they are in her classroom. She is claiming that she is able to enter an elevated state of teaching and learning. She accepts responsibility, faces challenges, and adapts. She does this with confidence, knowing that she can form a relationship with every child; and because of her capacity to do this, she is able to move each child and the class as a whole further than would normally be expected. Kelli has mastered something that can help every teacher become the best teacher they can be. That is why we have written this book.

Two Views of Teaching

Kelli kept surprising us. She kept recounting stories that exceeded our expectations and challenged our assumptions. The same thing happened in our interviews with other HETs, so we began to ask what assumptions are commonly made about the process of teaching.

Because the conventional assumptions of a culture are often reflected in that culture's language, an examination of the dictionary is a good place to start. To teach is to instruct, train, school, discipline, drill, or educate. Consider the meaning of each word.[4]

- *Teach:* to impart knowledge or skill to
- *Instruct:* to provide with knowledge, especially in a methodical way
- *Train:* to coach in or accustom to a mode of behavior or performance
- *School:* to discipline or control
- *Discipline:* to train by instruction and practice, especially to teach self-control to
- *Drill:* to instruct thoroughly by repetition in a skill or procedure
- *Educate:* to develop the innate capacities of, especially by schooling or instruction

These definitions suggest that a teacher directs and controls the classroom. Teaching is a process in which a more expert person imparts knowledge or skill to a less expert person. The student is in a lower position in a knowledge hierarchy. The student is expected to perform to an existing standard or acquire an accustomed mode of behavior or performance. The provision of knowledge is methodical. The student is subjected to discipline and control. The process may be repetitive and should lead to the development of self-control on the part of the student. We call this view the *directive perspective.*

In books it is common to create an image or list and then use it as a straw man. The image is then attacked and replaced by a better image. This book offers a second image, but it does not denigrate the directive perspective. Great teaching is built on a solid foundation of expertise, direction, control, discipline, and repetition. We need the assumptions and the skills of the directive perspective. They are essential to teaching.

The second perspective that we develop later in this chapter is not better than the first. Instead it supplements the directive perspective with additional capacities that make teaching more effective. It values the directive perspective but moves beyond notions such as discipline and repetition. Great music, for example, is a product of more than mechanics, scales, and simple melodies—it is ultimately about finding a unique musical voice and the courage to express it. To do this musicians have to risk, experiment, learn, and create. In their performances great musicians are deeply and dynamically connected to their instrument, their music, and their audience. Similarly, great teachers are deeply and dynamically connected to their subject, their content standards, their evolving practice, and their students. In these dynamic connections, there are feedback loops. Knowledge is not only disseminated but also co-created. e teacher and the student join together to generate knowledge. In this process both the teacher and the student grow.

FROM NOVICE TO MASTER

Novelist and philosopher Robert Pirsig asks why, in a given activity, some people obtain normal outcomes while others generate outcomes of higher quality. To answer the question, he uses the metaphor of the motorcycle mechanic. He suggests that not all mechanics are the same; the quality of their work varies:

> Sometime look at a novice workman or a bad workman and compare his expression with that of a craftsman whose work you know is excellent and you'll see the difference. The craftsman isn't ever following a single line of instruction. He's making decisions as he goes along. For that reason he'll be absorbed and attentive to what he is doing even though he does not deliberately contrive this. His motions and the machine are in a kind of harmony. He isn't following any set of written instructions because the nature of the material at hand determines his thoughts and motions,

which simultaneously change the nature of the material at hand. The material and his thoughts are changing together in a progression of changes until his mind is at rest at the same time the material is right.[5]

Pirsig is claiming that there are master mechanics (just as there are highly effective teachers) who produce extraordinary outcomes. They do more than act upon an object with expertise. Just as Kelli is "with" her students, the mechanic is "with" the motorcycle in a relationship of reciprocal influence: "The material and his thoughts are changing together in a progression of changes." In this learning relationship, the machine and the mechanic are both altered. The machine is being repaired with excellence while the mechanic is also becoming more excellent. The work of the master mechanic is an intrinsically motivated labor of love because when he does his work, he also produces a better self. He is expressing the best mechanic in him.

MASTERY IN THE CLASSROOM

Excellence is a dynamic process. We take the liberty to rewrite and then elaborate on Pirsig's account with respect to a master teacher to describe what these dynamics look like in the classroom:

> Sometime look at a novice teacher and compare his expression with that of a master teacher whose work you know is excellent, and you'll see the difference. The master teacher isn't ever following a single line of instruction. He has a plan, but it soon becomes a rough guide as he begins to respond to students' needs and to improvise. He is fully present, making decisions as he goes. The master teacher is absorbed and attentive to what he is doing even though he does not deliberately contrive this. His actions and the actions of his students are in a kind of harmony. The master teacher's ongoing assessment of his students determines his thoughts and actions, which simultaneously change the nature of what and how students are learning. The teacher and the class co-create a process of reciprocal, real-time learning. In doing this they are becoming a learning community. This process continues until the teacher's mind is at rest and the particular lesson is concluded with excellence. Both the students and the teacher leave the lesson having had a deeply meaningful learning experience.

As this process unfolds, the teacher recognizes needs, facilitates discussion, builds trust, and inspires spontaneous contributions. The natural hesitancies within students and the natural disparities among students begin to diminish. The conversation becomes more authentic, more engaging, and more reflective. Listening becomes mutual, and students expect one another to contribute.

As in Kelli's story, the classroom becomes a place where students engage in activities that they find relevant and challenging. The teacher improvises and encourages creativity. As the teacher relaxes overt control, the students take ownership of their learning, and leadership shifts seamlessly from one participant to another. Through discussion they explore the big picture and continually question assumptions. Students begin to see from multiple perspectives. In this heightened, collective state, students arrive at creative, joint conclusions. Participating in the process not only builds knowledge but also increases self-effcacy. Students see more potential in themselves and in their world, and they begin to more fully believe in their own capacity to learn and create. They feel more empowered and experience the love of learning. So does the teacher.

As you read our adaptation and the accompanying detail, how did you respond? Did it challenge some of your basic assumptions? If it did, you may have felt skepticism and disbelief. Yet most of us have been part of a group in which this kind of "magic" emerges. We invite you to keep an open mind. As you read *The Best Teacher in You*, if something surprises you, first note exactly what it is. Suspend judgment and then open yourself to possibility. Ask yourself how the surprise might help you enlarge your assumptions and expectations regarding the practice of teaching.

Interconnected Perspectives

Our elaboration of Pirsig's account suggests that teachers—like motorcycle mechanics—need the directive perspective. But if they seek to accelerate learning and change lives, they need to do what Kelli did. They need to be able to transcend their directive assumptions and move into the realm of co-creation. These two perspectives are shown in figure 1.

TWO VIEWS

Each of these perspectives provides a set of assumptions or lenses for making sense of teaching. Looking through the lens of the directive perspective, learning is a technical process managed

Directive Perspective	Co-Creative Perspective
• Conveying high standards	• Understanding needs and interests
• Encouraging achievement	• Encouraging collaboration
• Focusing on individuals	• Focusing on the collective
• Assessing performance	• Facilitating discussion
• Providing challenge	• Building trust
• Emphasizing urgency	• Taking time to listen
• Being in control	• Shifting leadership
• Planning	• Improvising
• Knowing the details	• Seeing the big picture
• Expecting compliance	• Expecting creativity
• Covering required content	• Questioning assumptions
• Expecting the right answer	• Examining multiple perspectives

Figure 1. Two Perspectives of Teaching

by a teacher. It tends to be about content and control. The teacher is in charge—a person in a position of hierarchical authority, who sets high standards while maintaining order. Planning, assessment, and achievement are emphasized. We use the acorn as a metaphor to capture the essence of the directive perspective because it provides the foundation for good teaching. A new teacher often uses the directive perspective to build his or her confidence and capabilities to create an orderly classroom. While the acorn or directive perspective is an important starting point, it comes to life only when it grows into something more dynamic. The directive perspective can be broadened over time to grow into the *co-creative perspective*.

As the teacher and the students commit to a common purpose and form high-quality relationships, they become a system that has emergent possibilities. *Emergent* means something that is embryonic, like a seed, that can then sprout, grow, or develop into something more complex, like a tree. We include the image of the seedling to reinforce that the more dynamic perspective emerges from the acorn. Without the acorn the tree cannot sprout and flourish.

When individual minds become fully engaged and integrated around a common purpose, collaboration can move to a higher level. Learning can grow into something more complex. The group can learn in ways that the individual cannot. When the group is functioning at a high level, the individual may feel that he or she has become part of something bigger than self, something worthy of sacrifice.

When this happens the social structure can transform. In the conventional hierarchy, the belief is that the teacher must hold students accountable. When collaborative learning occurs, students may begin to hold one another accountable. At this moment of transformation, the teacher can move beyond the role of disciplinarian. The network of relationships becomes more flexible, and the classroom, as a functioning whole, can acquire the capacity to co-create and learn more deeply.

To bring about the co-creative process, the teacher becomes a facilitator of learning. In this role the teacher pays attention to relationships and works to create a culture of collaboration, a context that is more likely to give rise to full engagement and accelerated learning.

Kelli gives an example. To establish a culture of "what it is to be a learner" at the beginning of the year, Kelli sets a tone of respect, teaches her students how to be effective listeners, and makes them feel valued. Facilitation involves providing challenge and support, asking questions, and moving back and forth in directive and nondirective ways to enable students to join together in the process of co-creation.

Teacher's Tip

Kelli: Challenge yourself as a teacher to change what you view about your role. Is your view of teaching a "true barrier" to moving forward with students? If our view of teaching is limited, we will often become disengaged and unhappy with our job.

CONNECTING THE TWO VIEWS

The kind of improvisation a master teacher employs cannot occur without sufficient underlying structure. Teachers still must teach content. They still strive for high achievement. They continue to focus attention on individuals, assess performance, and engage in all the aspects of practice listed on the left side of figure 1.

What changes in the co-creative perspective is the teacher's stance relative to students. The teacher is willing to surrender control until it is again necessary to take control. In the directive perspective, the focus is on the teacher and the teaching. In the co-creative perspective, the attention is on the learning of the student rather than the knowledge of the teacher. The co-creative perspective focuses on who the student is becoming and how the teacher can serve as a mediator between where things are and where things could be.

Kelli provides an example of the interconnectedness of the two perspectives. At the beginning of the year, she tries to quickly acclimate students to the rules and the routines of her classroom. Kelli helps students understand the parameters for what and how they will learn. Efficient learning depends on the structures and the xed processes of the directive perspective. At the same time, Kelli invites students into conversations about "how much you learn, how fast you learn, and the ways in which you learn." She wants to give students a sense of purpose for their own learning. Learning progresses as a journey that Kelli and her students take together.

Teacher's Tip

Kelli: Take the time to figure out what students are interested in and use that interest to build a relationship. If it is not something you know about, approach the child as if you are the learner and you want the child to teach you about his or her passion.

Teacher Development

The two perspectives also have implications for how to help teachers improve. From a directive perspective, teacher development is more likely to focus on honing skills related to planning, classroom management, and pedagogy. This perspective assumes that particular practices reliably produce particular outcomes. Professional development in this perspective relies on experts to provide teachers with scientifically validated solutions to predictable pedagogic problems. All of this is true, but it is also partial by itself.

In the co-creative perspective, a classroom becomes an adaptive organization. It consists of people in relationships with one another. Each student is an interdependent actor with the potential to learn, teach, and know. Learning accelerates and is deepened when a teacher forms high-quality relationships with students. Learning accelerates further when students form high-quality relationships with one another. To achieve this level of relationship, the teacher continually clarifies purpose, increases authenticity, practices empathy, and opens to the co-creative journey.

Teacher development, in the co-creative perspective, is likely to focus on reflection, self-assessment, interaction, experimentation, and learning from experience.[6] Teachers engage in activities that challenge them and invite them to examine their own assumptions and beliefs. They are encouraged to empower themselves to explore, appreciate, and integrate alternative assumptions. These experiences enable them to think and act in more complex ways. As they build these capacities, they better understand how to empower students and accelerate learning. Here a teaching practice is not so much a solution to a problem as an opportunity for experimentation, engagement, and learning.

In the co-creative perspective, development is not teaching teachers to know; it is teaching teachers to learn. As a teacher develops the capacity to think and act in more complex ways, his or her effectiveness increases because effectiveness is a function of being in the present and learning to adapt and create in real time. The objective is for the teacher to acquire adaptive confidence and transformational influence.

REALITY

Researchers suggest that 10,000 is the magic number of hours needed to attain mastery.[7] If a gifted pianist, for example, puts in 9,000 hours of practice, that person is likely to have a less luminary career than a gifted musician who puts in 10,000 hours. Ten thousand hours seems to be a threshold.

By the time we graduate from college, we all have more than 10,000 hours in classrooms observing teachers. This extensive socialization means we are all deeply rooted in the directive view of teaching. As we have seen, the directive perspective is at the heart of our experiences, language, and culture. To access the co-creative perspective, we have to undergo deep change and experience transformative learning. In this book you will find stories, concepts, and tools to help you do just that.

Summary

Highly effective teachers like Kelli have daunting challenges. They work with the same students in the same schools with the same resources as other teachers. Their organizational context is hierarchical, conflictridden, and politically charged. And while these challenges lead some teachers to feel frustrated, discouraged, and dissatisfied, highly effective teachers somehow learn to perform at high levels.

Through our work with HETs, we have tried to make sense of what accounts for their extraordinary impact. To do this we have drawn from a number of different scientific literatures to develop some hypotheses about the integration of the directive and co-creative perspectives. This book shares our theories with you. Chapter 2 introduces a framework that will help you more deeply examine and reflect on HETs' journeys from novice to master teacher so that you can begin to apply these lessons to your own teaching practice.

Planting Seeds

1. Kelli says, "It is not about teaching math. It is about getting them to want to learn." What are the implications of working toward the one purpose versus the other? How might the two purposes be integrated?

2. Kelli started out well, but her students changed and her assumptions did not. This led to failure and frustration. Her friends advised her, "You have to realize early on that you are not the key to every door." When have you received or given such advice? What arguments justify this advice? How is accepting such advice conspiring in your own diminishment?

3. Kelli made a vow that took her on a new path. She states:

   I needed to pay more attention to those types of kids. I had to figure out what works for them, how to have respect for them, how to use humor to diffuse explosive situations. I learned how to make those kinds of kids feel safe in my room, and I learned how to teach them social skills so the other students would feel safe in the room with such a child. And then I learned that I have to be very parent-savvy. I have to sit down and get the parents on my side very early on. So I learned those techniques, and I've never had another year like that.

How is this kind of learning different from the procedural learning to which we are more accustomed? What are the key requirements for this kind of learning? What does this suggest about your most pressing frustrations?

Growing Your Practice

1. What is one specific practice you can undertake in your next week of teaching to build momentum on the journey to the co-creative perspective? Use the right-hand column in figure 16 to help you identify a specific practice. Be specific about when, who, what, and how you will get started.

2. Following Kelli's advice, identify one student whom you would like to reach in a deeper way. Find out what he or she is interested in and use that interest to build a relationship. If it is not something you know about, approach the child as if you are the learner and you want the child to teach you about his or her passion.

CHAPTER 17

The Challenges of Becoming a Teacher

INTRODUCTION

BY KISHA R. CUNNINGHAM, PHD

"When you study great teachers ... you will learn much more from their caring
and hard work than from their style."

—William Glasser

Struggles and Strategies in Teaching: Voices of Five Novice Secondary Teachers

BY YE HE AND JEWELL COOPER[1]
TEACHER EDUCATION QUARTERLY

As most teachers and teacher educators would concur, the journey of becoming a teacher is not always smooth. Beginning teachers bring their personal experiences and beliefs with them into teacher education programs (Beijaard, Meijer, & Verloop, 2004; Clandinin & Connelly, 1996; He & Levin, 2008; Levin & He, 2008; Lortie, 1975; Richardson, 2003). Consequently, their beliefs and prior experiences filter what they encounter in the teacher education program, which impacts the beliefs they develop that guide their classroom practice (Chant, 2001; Chant, Hefner, & Bennett, 2004). With shifts and changes in the social and professional context of 21st century education (Clandinin, Downey, & Huber, 2009), however, beginning teachers are especially challenged by conflicts between their personal beliefs and the reality of teaching, in addition to the struggles first-year teachers often encounter (Brown, 2006; Day, 1999; Veenman, 1984; Vonk, 1993).

While there is an established body of literature in teacher education that examines teachers' concerns (Adams, 1982; Boccia, 1989; Conway & Clark, 2003; Fuller, 1969; Marso & Pigge, 1989, 1995; Pigge & Marso, 1987; Watske, 2007), studies exploring the emergence of such concerns and beginning teachers' strategies to survive during their first year of teaching is limited. Specifically, more studies that focus on the professional development of secondary teachers are needed.

In this study, we followed five secondary preservice teachers for two years during their teacher education program and their first year of teaching. Using interviews and their written narratives, we described: (1) major concerns of our preservice teachers; and (2) strategies they used to help them face their concerns. Identification of their concerns and especially the strategies they used as they better understood their students and their students' families and became more aware of their identities as teachers also shed light on reforms in current teacher education efforts.

---

1   Ye He and Jewell Cooper are professors in the Department of Teacher Education and Higher Education of the School of Education at the University of North Carolina at Greensboro, Greensboro, North Carolina.

Literature Review

In 1969, Frances Fuller identified a stage-related and concerns-based model of teacher develop-ment. In this model, she sequenced concerns of beginning teachers as related to themselves, their tasks, and the impact they were having on their students. While Fuller's model has been critiqued over the years, Conway and Clark (2003) suggested that within teacher development, teachers not only experience a "journey outward" as determined by Fuller, but they also have a "journey inward" when considering the self during the period of student teaching.

There are various theories and models of teacher development that have emerged since Fuller's model (Berliner, 1988; Bullough & Knowles, 1991; Hollingsworth, 1989; Huberman, 1989; Kagan 1992; Nias, 1989; Ryan 1992; Sprinthall & Thies-Sprinthall, 1980). However, Grossman (1992) examined and acknowledged that some learning-to-teach research models on teacher education are viewed through the context of subject matter content instruction and oth-ers are explored from a moral and ethical stance. As an alternate view on professional growth in teaching, she recommended that we as teacher educators not immediately accept prevailing prac-tices and developmental models but "challenge the lessons learned during prospective teachers' apprenticeships of observation" (p. 176). Moreover, we should encourage our teacher candidates "to ask worthwhile questions of their teaching, to continue to learn from their practice, to adopt innovative models of their teaching, and to face the ethical dimensions of classroom teaching" (p. 176). By providing strategies for thinking about teaching experiences beyond subject matter content and ethical and moral issues, teacher educators offer additional, more meaningful, and lasting preparation for professional life beyond the security of teacher education programs.

Furthermore, while many studies confirmed or built upon the stage-based theories regard-ing teacher development, recent research has also indicated that teacher professional identity development is more complex and context-based than previously thought (Beijaard, Meijer, & Verloop, 2004). Thus, in addition to large-scale survey studies on teacher growth (Melnick & Meister, 2008; Watzke, 2007), case studies are also a commonly used method in the examination of teacher development (Levin, 2003).

Recognizing that teachers are not often followed longitudinally over long periods of time but should be (Sleeter, 2004), Robert Bullough and his colleagues (i.e., Bullough, 1989; Bullough & Baughman, 1997; Bullough, Knowles, & Crow, 1991) authored several case studies related to first year teachers' professional growth. In their attempt to explain factors that influenced begin-ning teachers' growth, Bullough, Knowles, and Crow (1991) determined that metaphors helped to predict the success or difficulty of beginning teachers' adjustment to teaching. In essence, the more positive the teachers' metaphors, the greater the likelihood of a good adjustment to teaching would be. On the other hand, the more negative the metaphors, the more likely beginning teachers would have difficulty unless they changed their points of view.

Earlier, Bullough (1989) conducted a longitudinal case study of one teacher, Kerrie, and described her development during her first year of teaching. In this study, teaching context was one factor that was highlighted. Additionally, Bullough and Baughman (1997) chronicled the professional development of the aforementioned teacher across eight years. The study was important in that the authors shared not only changes in Kerrie's life, but also changes in her professional practice, her pedagogical thinking, and her teaching context, as well as her participation in a longitudinal study.

More recently, Levin (2003) chronicled the results of a 15-year study of how the pedagogical thinking of four elementary school teachers developed over time. Her teacher participants provided an in-depth understanding of how they think about their students' behaviors, development, and learning as well as their own learning and teaching as they intersect their personal and professional lives. Levin found these factors started out being very global but gradually became more sophisticated; also, "their thinking and actions become more congruent" (p. 283) over time. In addition, their personal and professional contexts continuously influenced the development of the professional self. These teachers constantly sought to express a "deep understanding of children's development" (p. 283), and they requested assistance from other professionals as they continually reflected on both their joys and difficulties in teaching.

Similar to the effort to depict the journey of elementary school teacher development (Levin, 2003), in this study we explored the journey of five secondary teachers for two years through their teacher education program and their first year of teaching. In addition to examining participants' developmental change in their concerns, we also uncovered the strategies they used to face those challenges.

Methodology

Two major research questions guided the data collection and analysis in this study: (1) What, if any, are participants' concerns and struggles as they develop from student teachers to first-year teachers? and (2) What strategies did participants utilize to face their concerns or struggles and sustain their passion for teaching?

PARTICIPANTS

Qualitative data were collected from five participants over the course of two years during their field experiences in a secondary teacher education program and their first year of teaching. The participants in this study included two males and three females. All of the participants were White; however, two of them proudly recognized their Italian heritage in their autobiographies. The pedagogical content subject areas included English, social studies, and history (see Table 1). At the time of the study, four of the five participants were 22–23 years of age; the fifth participant, age 28, had been a non-traditional student during his preservice teacher years. Only one of the participants was married.

As in many other teacher education programs, participants took general education college courses during their first and second year and started taking teacher education courses during their third year. In addition to the teacher education courses, participants also participated in two one-semester internships in 2006 (at least 80 hours) and one-semester of full-time student teaching in spring 2007 (450 to 500 hours) before they graduated from the program. In other words, they experienced three sequential semesters of student interaction through internships and student teaching. Table 1 provides a general description of participants' field experience settings and their final job choice for their first-year teaching from fall 2007 to spring 2008.

DATA COLLECTION AND ANALYSIS

Data were collected through participants' autobiographies, interviews, and focus group discussions. In spring 2006, participants entered the School of Education and completed an autobiography project in one of the required education courses, where they wrote about their family backgrounds, learning experiences, and their visions for teaching. During fall 2006, all participants had internships, coordinated in conjunction with another required education course, in high school classrooms. During their internships, participants were required to conduct a biography project with one of their students whose cultural background was different from their own. This assignment required that they consult with the parents or other family members to get biographical information about the student they worked with and compare the

Table 17.1. Description of Participants

Name	Major	Background	Internship-Spring 2006	Internship/Student Teaching-Fall 2006-Spring 2007	First-Year of Teaching-Fall 2007-Spring 2008
Bill	English	Growing up in a rural town in the western region of his state, Bill had a great high school experience, which is the main reason why he decided to become an English teacher. He is very interested in Shakespeare and wants his students to "understand and appreciate just how amazing William Shakespeare was." (Autobiography, spring, 2006)	Rural high school! Majority White population.	Suburban school setting with an ethnically diverse population. School was renown from football victories.	Rural high school in the mountains of the state. Student population was predominantly White. Large socioeconomic divide.
Ellen	English	Considered a "mountain girl," Ellen was eager to leave her hometown to experience "city life," though she desired to return to the mountains to instill a love of learning not only English but also she wanted students to be true to themselves. (Autobiography, spring 2006)	Suburban high school. Ethnically diverse; however, mostly White.	Suburban school setting with an ethnically diverse population. School was renown for its football victories.	Rural high school in the mountain region of the state. Student population was not very ethnically diverse. Large socioeconomic divide.
Mary	Social Studies	Mary grew up in the same city where she attended high school. She is socio-politically engaged and cared about what happened to those less fortunate than she is. (Interview, fall 2006).	Urban high school. Predominately African American.	Ethnically diverse urban setting. School was not well known for its academic reputation.	Ethnically diverse middle school. Recent redistricting caused the school to become more culturally diverse than before.

Karen	History	Growing up in the largest city in the state, Karen is proud of her Italian heritage and her understandings of different cultural groups. As a teacher, she wants to "help students realize the power of their knowledge." (Autobiography, spring, 2006)	Urban high school. Predominately African American.	Ethnically diverse urban setting. Large international population.	Flagship high school of the city. Redistricting strengthened its ethnic diversity.
Charles	English	Born in the "Big Apple", Charles enjoys working with students from diverse backgrounds and views his responsibility to "get students ready for dealing with different people" (Interview, fall, 2006).	Rural high school. Majority White population.	Ethnically diverse urban high school. Title I status.	Remained in the same high school as he was in for student teaching.

student biography to their autobiography for similarities and differences. This ABCs project (Autobiography, Biography, and Cross-cultural Comparison) (Schmidt, 1999) provided participants with opportunities to interact with diverse student populations and their families beyond classroom settings. Participants' autobiographies, their students' biographies, and participants' cross cultural comparison assignments were used as data for this study. Interviews with individual participants were then conducted at the end of the semester.

Participants were student teachers during the following spring 2007 semester, at the end of which a focus group discussion was convened to discuss their needs and concerns. During their first year of teaching, participants wrote about their beliefs about teaching in the format of autobiography (fall 2007); and interviews were conducted with participants, inviting them to share their experiences as first-year teachers (spring 2008). Finally, a focus group was conducted with participants, enabling them to reflect on their first-year teaching experiences. Member checking was conducted by sending interview and focus group transcripts back to each participant for their individual feedback. All the qualitative data, including participants' autobiographies, field experience reflections, individual interviews, and focus group discussions were analyzed in this study.

357

Data were analyzed in both a vertical and a horizontal manner (Miles & Hu-berman, 1994). First, each participant's autobiography, interview, and focus group responses were analyzed separately as five different cases. During the second phase of analyses, constant comparative analysis was conducted to seek patterns and themes across the five cases (Glaser & Strauss, 1967). Two researchers analyzed and coded the data independently, and memos were kept to track emerged themes and patterns. Discrepancies in coding and analysis memos were resolved through discussions between the researchers.

Findings

In this section, we describe participants' reported concerns and challenges in a chronological order, first as student teachers and then as first-year teachers. Then, a comparison is conducted to synthesize participants' concerns. The strategies they used to face the challenges are then summarized.

STUDENT TEACHERS' CONCERNS AND CHALLENGES

During their internships and student teaching, all five participants had the opportunity to interact with diverse student populations in high school settings and to teach lessons to students at different grade levels. Based on their autobiographies, individual interviews, and a focus group discussion after their student teaching, three major themes of concerns merged: (1) classroom management, (2) student motivation, and (3) parent involvement.

While all five participants commented on their concerns related to classroom management, there was a difference in the degree to which they viewed it as a challenge. Ellen, for example, in her interview before she student taught, stated explicitly that classroom management was one of her major challenges. She commented: "Classroom management is an area that I felt especially weak in, regardless of the training I had received. This is where most of my struggles lie and the main source of frustration" (Interview, fall 2006).

Mary, Karen, and Charles commented on their concerns with classroom management in terms of establishing themselves as teachers that "the students could respect and expect respect from" (Mary, Autobiography, spring 2006). Reflecting on his role as an intern in the classroom and comparing himself to other teachers,

Charles, for example, commented that he was not "a big strict disciplinarian" (Interview, fall 2006). Instead, he wanted to "be somebody they [students] can trust and come to and that…they [students] will be able to respect that" (Interview, fall 2006). He did believe that as he became the teacher in the classroom, rather than an intern or student teacher, he would have the respect from his students: "Although I know that I'm just the intern…I think once I start teaching then it [student respect] will be there anyway" (Interview, fall 2006).

Bill also commented that he "may not be terribly well-prepared when it comes to classroom management (none of us really are until we actually get into the classroom)" (Autobiography, spring 2006). However, he added that he had "a great deal of leadership experiences" and that experience made him feel "comfortable and confident when placed in front of a group of people" (Autobiography, spring 2006).

In addition to classroom management, motivating students in content areas they taught was another challenge that student teachers reported. In their individual interviews and focus group discussions, all participants emphasized that it was important for them to "make the class interesting and engaging" (Bill, Interview, fall 2006), and "make the classroom student-centered to make the students responsible for their learning" (Karen, Focus Group, spring 2007). Recognizing that students might not see the content relevant, Mary, Karen, and Charles considered it teachers' responsibility to make the real-life connections for their students and "for them [students] to understand what happened in the past and be able to apply that information to their current lives" (Karen, Interview, fall 2006), in order to "get them [students] ready for the real world" (Charles, Focus Group, spring 2007). Describing her experience motivating her students and making her lessons more relevant, Mary gave an example of teaching her third block U.S. history class during student teaching:

> I just kind of switched gears halfway through and had a little conference with them and said: "Look, we've got to find something that's going to work a lot better; and you tell me what [you] want to do this semester, and I'll incorporate a lot of that into my lessons." So we had a little sit-down talk for like fifteen minutes and they told me exactly what they wanted. So each day I tried to put something in there. (Focus Group, spring 2007)

To make their lessons more interesting to their students, all participants recognized the importance of making connections with students and respecting students' input and opinions.

While all participants reported having opportunities to work with students in both small group and one-on-one settings to get to know them through projects during the teacher education program (such as the ABCs project), they recalled that they rarely had the opportunity to interact directly with parents. Ellen, Karen and Bill all reported that they had not personally interacted with parents. Their only interactions with parents were through emails or letters. Based on the limited interactions, Karen was concerned that "some of the parents just don't have a general sense of what's going on in the classroom" (Interview, fall 2006). Mary further commented on the difficulty of getting in touch with the families, and said one of the things she has learned is "they [school administrators] tell you, you know, you need to call home and talk to parents and a lot of times you can't. A lot of times you're just going to have to get in your car and go" (Interview, fall 2006). Although all participants were required to conduct community-based service-learning projects during their teacher education curriculum and several of them even conducted home visits, participants still considered it a challenge to contact and involve parents in schools.

Though all participants successfully completed their internship and student teaching requirements despite their common concerns and struggles, they also stated their individual concerns for their first-year of teaching. Charles and Mary both mentioned that they would like to be more confident in front of their students. Being from another state, Charles reported he felt he needed to be more familiar with the curriculum. Mary, on the other hand, wanted to enhance her confidence in dealing with the "hurtful things students would sometimes say" (Autobiography, spring 2006). Ellen and Karen commented on their struggles between their ideal goals for teaching and the reality of teaching. Both of them admitted that they chose to be teachers because they "want to change the world" (Ellen, Focus Group, spring 2007), or viewed themselves as "a person of influence" (Karen, Focus Group, spring 2007).

However, in reality, Karen recognized that "it's okay to mess up." As she commented:

> You're going to mess up a lot. And you have to take it, roll with the punches, and I would hope that I'm getting better at that. We have a long way to go and we're going to have ups and downs. Things are going to go well and things are going to go badly, but you have to see yourself as somebody that's going to influence these kids no matter what you do. (Focus Group, spring 2007)

Recognizing the gap between her ideal and the reality of teaching, Ellen also reported that she was not happy with who she was as a teacher and even questioned herself as to whether she really wanted to become a teacher. Like Karen, Ellen also commented that "teachers can only bring so much idealism inside the door with them" (Autobiography, spring 2006). Different from other participants, Bill viewed teaching as "about which act you should run on a particular day" and "the person you are in the classroom isn't necessarily the person you are outside of the classroom" (Focus Group, spring 2007). He reported that he was finally "happier at the end of the day as I haven't been putting on as much of an act to hold them [students]" (Focus Group, spring 2007). After student teaching, he stated that he had not decided exactly what he wanted to do and just felt like he put on different masks in front of different groups of students.

FIRST-YEAR TEACHERS' JOYS AND CHALLENGES

All participants successfully finished their first-year teaching in spring 2008, with four of them being selected as Rookie Teacher of the Year in their schools, and one emerging as Rookie Teacher of the Year for the school district. After their first-year of teaching, all participants reported they were more confident as teachers and "much more comfortable in front of a classroom full of students" (Charles, Focus Group, spring 2008). Compared to their concerns during the teacher education program, classroom management became less of a concern for our participants; but all participants continued to strive to make the content relevant for their students in an effort to enhance student motivation.

While all participants had positive impacts on their students in terms of test scores, participants unanimously commented on the restrictions that standardized testing places on teaching—restrictions that prevent teachers from offering "things that they [students] really get into and look into real-world applications and issues" (Ellen, interview, spring 2008) and that allow students to "have some say in their own education and actually become engaged in works that they want to read" (Karen, Interview, spring 2008). Among the five participants, Bill is the only one who taught a communication-skills class, one that did not require a state-mandated assessment. He really enjoyed it and commented that without the testing pressure, he realized "how much I [he] could go outside the box" (Focus Group, spring 2008). Even though he did not face testing pressure as much as the other participants, he still commented: "If there was one thing I could change it would be to focus on a more realistic and a real-world approach to education instead of focusing on padding numbers for somebody in an office somewhere" (Focus Group, spring, 2008).

Since they were teaching at very different school settings, our participants also faced unique challenges due to contextual factors. Located at schools with high ethnic minority populations that were cited in the media as having student behavioral problems, Karen and Charles mentioned the desire for consistency of administrative support where disciplinary issues were concerned. Charles reiterated:

> There would be times that I would write up kids for cursing or cutting [skipping class] or [what] they're not supposed to be doing, and first—the write up that I would give sometimes, it would take a week, two weeks, for it even to get read. And then, punishment that they would be given would be little to nothing at all. So, I get to the point where I'm just like, "OK, why do I even bother … ." I just wish that the administration would put their money where their mouth is sometimes and actually follow through on things that they say they're going to and not just expect us to follow through on things and then do nothing. (Focus Group, spring 2008)

Contrasting her situation with that of her students, Karen was especially frustrated when students are not held accountable for their behavior in school as teachers typically are. She was concerned that what happens to students in school can have consequences later in their lives. She said:

> If I'm not signed in by 8:15 am, you [administration] put a note in my file. I am held accountable. But when a student is consistently late or when they are walking right in front of you smoking on campus, when all public schools are 'Tobacco-Free,' and nothing gets done about it, it's kind of like, "How can you hold me accountable when you're not holding students accountable?" How many chances are you going to give a student when the lesson should be that there are consequences for their actions? When they go out into the real world and they have a job where they are consistently late, they are going to be fired. And then they will look at their employer and say, "Where's my second chance?" They're not going to get one. By not holding them accountable, we're not helping prepare a lot of these students for what really happens in the real world. (Focus Group, spring 2008)

Mary agreed with Charles and Karen about feeling unsupported when she admitted that the assistant principal assigned to her grade level was "very unsup-portive." She explained that "there would be extreme situations in a classroom, and we would never see paperwork about it. And that's the big thing that bothered me about my first year-[it] is that I almost felt like we were kind of unsupported" (Focus Group, spring 2008). She confessed, though, that her classroom management initially suffered but went on to admit that "I'm getting better at it" (Interview, spring 2008).

Related to school context, having more resources was cited by Bill. He wanted his students to be more in tune with 21st century technology that was located at the school. He wanted to integrate more technology in his teaching. He would love to have a Smart Board, a projector, a document camera, and a laptop lab "where they had computers connected to the Internet. The kind of lessons I could design with a technology focus could be really a lot of fun" (Interview, spring 2008).

Four of the five participants hoped for more parent involvement where their child's academic success and behavior management were concerned, especially with parents of students who were on the borderline of not passing their courses or students who were having behavioral difficulties that impeded their academic progress. Ellen commented, "The parents whose children really don't need intervention, you see them more so than you see the parents whose children do need it. I never get in touch with the parents I need to talk to" (Focus Group, spring 2008). In fact, all of the participants wanted to get to know the students and their parents better, even though they realized that "parents can be your greatest ally or your biggest enemy" (Ellen, Interview, spring 2008). Furthermore, all of the participants wanted to gain better control over the balance of their professional and personal lives. The first year of teaching was "exhausting and yet kind of fun at the same time" (Bill, Interview, spring 2008).

While they enjoyed their first-year of teaching, four of the participants explicitly commented that it was "exhausting" (Bill, Interview, spring 2008). Participants commented on how they typically stayed late at school and still brought work, such as grading and planning, to finish at home, which sometimes made them resent going back to work some mornings (Charles, Focus Group, spring 2008). As Karen put it: "You leave school late, and then you take stuff home, and then you sit there and just resent the fact that you have to do it…I think that makes the whole thing [teaching] unenjoyable" (Focus Group, spring 2008).

Reflecting on their first-year of teaching, while proud of what they had accomplished, our participants did report new challenges, including testing pressures, lack of administrative support, lack of up-to-date resources, lack of parent involvement, and the difficulty of balancing their teaching responsibilities and their personal lives. In addition to discussing the challenges, we uncovered some of the strategies our participants used to face challenges in their first-year teaching.

STRATEGIES USED TO FACE CHALLENGES

Following our participants from their teacher education program through their first-year of teaching, we noted that when facing challenges in their teaching, our participants developed various strategies including: (1) learning from their students in order to better motivate them in content area learning; (2) using assignments, observations, and class discussions to better get to know students and their families; (3) sustaining their passion for teaching through focusing on positive experiences such as student accomplishments and statements of appreciation from parents; and (4) adopting individual ways to manage stress and frustration.

At the end of their first-year of teaching, participants reported on the connections they saw between their students and themselves and the efforts they made to create those connections. Charles, Bill, and Karen commented on how they were able to relate to their students because they are close in age and they "listen to the same music and watch the same movies ... and in a sense identify with the things they like to do" (Karen, Interview, spring 2008). Bill recognized that as a teacher, he could relate to students at a "social level" and that one way he earned respect from his students was "by knowing and understanding—knowing and understanding what Facebook and My Space are, for example" (Interview, spring 2008).

Charles admitted that sometimes his students were not familiar with the movies and TV shows he wanted to use as examples. For instance, when using *Indiana Jones* to explain "Epicurus," his students "did not have a clue who that is." He started to ask his students for examples and said that he was going to "listen to a little bit of their music, their movies and ... try to get into their minds a little bit more so that I can connect to them a little bit more" (Focus Group, spring 2008). Mary and Ellen mentioned their personal relationships with students especially because they found many students were "very much like" them (Mary, Interview, spring 2008) and "struggle with the same exact things" they had experienced (Ellen, Interview, spring 2008). Interestingly, all five participants also reported student motivation in content area learning as the most exciting aspect during their first-year of teaching.

Ellen, for example, cited her students' growing interest in grammar as the most exciting thing for her:

> When the kids beg me to have more grammar on Friday [weekly grammar exercises that precede daily instruction], because they know Grammar Fridays. That was exciting. And we had a Grammar Olympics ... they're going to write their research papers, and they don't have atrocious grammar. That was incredibly exciting for me, because it actually made me feel like I had accomplished something with those silly games that people would make fun of me for. So, that was pretty exciting for me. (Focus Group, spring 2008)

To better connect with their students' backgrounds and understand students' families, all five participants in our study tried to use different strategies in addition to talking with students and/ or other teachers, and having teacher-parent conferences. Bill, Charles, and Karen used writing projects, such as introduction letters, information sheets, and personal narratives, to encourage students to share personal information with them. At the same time, they also shared their own stories with their students through demonstration/modeling or through feedback to students' writing. Ellen, Mary, and Bill also stated that they learned about their students and their families through observation of "how they acted in class and their interactions with others in and out of the classroom" (Ellen, Interview, spring 2008), and through classroom discussions. As Bill mentioned, "You really get to know a lot about these kids when you get them to talk about a subject they feel passionate about" (Interview, spring, 2008). Through using different ways of communication, all participants reported learning more about their students and their families.

Discussing his perspective on different degrees of parental involvement, Charles commented:

> Getting to know all the students, and getting to know all their situations, you learn that, yes, there is a reason for a lot of it ... most of them do care. It's just they have other circumstances that they have to deal with. So, it's not just our job, again, to teach them. (Focus Group, spring 2008)

Facing various challenges in their first-year teaching, all participants reported receiving recognition and support from their students and parents with whom they worked. In addition to most of them being selected as Rookie Teachers of the Year in their individual schools, all participants reported they regained their energy from their students even when they had "bad days." Ellen, for example, a Rookie Teacher of the Year for her school district, described how her students made her feel needed:

> ... to like walk in late or to walk in right before the bell rings, and my period [students in that period] go, "Oh, God, you're here. Thank God. We thought we had a sub." And, then, to look at them and go, "You would have been so happy?" "No, we really wouldn't have." That lets me know that I'm doing something right—that I do need to come here. (Focus Group, spring 2008)

Although all participants commented that they wanted to get to know parents better and establish relationships with more parents, they did recognize that their established relationships with parents were reassuring. Charles commented that one of the parents, who was also a teacher herself, would thank him for what he did for the students and told him how she knew "what it is like to be a first-year teacher." "Her simple thank you helped at least to validate what I was doing and kept me sane during the rough patches throughout the year" (Interview, spring 2008). Similarly, Karen reported getting thank you emails from parents and felt being appreciated: "If you try hard enough, I think they recognize that. And they would appreciate it even if you weren't in the end successful" (Interview, spring 2008).

Ellen also commented on her relationships with some students' families and how such relationships helped her working with students in her class:

> I struggled with Brandon [the student] at first; nothing was hard for him. I became very close to his mother, who helped me find things for him to do. By the end of the first semester, I was able to scaffold for him and, in the process, built a great relationship with him. (Interview, spring 2008)

Individually, they also developed different coping strategies to unwind after having "a stressful day." Both Ellen and Karen found sharing with other people was a way to cope with difficult situations. Karen said she shared her frustration with "a small group in my department," while Ellen "called on a few friends of mine from college who are not teachers" (Focus Group, spring 2008). Bill, on the other hand, said going home and playing videogames was his "system of unwinding" (Focus Group, spring 2008).

Discussion and Implications

During their student teaching experiences, participants were concerned about classroom management, keeping students motivated in learning the content, and parent involvement through knowledge of their children's academic progress or nonprogress as well as of their behavioral issues. After the first year of teaching, classroom management became manageable, albeit, three of five of them would have liked more administrative support in their decision making where disciplinary procedures were concerned. Parent involvement remained as one of the major challenges during first-year teaching, and new challenges, including testing pressures, lack of administrative support, lack of resources, and keeping the balance between teaching and their personal lives, were emerged.

Given these findings, we observed that the teachers' shifting concerns were not restricted to the traditionally defined domains such as self, task, and students. Although our findings also indicated that classroom discipline and student motivation were two major concerns of our student teachers, which are consistent with Veenman's (1984) findings, we also noted that instead of focusing on organization of class work and daily routines, our participants expressed concern for making connections with diverse student populations. In addition, after their first year of teaching, they used various strategies to motivate students in content areas, and viewed building relationships with students and making content relevant for their students to be their strengths.

Through internships, student teaching, and required assignments such as the ABC's project, participants had the opportunity to interact with culturally and ethnically diverse student populations during the teacher education program. It appeared that they developed an open and welcoming attitude toward diversity of all kinds, not just ethnic diversity (He & Cooper, 2009). As first-year teachers, they fully understood their multiple roles as teachers and perceived teaching as more than content delivery. While there is increasing focus on content and content pedagogy courses in secondary teacher education programs, it remains critical that teacher candidates are provided with opportunities to interact with diverse student populations, students' parents, and members of the community to better understand their responsibilities beyond academic content instruction.

In building relationships with their students and learning from their students, our participants also used positive connections they could make given the proximity of their ages and their students'. Bill, for example, related current music to his teaching of composition. Such connections sometimes also transcended differences in cultural preferences and made more visible the links between the cultural identities of both students and teachers. Through these connections, common ground was discovered, cultivated, and used as strategies to engage students in learning content and relating it to their current lives. These types of strategies, including ways to explore the teachers' own backgrounds and assets through guided reflection or assignments such as the ABC's project, taught them to make connections with students and enhanced the teachers' awareness of their own assumptions and preferences. Therefore, we believe such strategies need to be highlighted through courses and field experiences in the teacher education program. In other words, as teacher educators, we need to move beyond the discussion of what constitutes student diversity to explore the how and why in our teacher education programs (Nieto, 2003). Teacher candidates need to be equipped with ways to better understand others and to become more aware of their own identities in an effort to better serve the needs of all students in diverse settings.

Based on our findings from listening to our participants across two years, we also recognized the impact of the school context and questioned how we could effectively prepare our teacher candidates for different teaching contexts (Beijaard, Meijer, & Verloop, 2004; Bullough, 1989; Bullough & Knowles, 1991; Grossman, 1992). We believe that the first step is for us, as teacher educators, to experience diverse school settings ourselves and face some of the challenges mentioned by our teachers. Perhaps teacher educators should spend more prolonged time in school and community settings, especially in urban settings in which poverty has a severe impact on students' learning.

We also need to not only learn to empathize with some of our teacher candidates' fear of diversity but also to explore with them strategies they could use to respond to it. Further, we need to more fully understand their fears of standardized testing as a chief mechanism for system-wide, state, and national accountability, and develop with them strategies to sustain their passion for teaching even while facing assessment pressures. In other words, teacher educators should observe and work, in some cases, in the same schools as do their teacher candidates to experience diverse teaching contexts for the purpose of better facilitating teachers' development in facing challenges and concerns in those specific contexts (Darling-Hammond & Snyder, 2000).

With all participants being successful in their first year teaching, we also wondered if participation in the research itself served as a venue for teachers to reflect on their practice and discuss their concerns as first-year teachers. In their focus groups, they had opportunities to learn from each other, and they found that they were not alone in their journeys. The focus groups appeared to allow them to create their own professional learning community, where they gained strength and support from each other. Our teacher education programs should encourage building of such communities among our graduates and support such sharing and reflection in their first-year. This can be done by following up our graduates for not only the purpose of program effectiveness (Sleeter, 2004) but also to help form such professional communities for our former teacher candidates. There are additional potential benefits for following up with our graduates. By bringing our graduates together, we can promote and support teacher retention and also strengthen our own practice, for we can learn from former students, our new colleagues. Maybe by turning the tables in education, our graduates can teach us how to respond to future teacher candidates better and respond to their needs in ways never done before.

Therefore, in order to better prepare secondary teachers, we believe that as teacher educators we need to:

1. Continue engaging teacher candidates in the exploration of and reflection on their own identities—both the personal self and the professional self as related to diversity—through intentional, cohesive assignments in teacher education programs;
2. Provide teacher candidates various opportunities in teacher education programs to interact with and learn from diverse K-12 students and their families, and encourage them to develop various strategies to build relationships with the 21st-century students they teach and with their families;
3. Provide teacher candidates with structured opportunities to reflect upon the realities of today's college and university students as these realities relate to the preparation of effective teachers and transition to professional roles and responsibilities;
4. Be more involved in diverse school settings ourselves so that we could be better aware of and more responsive to teacher candidates' changing concerns and struggles as they work with the increasingly diverse student population in the 21st century;
5. Engage teacher candidates in professional learning communities where they can learn from and provide support for each other, not only for the purpose of teacher retention but also to give our new colleagues tools to create their own such communities after they leave our programs; and
6. Continue our efforts to conduct multi-year longitudinal studies and purposefully collect program evaluation data through course assignments, follow-up interviews, and focus group

discussions with our graduates, so that we could gain insights from our teacher candidates to improve and refine our teacher education programs.

Conclusions

The findings of this study revealed the development of five secondary preservice teachers over the course of two years, during their teacher education program and their first year of teaching. Their concerns at different points of their teacher education program and the strategies they employed to face challenges are informative for teacher educators. Additionally of significance, this study calls attention to teacher educators' following their graduates into the classroom to explore, document, and make public the explicit connection between what is taught in teacher education programs and the reality of instructional practice (Sleeter, 2004).While participants' expressed concerns confirmed the value of field experiences and self-reflection in teacher education programs, the case descriptions provided in this study also focused our attention on specific areas for improvement in our own pedagogy and teacher education programs.

However, to better prepare our teacher candidates for the reality of today's classroom, as teacher educators, we need to familiarize ourselves not only with the changing needs and characteristics of today's college students, but also with the needs of the 21st century K-12 students they will teach. Further, recognizing the new reality of teaching, teacher education programs need to move beyond introducing teacher candidates to diversity, accountability, and other complex issues in schools, to more thorough discussions and analyses of the realities of diversity as we, both teacher educators and teacher candidates, experience it in particular school contexts.

Considering multicultural education, the central question is how do we teach teacher candidates to be actively involved in shaping their professional identities not only as experts in content knowledge, but also as teachers who build relationships with their students and their families for the purpose of enhancing student achievement and becoming more culturally competent themselves. How do we engage them in ways of teaching to the diverse needs of their students? Teachers tend to focus their reflection on diversity in terms of how they could involve all students in academic learning. However, little effort/reflection is placed on the means and manner to educate for globalization and utilizing diversity as an asset. Perhaps we as teacher educators should educate ourselves and step out of our secure communities of practice to explore the reality of teaching to globalization. If we do not, our teacher candidates will not be the only ones left behind.

If we were to continue following up with our participants into their second and third year of teaching, we would like to further examine the impact of various contextual factors, such as urban versus rural school settings, on our participants' professional development as beginning teachers. Further, we are more curious to also learn about strategies beginning teachers use to make sense of their school context and community and how they integrate various resources to become good teachers in their efforts to better serve the needs of the diverse student population. Finally, we would like to collect additional data from school administrators, parents, and K-12 students to obtain their perspectives on the development of our teacher participants.

References

Adams, R. D. (1982). Teacher development: A look at changes in teacher perceptions and behavior across time. *Journal of Teacher Education, 33*(44), 40–43.

Beijaard, D., Meijer, P., & Verloop, N. (2004). Reconsidering research on teachers' professional identity. *Teaching and Teacher Education, 20,* 107–128.

Berliner, D. C. (1988). Implications of studies of expertise in pedagogy for teacher education and evaluation. In *New directions for teacher assessment. Proceedings of the 1988 Educational Testing Service Invitational Conference.* Princeton, NJ: Educational Testing Service.

Boccia, J. A. (1989). *Beginning teachers speak out: A study of professional concerns in the first three years of teaching.* ERIC Document ED 316555.

Brown, T. (2006). Negotiating psychological disturbance in pre-service teacher education. *Teaching and Teacher Education, 22,* 675–689.

Bullough, R. V., Jr. (1989). *First-year teacher: A case study.* New York: Teachers College Press.

Bullough, R. V., Jr., & Baughman, K. (1997). *"First-year teacher" eight years later.* New York: Teachers College Press.

Bullough, R. V., Jr., & Knowles. J. G. (1991). Teaching and nurturing: Changing conceptions of self as teacher in a case study of becoming a teacher. *Qualitative Studies in Education, 4,* 121–140.

Chant, R. H. (2002). The impact of personal theorizing on beginning teachers: Experiences of three social studies teachers. *Theory and Research in Social Education, 30*(4), 516–450.

Chant, R. H., Heafner, T. L., & Bennett, K. R. (2004). Connecting personal theorizing and action research in preservice teacher development. *Teacher Education Quarterly, 31*(3), 25–42.

Clandinin, D., & Connelly, F. (1996). Teachers' professional knowledge landscapes: Teacher stories—stories of teachers, school stories—stories of schools. *Educational Researcher, 25*(3), 24–30.

Clandinin, D. J., Downey, C. A., & Huber, J. (2009). Attending to changing landscapes: Shaping the interwoven identities of teachers and teacher educators. *Asia-Pacific Journal of Teaching Education, 37*(2), 141–154.

Conway, P. F., & Clark, C. M. (2003). The journey inward and outward: A re-examination of Fuller's concerns-based model of teacher development. *Teaching and Teacher Education, 19,* 465–482.

Darling-Hammond, L., & Snyder, J. (2000). Authentic assessment of teaching in context. *Teaching and Teacher Education, 16,* 523–545.

Day, C. (1999). *Developing teachers: The challenges of lifelong learning.* London, UK: Falmer Press.

Fuller, F. F. (1969). Concerns of teachers: A developmental conceptualization. *American Educational Research Journal, 6,* 207–226.

Glaser, B. G., & Strauss, A. L. (1967). *The discovery of grounded theory: Strategies for qualitative research.* Chicago, IL: Aldine Publishing Company.

Grossman, P. L. (1992). Why models matter: An alternate view on professional growth in teaching. *Review of Educational Research, 62*(2), 171–179.

He, Y., & Cooper, J. E. (2009). The ABCs for preservice teacher cultural competency development. *Teaching Education, 20*(3), 305–322.

He, Y., & Levin, B. B. (2008). Match or mismatch? How congruent are the beliefs of teacher candidates, cooperating teacher, and university-based teacher educators? *Teacher Education Quarterly, 34*(4), 37–55.

Hollingsworth. S. J. (1989). Prior beliefs and cognitive change in learning to teach. *American Educational Research Journal, 26,* 160–189.

Huberman, M. (Ed.). (1989). Research on teachers' professional lives. *International Journal of Educational Research, 13*(4), 343–466.

Kagan, D. M. (1992). Professional growth among preservice and beginning teachers. *Review of Education Research, 62*(2), 129–169.

Levin, B. B. (2003). *Case studies of teacher development: An in-depth look at how thinking about pedagogy develops over time.* Mahway, NJ: Lawrence Erlbaum Associates. Levin, B. B., & He, Y. (2008).

Investigating the content and sources of teacher candidates' personal practical theories (PPTs). *Journal of Teacher Education, 59*(1), 55–68.

Lortie, D. (1975). *Schoolteacher: A sociological perspective.* Chicago: University of Chi-cago Press.

Marso, R. N., & Pigge, F. L. (1989). The influence of preservice training and teaching experience upon attitude and concerns about teaching. *Teaching and Teacher Education, 5*(1), 33–42.

Marso, R. N., & Pigge, F. L. (1995). Outstanding teachers' concerns about teaching at four stages of career development. *Educational Review, 18*(2), 1–11.

Melnick, S., & Meister, D. (2008). A comparison of beginning and experienced teachers' concerns. *Educational Research Quarterly, 31*(3), 39–56.

Miles, M., & Huberman, M. (1994). *Qualitative data analysis: An expanded sourcebook* (2ne ed.). Thousand Oaks, CA: Sage.

Nias, J. (1989). *Primary teachers talking: A study of teaching as work.* New York: Rout-ledge.

Nieto, S. (2003). *What keeps teachers going?* New York: Teachers College Press.

Pigge, F. L., & Marso, R. N. (1997). A seven year longitudinal multi-factor assessment of teaching concerns development through preparation and early years of teaching. *Teaching and Teacher Education, 13,* 225–235.

Richardson, V. (2003). Perservice teachers' beliefs. In J. Raths & A. McAninch (Eds.), *Teacher beliefs and teacher education. Advances in teacher education* (pp. 1–22.). Greenwich, CT: Information Age Publishers.

Ryan, K. (1992). *The roller coaster year.* New York: HarperCollins.

Schmidt, P. (1999). Know thyself and understand others. *Language Arts, 76,* 332–340.

Sleeter, C. S. (2004, Fall). From the Vice President. In *Teaching and Teacher Education: Division K Newsletter.* Washington, DC: American Educational Research Association.

Sprinthall, N. A., & Thies-Sprinthall, L. (1980). Education for teacher growth: A cognitive developmental perspective. *Theory into Practice, 29,* 278–286.

Veeman, S. (1984). Perceived problems of beginning teachers. *Review of Educational Research, 54*(2), 143–178.

Vonk, J. H. C. (1993). Mentoring beginning teachers: Development of a knowledge base for mentors. Paper presented at the annual meeting of the American Educational Research Association, Atlanta, GA, April.

Watzke, J. (2007). Longitudinal research on beginning teacher development: Complexity as a challenge to concerns-based stage theory. *Teaching and Teacher Education, 23,* 106–122.

CPSIA information can be obtained
at www.ICGtesting.com
Printed in the USA
LVHW05s0423280818
588291LV00001B/3/P